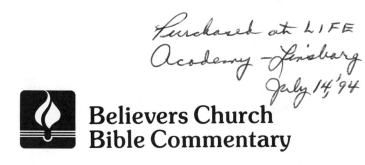

Believers Church
Bible Commentary

Elmer A. Martens and Willard M. Swartley, Editors

Believers Church Bible Commentary

Colossians
Philemon

Ernest D. Martin

HERALD PRESS
Scottdale, Pennsylvania
Waterloo, Ontario

Library of Congress Cataloging-in-Publication Data
Martin, Ernest D. (Ernest Daniel), 1924-
  Colossians, Philemon / Ernest D. Martin.
     p.   cm. — (Believers church Bible commentary)
  Includes bibliographical references.
  ISBN 0-8361-3621-7 (alk. paper)
  1. Bible. N.T. Colossians—Commentaries. 2. Bible. N.T. Philemon—
Commentaries. I. Bible. N.T. Colossians. English. New Revised Standard Version.
1993. II. Bible. N.T. Philemon. English New Revised Standard Version. 1993.
III. Title. IV. Series.
BS2715.3.M35   1993
227'.707—dc20   93-18790
                                                                                      CIP

The paper used in this publication is recycled and meets the minimum requirements of
American National Standard for Information Sciences—Permanence of Paper for
Printed Library Materials, ANSI Z39.48-1984.

Unless otherwise indicated, Scripture is from the *New Revised Standard Version
Bible,* copyright 1989 by the Division of Christian Education of the National Council of
the Churches of Christ in the USA. It is used by permission, as are other versions used
in making comparisons: GNB, *Good News Bible;* JB, *The Jerusalem Bible;* KJV, *King
James Version;* NASB, *New American Standard Bible;* NEB, *The New English Bible;*
NIV, *New International Version;* Phillips, *The New Testament in Modern English;*
RSV, *Revised Standard Version.* Scripture translated by the author is identified by his
initials, EDM, or the term *literally.*

BELIEVERS CHURCH BIBLE COMMENTARY: COLOSSIANS, PHILEMON
Copyright © 1993 by Herald Press, Scottdale, Pa. 15683
   Published simultaneously in Canada by Herald Press,
   Waterloo, Ont. N2L 6H7. All rights reserved
Library of Congress Catalog Card Number: 93-18790
International Standard Book Number: 0-8361-3621-7
Printed in the United States of America
Cover by Merrill R. Miller

02 01 00 99 98 97 96 95 94 93 10 9 8 7 6 5 4 3 2 1

To my children
and grandchildren,
to feed their interest
in the Word

Abbreviations

EDM	Author's translation
lit.	Author's literal translation
NT	New Testament
OT	Old Testament
TBC	Text in Biblical Context
TLC	Text in the Life of the Church

Also see "Abbreviations" on pages 280-281.

Contents

* = The Text in Biblical Context
+ = The Text in the Life of the Church

Contents   **9**

Contents

Series Foreword

The Believers Church Bible Commentary Series makes available a new tool for basic Bible study. It is published for all who seek to understand more fully the original message of Scripture and its meaning for today—Sunday school teachers, members of Bible study groups, students, pastors, or other seekers. The series is based on the conviction that God is still speaking to all who will hear him, and that the Holy Spirit makes the Word a living and authoritative guide for all who want to know and do God's will.

The desire to be of help to as wide a range of readers as possible has determined the approach of the writers. Since no blocks of biblical text are provided, readers may continue to use the translation with which they are most familiar. The writers of the series use the *New Revised Standard Version,* the *Revised Standard Version,* the *New International Version,* and the *New American Standard Bible* on a comparative basis. They indicate which of these texts they follow most closely, as well as where they make their own translations. The writers have not worked alone, but in consultation with select counselors, the series' editors, and with the Editorial Council.

To further encourage use of the series by a wide range of readers, the focus is on illumination of the Scriptures, providing historical and cultural background, sharing necessary theological, sociological, and ethnical meanings and, in general, making "the rough places plain." Critical issues are not avoided, but neither are they moved into the foreground as debates among scholars. The series will aid in the interpretive process, but not attempt to provide the final meaning as authority above Word and Spirit discerned in the gathered church.

The term *believers church* has often been used in the history of the church. Since the sixteenth century, it has frequently been applied to the Anabaptists and later the Mennonites, as well as to the Church of the Brethren and similar groups. As a descriptive term it includes more than Mennonites and Brethren. *Believers church* now represents specific theological understandings, such as believers baptism, commitment to the Rule of Christ in Matthew 18:15-18 central to church membership, belief in the power of love in all relationships, and a willingness to follow the way of the cross of Christ. The writers chosen for the series stand in this tradition.

Believers church people have always been known for their emphasis on obedience to the simple meaning of Scripture. Because of this, they do not have a long history of deep historical-critical biblical scholarship. This series attempts to be faithful to the Scriptures while also taking archaeology and current biblical studies seriously. Doing this means that at many points the writers will not differ greatly from interpretations which can be found in many other good commentaries. Yet basic presuppositions about Christ, the church and its mission, God and history, human nature, the Christian life, and other doctrines do shape a writer's interpretation of Scripture. Thus this series, like all other commentaries, stands within a specific historical church tradition.

Many in this stream of the church have expressed a need for help in Bible study. This is justification enough to produce the Believers Church Bible Commentary. Nevertheless, the Holy Spirit is not bound to any tradition. May this series be an instrument in breaking down walls between Christians in North America and around the world, bringing new joy in obedience through a fuller understanding of the world.

The Editorial Council

Author's Preface

The aim of this commentary is to expose readers to the text of two closely related New Testament letters and to engage them in the fruits and joys of Bible study. Over forty years ago, seminary classes with Howard H. Charles and J. C. Wenger stimulated my interest in a careful search of the Scriptures. More recently a class with Gertrude Roten and Jacob Enz fanned this flame of delight. I have been both challenged and humbled by the invitation to write this commentary and the efforts that have gone into it.

For thirty years I have used my gifts and skills in writing many adult Sunday school lessons. Commentary preparation has been more of the same, only more intensive and extensive. I have used a similar study pattern, involving detailed work in the original language, and then living with the text and letting the message surface.

Colossians has been for me a focus of attention for many years. I have preached from Colossians and led studies in three settings, including one with a group of pastors. Philemon is a logical companion to Colossians. For both letters the rewards of careful study go far beyond what the size of the documents might suggest.

Fruitful Bible study is like the rule that in order to take a bath, one needs to get wet. To open ourselves to the biblical text, we need to do more than read a commentary that offers only the author's ideas and those gleaned from others. Therefore, I have attempted to take the reader and Bible student through some of the process of discerning what the text says and what it means for us. You will find suggestions for further study, questions, reviews of various interpretations, and helps for weighing the options along with my observations and findings. Greek words (transliterated) have been kept to a minimum, although word studies with the aid of a Greek concordance and the *Theological Dictionary of the New Testament* are important in my work. Scripture references dot the pages to enable you to compare the words and phrases of the text at hand with other biblical usage.

Unless otherwise indicated, the *New Revised Standard Version* is the quoted text. Quotations from other translations are indicated by standard abbreviations (see the back of the title page). Occasionally the author's personal translation (marked EDM) has been used to make details of the Greek text more explicit.

Additional material on especially relevant topics, for several references in these two letters, are arranged alphabetically as supplemental Essays, in the back of the book. These are indicated with headings enclosed in brackets, as follows: *[Before—After, p. 282.]* Several of the headings are shortened in the commentary text to conserve space, but the first word is always the same. Under the essay label *[Grammar Notes, p. 290]*, further items of grammatical significance are given according to verse references.

The help and encouragement of many persons have gone into the writing and refining of this volume. In addition to the members of the Editorial Council, I want to acknowledge the valuable contributions of Howard H. Charles (New Testament editor when I started the project), Willard M. Swartley (current New Testament editor), S. David Garber (theological consultant), Sara Wengerd (readability consultant), and Alan Beuscher (our son-in-law, whose perspective and expertise were valuable along the way). I am grateful to the Midway congregation for allowing me time to begin work on the commentary while I was then serving as pastor. As I learned basic word-processing skills, this became an important and stretching part of the whole endeavor. Thanks also go to S. David Garber, Herald Press book editor, for enhancing and fine-tuning the manuscript for publication.

My experience in the church, appreciation for it, and inclination to see things from a pastoral perspective have shaped what I have seen and highlighted in Colossians and Philemon. My prayer is that these pages may help you anew to encounter the all-sufficient, cosmic Christ, who is at the center of Colossians and of Christian faith and life, and that your experience in Christ and the church will move you to worship and to renewed service in the mission of the church.

> *Ernest D. Martin*
> *Columbiana, Ohio*
> *April 1992*

Colossians

A Letter Exalting Christ

Approaching Colossians

Students of Colossians are soon in for a surprise. How can one small, obscure, ancient letter be so potent? For many people, memorizing the names of the New Testament (NT) books involved the rote mastery of the sequence: Galatians, Ephesians, Philippians, Colossians. Colossians is the shortest of the four and for many persons the least familiar. However, one quickly discovers that Colossians is high-voltage material. Names, places, issues, and thought forms give evidence of it being written to a historically specific situation in the interior of Asia Minor. Yet this contextualized document has a way of spanning the centuries and cultures and yielding a powerful message for the modern church scene.

Cursory reading of the text reveals to us that Colossians is packed with words common to the vocabulary of biblical theology. With serious study we learn that Colossians touches on an amazingly broad range of topics. It also contains a number of more or less technical terms, the meanings of which are not obvious to the modern reader. As a result of his studies, William Barclay has said of Colossians, "There is no more difficult book in the New Testament" (1963:8).

The challenges, however, are more than balanced by the rewards of careful study. Colossians yields insights into the apostle's pastoral way of confronting a potentially ruinous religious development. The church today is faced with movements and teachings that also challenge the sufficiency of divine revelation and power in Jesus Christ. Colossians is about Christ, although not an exhaustive treatise on Christology (an organized understanding of the person and work of Christ). However, the inclusion of this letter in the NT canon makes the church the beneficiary of the creative expression of one who was thoroughly convinced in mind and heart of the supremacy and sufficiency of the cosmic Christ.

One of Several Letters to Colossae

Two of the NT letters are written to Colossae, a city in the Roman province of Asia, in what is now Turkey. Similarities in mentioned circumstances and names link Colossians and Philemon to the same city and church community (see the introduction to Philemon). The most natural meaning of the reference to the *letter from Laodicea* (4:16) is that a third letter from Paul also came into the Lycus Valley and was passed on to be read at Colossae. Therefore, the church at Colossae (with the churches at nearby Laodicea and Hierapolis) is of more than passing interest to students of the NT. Colossae is on maps of first-century western Asia Minor because of two NT letters.

The map on the next page shows Colossae situated slightly south of a point 100 miles east of Ephesus and 135 miles west of Antioch in Pisidia. Note the rivers and major ancient highways, especially the important east-west route that went through Colossae and connected Ephesus (close to the Aegean coast), the cities of the Lycus Valley, Antioch in Pisidia, Iconium, Lystra, Derbe, Tarsus, Antioch in Syria, and points east in Mesopotamia.

The now uninhabited location of ancient Colossae was discovered in A.D. 1835 by William J. Hamilton. The city had straddled the Lycus River about twenty miles upstream from where the Lycus River flows into the Meander River. Among other surface remains, Hamilton found ruins of the acropolis and theater on the south side of the river, and burial sites on the north side. The location of Colossae relative to the rivers and mountains and two other nearby cities on the Lycus River can be seen on the map of the Lycus Valley.

Several features of the Lycus Valley are of interest. Rich volcanic soil provided good grazing, and consequently a thriving wool industry developed. Colossae was known for wool dyed a deep red. The topography was marked with chalky calcium deposits and travertine. The area was subject to earthquakes. A major quake in A.D. 60-61 is known to have destroyed Laodicea. Less explicit evidence implies that Colossae and Hierapolis were also devastated at the same time. Laodicea and Hierapolis were soon rebuilt, but Colossae apparently was left in ruins, since later historical records do not mention it. This provides strong support for dating the writing of Colossians prior to that earthquake.

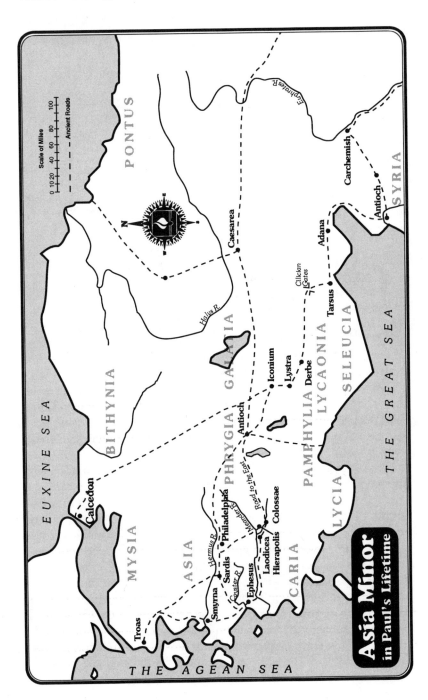

Asia Minor in Paul's Lifetime

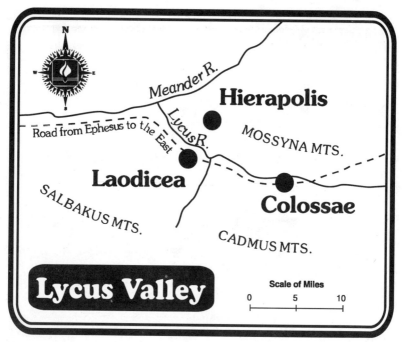

In pre-Christian times Colossae was the most prominent of the three Lycus Valley cities. Colossae is listed in the annals of Herodotus and Xenophon (both in the fifth century B.C.) as being a large, prosperous city. However, in Roman and Greek times Laodicea and Hierapolis surpassed Colossae in size and significance. Colossae may have been one of the least of the cities in which a church received a letter from Paul.

When the gospel came to Colossae, the populace was made up of a diverse cultural and religious mixture, including the indigenous Phrygian people, Greek settlers, and likely a significant Jewish population. Josephus records that in the early part of the second century B.C., Antiochus III transplanted two thousand Jews from Mesopotamia to the districts of Lydia and Phrygia (*Ant.* 12.147-153). A Roman governor in the Lycus Valley district intercepted a shipment of gold being sent to Jerusalem to pay the temple tax. Calculating from the amount, the Jewish population has been estimated to be as high as 50,000 (Barclay, 1975a:93). Colossae, being located on a major east-west highway, was undoubtedly a cosmopolitan city.

The religious landscape in the Lycus Valley was even more diverse. Research has identified Persian and other Asian religious elements as well as Roman and Greek religious ideas and practices. [*Religions, p. 313.*] A blending of various cultic beliefs and ceremonies is known as religious syncretism. Into just such a pluralistic cultural and religious environment, the gospel of Jesus Christ was proclaimed and was *bearing fruit and growing* (Col. 1:6).

The Church at Colossae

How and when the church began at Colossae is not clear. Neither Colossians itself nor Acts supplies an explicit account of the origin of the congregation. According to Colossians 1:7, Epaphras, not Paul, brought the gospel to Colossae. Yet Paul knew a number of persons in this church. The reference in 2:1 to those who had not seen him *face to face* could refer to new persons who came into the church later or mean that he had never been there.

Although there were Jews from Phrygia present on the day of Pentecost (Acts 2:10), the biblical record contains no hint that they took the gospel to the Lycus Valley. Acts 13:49 reports that "the word of the Lord spread throughout the region" (around Antioch in Pisidia). Because a major highway went from Antioch in Pisidia through Colossae, it is possible but not probable that disciples spread the good news as far as Colossae, 135 miles westward in the province of Asia. Reference to Barnabas (4:10) fits this option. Paul went through the region of Pisidia again on his second missionary campaign (Acts 16:6), but seems to have taken a northern route to Troas rather than the one through Colossae. On the third campaign the most direct route (but not the only one) from Antioch in Pisidia to Ephesus was through Colossae, but Acts does not indicate a ministry there (Acts 18:23; 19:1).

The most likely scenario is that during Paul's three years at Ephesus (ca. A.D. 53-56), Epaphras, a native of Colossae who had become associated with Paul, introduced the gospel to the people of the Lycus Valley. If the reading *on our behalf* (1:7) is accepted [*Text, p. 320*], Paul may have been behind the evangelizing efforts of Epaphras. All this means that when this letter was written, the church at Colossae was probably not more than about eight years old, and perhaps younger. If, as the evidence suggests, life in Colossae came to an end with the major earthquake in A.D. 60-61, the congregation there was rather short-lived. Yet out of this small chapter in the story of the spread of the gospel, a letter has been preserved that is of immense value and interest for the Christian church universal.

Several details of the letter imply that most of the members of the church at Colossae were of Gentile background. For example, there is little reference to the Old Testament. Colossians 1:12, 21, 27 refer to outsiders (Gentiles) being brought in. Also, the vice lists in chapter 3 include sins associated with Gentiles more than with Jews. In most cities where Paul preached Christ, a few Jews responded along with Gentiles, and we assume that to be true also in the Lycus Valley.

The Author and His Circumstances

Traditionally the apostle Paul has been accepted as the author of Colossians (and Philemon). Except for occasional greetings in his own handwriting, the actual writing of all of Paul's letters was probably done by a secretary. (See Rom. 16:22; 1 Cor. 16:21; Gal. 6:11; Col. 4:18; 2 Thess. 3:17; Philem. 19.) For Colossians, the secretary may well have been Timothy.

Pauline authorship of Colossians has been challenged along several lines. Analysis of the vocabulary reveals that Colossians contains thirty-four words not found elsewhere in the NT. Before jumping to conclusions about authorship, we also note that Galatians has thirty-one words not found elsewhere in the NT. Vocabulary differences are largely accounted for by differing subject matter. Similarly, we can readily explain differences of style in the letters attributed to Paul by taking into account that Paul had new matters to address and found new ways of expressing his responses. Along with elements of style peculiar to Colossians, many similarities of style are also found in comparing Colossians with the undisputed writings of Paul.

Based on the assumption that the false teachings addressed in Colossians come from Gnosticism, some say that a later date of writing is required because Gnosticism did not come into full bloom until the second century. However, that argument holds true only if full-scale Gnosticism is read back into Colossians. [Gnosticism, p. 289.] If what we have in Colossians are first-century ideas, some of which in time developed into Gnosticism, then Pauline authorship is not thereby a problem.

Certain interpreters contend that Colossians reflects a much more highly developed Christology than could have been the case in Paul's time. But that conclusion presupposes a well-defined development of the doctrine of the person and work of Christ. Who is to say what Paul could or could not have understood about Christ at a given time? [History of Christology, p. 295.]

Although some scholars continue to consider Colossians as written by someone else in Paul's name (deutero-Pauline), scholarly opinion seems to be moving toward greater acceptance of Pauline authorship. Philemon is almost indisputably Pauline. Colossians and Philemon are linked together in several ways, and these connections strongly favor Paul as author of Colossians. The lists of persons in the greetings of both letters are almost identical. Both mention similar circumstances of imprisonment, and both have Colossae as their destination. The self-evident authenticity of Philemon gives convincing support to the same authenticity for Colossians.

Paul was in custody when he wrote Colossians and Philemon (Col. 4:3, 18; Philem. 13). But which imprisonment? Where? Traditionally, commentators thought that four of the so-called prison epistles—Ephesians, Philippians, Colossians, and Philemon—were written during Paul's first imprisonment at Rome. Philippians conveys an uncertainty about the future not found in the others. But the other three accord well with the circumstances of custody described in Acts 28:30, a relative freedom for friends to come and go. Paul does not include a trip to Colossae in his projected plans in Romans 15, but contact with Onesimus could well account for a change in itinerary. (Also written from prison, 2 Timothy has traditionally been understood as coming out of a second Roman imprisonment.)

Various opinions prevail concerning the place and time of writing of Colossians and other Pauline letters. Paul's imprisonment at Caesarea for two years (Acts 24:27) is proposed. One scholar concludes that Colossians and Philemon were sent from Caesarea in about A.D. 59 (Reicke: 429-438). But some features implied in the correspondence do not fit well with Paul's detention at Caesarea: associations with co-workers, opportunities for proclaiming the gospel (Col. 4:3-4), and the likelihood of Onesimus seeking shelter there.

A possible imprisonment in Ephesus offers another alternative location. Although not mentioned in Acts, such an imprisonment may perhaps be inferred (1 Cor. 15:32; 2 Cor. 1:8-10; 11:23) and supported by several extrabiblical witnesses (cf. Martin, 1978:27). If an extended incarceration in Ephesus is granted, several factors favor Ephesus over Rome as the writing place of Colossians. Ephesus was only 100 miles from Colossae, whereas Rome was 1,200 miles away. There is evidence that Colossae had been only recently evangelized when Paul wrote, and this fits with the period of Acts 19-20. Ralph P. Martin (among others) argues at length for Ephesus as the writing place of Colossians, within the period of A.D. 54 to A.D. 57

(1978:26-32). However, two factors raise cautions against this theory: the silence of Acts about imprisonment in Ephesus, and the fact
that Paul's ministry at Ephesus is not in the *we* sections of Acts—indicating when the writer Luke was with Paul (cf. Col. 4:14).

Thus I settle on an option which is still defensible: Rome as the
place of writing, early in Paul's imprisonment and before the devastating earthquake in the Lycus Valley. Precise chronology of Paul's life
is not available, but a date of A.D. 59 or 60 for the writing of Colossians is a reasonable conjecture. Even though these matters may
intrigue us, knowing the place and time of writing does not significantly affect an understanding of the message of Colossians.

One Side of a Conversation

We encounter a major limitation in our attempts to piece together the
purpose of the letter and the situation at Colossae that occasioned
the writing. In reading the letter, we are hearing only one side of a
conversation. As it is with hearing only one side of a telephone conversation, sometimes we can only surmise what is happening at the
other end. Assumptions are especially risky because it is easy to reason in circles. That is, we might take a few clues, fabricate a picture
with guesses and projections, and then look for more clues in the material that fit the hypothesis. This kind of exercise is tempting, but the
hazards require extreme caution.

Proceeding under the yellow caution lights, however, we can discern some features of what troubled Paul about winds of teaching in
the Lycus Valley. Although we have only Paul's answers to work with,
we can identify important elements of the questions. In keeping with
the approach in this commentary series, synthesis will come after in-
ductive analysis. It is clear that Paul had a deep pastoral concern for
the church at Colossae. The nature and content of that concern will
take shape as we consider the particulars of his response.

For the church today, it is not as important for us to figure out the
details of the potentially dangerous teaching which concerned Paul
as to learn from the manner in which he responded. We can see certain similarities between the deviant beliefs and practices endanger-
ing the church in Colossae and the contemporary revival of Eastern
mysticism, witchcraft, parapsychology, and pseudo-Christian cults.
But the greatest help from Colossians will be realized by making use
of Paul's strategy of preventive maintenance and encouragement to
grow in Christ. Let us grasp what is central in this pastoral letter to the

church at Colossae: Paul's constructive teaching about the excellency and sufficiency of Christ and the gospel.

Correlation Between Colossians and Ephesians

A close relationship between Colossians and Ephesians is evident. The similarities are striking, and parallels in concept and wording are numerous. We readily observe likenesses in style and general structure. While we cannot ignore the parallels between Colossians and Ephesians, let us also observe notable differences. Verbatim agreement is not all that extensive. Words common to both do not always have the same meaning. Examples are *fullness* and *mystery*. Yet the affinity between these two letters is greater than one finds between any other two Pauline letters. Making this observation is one thing. Explaining it is an entirely different matter.

Much of what has been written on the subject deals with questions of the authenticity of one or both epistles and with evidence of the dependence of one on the other or on a common source. *[Col. and Eph., p. 284.]* This commentary accepts the Pauline authorship of both Colossians and Ephesians. Beyond the obvious and significant factor that they were written to different church situations (contextualization), precise reasons for differences are speculative. We will regularly note points of similarity and difference between the two texts.

As You Enter the Text and World of Colossians

Wading into Colossians, beyond the familiar shoreline, will broaden your biblical insights, stretch your theological muscles, and prompt you to reflect on your experience of Jesus Christ in the church. Be prepared to hear the Word of the Lord and to integrate what you hear into your disciple life and ministry as servants of Christ, the gospel, and the church.

Paul's Letter to the Colossians

A block chart portrays some of the relationships of the several sections of Colossians, as outlined and perceived in this commentary.

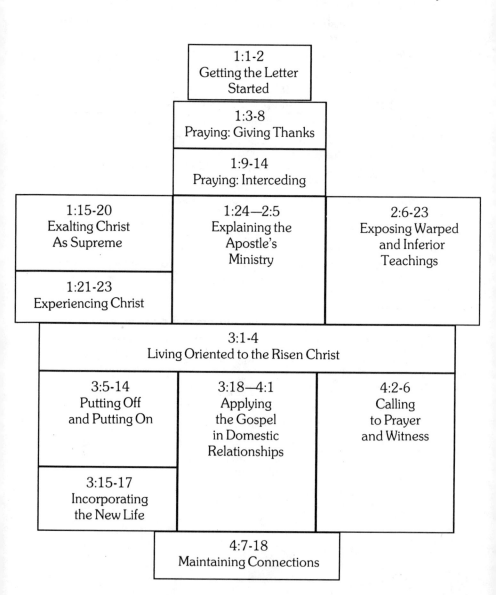

Colossians 1:1-2

Getting the Letter Started

PREVIEW

Paul began Colossians the way letters usually began in his time. Daniel 4:1 gives an earlier example of a widely used salutation form:

> King Nebuchadnezzar to all peoples, nations, and languages that live throughout the earth: May you have abundant prosperity!

First-century Christian usage followed the same form. In simplest terms, the greeting of Colossians and other NT letters follows this outline:

From _____; to _____; blessing.

Although basically using this traditional form, NT letters include specific Christian content in their salutations.

No two of Paul's letters begin exactly alike. The differences are worth noting. Already in the greetings we see that Paul is writing to specific readers. The individualized greetings provide clues about the tone and content of the letters. The greeting in Colossians, which is neither the longest nor the shortest of Paul's greetings, sets the stage for what follows.

OUTLINE

Author, 1:1

Recipients, 1:2a

Blessing, 1:2b

EXPLANATORY NOTES

Author 1:1

In eight of the NT letters attributed to him, Paul identifies himself as an *apostle*. Although his apostleship is not under attack at Colossae, as it was at Corinth and in Galatia, Paul is candid in giving his credentials at the top of this letter of warning against false teaching. An apostle is more than a commissioned deliverer of a message. An apostle represents the sender with authority. Two elements of apostleship as practiced by Paul stand out in Colossians: teaching and pastoral care.

Paul frequently uses the title *Christ Jesus*. The word order indicates that Christ has become a proper name, more than a modifying word to indicate which person named Jesus is the Messiah (as the word order Jesus Christ may signify). *[Titles, p. 323.]*

Adding to his credentials, Paul sets his commission in *the will of God* (see also 2 Cor. 1:1, Eph. 1:1; 2 Tim. 1:1). Paul's apostleship does not come by self-appointment. *The will of God* (occurring also in 1:9; 4:12) is best understood when associated with God's grace (Eph. 3:1-13). Paul does not mention in his self-introduction that he is in prison, although that fact becomes clear from 4:18.

Timothy is included in the greeting (as also in 1 and 2 Thess., 2 Cor., Phil., Philem.) but is not mentioned again in the letter. Persons named with the sender in letter introductions are not necessarily coauthors, but rather companions of the author at the time. Possibly Timothy serves as secretary to Paul. Since Paul identifies Timothy as *our brother*, he likely is already known in the area. Thus, including his name buttresses Paul's authority in addressing issues at Colossae, especially if he himself has not been there, as 2:1 seems to imply.

Recipients 1:2a

The way Paul identifies the addressees emphasizes a built-in tension. Literally, verse 2a reads: *to the in-Colossae saints and faithful broth-*

ers in Christ. The reality of two kingdoms becomes explicit in 1:13, but the concept is implicit here in 1:2. The dual environment is that of being in Colossae and also being in Christ. [In Christ, p. 299.] The words between allow a choice of translation. NIV has holy and faithful as adjectives modifying brothers. NRSV, RSV, and NASB take the first word to be a noun, saints (holy ones). The word is a noun in the greetings of other letters of Paul, and those greetings also show that saints is another name for church (1 and 2 Cor.). Saints does not mean being superholy; it means being set apart. [Holy, Saints, p. 296.] Faithful adds the quality of steadfastness to believing.

By calling them brothers and sisters, Paul draws attention to their link with others of the Christian family. Christians are not meant to be alone or unattached. Here, as in many other occurrences in the NT, brothers (in the Greek text) is best taken in a generic sense, including brothers and sisters. The NRSV rendering makes explicit what is implicit in the text. The relationship of the components of this phrase is thus:

$$
\textit{to the } \textbf{in-Colossae} \left\langle \begin{array}{c} \textit{saints and} \\ \textit{faithful brothers} \\ \textit{and sisters} \end{array} \right\rangle \textbf{ in Christ}
$$

Although in general Paul's greetings are in the contemporary style for letters, the content is distinctly Christian.

Blessing 1:2b

The salutation concludes with words of blessing, Grace to you and peace. The word grace is similar to a common Greek greeting (cf. 1 Macc. 10:18, 25; Acts 15:23; 23:26; James 1:1) but distinctly Christian. In the NT grace is the unmerited favor by which God in Christ bridges the gap between himself and humankind (cf. Eph. 2:8). Peace describes the new relationship between God and his people (cf. Eph. 2:14-18; 6:15). The word peace, occurring 91 times in the NT, represents the Greek equivalent to the Hebrew word and greeting, shalom, found 250 times in the OT. In biblical usage, peace has a richer, broader meaning than it carries in common English usage—expressing total well-being, wholeness. The theme of peace comes up again in Colossians in 1:20 and in 3:15.

Grace and peace come from God our Father. By virtue of being the giver, God gives special value to his gifts of grace and peace. Jesus taught his disciples to address God as Father. Yet the imagery of God as Father is also evident in the OT (Deut. 32:6; Isa. 63:16; Jer. 3:4; 31:9; Mal. 1:6; 2:10). Speaking of God as Father should not, however, lead to thinking of God as male. Occasionally maternal imagery also carries the biblical revelation of God. As examples, note Numbers 11:12 (where Moses implies that God conceived the people and brought them forth) and Luke 15:8-9 (Jesus' parable of the woman searching for a lost coin). However, this imagery does not infer that God is female. God transcends the sexuality associated with male and female. In this text, reference to God as our Father conveys the common family identity under God that brings Christians together and holds them together.

Summary

No hint of any problem at Colossae can be found in the greeting. Paul is not tentative in claiming apostolic authority as he writes to a church he presumably has not started or visited, but the reason for establishing his credentials is not immediately evident. However, affirmations made with a few key words and phrases stand out. Colossians is to be read in the assembly (4:16). The carefully worded greeting is more than a customary formality. Note these assurances already set forth in the first two verses:

- affirmation of a special relationship with God: *saints*
- affirmation of loyal allegiance to Christ: *faithful*
- affirmation of the family nature of the church: *brothers and sisters, Father*
- affirmation of a tension with culture: *in Colossae and in Christ*
- affirmation of God's blessings: *grace and peace*
- affirmation of a common bond: *our Father*

THE TEXT IN BIBLICAL CONTEXT
Pauline Salutations

A number of useful observations arise through making a chart of the salutations of the letters attributed to Paul—Romans through Titus. For each of the thirteen letters, the chart should include five categories: (1) writer-author, (2) descriptive identification of the writer-author, (3) associate(s), (4) addressee(s), with identification, and (5) blessing. By using a translation that renders words fairly uniformly (such as NASB), you will be able to note precise similarities and differences. Watch for repeated terms: apostle, slave (bond servant), by the will of God, Timothy, church, saints, grace, and peace.

Blessing as a Christian Tradition

A blessing of "grace and peace" appears in the salutation of all of Paul's letters, and also in 1 and 2 Peter and Revelation. Wherever this form of blessing originated, with Paul or in the early church before Paul, it became a standard form of Christian greeting. Variations of the form show that Paul and others adapted a conventional greeting to Christian use. While NT blessings follow the customary form of the culture, the *practice* of blessing rests on the biblical tradition of conferring a benediction of God's favor on others (Num. 6:24-26).

Blessings (and cursings) had a primary place in Israelite worship (IDB, 1:446-448). The priests officially pronounced powerful verbal blessings aligned with divine purposes and people conferred the same mutually. In the OT and NT, blessings are closely associated with greetings, both in meeting and parting. The blessings at the beginning and end of NT letters may reflect worship practices of the early church (Barth: 71; C. Westermann: 96-98). The benedictions with which letters begin and end show signs of intentions that go beyond the conventions of the day.

THE TEXT IN THE LIFE OF THE CHURCH
God-Talk in Our Greetings

References to deity were apparently normal in greetings in the NT era. Non-Christians made reference to their gods, and Christians addressed each other in the name of God the Father and Jesus Christ.

In secularized Western culture, people tend to mention God only in profanity and spontaneous exclamations and in an occasional "God bless you" when someone sneezes. Christians seem less disposed to greet each other in the name of Jesus than was true in times past. Does the change mean that earlier greetings were largely cultural, or that modern Christians have become so secularized that they drop God-talk out of their conversations?

God's people need to rediscover the power of blessing and reintroduce explicit references to God, Jesus Christ, and faith in greetings, conversations, and benedictions. The words need not be identical with NT patterns, but we need to learn and practice the naturalness and integrity of the biblical examples.

Colossians 1:3-8

Praying: Giving Thanks

PREVIEW

Samples of Paul's praying, as found in his letters, continue to challenge the believing community today to higher levels of prayer. Thanksgiving and intercession make up the threads in the fabric, the warp and woof, of Paul's prayers. Although these two aspects of the apostle's praying will be treated separately, together they comprise a coherent unit in 1:3-14. We can see four related functions of this combined section: (1) Pastoral—as an integral part of the purpose for the letter as a whole. (2) Teaching—adding to the instruction already received. (3) Exhortation—encouraging and calling the readers to further steps of growth in faithfulness. (4) Introduction—as a way to introduce concepts to be elaborated in the body of the letter.

Several features of verses 3-14 may be noted by way of overview. Nine words and phrases in the thanksgiving part of Paul's prayer have close parallels in the intercession part (EDM translations):

3	*giving thanks*	*giving thanks* 12
	praying	*praying and asking* 9
	the Father	*the Father* 12
4	*having heard*	*we heard* 9
	the saints	*the saints* 12
6	*bearing fruit*	*bearing fruit* 10
	growing	*growing* 10
	from the day	*from the day* 9
	knew (verb form)	*knowledge* 9-10

The word *all* (or an equivalent translation) is also a unifying thread in 1:3-14: *for all the saints* (1:4), *in the whole world* (1:6), *in all spiritual wisdom and understanding* (1:9), *fully pleasing* (1:10), *in every good work* (1:10), *with all the strength* (1:11), *to endure everything with patience* (1:11).

All of Paul's letters, except Galatians, have a thanksgiving following the greeting. As is typical, this thanksgiving has the marks of being composed specifically for the believers at Colossae. The main part of the letter begins with thanksgiving, not with a rebuke or correction. Here are affirmations of solid experience in Christ and confirmation of the message of the gospel received through Epaphras. These expressions tie the text to a particular time and place. We are privileged to listen in on the apostle's prayer thoughts.

In the UBS (United Bible Societies) edition of the Greek text, verses 3-8 are one long, complex sentence of 102 words. *[Grammar, p. 290.]* (NASB keeps verses 3-8 as one sentence.) The thought flows more by association than by logic. This complex sentence contains a number of words found in the favored vocabulary of Colossians. Of particular interest is the triad—faith, love, and hope.

OUTLINE
Always Thanking God, 1:3

Experience of the Gospel, 1:4-5
    Faith in Christ
    Love for All the Saints
    Hope Laid Up in Heaven
    The Word of the Truth

Spread of the Gospel, 1:6
    Bearing Fruit
    Growing

Teacher of the Gospel, 1:7-8
    Epaphras

EXPLANATORY NOTES
Always Thanking God 1:3
Following a blessing from God, 1:2b, Paul's thoughts move to giving

thanks to God. By including a thanksgiving near the beginning of
Colossians, Paul follows the customary letter style of the Greek
world. One example will illustrate a common practice of the period.
In a letter to her husband, a woman wrote:

> If you are well and other things are going right, it would accord with the
> prayer which I make continually to the gods. I myself and the child and all
> the household are in good health and think of you always . . . for the
> news that you are well I straightway thanked the gods (Lohse: 12).

However, to whom and for what Paul gives thanks is thoroughly
Christian. The plural, we, may mean that Timothy and others with
Paul are also giving thanks. Praise goes to God rather than to the
Colossian believers for their faithfulness.

This is the first of seven references to the giving of thanks in
Colossians (1:3, 12; 2:7; 3:15-17; 4:2). Such a strong emphasis on
praise and gratitude is noteworthy in itself. In terms of what prompts
thanks or should be the reason for giving thanks, these seven examples expand the horizons of the thanksgiving aspect of prayer.
[Thanksgiving, p. 322.]

Paul confesses, *we always thank God, the Father of our Lord Jesus Christ.* Implicit in this statement is the claim that the bridge between believers and God is complete. Believers are in Christ. God is
the Father of the Lord Jesus Christ. It therefore follows that God is
also the Father of the believers. Jesus Christ is the linkage and bond.

This letter focuses on Christ and Christology, and thus the full title, *Lord Jesus Christ*, emerges early. Paul's case for the preeminence and the supreme authority of Jesus Christ as Lord begins
here in verse 3. You will find it worthwhile to survey the several titles
for Christ in Colossians. *[Titles, p. 323.]*

By its location in Greek, the word *always* may refer to either *thank*
or *pray*, or both. NRSV has *we always thank God.* NASB has *praying
always for you.* Both prayer and thanksgiving were regular activities
of the apostle. This prayer includes three reasons for gratitude.

Experience of the Gospel 1:4-5

Most likely Paul heard through Epaphras about the progress of the
Colossians in their experience of the gospel. Paul's thanksgiving to
God focuses in this case on the familiar NT threesome, faith, love,
and hope. *[Triad, p. 324.]* The more familiar order is faith-hope-love
(1 Cor. 13:13). But the sequence faith-love-hope is the same as in

1 Thessalonians 1:3 and 5:8. By word order, sentence structure, and number of words, Paul here gives the greatest emphasis to hope. The reason for the stress on hope will become clearer.

① *Faith in Christ.* As in other examples of *faith in* _____, *in* refers more to the sphere in which faith is exercised than to the object of faith. Christ is also the object and center of the Christians' faith. But here the emphasis is on the faith of those who are *in Christ,* living in him as well as believing in him. The other occurrences of *faith* in Colossians are in 1:23; 2:5, 7, and 12.

② *Love for all the saints.* The evidence of a continuing experience of God's love is the outward flow of love to others, especially in the community of Christ. *[Holy, Saints, p. 296.]* Although not fully explicit from the wording here, love is not to be regarded as a feeling of kindness that Christians have, but rather as an activity directed toward the well-being of others. The word *love* also occurs in 1:8, 13; 2:2; and 3:14.

③ *Hope laid up in heaven.* The content of the Christians' hope is not explained or elaborated here, as it is in 1 Peter 1:3-5, but Peter's expression "kept in heaven for you," sounds much like *laid up for you in heaven.* The two other occurrences of *hope* in Colossians are in 1:23 and 1:27.

Notice that Paul does not give thanks for these three graces as abstract concepts, but as elements of the Colossian believers' experience. The personal dimension comes out in *your* faith, love that *you* have, and hope laid up for *you.*

How, then, are faith, love, and hope related? NIV expands verse 5 to bring out the relationship implicit in the text: *the faith and love that spring from the hope that is stored up for you in heaven.* Faith and love are grounded in a sure hope, rather than hope being a reward for faith and love. This is why, in Colossians, *hope* is the most important element in the faith-love-hope triad. The now experience of God's working in Christian experience takes on even more meaning when tied to the sure, future consummation of salvation.

Reports about new teachings in the Lycus Valley may have prompted Paul to emphasize hope in the Colossian letter—but that is somewhat speculative. *[Problems, p. 310.]* However, a solid hope is good protection against the enticements of foreign teaching of any kind. Paul has good reason for thanksgiving to God after hearing that faith, love, and hope were imbedded in the Colossians' ongoing encounter with the gospel.

When Paul puts a special emphasis on hope, he is not introducing an unknown dimension of the gospel, but underscoring an integral part of the gospel they have already received (1:6). His thoughts of how the Colossians have heard the gospel lead into thoughts about the gospel itself.

The word of the truth. This phrase also appears in Ephesians 1:13; 2 Timothy 2:15; and James 1:18, with essentially the same meaning. By wording and punctuation (in NRSV and other translations), *the gospel* and *the word of the truth* are two ways to say the same thing. The construction of the expression as a whole allows also for the rendering of NEB, *the message of the true Gospel*; or of GNB, *the true message, the Good News*; both of which emphasize the truth of the apostolic gospel (cf. Gal. 2:5, 14).

The gospel (euangelion) means good news. In the LXX *[Septuagint, p. 316]*, the term is used of tidings of the birth of a child (Jer. 20:15) and news of victory (1 Sam. 31:9). The word occurs twice in Colossians (72 times in the NT; 57 times in Paul's letters). *Gospel* "is the word which is the summation of the whole Christian message. . . . The good news is *of* God and *from* God" (Barclay, 1964:101-102). The concept includes both the church's message about Christ and God's revelation in Christ (what Christ proclaimed).

In verse 5, *the gospel* is viewed as the source of *hope*. As the significance of the gospel is elaborated in verse 6, it is described as a gospel for *the whole world,* a gospel that bears fruit, and a gospel of grace.

Spread of the Gospel 1:6

In verse 6 the apostle's thanksgiving moves from experience in the gospel to the expansion of the gospel *in the whole world.* The authentic power of the gospel is evident in what it does. The gospel is *bearing fruit.* The verb form translated *bearing fruit* conveys the idea of intensity: fully bearing fruit. *[Grammar, p. 290.]* The gospel is not like many flowers that regress after producing seed pods. It keeps on bearing fruit. Mention of the fruitfulness of the word of truth recalls the words of Isaiah 55:10-11, the promise that the word of the Lord will not return empty, but will accomplish its purpose and prosper.

The gospel is also *growing. [Text, p. 319.]* The phrase that follows, *among yourselves,* could refer to inner spiritual growth and fruit bearing, as in 1:10. But in the context of verse 6, *bearing fruit and growing* (or increasing) have to do primarily with the spread of the gospel. The gospel has been reaching out effectively *in the whole world*, including Colossae. The expression *whole world* is an example of what is called hyperbole (as in Rom. 1:8 and 1 Thess. 1:8) and is not to be pushed to its literal limits. The point is that what they are experiencing at Colossae is not an isolated, localized phenomenon. The early Christians are not withdrawing and secluding themselves from the world, but everywhere they are penetrating their world with the gospel of Jesus Christ. The fact that the gospel works so effectively everywhere supports its integrity and gives reason for thanks to God.

Paul explains how and why the gospel takes root and grows into fruitfulness by saying they *heard* and *truly comprehended* the message of the gospel, here identified as *the grace of God*. Coming to a knowledge of the truth is a NT way of speaking about becoming a Christian. God "desires everyone to be saved and to come to the knowledge of the truth" (1 Tim. 2:4; cf. 2 Tim. 2:25; Heb. 10:26; 2 John 1). Knowledge and knowing in these texts go far beyond intellectual perception. [*Know, p. 304.*] Paul's whole being is caught up in testifying to the gospel of the grace of God (Acts 20:24).

The phrase *in truth* describes how the gospel of God's grace is received as well as the reliability of the message. NRSV has the rendering "truly comprehended the grace of God." Understood this way, Paul thanks God that they have truly, genuinely experienced God's grace.

Teacher of the Gospel 1:7-8

The one through whom the Colossians have learned the gospel, Epaphras, is now added to the thanksgiving list. Epaphras is a shortened form of Epaphroditus, but we are not to confuse Epaphras with the Epaphroditus of Philippians 2:25 and 4:18. According to Colossians 4:12, Epaphras was a native of Colossae.

As Paul thinks of Epaphras, a number of associations come to mind. Their relationship is warmly affectionate. He calls him *beloved* (dear). He also identifies him as a *fellow servant* (slave), as he does Tychicus in 4:7. In 4:12 Paul calls Epaphras a *servant* (slave) *of Christ Jesus*. He also thinks of him as a *faithful minister of Christ*. Thus Paul is expressing his appreciation for Epaphras in a prayer to God. However, the Colossian church would sense a clear affirmation both of the person and the ministry of Epaphras. A reliable communicator assures a reliable gospel. Epaphras is also the source of Paul's information about the Colossians. Through him Paul knows of their spiritual progress.

The finishing touch on Paul's prayer of thanksgiving is a recognition of the Colossians' *love in the Spirit.* It is left open whether the object of their love is God, each other, or Paul. Regardless of the object, Paul rejoices to know of their love, for love comes by the Spirit (Rom. 5:5; 15:30; Gal. 5:22). Love functions as the crowning evidence of the Colossians' solid grounding in Christ.

The only direct reference in Colossians to the Spirit is in 1:8. The adjective *spiritual* in 1:9 and 3:16 provides an indirect reference. In 2:5 the human spirit is the meaning. In Colossians we find experience in the gospel described with a minimum of reference to the Holy Spirit. *[Col. and Eph., p. 284.]*

Summary

Reviewing the items for thanksgiving, we find gratitude expressed for the following:

1. The Colossians' faith exercised *in Christ.*
2. Their love for all the saints.
3. Hope being stored up for them.
4. The gospel, the word of truth, coming to them.
5. The gospel bearing fruit/growing in the whole world.
6. Their having heard and fully understood God's grace in truth.
7. Epaphras as a faithful evangelist, teacher, minister.
8. Their love in the Spirit.

We can try to imagine how these specifics of thanksgiving to God may have been heard and felt at Colossae. *[Thanksgiving, p. 322.]*

THE TEXT IN BIBLICAL CONTEXT
Biblical Themes Early in Colossians

Several themes in addition to thanksgiving surface in 1:3-8. They set the tone and message of Colossians. The following topics have significant interrelationships with Colossians as a whole, with other passages of the Bible, and with the biblical message as a whole.

1. *The Grace of God.* Grace, a concept prominent in the NT, has only limited visibility in Colossians (compared, for example, with Romans and Ephesians). The Greek word *charis*, often translated as grace, appears in Colossians in the greeting (1:2) and in the closing benediction (4:18). In 3:16 it carries the meaning of gratitude or thanksgiving. In 4:6 it has the meaning of graciousness. However, 1:6 has grace in the sense of the gospel being the message of God's gra-

cious action in Christ (cf. 2 Cor. 6:1; 8:9). Although not expressed in
the theological language of Romans 3:24 and 5:15, the grace base of
the good news is clear. When grace is not at the core of the gospel,
something else takes its place. Some of the substitutes for grace can
be found later in the Colossian letter.

2. *Truth.* In the OT, truth carries the ideas of integrity, faithfulness,
and reliability. What God says is "the word of truth" (Ps. 119:43).
"The ordinances of the Lord are true and righteous altogether" (Ps.
19:9b). God's word is truth because of who God is.

The NT view of truth adds the experiential dimension of trustwor-
thiness to the meanings of factual, accurate, and conceptual. In this
biblical sense, truth is much more than correct doctrine which Christians may possess. It is not elusive, relative, the possession of only a
few, or something to argue about. As it is with the biblical meaning of
knowledge *[Know, p. 304]*, truth is not discovered in intellectual abstractions but in an encounter with Jesus Christ, in whom God has revealed himself. Ephesians 4:21 says it succinctly: "as truth is in Jesus." John 1:14 declares that the Word who became flesh was "full of
grace and truth."

3. *Fruitfulness and Growth.* Paul's comments about the gospel
echo what Jesus said about the kingdom, "Other seed fell into good
soil and brought forth grain, growing up and increasing and yielding
thirty and sixty and a hundredfold" (Mark 4:8). Several other kingdom parables emphasize growth: the seed growing secretly (Mark
4:26-29) and the mustard seed (Mark 4:30-32). Growth is an inherent characteristic of the gospel.

Paul as a Team Person

Although retaining the designation of apostle for himself in Colossians, Paul recognizes and rejoices in the ministry of Epaphras (and
others). There is no taint of jealousy, competition, or superiority in
Paul's comments about a fellow servant. The same spirit shows in
Paul's words, "I planted, Apollos watered, but God gave the growth"
(1 Cor 3:6). It would not be like Paul to say to the Colossians, Now, if I
had brought you the gospel in the first place, things would be different. Although Paul has a strong pioneering spirit, he is a team person
in Christ.

THE TEXT IN THE LIFE OF THE CHURCH
The Noble Vocation of Thanksgiving

All Christians could take a lesson from Paul in the regular practice of thanksgiving. Too often we limit prayer to asking God to fix something or someone, and neglect to thank God. What difference might it make in the life of the church if members majored in thanking God? Following Paul's example in Colossians 1:3-8, that would include rejoicing in the following:

1. the fruitfulness of the gospel in others' lives
2. the wonder of kingdom growth
3. faithful communicators of the gospel

Keeping Faith, Love, and Hope in Balance

Each member of this triad needs the other two. [Triad, p. 324.] Any one of the three may appropriately receive emphasis in a given era or circumstance, but never to the exclusion of either of the other two. Experience (the here and now) and expectancy (the not yet) need to be kept in balance. An eschatology of hope takes on added relevance when the church encounters hardship and persecution. In an age of aimlessness and despair, a gospel that majors in hope will be attractive, not simply as a fantasy of escape, but as a stabilizing goal.

An Unbounded Gospel

Discovery that the gospel is for all people caused growing pains in the early church. As the gospel leaped over the boundaries of language, culture, and social class, some people were faced with difficult adjustments in their thinking and in their relationships. In one sense the gospel is exclusive. It demands personal response, which separates believers from unbelievers. In another sense the gospel is inclusive. The invitation is for all. Some "Christians" have at times represented the gospel as exclusive for the wrong reasons. Thus they have missed the insight of Frederick W. Faber (1862):

> There's a wideness in God's mercy,
> Like the wideness of the sea;
> There's a kindness in His justice,
> Which is more than liberty.

> But we make His love too narrow
> By false limits of our own;
> And we magnify His strictness
> With a zeal He will not own.

The Christian church still struggles with the implications of Paul's phrase, *all the saints*. Paul's faithfulness to a vision of the gospel moving out and bearing fruit in the whole world still challenges the church to be as excited as he was about the power and potential of the gospel.

The Human Element in Communicating the Gospel

Romans 10:14-15 makes the point that believing comes by hearing, and hearing by someone preaching. Epaphras was the one through whom the Colossians had *heard* and *learned* the grace of God. God continues to use human instruments in transmitting the gospel. The church needs to remember that God has not chosen to bypass the human element. The responsibility for passing on the good news rests with the Epaphrases who will be faithful servants of Christ.

Colossians 1:9-14

Praying: Interceding

PREVIEW

Continuing in the mode of prayer, the writer's focus shifts from thanksgiving to intercession. One might ask why Paul includes references to his praying in Colossians and in his other letters. Technically we do not have here a verbatim prayer, but a listing of what he has prayed about. Although elements of exhortation and teaching shine through, the primary purpose seems to be pastoral.

The sentence construction of this block is complex. Some editions of the Greek text have verses 9-20 all in one sentence! Differences between translations raise several questions to be investigated.

If we underline the significant words in verses 9-14, we can easily find more than thirty of them. That's more than 25 percent of the words! (Refer to the Preview of 1:3-8 for features of 1:3-14.)

OUTLINE

The following simplified outline shows the general flow of the string of thoughts making up the intercessory part of Paul's prayer. The flow of thought in this complex combination of clauses can be seen more readily in a structural analysis of 1:9-14 that closely follows the Greek text and grammar. *[Grammar, p. 290.]*

Asking Deliberately, 1:9

Asking Specifically, 1:10-11

Asking Confidently, 1:12-14

EXPLANATORY NOTES

Paul's intercession is not prompted by an awareness of coldness or decline at Colossae, but by news of the church's vigor, as implied by the link, *for this reason.* Paul does not reserve intercession for when things are going badly for churches. The good report he has received gives rise to intercession as well as to thanksgiving. Although the intercessory requests in this prayer are pertinent to individual Christian experience, the application to congregational life must not be ignored or neglected.

Asking Deliberately 1:9

Nonstop praying. We can imagine what it must have meant to the saints at Colossae to hear from the apostle Paul the words *we have not ceased praying for you.* The plural subject, *we,* is probably meant to include Paul's associates. The use of both words, *praying* and *asking,* coupled with the claim of not stopping the activity (cf. Eph. 1:16-19), emphasize the intensity and earnestness of the apostle's prayer life. Paul practices what he urges others to do (4:2). Jesus' teaching in Mark 11:24 has the same two words for prayer, "all things for which you pray and ask" (NASB).

Filled. The concepts of fullness and being filled, as applied to Christ and Christian experience, are prominent in Colossians. *[Fullness, p. 288.]* Paul's specific request, *that you may be filled,* employs a passive verb, which indicates that it is not a do-it-yourself exercise. Restating it actively as *asking God to fill you* (NIV) makes the point clear. In addition, to *be filled* implies elements of completeness (that a knowledge of God's will is to shape the whole of life) and of exclusiveness (that only God's will be allowed to shape life).

Knowledge, wisdom, understanding. The compound word *epignōsis,* translated *knowledge,* as found here (and most times in Colossians), may carry a richer meaning than the simple word *gnōsis,* although that distinction is seriously questioned. Certainly the words associated with it have a rich meaning. The phrase *in all spiritual wis-*

dom and understanding reinforces the biblical concept that knowledge is much more than acquired information. *[Know, p. 304.]* Paul does not depreciate knowledge but asks that Christians participate fully in what they may know and understand. His perspective is not that the Colossians already know too much, but that they know too little of what is spiritually important. The word *spiritual* implies a recognition that wisdom and insight are given by the Spirit.

God's will. What Paul desires the Colossians to know fully is God's will. In line with the biblical concept of knowledge, God's will is not a piece of isolated information, a predetermined mold, or a pre-packaged plan for the future. According to the wording of Jesus' model prayer, "Your will be done" (Matt. 6:10), God's will is for doing. Therefore, to know God's will is to experience what God wants his people to do, individually and corporately. As Jesus explained, insight comes through commitment to do God's will (John 7:17). The close connection between knowledge and behavior is made abundantly clear as the prayer goes on.

Paul's asking has been regular, intense, focused, and intentional. Such deliberateness stands in sharp contrast to the bland suggestion of prayer in the comment, I'll be thinking of you.

Asking Specifically 1:10-11

A worthy and pleasing life. According to this text, the result of being filled with the knowledge of God's will is appropriate living. Paul often refers to the manner of life as *walking,* using a word that also means physical walking (*peripateō*). Three other examples are found in Colossians: 2:6; 3:7; and 4:5. The gospel requires a radical change in the conduct of life.

Two phrases describe this walk in relational terms. (1) *Worthy of the Lord* identifies living that is appropriate to those who own Jesus as Lord. (The phrase is found in a similar context in 1 Thess. 2:12; cf. Matt. 10:37; Eph. 4:1; Phil. 1:27.) *Worthy* does not imply merit, which is excluded by the gospel of grace, but a manner of living in keeping with confessing Jesus as Lord. (2) *Fully pleasing to him* sets the goal for all Christian action. (See 1 Thess. 2:4; 4:1; and 1 Cor. 7:32-35 for other examples of this motivational goal.) Living to please the Lord is not a tactic for getting favors, as pagans would view it, but a loving, obedient response to grace.

Four facets of walking in the will of God follow. The sequence of four Greek participles *[Grammar, p. 290]* is retained in the NIV wording:

1. *Bearing fruit in every good work.* Fruit bearing has a somewhat different meaning here from what it has in 1:6, where Paul emphasizes the fruitfulness of the gospel in the world. Here in 1:10 the focus is on the believers' experience, parallel with Jesus' emphasis on fruit bearing in John 15. Experiencing the gospel leads to practical goodness, without any hint of merit. Grace is intended to lead to good works, and not the other way around (cf. 2 Cor. 9:8; Eph. 2:10; and 2 Tim. 2:21).

2. *Growing in the knowledge of God.* Personal growth in those receiving the gospel is the point here, rather than the growth of the gospel, as in 1:6. In line with Paul's dynamic view of Christian experience, a pattern of progress emerges here in Colossians:

To receive the gospel is to come to know God.

To know God is to do his will.

To do his will is to know more and more of God.

3. *Being strengthened with all power according to his glorious might.* From an emphasis on living out God's will, the prayer moves to receiving power to do God's will. Literally, the wording of the phrase is *with all power being empowered.* The request implies an available, adequate, steady flow of power to enable appropriate living by the Lord's people.

The accompanying words, *according to his glorious power,* reveal the source and measure of available power. In the literal rendering of the phrase, *according to the might of his glory* (NASB margin), we encounter the word *might,* which is never used of human power in the NT. Several other references shed light on the meaning. In Ephesians 1:19-20 three Greek words—*power, strength,* and *might* (NASB)—are associated with Christ's resurrection as a demonstration of God's power. Romans 6:4 says, "Christ was raised from the dead by the glory of the Father." Power and glory are associated also in some NT doxologies (e.g., Rev. 1:6; 5:12; 19:1).

God's *glory* (NASB margin), in addition to a connotation of splendor, has the meaning of essential character. A display of God's glory is, in that sense, a revelation of what God is really like. Piling up related words (power, might, glory) and adding an *all,* has the net effect of making the strongest kind of statement about God being adequate to enable believers to walk the new life.

Paul asks that the Colossians be empowered by God for a specific reason. When Paul identifies the two intertwined needs, *to endure everything with patience,* he is reminding them of resources that as yet they may not know they need. Although distinctions in meaning between endurance and patience are not absolute, endurance (*to endure*) emphasizes holding up in all circumstances and attacks without complaint or resentment, and *patience* emphasizes a long-suffering attitude toward all people without growing weary in love (3:12). *[Endurance, Patience, p. 286.]* Paul recognizes that these desired Christian responses to life go beyond the potentials of the human spirit. They are imparted by God (cf. Rom. 15:5; Gal. 5:22).

Verses 11-12 present several problems in understanding the text. The words translated *while joyfully* (literally, *with joy*) can be taken with what precedes or with what follows. *[Text, p. 319.]* The NRSV rendering, *joyfully giving thanks*, commends itself (cf. NIV, NASB, and GNB). Thanks is to be given joyfully, not merely dutifully.

A related question is whether verses 12-14 are part of the prayer or a preface to the following section. The phrase *giving thanks to the Father* is not closely tied to the previous parallel phrases. The GNB rendering, *And with joy give thanks*, is an example of taking the phrase as an injunction to give thanks, rather than as part of Paul's request to God. The inclusion of conversion language in verses 12-14 leads some commentators to see these verses as "confessional liturgy," statements of faith used in worship by the early church. The style is a bit different from that of verses 9-11. But if we recognize that Paul's dictation flows at times by association rather than by precise outline, we can see how he leads into the thoughts of verses 12-14.

4. *Giving thanks* (the fourth in the series of participles). Giving thanks is a prominent theme in Colossians. *[Thanksgiving, p. 322.]* It is not out of character for Paul to include the need for expressing gratitude as an essential part of his prayer concern that the Colossian believers please God (1:10). As in 3:17, *the Father* receives the thanks. Designating God as Father assumes that readers and hearers of the letter understand something of Jesus' use of that term. Next follows a list of reasons for gratitude.

Asking Confidently 1:12-14

Three actions of the Father and two benefits by way of the Son make up the conclusion of Paul's prayer. They spell out why the Colossian believers should be thankful. Even more, they make up Paul's reasons for confidence in his intercessory prayer. God in Christ has already acted and is acting on behalf of all believers. The conclusion of the prayer returns to the theme with which it began—thanksgiving.

The Father . . . has enabled you (or us). *[Text, p. 319.]* The word translated *enabled* means to authorize, make fit, qualify. The same word (including the adjective form) occurs three times in 2 Corinthians 3:5-6, translated as competent or sufficient.

Paul uses OT words and images in explaining for what the Father enables or qualifies believers. The same words translated here as *share* and *inheritance* are found in a number of places in the LXX *[Septuagint, p. 316]* as "allotment/portion" and "inheritance" (Deut. 10:9; Josh. 19:9). The imagery is that of God allotting the Promised Land to the tribes (Josh. 13ff.). The inheritance of the new Israel is the moreness to which Abraham looked (Heb. 11:8-12). The believers' inheritance is both a future certainty and a present experience. Christians are assured of a glorious future, but that is not the point of this text, which speaks of the believers' present possession. "This Canaan is not in the distance, beyond death; it is about us to-day, in our home, in our family, in our business, in our worship, in our company, in our solitude, in our joys, in our tears, in all that makes up mortal life" (H. Moule: 65-66). Acts 20:32 offers similar wording: "A message that is able . . . to give you the inheritance among all who are sanctified."

The inheritance belongs to *the saints in the light*. The saints (literally, *the holy or sanctified ones*) *[Holy, Saints, p. 296]* are those whom God calls his own (1:2, 4, 26). A similar connection between inheritance and saints appears in Ephesians 1:18: "That you may become aware of the hope to which he is calling you, what glorious riches are to be inherited among the saints" (as rendered by Barth: 145).

Light is the new context in which God's saints live. Other NT texts also refer to *light* as the believers' new arena (2 Cor. 4:4, 6; Eph. 5:8; 1 Thess. 5:5; 1 Pet. 2:9; and 1 John 1:5-6). Note the similar wording in Paul's statement of his calling (cf. Acts 26:18; Col. 1:12-14).

A striking interplay of words in the last part of verse 12 and in verse 13 can be caught by marking or arranging the text to show the parallels and contrasts in this compact text.

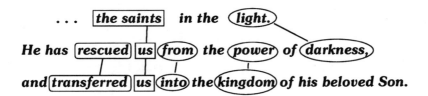

. . . the saints in the light.
He has rescued us from the power of darkness,
and transferred us into the kingdom of his beloved Son.

He has rescued us. To rescue is to deliver, to save. God's deliverance is a prominent theme of the OT. The concept is more frequently expressed in the NT by *save.* Here (1:13) the vivid picture portrays God's initiative and power in response to human captivity, helplessness, and frustration. Even though the human spirit apart from God is not totally unresponsive to him, and not everyone goes to the extreme of depravity, only God can effect the needed rescue. The word translated *rescued* always has God as the subject in the NT, and most of the occurrences appear in prayer contexts (e.g., Matt. 6:13; Rom. 7:24). We find the word in Luke 1:74 (Zechariah's prophecy), and in 2 Corinthians 1:10 (three times).

God's rescue is *from the power of darkness.* The word translated *power* (*exousia*) has the meaning here of jurisdiction, thralldom, tyranny. The plural form of the word in 1:16; 2:15; and Ephesians 6:12 calls attention to the agents of that tyranny: *powers.* The same words (in Greek) are part of Jesus' response to those who came to arrest him: "But this is your hour, and the power of darkness" (Luke 22:53). The phrase identifies a condition of captivity under the jurisdiction of moral and spiritual darkness.

[God] transferred us. The verb *transferred* conveys the sense that God brought us over into a different realm. The Jewish historian, Josephus, used the word with reference to Tiglath-pileser's relocation of Israelite tribes into his own kingdom (*Ant.* 9.235). That connotation is closer to the meaning here than any of several other NT references (e.g., Acts 13:22; 1 Cor. 13:2). However, the phrase, *the kingdom of his beloved Son,* does not describe a new location, but a new Lord, a new citizenship. In contrast to the tyranny of darkness, the new kingdom is experienced when the Son is honored as Lord. *[Titles, p. 323.]* The change is from slavery to freely given service to the new Sovereign.

Rather than describing the transfer in terms of an abstract darkness-light dualism, Paul puts it in personal terms: the rule of *his beloved Son,* literally, *the Son of his love.* Some scholars consider this phrase to be a Hebraic expression equivalent to God's affirmation of his Son, as for example in Mark 1:11; 9:7; 12:6 (Blass-Debrunner, sect. 165). However, Lightfoot (142) contends that *Son of his love* says more, that love is the essence of the Son as well as of the Father. What follows (1:14) springs from love.

The kingdom, as used here, is present reality and experience, with the fullness of realization yet to come. Christ is King. His reign began with his ascension. His kingship and kingdom are inherent in the confession, "Jesus is Lord" (as in 1 Cor. 12:3).

In review, as reasons for thanksgiving, Paul names three actions of God—*enabled, rescued, transferred*—with accompanying blessings. With all that God has already done, there is no need for the Colossian believers to search elsewhere for what is already theirs in Christ.

Mention of *the Son* leads Paul to include two benefits particularly identified with Christ. The sequence of *kingdom, redemption,* and *forgiveness* moves from the broad general concept to a specific part of the whole. Redemption includes more than forgiveness, and kingdom includes more than redemption. The relationships may be thought of this way:

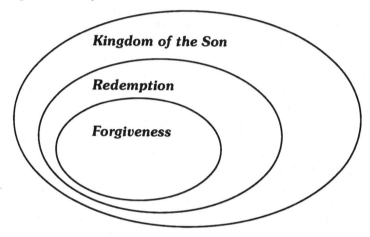

Redemption is viewed here (and in Eph. 1:7) as a present benefit of union with Christ. A literal translation is *in whom we are having redemption*. In other NT passages, redemption is a future promise (e.g., Rom. 8:23; Eph. 1:14; 4:30). The basic meaning of *redeem* is to set free for a ransom, as with a slave being freed for a price. Mark 10:45, using a related verb, speaks of the Son of Man offering himself to buy back many. The ransom factor is minimal here because the focus is on the source of redemption and the resultant liberation rather than on how it was accomplished. In Paul's vocabulary, *redemption* is not as comprehensive a theological term as *reconciliation* (1:20). Yet it is a significant word in the constellation of terms Paul uses to describe the riches of the gospel.

Redemption is directly tied to Jesus Christ. We should not view redemption as something previously accomplished by Christ that is now available apart from Christ. Experience of redemption, in past, present, and future aspects, comes through the "in Christ" relationship. The person and ministry of Christ includes both the historical Jesus who taught, lived, and died, and the risen, reigning, returning Lord.

As a consequence of redemption, those in Christ receive *the forgiveness of sins*. An association between forgiveness and redemption is also explicit in Ephesians 1:7. Here in Colossians we have the most common word for forgiveness in the NT: *aphesis*. It has the meaning of letting go, leaving behind, remitting. The Jubilee principle of releasing indebted servants (Lev. 25) seems to be part of the imagery. Other examples of usage are found in Luke 24:47 and Acts 10:43. A synonym appears in 2:13 and 3:13. The Son provides forgiveness of *sins*, a forgiveness that is specific, personal, and inclusive.

Forgiveness, particularly when coupled with redemption as it is here, includes more than canceling the guilt of sins. Thinking of forgiveness only in a narrow judicial sense (of removing penalty) blocks an appreciation for its more comprehensive meaning. Forgiveness includes breaking the hold and power of sin (cf. 2:13-15). In John 8:11, Jesus' words to the woman, "Go your way, and from now on do not sin again," imply that she could do just that because she was forgiven. A line in a Charles Wesley hymn captures this fuller meaning of forgiveness, "He breaks the power of canceled sin."

A footnote on verse 14 (in some versions) states that a few late manuscripts read "redemption through his blood." *[Text, p. 319.]* The phrase is found uniformly in the Greek texts of Ephesians 1:7, and was likely borrowed from there by some copyists. The Greek text followed by RSV, NRSV, NIV, NASB, and others does not include the phrase. Note that *through the blood of his cross* is found a few verses later in Colossians (1:20).

Summary

Verses 9-14 are packed with rich material for the Bible student. As we look back over the prayer of intercession, the concepts of goodness, power, and gratitude stand out. Even more of what is available in Christ will come out in later sections of Colossians.

THE TEXT IN BIBLICAL CONTEXT
Understanding Is Not Enough

The NT consistently connects understanding and doing. Jesus said that only those who do the will of his Father enter the kingdom of heaven (Matt. 7:21). The difference between the wise man and the foolish man in Jesus' story was in acting or not acting on the words they heard Jesus say (Matt. 7:24-27). The servant who knows his master's will but does not make ready or do what is wanted, shall receive a severe beating (Luke 12:47). Paul's warns, "So do not be foolish, but understand what the will of the Lord is" (Eph. 5:17). The context shows that he does not assume understanding without obedience. Doing the will of God is the way to receive what is promised (Heb. 10:36). "Those who do the will of God live forever" (1 John 2:17). The NT writers leave no room for speculative wisdom apart from lived wisdom. There is an intellectual element, right knowledge, which has value in combating error, but it must lead to right conduct.

Good Works Have a Place

From the NT it is abundantly clear that good works are an integral part of Christian experience. The only specific reference to good works in Colossians is in 1:10. In this text, as is true in the many instances scattered throughout the NT, good works are in no way a matter of human achievement or merit. Ephesians 2:8-10 is explicit about what is implicit in Colossians: we are not saved by our good works, but we are created in Christ Jesus for good works. That's the way it is in God's blueprint for his people.

Paul contrasts works of righteousness with justification by faith in the context of opposing the imposition of certain Jewish regulations on Gentile believers. Never in the NT is the contrast drawn between faith and good works (the issue in James 2:14-26 is faith and action).

The biblical perspective on works rests on God's good works and Jesus' claim that he was doing the works of the one who sent him (Ps. 145:4-6; John 5:17; 10:31-39). Hence, those following Christ will be actively engaged in good works.

The Purpose of God-Given Power

Viewed broadly, the prayer of Colossians 1:9-14 has a request for discernment of God's will, followed by a request for power to perform that will. Paul's concern (1:11) was that the Colossians have power to survive under pressure. That practical use for power from God, a power that excels at the point of human weakness, is also mentioned in 2 Corinthians 12:9 (cf. Eph. 6:10-12; 2 Tim. 1:7-8). God's power is also needed to cast out demons and to heal diseases (Luke 9:1; 10:19), to witness (Acts 1:8; 4:23-33), to speak and preach (1 Cor. 2:4-5), to excommunicate (1 Cor. 5:4-5), and to minister (1 Pet. 4:11). For any of these purposes, God-given power is not a luxury but a necessity. The good news is that abundantly adequate power is available to all those in Christ, and as Paul's prayer demonstrates, it can be requested for others as well as for oneself.

A Before-and-After Theme

In 1:12-13, Paul expresses the radicalness of the changed life and re-lationships by the contrast between light and darkness. Later in the letter the theme surfaces as alienation and reconciliation (1:21-22), dead and alive (2:13, 20; 3:1), and the old nature being put off and the new nature being put on, like a garment change (3:9-10). Other ways of describing the contrast include slavery and freedom (Rom. 6), flesh and Spirit (Rom. 8), enmity and peace (Eph. 2), and strangers and family members (Eph. 2). [Before—After, p. 282.]

The Kingdom

Jesus came announcing the kingdom of God. He spoke much about the kingdom. Paul preached the gospel of the kingdom (Acts 19:8; 20:25; 28:23, 31). Some texts refer to a future kingdom, while others refer to a kingdom that is present as well as future. The kingdom of the Son, or the kingdom of Christ, sometimes has a more limited meaning than the kingdom of God (cf. 1 Cor. 15:24), but a distinction is not always made (Eph. 5:5). Although the kingdom of Christ fre-quently refers to the present manifestation of the kingdom, the term is also used for the future phase of the kingdom. Colossians 1:13 is a key text in kingdom understanding. Without detracting from the es-chatological fulfillment of the kingdom, it speaks clearly of a present reality.

Behind the concept of the kingdom of Christ is the affirmation that Jesus is King. The confession "Jesus is Lord" has the same meaning. The term kingdom of Christ conveys a profound sense of who Christ is. One who is being transferred into the kingdom of the Son experiences change in fundamental relationships.

Kingdom theology takes into account two kingdoms, the kingdom of God/Christ and the kingdom of the world. Although we can be "in Christ" and "in the world" at the same time, the nature of Christ's kingdom precludes its citizens from also giving full allegiance to another kingdom. Some kingdom theologies blur the distinction between the two kingdoms.

Being "born again" or "born from above" (John 3) rightly involves coming into the kingdom of the Son. Coming into the kingdom also means coming into the Christian community as an integral part of being in Christ. Being called into the fellowship of the Son (1 Cor. 1:9) includes coming into fellowship with other believers. The concept of kingdom, a corporate reality, excludes all limiting notions of redemption being a private matter between the individual and God.

The kingdom of Christ encompasses and shapes a value system, a view of history, social ethics, personal discipleship, and an understanding of church. The kingdom of Christ is an upside-down kind of kingdom. Values that are scorned in the kingdom of this world, because of sin and disobedience, are given high value in Christ's kingdom, and vice versa (Matt. 5:3-12; Mark 10:31, 42-45; Luke 1:51-53). Since the two kingdoms do not have the same goals and methods, the church may expect to experience tensions and even clashes with the kingdom of this world. Jesus makes it clear that the church is in the world by divine design (John 17:14-18). When we are transferred into the kingdom of God's Son, the gospel calls us to be intentional and proactive, not merely defensive and reactive. [Kingdom Theology, p. 300.]

Thanksgiving Again!

This second reference to thanksgiving in Colossians [Thanksgiving, p. 322] focuses on gratitude in response to God's actions. Gratitude is a vital part of the Christian walk in Christ. We maintain awareness of God's initiative and grace by the practice of thanksgiving for what God has done in enabling, rescuing, and transferring us. If we remember the Father's blessings, this serves as an antidote to heresy and a defense against perversions of the gospel. Such thanksgiving is not an exercise in ignoring problems, but a way to maintain equilibrium and perspective in the midst of problems.

THE TEXT IN THE LIFE OF THE CHURCH
A Community Frame of Reference

One striking emphasis of Paul's prayer in Colossians is that the frame of reference is the Christian community rather than isolated individuals. We can readily miss the community application that Paul takes for granted if we adopt the largely unchallenged assumptions of individualism that those of Western orientation bring to Bible study. When we read Colossians and other NT letters with an eye to the applications and implications for Christian community, new vistas open for us to appreciate the richness of the gospel.

A Model for Intercessory Prayer

The church could learn a lot about prayer by absorbing more of Paul's style. Colossians 1:9-14 along with prayers in other letters (e.g., Eph. 1:15-19; 3:14-21; Phil. 1:9-11; 1 Thess. 5:23) show the praying church how to rise to higher levels of mutual intercession. Paul's prayers are examples of how to make specific requests on behalf of others.

Paul prays that the Colossian believers might enter more fully into what already is theirs. One does not get the impression that he senses they need an additional experience of a different kind, but more of the same. Correction and renewal are needed from time to time in the Christian community, and persons are at different stages of maturity. However, it is always appropriate and needful for us to pray that persons and congregations experience their potential in Christ.

The samples we have of Paul's intercession for the churches do not have him asking God to "fix" people. Instead, he seeks to strengthen them for future testings, exercising preventive maintenance. Too often intercession waits until there is a problem.

A number of Paul's specific requests appear to be asking God to do for persons what they have responsibility to do themselves. When we ask God to make people live worthy of the Lord, we can hardly bypass their own desire to please the Lord with their lives. Paul's understanding is not that God imposes himself on persons or circumvents human responsibility. Paul brings spiritual requests that reveal his concern and his vision for a young congregation. By sharing his prayer with them, he reminds the Colossian believers of their privilege, duty, and potential in Christ.

Discipleship: Doing the Will of God

Whenever we separate knowledge and obedience, distorted theology results, and that problem is still with us. A fresh discovery that salvation is by grace instead of merit has at times resulted in laxness with regard to behavior. In the sixteenth century, Hans Denck (d. 1527) was repulsed by the lack of moral improvement in the lives of most of the new Protestants. He was attracted to the Anabaptist emphasis on discipleship. Later Denck wrote, "But the medium is Christ whom no one can truly know unless he follow him in his life, and no one may follow him unless he has first known him. . . . For whoever thinks he belongs to Christ must walk the way that Christ walked" (Klaassen, 1981:87).

An emphasis on good works can lead to legalism and a works religion. The reason for the right behavior the gospel demands must always be clear. When the Anabaptists challenged what they perceived to be a lopsided emphasis on "faith only," they were accused of being legalists and of returning to works-righteousness. In an extensive *Reply to False Accusations* (1552), Menno Simons attempted to put to rest a number of false charges he considered slanderous. One reply was as follows:

> As to being heaven-stormers: Because we teach from the mouth of the Lord that if we would enter into life, we must keep the commandments; that in Christ, neither circumcision nor uncircumcision avails anything but the keeping of the commandments of God, and that the love of God is that we keep his commandments, and His commandments are not grievous; therefore the preachers have to call us heaven-stormers and merit-men, saying that we want to be saved by our own merits even though we have always confessed, and by the grace of God ever will, that we cannot be saved by means of anything in heaven or on earth other than by the merits, intercession, death, and blood of Christ. . . .(569)

Failure to keep knowing and doing together can lead to several other dangers. One is a one-sided pietism that majors in the exhilaration of religious fervor without connecting faith to the issues of living. Another is creedalism, putting almost exclusive emphasis on having correct statements of biblical truth to the neglect of obeying the truth of the Bible. Colossians presents a balance between gospel truth, spiritual experience, and good works and behavior. Balthasar Hubmaier had confidence that God would give sufficient strength for faithful living to those who have experienced the Spirit's regeneration. He said (in 1524), "Such faith cannot be idle, but must break

forth in gratitude toward God and in all sorts of works of brotherly
love toward others" (32).

Theology and Life

At times people devalue theology in preference for "the more important issues of life." Repeatedly, early activists in a particular social
concern become involved out of convictions arising from a solid theology. But then, in the urgency of the cause, they do not talk much
about their undergirding theology. Later joiners caught up in the
cause may not have the moorings of a good theological base. Much
theology appears in Paul's prayer in Colossians, as well as in the
whole letter. An intense interaction between theology and life characterizes Paul's writings. He is not interested in theology for the sake of
theology, nor can he write about life without becoming theological.
Blending theology and life is the Bible's way.

> Grateful feelings stir within
>   When God's grace we see.
> He, in Christ, removed our sin;
>   Now in him we're free.
>
> Thanks to Christ the Lord we give,
>   For his strength we know.
> Now that unto him we live,
>   Praise to him must flow.
>
> Yet our gratitude will show
>   By the way we live.
> Daily we should seek to grow
>   In the thanks we live.
>   —EDM

Colossians 1:15-20

Exalting Christ as Supreme

PREVIEW

Stepping into this section of Colossians is like stepping into a different room in a house. Although many features of the decor are different from the adjoining rooms, this room is integral to the house, like a central foyer with direct linkage to other rooms.

No proper name for Christ is found in this new section, only the pronouns *he and him*. Unquestionably the references are to *his beloved Son* (1:13). A connective word *and* carries the reader over into the next section (1:21-23). In reading from verses 13-14 to verses 21-23, we go by way of the special, unique section, verses 15-20.

Several stylistic features stand out. The previous section (1:9-14) is cast in first-person experience (rescued *us*, transferred *us*, *we* have redemption). The following section (1:21-23) is in the form of second-person address (*you, you, you, you*). But verses 15-20 focus on a subject identified by third-person pronouns (*he, him*). These six verses have a distinctively different literary style. Although frequently referred to as a hymn (and set as poetry in JB), it is not a hymn in our usual sense of the term, with precise meter and rhyme. Yet the passage has a poetic quality about it, suitable for a faith confession intended to be repeated as a liturgy. When read aloud, it has a rhythmic lilt, even more so in Greek than in most translations. There are word and phrase parallels, repetitions, a precise use of prepositions (*in*,

59

through, for), and a highly select vocabulary; these all point to it being the product of careful composition.

This fascinating passage stands out as special in its own right. At the same time it is neatly woven into its context. Some of the outstanding details of structure (in the Greek text) that bear on understanding the text can be observed in my rather literal translation, below. Indentations and type styles call attention to parallels and relationships. *[Literary Structure, p. 305.]*

(15) **WHO IS** the image of the invisible God,
          THE FIRSTBORN of ALL creation,
(16)   *for* **in him** were created ALL things
              in the heavens and on the earth,
              things visible and things invisible,
                  whether thrones **or** dominions **or** rulers **or** authorities;
          ALL things **through him** and **for him** were created;

(17)   and *HE IS* before ALL things,
          and ALL things **in him** hold together,
(18)   and *HE IS* the head of the body, the church;

          WHO IS the beginning,
          THE FIRSTBORN of the dead,
              so that in ALL things he might be first,
(19)   *for* **in him** ALL the fullness was pleased to dwell,
(20)   and **through him** to reconcile ALL things to himself,
              having made peace through the blood of his cross,
                  through him (that is),
                  whether things on the earth **or** things in the heavens.

These lines form the core of the Christology of Colossians. They make up the most inclusive passage about Christ in the NT. Yet it is not a fully comprehensive Christology. This major teaching about Christ is included in the letter because of a perceived need. Also, the hymn should be seen as a worship expression more than as a logical doctrinal statement.

The passage defies consistent outlining. If we force it into a rigid intellectual mold, we spoil the splendor of the hymn. Dissecting such a beautiful piece of art is in some respects an irreverent exercise. Yet our appreciation of its beauty and meaning depends on our understanding of crucial details. For example, we need carefully to observe the precision and balance in these lines. After analysis comes the important task of synthesis, reassembling the pieces and viewing the whole.

OUTLINE

Analysis of the text in scholarly commentaries is far from uniform. Interpreters debate over how many strophes (or stanzas) it has and where the breaks are placed. The outline below has its rationale in the close parallel between verse 15 and verse 18b, and in other construction details illustrated in the form of the translation above.

Exalting Christ as Supreme, 1:15-20

    First Stanza—Christ, God, and Creation, 1:15-16
        1:15   Christ, the Image of God
        1:16   Christ, the Creative Agent and Goal of All
    Bridge—Christ, the Central Figure, 1:17-18a
        1:17a   Christ, the One Before All
        1:17b   Christ, the Sustainer of All
        1:18a   Christ, the Head of the Church
    Second Stanza—Christ, God, and the New Creation, 1:18b-20
        1:18b   Christ, the Founder of the Church
        1:19   Christ, the Fullness of God
        1:20   Christ, the Means of Reconciling All

EXPLANATORY NOTES

References to specific words and phrases from verses 15-20 will follow the author's translation (above) rather than NRSV.

Christ, God, and Creation 1:15-16

1:15 Christ, the Image of God

Verse 15 (in Greek) begins with the relative pronoun, corresponding to the English *who*, rather than with the definite pronoun *he*. The closest antecedent of *who* is *Son* in verse 13. Other NT passages with a similar confessional and hymnic quality also characteristically begin with a Greek relative pronoun (Phil. 2:6; 1 Tim. 3:16; Heb. 1:3; 1 Pet. 2:22).

Image of the invisible God. Other texts also describe God as the invisible one (John 1:18; Rom. 1:20; 1 Tim. 1:17; 6:16; Heb. 11:27). We might think it is a logical contradiction to speak of a visible representation of what is invisible, but this is true to other biblical affirmations that God can be seen in Jesus Christ (John 12:45; 14:9). The point of *image* is not exact likeness, much less resemblance, but revelation and representation. The reality of God is in the image of God, in Christ. God is invisible, but not unknowable, or knowable only to an elite few. The means through which Jesus made the Father known include his incarnation (becoming flesh), life and example, ministry, teaching, response to evil, suffering, death, and resurrection.

Many interpreters have noted striking similarities between the terminology and thought forms of Colossians 1:15-20 and Jewish wisdom theology. *[Sources, p. 318.]* However, beyond the similarities, important differences mark Paul's teaching as distinctly Christian. Wisdom theology has wisdom as the image of God and the creator of the world. Paul can utilize familiar thought forms for proclaiming the person of Christ. The Greek philosophers thought of the world (the cosmos) as God's image. Paul does not say anything like that. He rises above all of those ideas and declares the Son of God to be the visible manifestation and presence of God. *[Image, p. 298.]*

Firstborn of all creation. Taken by itself, out of its immediate and larger biblical context, this phrase could be construed to mean that the Son was the first of God's creations. But biblical usage of *firstborn* indicates a predominate emphasis on being first in rank and honor.

The relationship in view is Christ and creation, *all creation.* The implicit affirmation of the text is caught in the renderings *the firstborn over all creation* (NIV) and *his is the primacy over all created things* (NEB).

The next phrase, *for in him were created all things* (EDM), gives the reason for declaring that Christ deserves the title *the firstborn.* To say that Christ is the one in whom all things are created makes no sense if the point of the previous phrase is that he is the first of created beings. The thrust of this faith statement as a whole is that Christ is the creator of all, and separate from it.

1:16 Christ, the Creative Agent and Goal of All

In him were created all things. The expressions *in him, through him,* and *for him* further define the relationship between Christ and *all things.* In contemporary language we speak of *all things* as the universe. The three prepositions broaden our understanding of the

Son of God as the cosmic Christ, not limited to existence on earth as we know it. We rightly speak of God as the Creator. But to be true to this and related texts, when we speak of the action of creation, we need also to say that Christ participated directly in that creating work. *In* defines the sphere of activity and conveys that God's creative activity does not take place apart from Christ. *Through* suggests that he is the means or agent of creation. *For* defines the goal of all of creation (cf. 1 Cor. 8:6 and Heb. 2:10).

Christ's supremacy over all things, in harmony with his participation in the creation of all things, is not limited to the material universe and human beings. It includes also the cosmic powers, often referred to as "principalities and powers." *[Powers, p. 308.]* Four of the many terms used to designate these powers appear here as representative of all such: *thrones, dominions, rulers, authorities.* Colossians clearly says that the powers derive their existence from Christ. The powers are the structures through which evil forces can and do work, and thus they often become hostile toward Christ and his kingdom. To the extent that the powers become hostile, Colossians also assures us that Christ has stripped them of their power by his death (2:15). The universe, inclusive of all, is Christocentric (cf. Eph. 1:10, 20-21).

A literary feature of verse 16 is of interest. In the following phrases, notice that visible corresponds to earth and invisible corresponds to heavens: *in the heavens and on the earth, things visible and things invisible* (EDM). The order is A B B[1] A[1], a literary device called chiasmus. A less obvious example is found in verses 16c and 20: *all things . . . through him . . . through him . . . all things.* Such chiasmus adds to the rhythmic quality of the hymn already evident in other parallels and repetitions.

Christ, the Central Figure   1:17-18a

These three lines are similar to each other in construction and serve as a bridge between the two main stanzas. The two phrases, *and he is,* are unique in the hymn. (Review the structural analysis above.)

1:17a   Christ, the One Before All

In what sense is Christ *before all things*? The preposition *before* has several meanings in biblical usage. In Acts 12:6 it has to do with space, meaning "in front of." In Matthew 24:38; John 5:7; and 17:24 it has to do with time, meaning "prior to." In James 5:12, coupled with "all things" (as in Col. 1:17), it denotes preference, meaning "above all things" (in importance). Here in Colossians 1:17, the word denotes priority of time (preexistence) and importance.

1:17b Christ, the Sustainer of All

The next phrase, *and all things in him hold together* (EDM), adds the role of Sustainer to that of Creator. At a minimum it says that all things have their existence in him. Most translations pick up the thought of preservation and coherence, attributing to Christ the active power that holds all things together. As Lightfoot put it, "He is the principle of cohesion in the universe. He impresses upon creation that unity and solidarity which makes it a cosmos instead of a chaos" (156).

With different wording Hebrews 1:3 makes a similar affirmation: "He is the reflection of God's glory and the exact imprint of God's very being, and he sustains all things by his powerful word." Somewhat similar statements come from Greek philosophers and writers of the intertestamental period. But Paul went beyond them in identifying *Christ* as the active integrating principle of the universe, yet separate from the universe. The Greek word translated *hold together* is related to our word "system." "Christ—and not the Powers themselves—is the system of creation" (Berkhof: 28). Christ is "the System of the systems" (Wink, 1984:115). *[Powers, p. 308.]*

1:18a Christ, the Head of the Church

The obvious parallel between *who is the image . . . the firstborn . . .* (1:15) and *who is the beginning . . . the firstborn . . .* (1:18b) indicates a division at verse 18b, rather than at the beginning of verse 18 (EDM). *The church* (1:18a), appearing as it does in the bridge lines, is thus related both to the first stanza, in which Christ is honored as Creator, and to the second stanza, in which he is honored as Re-creator.

The head of the body, the church. All three terms (*head, body, church*) call for careful consideration. With respect to *head* and *body*, modern readers find it "natural" to read into the term *head* their understandings of the brain and nervous system. Thus they assume that the image refers to what controls the body. However, biblical usage offers another way to understand the term. *[Head, p. 293.]* In the context of 1:18a, *head* connotes beginning, source, and prototype more than control and rule (Bedale: 213). Since the hymn as a whole celebrates Christ's priority and superiority, the term *head* must be seen within that perspective. In 2:10 *head* emphasizes these qualities in relation to the powers.

"The body of Christ" is one of many figures for the church in the NT. The body concept of the church is a figure from anatomy and needs to be respected, without making either too much or too little of it. This analogy, found only in the letters of Paul, conveys the thought that those who are in Christ become a living organism. *Church* in 1:18 refers not to a local congregation but to the inclusive body of Christ. This sense fits with the context in which the word *(all things/ everything)* is prominent. *[Church, p. 283.]*

Paul has asserted that Christ has priority and supremacy over all created things because they were created in, by, and for him. Now he can say in the same vein that Christ's primacy also includes his relation to the church. Christ is both source and sustaining power for his body, the church, as well as for the created order. This is a weighty affirmation: the one who is head of the church also holds supremacy over the powers (1:16).

Christ, God, and the New Creation   1:18b-20

The second stanza echoes the tones and thoughts of the first stanza and adds new themes.

1:18b   Christ, the Founder of the Church

The first phrase, *who is the beginning*, involves a translator's decision with respect to the final word of the phrase (EDM). The same word *(archē)* is translated *ruler* in 2:10. When it has the meaning of rule or power in the NT, it is always coupled with the word "authority" (except for Jude 6). Two other examples in Colossians are 1:16 and 2:15. If we give *head* the meaning of ruler in verse 18a, then a possible meaning of this pivotal word *head (archē)* in verse 18b could be ruler. But *head* (in context) emphasizes origin, and the associated phrase, *firstborn of (from, NRSV) the dead*, is a clear reference to Christ's resurrection. Therefore, the implied meaning here is *beginning* rather than ruler. (Further usage of the word *archē* can be observed in a beginning-end combination in Rev. 21:6 and 22:13.)

Beginning of what? This is not a repetition of the thought from previous verses on the beginning of creation. Linked as it is with resurrection, the term *beginning* means Christ is the founder of the new creation of the resurrection age—the church. Thus, in this Christ-hymn, the celebration of Christ's creative work reaches its climax in the creation of a new people by means of the resurrection of Jesus from the dead (Wright, 1990:457).

The phrase *the firstborn of the dead* carries the meaning (and more) that Christ's resurrection is unique. (Lazarus and others were resuscitated, and died again.) Resurrection means being raised to a new kind of existence. The risen Christ is, by these phrases in Colossians 1:18b, the founder of the resurrection community of life. Christ's resurrection also prefigures the resurrection when he comes again (1 Cor. 15:20-23; 1 Thess. 4:13-17).

Where all this leads becomes clear in the purpose clause that follows, *so that in all things he might be first* (EDM). The first stanza of the hymn celebrates the confession that Christ has first place in the old creation. The second stanza now affirms that Christ is also first in the new creation. Thus he has become and is in first place with respect to everything. The dominant strain running throughout the hymn can be traced in four related words (each with the same initial Greek letters, *pro/prō*): *firstborn* (1:15), *before* (1:17), *firstborn* (1:18), and now *first* (1:18) as the climax. Christ holds first place; he is supreme above all. The significance of the repetition of *all* can now be appreciated.

1:19 Christ, the Fullness of God

Verse 19 explains the basis for Christ's supremacy from another perspective. However, it is not easy to discover the subject of *was pleased* and the meaning of *all the fullness*.

In the Greek text we discern three possible subjects to produce the action, *was pleased:* (1) Christ, (2) God, and (3) all the fullness. Although grammatically possible, the first option makes no sense. NIV, NASB, and many other translations supply God as the subject, *For God was pleased to have all his fullness dwell in him* (NIV). In the third option (NRSV and the translation above), *all the fullness* is seen as equivalent to *God in all his fullness*. Phillips has, *It was in him that the full nature of God chose to live*. Of the options, both (2) and (3) convey the thought satisfactorily. The meaning here is essentially the same as in 2:9, *for in him the whole fullness of deity dwells bodily*.

The words *was pleased* express God's resolve and good pleasure, a concept found frequently in the OT. This same verb in the Septuagint has the meaning of choice, election, and delight. Several times the combination of *was pleased* and *to dwell* is found (Pss. 68:16; 132:13-14). The voice from heaven at Jesus' baptism has a similar thought: "This is my Son, the Beloved, with whom I am well pleased" (Matt. 3:17). (Cf. Gal. 1:15-16, "[God] was pleased to reveal his Son to me," and Eph. 1:5, 9, "good pleasure.")

In biblical usage *fullness* has several meanings: having to do with what fills, the concept of completeness, and the sum total. *[Fullness, p. 288.]* A connection can be traced between *fullness* and the *shekinah* manifestation of God's presence and glory. The shekinah cloud of glory filled the tabernacle (Exod. 40:34-35) and Solomon's temple (1 Kings 8:10-11; cf. Isa. 6:1-4.) Although *fullness* may have roots in shekinah, Paul's teaching that Christ is the complete, undiluted manifestation of the fullness (*plērōma*) of God goes beyond the concept of shekinah. Christ supplants the tabernacle and the temple, and he represents God in person.

We wonder to what extent Paul in Colossians is countering proto-Gnostic ideas. *[Problems, p. 310.]* His use of *fullness* may be an illustration of using the vocabulary of an early form of Gnosticism, but redefining the terms to express gospel truth. *Fullness* was a favorite word with Gnostics in the second century. Gnostic teaching, however, did not associate fullness (*plērōma*) with God himself, but with intermediary emanations from God (a term Gnostics used for lower levels of beings separating deity from the evil material world). *[Gnosticism, p. 289.]*

Colossians 1:19 is the apex of Paul's Christology. He declares in the clearest language that *all* the fullness of God was and is in Christ. In the Son, God comes to humans with all grace and truth, fully sufficient for self-revelation and redemption (cf. John 1:14-18).

To dwell carries the sense of taking up permanent residence, in contrast to a temporary stay. Here, with the past tense (aorist) used, the focus is on Christ's incarnation, including the whole Christ-event. The same word, *dwell,* is used to speak of residing at a particular geographic location, for example, to dwell in Nazareth. The word appears in Acts 7:48 and 17:24: God does not dwell in houses made with hands. Paul uses it here to affirm what Jesus said to Philip, "Whoever has seen me has seen the Father" (John 14:9).

Although these lines are in the motif of worship rather than argument, the Christ-hymn leaves no room for Christ to be considered a lower-level intermediary. It affirms a separate identity for Father and Son, without attributing lesser significance to the Son.

1:20 Christ, the Means of Reconciling All

The first clause of verse 20, *and through him . . . to reconcile to himself all things*, stands parallel to verse 19. (Refer to the structural analysis above.) This means, first of all, that *the fullness* that is in Christ is seen in what he does. It is well pleasing to God to reconcile *all things* to himself through Christ (cf. 2 Cor. 5:19, "in Christ God was reconciling the world to himself"). These texts open a window to the heart and purpose of God. To express God's purpose, Paul selects the word *reconcile* to be coupled with *create*. *[Reconciliation, p. 311.]*

Reconciling activity has to do with relationships. A previous estrangement is presupposed. Verse 21 explores the hostility addressed by God in Christ. God has taken the initiative in restoring broken relationships. Verse 18, with its emphasis on the new resurrection community, guards against taking a narrow, individualistic concept of reconciliation. It took no less than the very Son of God to do it, and he is adequate to re-create as well as to create.

The scope of reconciliation is *all things*. Considerable consistency should be assumed in the meaning of the several occurrences of *all things* in verses 15-20. Colossians gives us no liberty to construe *all things* as less inclusive in reconciliation than in creation. God's intent is clear. Yet this passage does not address to what extent and in what manner God's intentions become full reality. *[Reconciliation, p. 311.]*

As we remember, this passage is a worship expression more than a precise doctrinal statement. In an oft-omitted stanza of "Joy to the World," Isaac Watts catches the thrust of Colossians 1:20:

> No more let sins and sorrows grow
> Nor thorns infest the ground,
> He comes to make his blessings flow
> Far as the curse is found.

God's intent *to reconcile* is restated as being already accomplished in the phrase *having made peace* (EDM). *[Grammar, p. 290.]* In a similar way Jesus, before his suffering and death, spoke of the effects of his death as already accomplished (John 12:31). The compound word translated *having made peace* (EDM), occurring only here in the NT, matches the noun form, peacemakers, in Matthew 5:9. The concept of peace, following that of *shalom* in the Hebrew Scriptures, "points to a positive state of affairs where things are as they should be, as God wills them to be" (P. Yoder: 21). Peacemaking, then, is making things as they ought to be. This goes significantly beyond the popular connotation that peace is the absence of strife and war. Acts 10:36 identifies peace as a major theme of apostolic preaching.

Peace is accomplished *through the blood of his cross*, Christ's cross. (Although this phrase is unique in the NT, Eph. 1:7 has "redemption through his blood," and Eph. 2:13-18 connects *blood, peace, reconcile*, and *cross*.) Including both *blood* and *cross* is not a case of redundancy. The effect of this phrase is to bring the reader down from the lofty thoughts of preeminence and fullness to the plain of history and human experience. Christ's firstness is demonstrated in his reconciling work, and that has been accomplished by way of *the blood of his cross*, through suffering and death. The phrase emphasizes the cost of reconciliation, who bore that cost, and when.

Although blood is commonly associated with sacrifice, let us not overlook another biblical meaning. "In the OT 'blood' signifies death by violence in over half of its uses" (Finger, 1985:334). Finger refers to one occasion when Jesus spoke of his coming death and its meaning: "Jesus was identifying his coming murder as the climax, the summing up, the recapitulation of all violent resistance against all God's righteous representatives throughout history" (1985:334). Human minds can only begin to fathom the significance of peace (reconciliation) being made through the shedding of blood, which was in itself the violent reaction of unbelief.

Although the Son of God is described in ultimate language in Colossians 1, he also amazingly had blood. The cross connotes humility and shame (Phil. 2:5-11). Paul sees nothing incompatible in Christ being *before all things* (EDM) and his coming in a body of flesh (2:11) and dying on a cross. In fact, his excellence is demonstrated in the combination of all that he has done.

The import of this passage is expressed vividly in Paul Scherer's words:

> I submit to you—if we're going to be pessimistic, let's be pessimistic about the right thing! That may at least give us the clue we need to life: not that it seems so short or looks so futile or feels so hard; just that there's something so abysmally wrong about it that nothing but a gospel with Almighty God in the middle of it, and a Man on a cross, could ever really be appropriate to our condition or relevant to our need. (60)

Clearly, God has taken the initiative in making peace through Christ. The notion of appeasement of an angry deity is totally absent in Paul's teaching about reconciliation. [Reconciliation, p. 311.]

Paul does not see Christ's reconciling and peacemaking work as an obscure, off-to-the-side enterprise. Reference to the *things on the earth* and the *things in the heavens* (EDM) parallels similar wording in 1:16. The same mind-stretching thought is found in Ephesians 1:10. With respect to the principalities and powers, 2:15 implies their compulsory rather than voluntary acceptance of Christ's victory. Philippians 2:10-11 also expresses God's purpose that Jesus be universally acknowledged as Lord.

In this section Paul uses some of the same words and phrases as are found in rabbinic Judaism, Hellenistic Judaism, and in Gnostic writings. [Sources, p. 318.] However, rather than taking this as sure evidence of the sources of these lines, we maintain that the apostle took the familiar thought forms of the day and poured gospel truth into them.

The uniqueness of the hymn is in the way it integrates sweeping, cosmic dimensions of Christology with down-to-earth experience of what God has done in Christ. What we have is a vehicle for understanding and praise that brings together the spheres of creation and redemption, for the faith community lives in both spheres.

Summary

Paul brings five relationships together in this brief hymn:
1. Christ and God
2. Christ and the creation
3. Christ and the powers
4. Christ and the church
5. Christ and all things

With this broad range of relationships, Paul will teach us much as he builds on the lofty thoughts of the hymn. The hymn accents words occurring later in the letter: *head*, *body*, *church*, and *reconcile*. Verses 21-23 reveal what Paul considers the primary, immediate significance of Christ's person and accomplishments.

THE TEXT IN BIBLICAL CONTEXT
Christ as the Firstborn

Biblical usage of the term *firstborn* illuminates its meaning in Colossians 1:15, 18. Occurring rarely outside the Bible, it is used extensively in the LXX. *[Septuagint, p. 316.]* Sometimes it has the literal sense of the oldest child and heir. As applied to Israel, it refers to a special place in God's love, a place of privilege (e.g., Exod. 4:22; Jer. 31:9). Psalm 89:27 is a prime example of *firstborn* in the sense of supremacy in rank. Speaking of a king in David's line (the Messiah), God said, "I will make him the firstborn, the highest of the kings of the earth." Other OT usage, with family or political imagery, also supports the meaning of supremacy and position of honor, without any suggestion of procreation.

Six of the eight occurrences of *firstborn* in the NT refer to Christ. In Luke 2:7 it is used in the literal sense, Jesus as Mary's first child. In the other five it is a title for Christ (Rom. 8:29; Col. 1:15, 18; Heb. 1:6; Rev. 1:5). Three of these have the term *firstborn* linked with Jesus' death. In none of the five is it associated with his birth. The overwhelming emphasis in biblical usage is on supremacy or prominence in rank, a meaning that meshes well in Colossians 1. Although the term *firstborn* does not in itself denote Christ's preexistence (existence before creation), the concept is implicit in the emphasis on supremacy and priority over all of creation. Being first in time goes hand in hand with being first in rank.

The identification *firstborn of the dead* (1:18) includes firstness in time. Christ's resurrection was a first. But the key element of primacy is also inherent in the context. Christ is the founder and chief figure in the new resurrection community. Two related texts using *firstborn* carry the same thought (Rom. 8:29 speaks of Christ as "the firstborn within a large family," and Heb. 12:23 of "the assembly of the firstborn"). In Acts 3:15 Peter called the one whom God raised from the dead "the Author of life." As *firstborn of the dead*, Christ holds first place in the new creation as well as in the universe.

The Contribution of the Christ-Hymn to Colossians

The Christ-hymn is not at all a digression in the thought flow of Colossians. Without verses 15-20, reference to being transferred into the kingdom of God's Son (1:13) would be robbed of much of its meaning. Without verses 15-20, reference to being reconciled in Christ's body by his death (1:22) would have a reduced meaning, and the appeal to steadfastness (1:23) would be considerably weakened. But with verses 15-20 in place, Colossians rings with rich meaning. Overtones of the Christ-hymn enhance text after text.

One of Several Christological Passages

Several NT passages stand out as especially focused on Christ. A capsule summary of the other main christological passages will help in sensing the contribution of the Christ-hymn of Colossians.

John 1:1-18. The prologue of the Fourth Gospel asserts that the Word (the Logos) is eternal, an active role in creation, and it emphasizes that the Word became flesh and that through him we receive God's glory and grace.

Philippians 2:5-11. Placed in a practical setting, this Christ-hymn focuses on Christ's self-emptying, his servant obedience even to the extent of death, and his subsequent exaltation and supreme lordship.

Hebrews 1:1-4. This first paragraph of Hebrews boldly proclaims God's Son as the ultimate of God's revelation of himself, the heir of all things, the Creator of the world, the upholder of the universe, and as superior to the angels in his exalted position.

It is wise for us to review such passages carefully and compare them with Colossians 1:15-20. We note similar and complementary concepts in these christological passages. Several elements are common to two or more of them: (1) Christ's existence prior to creation, (2) Christ's priority over creation, (3) victory by way of suffering and death, and (4) the relevance of it all for faithful living. To these four unique literary passages, we may add Hebrews 2:10-18 and Ephesians 1:3-23. They contain closely related christological teachings, although not in the same literary genre. The brief confessional statements about Christ in 1 Timothy 3:16 and Revelation 5:9-14 should also be included in the review. These passages make up a body of biblical tradition with respect to Christology, although they are not all that the NT has to say about Christ. Among them Colossians 1:15-20 is a gem.

The Contribution of the Christ-Hymn to Biblical Theology

Virtually all of the content of the hymn is also expressed elsewhere in the NT. A few examples will suffice. The teaching that Christ is the agent of creation is found in John 1:3, 10, and Hebrews 1:2. His preexistence comes out in John 8:58. An emphasis on incarnation stands out in John 1:14 and 1 John 4:2-3. The fact and importance of Christ's resurrection is at the heart of apostolic preaching (e.g., Acts 2:24-36; 4:10; 10:40-41; 13:30-37). His work of reconciliation finds classic expression in 2 Corinthians 5:18-19. In Ephesians 2:13-18 fuller expression is given to the assertion that peace is made by the blood of Christ. Philippians 2:8-10 clearly says that exaltation comes by the way of suffering. The confession in 1 Corinthians 8:6 also proclaims the cosmic Christ. Therefore, the contribution of the Christ-hymn of Colossians is more a matter of emphasis than of uniqueness. One peculiarity is that the words *Savior, save,* and *salvation* are not in the vocabulary of Colossians.

The dominant strain in the hymn is Christ's supremacy over all things, with special emphasis on his preeminence over the powers. The hymn points beyond personal redemption to include social and cosmic reconciliation.

A second strain is the declaration that what God has done, he has done through Christ. Likewise, what God is doing and will do, he does through Christ. This element of the confession is clear: the same one creates, sustains, and reconciles. Confessing that the same Christ is prominent in creation and in redemption precludes drawing a difference between the ethical implications of creation and those of redemption (as is sometimes done).

How the church is viewed is interwoven with the Christology of Colossians. References to body, church, beginning, and reconciliation add up to viewing the church as a reconciled community created and cherished by God. The new creation encompasses more than individual regeneration. This fact became evident immediately in the days following Pentecost, in Acts 2:42-47. Colossians 1:21-23 establishes a direct link between Christology and experience and holy living in the church. [*Church, p. 283.*]

The hymn from Colossians does not say all that can or should be said about Christ. For example, 1 Corinthians 15:20-28 with its mild subordination of the Son to God needs to be considered along with Jesus' assertion, "The Father and I are one" (John 10:30). We enrich our study of Colossians 1:15-20 by keeping the larger picture of biblical theology and of Christology in view.

THE TEXT IN THE LIFE OF THE CHURCH
Christology in the Life of the Church

Christology is crucial for theology and for life. Affirmations about the person and work of Christ appear in virtually all creeds and confessional statements. We note two reasons for such affirmations: The importance of Christology has been recognized throughout the history of the church. Also, in many cases some aspect of an accepted, traditional doctrine of Christ was being challenged at the time they were written.

Because historic statements of doctrine are to some extent reactions to false views, their limitations need to be recognized. Even creedal statements intended to be comprehensive show evidences of being dated. It is not that truth changes, but the challenges to truth vary from time to time, and our understanding grows. Therefore, it is important to go back to the NT as a primary source rather than to rely only on the formulations hammered out in the heat of challenge and controversy. [History, p. 295.]

The christological passages of the NT have their respective emphases along with common elements. The different highlights indicate that they are responses to specific challenges and needs. Thus John 1:1-18 emphasizes the full revelation of God by the Word become flesh. Philippians 2:5-11 speaks particularly to relationships in the Christian fellowship. Colossians 1:15-20 contends for the preeminence of Christ over all the powers and authorities. Hebrews 1:1-4 establishes Christ's superiority, particularly over angels. For the complete picture, we need all the biblical affirmations about Christ.

Beside the more formalized statements about Christ in the NT, we have the narrative records concerning Jesus. The first preaching of the early church about Christ was characteristically in narrative form (Acts 2:22-24; 10:36-41). Statements of faith developed out of the story of Jesus. That process commends itself to the church today. As we need to respond to challenges of the day, it is better to go back to the primary evidence (both Gospels and Epistles) rather than to rely only on historical responses.

Christology, rightly defined, includes more than the deity of Christ and finely tuned statements about his nature, and more than that he shed his blood for the sins of the world. His incarnation, humanity, servant life, ministry to persons, teachings, response to evil, suffering, death, resurrection, ascension, his relationship to his body (the church), his lordship over believers and the world, and his return and final triumph are all part of who he is.

The key role of Christology can be seen by noting how it bears on six subdivisions of theology:

1. The Bible (Revelation and Hermeneutics). When the Bible is seen as Christ-centered, we are led to different interpretations than when it is seen a "flat" document. We take the OT as looking forward to Christ, and the NT as reflecting back on Christ. Thus the outcomes are different from when isolated texts are given equal value. In the

sixteenth century, some church practices such as war and infant baptism were defended from OT texts. Anabaptists refuted these interpretations by appealing to Jesus as the highest authority for the church.

2. *Redemption/Salvation* (Soteriology). Christian understandings of redemption all give Christ and his death a prime place. However, by respecting the many images and motifs found in the Bible to describe Christ's work, we will avoid limited understandings of atonement that result from hanging all the meaning of Christ's death on one motif.

3. *Church* (Ecclesiology). When we take into account Christ's relationship with his body, we gain a better understanding of church than when Christ is viewed primarily as the Savior of individuals. We must acknowledge Christ's lordship and kingdom (in its present phase) if the church is to find its identity in the world.

4. *Morality* (Ethics). Christian behavior should be shaped by the teaching and example of Christ, although that connection is not always made. As we see who Jesus truly is, we discover the power of the way of the cross, which rejects violence and revenge in any form.

5. *Future consummation* (Eschatology). Whatever Christology people hold influences their views of the end. Some take the exaltation of Jesus as Lord and Christ to mean that the kingdom of God exists in the present as well as the future. They find a continuity and correspondence between these two phases of the kingdom because they are shaped by the same Lord. Others, however, look for a final triumph accomplished by violence and coercion toward sinners. That does not fit with an understanding of a victory accomplished by the Lamb.

6. *Creation theology.* Colossians does not separate the Christ of creation and the Christ of redemption (re-creation). In the Christ-hymn (and in Rom. 8:18-23), God's redemptive activity in Christ includes the created order. A vision of the cosmic Christ opens the way to an environmental ethic and provides incentive for involvement in ecological issues of the day.

Our views of Christ shape these and other aspects of theology. There will be disastrous effects if we separate Christology from other elements of doctrine, or work from too narrow a Christology. For example, some who begin with the Bible rather than with Christ may vigorously defend the inspiration and authority of the Bible. At the same time they may not take seriously what Jesus taught or demonstrated. One may build a case from the OT for engaging in war, and in so doing ignore how Jesus responded to evil and enemies, and not take into account how Jesus accomplished our redemption.

Frequently Christology has been limited to the person of Christ, his atonement, and his return, and then defined too narrowly in those important aspects. The church, to be true to the NT, must apply a full Christology to its use and interpretation of the Bible, to understandings and functioning of the church, and to ethical behavior. If we limit Christ's rule and ministry to a spiritual salvation, respect for the created order will seem unimportant. By beginning with Christ, God's people will discover an integrating center for theology and for life.

Pastoral Concerns

The overarching pastoral concern found in Colossians is relevant for the church in any age. The apostle's desire for maturity and fruitfulness in the Colossian believers is explicit in the intercessory prayer and pervades the whole letter. We see that same desire in the Christhymn. Paul's positive pastoral approach is especially apparent in this hymn that proclaims the excellencies of Christ. He is concerned that the saints not be distracted or subverted by seductive false teaching. This was apparently a major reason for the letter. [Problems, p. 310.] But not until 2:4 do we find specific mention of a problem. In Galatians and 1 Corinthians, by way of contrast, specific concerns surface early. Paul sees the teaching being countered in Colossians more as a potential threat than as a teaching that has already affected the faith community. "The epistle is a vaccination against heresy, not an antibiotic for those already afflicted" (Wink, 1984:73).

Sometimes it is necessary to expose error, as Paul did in Galatians. But generally the positive approach of undergirding, building, and feeding will be the best prevention against error. Christians who know and appreciate their faith will be equipped to recognize distortions of the truth of the gospel. The church's teaching diet needs to accentuate what it believes more than what it is against.

Another pastoral note may be observed. An important implication of Christ's supremacy is that there is no need to fear the powers. They have nothing to offer those in Christ. The world holds no ultimate terror for Christians.

To some persons, God seems distant, vague, incomprehensible, or perhaps frightening; the church can point such to Jesus Christ. If we present Christ as the image of God in whom the fullness of God dwells, this can help persons searching for an understandable revelation of God. Further, Colossians models a way of presenting Christ in experiential language rather than in abstract academic language.

In an age of exploding knowledge and high technology, the question can and does arise, Is Christ still adequate for these times? The pastoral response, growing out of Colossians, is that the supremacy of Christ assures also the sufficiency of Christ.

Christology and Ecological Concerns

Since Christ is the Creator and Sustainer of all of creation, it follows that Christ's people will be concerned about the created world. Disregard for ecological justice is inconsistent with worship of the Christ in whom all things hold together. Being an environmentalist does not make one a Christian, but Christians are rightly involved in environmental issues. Motivation for responsible use and management of Christ's creation stems from a biblical Christology.

The Christ-hymn of Colossians opens up a broad agenda for God's people. God's people participate in a reconciliation that includes all things. Thus they may expect to hear the call of God to be involved in Christ's reconciling work, including but not limited to helping persons be reconciled to God. Christ's ministry of peacemaking dictates both the agenda for those who bear his name and the way peacemaking is to be carried out.

Colossians 1:21-23

Experiencing Christ

PREVIEW

Like the ticktock of a pendulum clock, Paul's integrated gospel at one point emphasizes doctrine and at another point experience. References to experience frame the great theological passage, 1:15-20. Verses 21-23 focus on experience as applied theology. A definite attachment to the Christ-hymn (and to the prayer before it) is obvious. Although the sentence is grammatically independent, we need the previous sections to know who is meant by *he*, *his*, and *him* in verse 22. Three themes of verses 15-20 carry over into this section: reconciliation, the death of Christ, and Christ over all things.

Two features of this brief section stand out. First is the direct speech style, *And you*. Personal application of the truth about Christ is clearly intended. Second is the sharp contrast between *before* and *after* in the Colossian believers' experience.

OUTLINE

Then: Need, 1:21

Now: God's Action, 1:22a

Goal, 1:22b

Condition, 1:23

EXPLANATORY NOTES

Verse 21 is set alongside the all-encompassing grandeur of verse 20 and focuses on specific personal experience. With the words *and you*, the apostle relates the wonders of Christ's reconciliation to what the Colossian believers know best—their own transformation in Christ.

Then: Need 1:21

In order to appreciate the excellence of Christ, the believers need only to reflect on what they once were. Three phrases describe their former condition and predicament.

1. *Who were once estranged*. This assessment of the human problem, a persistent estrangement, is expressed similarly in Ephesians: "You were at that time without Christ, being aliens from the commonwealth of Israel, and strangers to the covenants of promise, having no hope and without God in the world" (2:12). Gentiles are "alienated from the life of God because of their ignorance and hardness of heart" (4:18). *Estranged* and *alienated* are translations of the same Greek word. As these parallel texts reveal, alienation from God also means alienation from God's people. The descriptive words in verse 21 are common designations for Gentiles, thus implying that the background of the church members at Colossae is mainly Gentile.

2. *Hostile in mind*, or more precisely, *enemies in the [your] mind* (EDM). In the LXX *[Septuagint, p. 316]*, this Greek term for *mind* is used frequently to translate the Hebrew word meaning heart (Deut. 6:5). In the NT, *mind* and *heart* are often put together (Luke 1:51) or used interchangeably (Heb. 8:10; 10:16). The concept is not limited to intellect; it identifies the center of the inner life, where ethical attitudes are determined. (See Eph. 2:3 and 4:18 for other negative connotations of *mind*, and 1 Pet.1:13 and 1 John 5:20 for positive connotations.) *[Mind, p. 307.]*

When the mind/heart is out of harmony with God, it is actively hostile toward God. Romans 5:10 and James 4:4 also refer to human hostility toward God. Although using a different word for mind, Romans 8:7 says, "The mind that is set on the flesh is hostile to God." Human minds need to change, not God's mind. In Ephesians 2:14-16, the hostility that is abolished by the cross of Christ is between Jew and Gentile, as well as between the estranged and God.

3. *Doing evil deeds*, or more precisely, *in [because of] the [your] evil works* (EDM). The relationship of the three phrases in verse 21 is

not entirely clear. NRSV and NASB make them parallel, while NIV suggests that alienation and hostility are the result of evil actions. Another possible meaning is that inner hostility toward God results in evil behavior. At any rate, mind and deeds interact, and human experience bears out that interaction.

Now: God's Action 1:22a

Notice that the counterpart of *you were once* is not "now you are," as might be expected; instead, the *now* focuses on God's intervening action. *[Text, p. 321.]*

The pronouns *he, his,* and *him* in verse 22 do not all have a clear reference. The phrase reads smoothly if taken in the sense, *Christ reconciled [you] in his body of flesh by his death.* Yet the larger context supports the meaning, *God reconciled [you] in [by] Christ's body of flesh by his death* (cf. 2 Cor. 5:18-19). Either way, the intervention of God in Christ is crucial for changing the alienation and hostility. The once—now contrast in these verses, movement from alienation to reconciliation, highlights the relational aspect of sin and salvation.

By using both *body* and *flesh,* the humanity of Jesus is established. Paul makes a clear distinction between Christ's physical body and the church as his body (1:18). Reconciliation was accomplished within human existence, not from a safe, antiseptic distance. It has been explicitly accomplished by means of Christ's death (1:20), and not by incarnation alone (cf. Eph. 2:16).

Goal 1:22a

The thought turns from the means of reconciliation to the purpose or goal of God's reconciling action. God's action *for* us is to be effective *in* us. Paul says his goal is *to present you holy and blameless and irreproachable before him.* Similar wording is found elsewhere (Rom. 14:10; 1 Cor. 1:8; 2 Cor. 4:14; 11:2; Eph. 1:4; 5:27; Phil. 2:15; Col. 1:28; Jude 24). In this phrase several questions beg for answers:

1. Who presents whom to whom? Since pronoun references in verse 22 are imprecise, context and similar expressions elsewhere carry more weight than strict grammar. The one doing the presenting may be Christ, but more likely God; and if God, the presentation is made to himself. Anyhow, what God does, he does in Christ. *You* may refer to individuals or the church (as in Eph. 5:27). Both are likely meant here.

2. When? Is a future judgment in view, or is the focus on the present? The conditions in verse 23 assume a future goal. Several parallel texts use similar language to speak of events at Christ's coming. However, Ephesians 1:4 and this text imply that present goals and activity are also being described. Even though the presentation is at Christ's coming, present growth and development are intended to be along these same lines.

3. Is this phrase speaking of status before God in his grace (as with Rom. 5:1-2) or of quality of character? That is, does the text speak of God considering a person righteous in Christ without reference to the person's life, or does it speak of the inner transformation that results in changed behavior? Philippians 2:15 and Colossians 1:28, along with this text, address what is characteristic of *lives worthy of the Lord* (Col. 1:10). Colossians 3:1-14 elaborates this here-and-now holiness that is to match the new relationship with God in Christ. Here in 1:22 a new standing is assumed, but the emphasis is on quality of life.

4. What imagery is to be associated with the descriptive words, *holy and blameless and irreproachable*? The first two suggest the imagery of sacrifice, while the third is court language. The three together describe completeness and purity, and they include both internal and external factors. One term is positive, and two are negative. In Greek, all three words begin with the same letter. This alliteration strengthens the effect of the phrase as a whole.

In summary, reconciliation has a moral factor. I am not permitted to say, God forgives me, so how I live does not matter. God's action aims at holiness—now. Although our measure of holiness does not achieve perfection now, we are not to postpone God's purpose to an ideal future. To use other vocabulary than found in this passage, we are not to regard sanctification as an optional extra, beyond justification. If we are reconciled, this must result in holy living. Paul keeps these several facets of Christian experience woven together.

Condition 1:23

The statement of God's intent has a proviso attached. Being in Christ calls for keeping the connection intact. What God has done and is doing must have continuing response. God's grace is not earned, but that does not remove the element of condition. Even a free gift must be kept. Paul in verse 23 says the saints must persevere, and he is optimistic that they will. The wording does not imply doubt about their continuing in the faith. [Grammar, p. 290.]

Therefore, Paul is not assuming that the Colossians have already strayed from the true faith, but neither does he assume that they cannot do so. The believers are not to take the wonders of the new relationship for granted.

The stated condition is continuing in the faith. The compound word translated *continue* emphasizes persisting (cf. similar use in Rom. 11:22; 1 Tim. 4:16). *[Grammar, p. 290.]*

The word translated here as *securely established* is identical with one in Ephesians 3:17: "As you are being rooted and *grounded* in love" (italics added). The figure is that of a secure foundation. "Foundation," in its figurative sense in the NT, has to do with Christ himself and the church as a building (1 Cor. 3:9-17). "When God confirms believers, or when believers are confirmed in faith and love, this is implicitly the assuring of the house or Church of God through its foundation, Christ" (TDNT, 3:64).

The word translated *steadfast* (cf. 1 Cor. 15:58) conveys a picture of being firmly seated in a chair, or of taking the solid stance of a football lineman. The phrase *without shifting* has the sense of not being moved away or off course, not being caused to drift.

The faith could mean "your" faith/faithfulness, as in 1:4. But here it most likely means the apostolic gospel, specifically mentioned later in the verse (as also in Gal. 1:23; 1 Tim. 1:2).

Paul's concern includes the persistence of individual believers, but we should not miss the reference to the church in this admonition. Jesus' parable of the wise and foolish builders (Matt. 7:24-27) focuses on individuals doing or not doing the will of God. However, the usual sense of the building figure in the NT is the Christian community, the church (as in Matt. 16:18; Eph. 2:20; 1 Tim. 3:15; and 1 Pet. 2:4-5).

What is not to be moved away from is *the hope promised by the gospel* (literally, *the hope of the gospel*). This is the only use of the phrase in the NT, although both hope and gospel are used in 1:5. In biblical usage, hope is not a flimsy wish, but a sure promise. In the Bible, *hope* has three types of use: (1) hope with a personal object (God, Ps. 65:5; or Christ, 1 Tim. 1:1), (2) hope with an expected reward or event (eternal life, Tit. 1:2; Christ's return, Tit. 2:13), and (3) hope as an active anticipation (Rom. 8:24-25; Phil. 1:20). This unique expression, *the hope of the gospel,* is further enriched in meaning by Paul's use of similar related phrases: *the hope of glory* (1:27), "the hope of righteousness" (Gal. 5:5), "the hope to which he has called you" (Eph. 1:18), and "the hope of salvation," meaning the hope that is part of salvation (1 Thess. 5:8).

The last part of verse 23 is strikingly similar to 1:5-7 in vocabulary: *hope, gospel, heard*. In both cases, Paul views the proclamation of the gospel, with hope as a key part of the gospel.

The gospel's universal application is evidence that it is authentic. How could it be truly good news if for only an elite few? This gospel-for-all fits with the cosmic Christ heralded in 1:15-20. Neither the phrase *to every creature*, nor the more literal rendering *in all creation* (NASB), is to be pushed to statistical precision. Yet the gospel applies to everyone everywhere. Paul subscribes to the vision and mandate of Jesus: "This good news of the kingdom will be proclaimed throughout the world, as a testimony to all the nations" (Matt. 24:14).

By identifying himself as a *minister* (EDM), Paul is not calling attention to an office, but to a function and stance. NRSV here translates the Greek word *diakonos* as *servant*, but in 1:7 as *minister*. By using *diakonos* for himself, Paul identifies closely with Epaphras (1:7) and Tychicus (4:7), also called ministers, thereby affirming their ministry. The last part of verse 23 provides a natural bridge into the next section, in which Paul writes more extensively about his ministry.

THE TEXT IN BIBLICAL CONTEXT
Conversion as Before and After

The change associated with experiencing Christ is commonly called conversion, although the terms *conversion* and *convert* occur infrequently in the text of the Bible. The language of the Bible, in both Testaments, is that of turning/repenting (such as turning from idols to the true God: 1 Thess. 1:9). In a similar vein, the wording of Colossians 1:21-22, *once . . . now*, is used frequently in the NT to describe the change, the difference between before and after.

In Colossians, the before-after contrast is expressed in several ways: from darkness to light (1:12-13), from hostility to peace (1:20-21), from estrangement to reconciliation (1:20-22), from dead to alive (2:13; 3:1-3), and from an old self to a new self (3:9-10). These are found elsewhere in the NT, plus others: from slavery to freedom, from far off to near, from no people to God's people. . . . *[Before —After, p. 282.]*

These graphic descriptions of before and after emphasize that God's action in Christ will produce a drastic change in human experience. Most of these expressions of radical change describe a basic change of identity and orientation (such as the change from slavery to freedom). Some of them also include descriptions of the change in behavior that is linked with experiencing Christ (e.g., Paul's change from persecuting to preaching).

Describing the Human Predicament

Colossians 1:21 describes the problem as human estrangement and hostility. The NT prominently portrays the need to be reconciled because of broken relationships and active enmity (Rom. 5:1-11; 2 Cor. 5:17-21; Eph. 2:13-16). But this is only one of a number of ways the problem is described. The following must be included in the broader picture of human need, combining explicit terminology used in the Scriptures and some implied descriptions of the human situation that requires God's action in Christ:

alienation	domination (by evil)	rebellion
anxiety/fear	guilt	shame
bondage/slavery	lostness	sickness
boredom	nobody	strayed
despair/without hope	outside/foreigner	
dirtiness	powerlessness	

Each of these descriptions helps to complete our understanding of why the gospel of Christ is needed. Christ meets persons in their hurting experiences. From whatever point of need persons encounter Christ, God wills to transform them so that they become holy, blameless, and irreproachable before him. Or, as Ephesians 4:13 puts it, God's intent is that we all come to "the measure of the full stature of Christ." (Cf. Shank: 137-156.)

THE TEXT IN THE LIFE OF THE CHURCH
Once—Now

The contrast in individual experience between *before* and *after* conversion is illustrated in the rich imagery of the song "Out of My Bondage," by W. T. Sleeper (to capture Paul's corporate outlook, one could change *my/I* to *our/we*):

> Out of my bondage, sorrow and night, Jesus, I come, Jesus, I come;
> Into Thy freedom, gladness and light, Jesus, I come to Thee;. . .
> Out of my sin and into Thyself, Jesus, I come to Thee.
>
> Out of my shameful failure and loss . . . ;
> Into the glorious gain of Thy cross. . . .

Out of unrest and arrogant pride . . . ;
Into Thy blessed will to abide, Jesus, I come to Thee.

Variations in Experiencing Christ

All persons do not experience Christ in the same way. When that encounter changes them from paganism to Christ rather quickly, the dramatic change from before to after is indeed a 180-degree turnaround. The term conversion means a reversal of direction. For some persons, however, conversion is a series of smaller but definite steps of encounter and response over a period of time, steps that result in assurance of being in Christ. For yet others, the experience of Christ is a gradual process of imperceptible degrees. They may not be able to identify conscious moments of crisis or decision, but the reality of the experience is undeniable.

Two general categories of Christian experience are identifiable. The one is the life-changing crisis of the first-generation Christian. That kind of conversion was the general rule in the early church, whether out of Jewish background or raw Gentile paganism. The other is the development of second- and third-generation Christians, those growing up with the benefit of Christian parents and grandparents, surrounded by the faith family of the church. Although both categories of experience are valid, they are obviously in contrast.

There is also a difference between the experience of rebels and seekers. Some persons have acted out their rebellion against God, and their trail of sin has left marks on body and spirit. Others have never been far from the kingdom, have been sheltered from the world, and are now discovering their God-given self. Faith development is not on the same track for those two types of persons.

Another kind of difference appears between those who are part of a culture that assumes individualism to be the norm, and those from a non-Western culture where conversions happen collectively, by families or tribes. NT references to households believing and being baptized (Acts 10:2, 33, 44; 16:15, 32-33) reveal a communal society setting. However, such multi-individual responses are not to be thought of as mass conversions.

The church needs to be on guard against taking any one of these tracks and attempting to impose that kind of conversion experience on everyone. Making the personal revolution of crisis conversion the norm does not take into account preconversion experience or individual needs. The church needs to be concerned with maintaining an emphasis on God's initiative and grace and yet not impose the same pattern of faith development on everyone. The issue is more complex when children of Christians are coming to faith in a congregational setting that is also calling and nurturing persons out of what is clearly the dominion of darkness. (For a discussion of the faith experience of children reared in a believing context, see Jeschke.)

In Western societies the believers church needs to counter the individualism that is often prevalent. The gospel message must make clear that although an experience of Christ is personal, it is not private. Coming to Christ means coming into community, just as it did for the disciples Jesus called to follow him.

The Gospel for Evangelism and Mission

How one understands and presents the gospel depends largely on how one understands the human problem. In both Catholicism and Protestantism, it has been common to define the human predicament almost exclusively as guilt resulting from sin. Along with an emphasis on guilt has come a preoccupation with punishment and retribution. Thus the church has focused attention on human guilt and a satisfaction view of Christ's atonement while neglecting the other NT images for salvation, including those in Colossians. (Driver: 1989 provides a helpful survey of the principal biblical images for the atonement.)

The cause of Christ is better served when the church takes a versatile approach to the good news, as does the NT. Paul packaged the gospel of Christ somewhat differently for different audiences. We can see those differences by reading Colossians alongside Acts, Romans, 1 Thessalonians, and Ephesians. Missionaries are now prodding the church to look again at its theology and examine its attempt to make the gospel message relevant to people of different cultures.

In North America, for example, the fragmentation of lives and of society makes people hungry for reconciliation and community. For many the gospel will have its strongest appeal in personal and relational terms. It is always the same gospel, but the emphases will need to be different when taking that gospel to cultures with a keen consciousness of the spirit world, or cultures where the family structure is outstandingly strong, or to a Muslim culture antagonistic to Christianity. If we fail to take the receptor culture into account, we contribute to nonsuccess and discredit of the gospel. For example, miscommunication is predictable when missionaries, themselves products of an anxiety-ridden culture, take a gospel they assume is in the guilt motif and give it to a tradition-oriented culture (e.g., Japan or Africa) where separation from God is experienced as shame (rather than guilt).

The Hope of the Gospel

Hope is essential for living at any time, especially in times of adversity and testing. Hope is living with a firm hold on the promise of life and salvation. Hope is the gift of looking forward with confidence, knowing that even if the future entails suffering, even unto death, it will be okay because Christ has gone on ahead. To hope is to have a secure future and know one has it.

Hopelessness is that feeling of futility and desperation in which there seems to be no prospect for an acceptable future. Human beings are most pitiable when their misplaced hopes disappoint and their empty hopes fade away. Responses to a variety of circumstances can contribute to a loss of hope. Extreme dangers, prolonged economic depression, and the threat of nuclear holocaust can cause people to slip into hopelessness. When people experience all losing and no winning, or a sense of being trapped in an unjust system, they may be pushed to give up in despair. Persecution severely tests hope, and yet it often strengthens hope.

An absence of the hope of the gospel produces some tragic results. Suicide, with a growing prevalence among the young and the aged (especially men), is evidence of hopelessness. Some people live without a sense of a future with God in it; as a result, they may shape life by distorted values derived only from the present. Life that is meaningless or has meaning only for today often becomes reckless. Morality is tossed aside. Life without hope is a dismal picture.

Into a world of hopelessness, Christ has placed his church as the custodian of the message of hope. Colossians reminds us to cling to Christ for hope for ourselves and others. The gospel of hope needs to be announced by the hopeful people of God and actualized in them. The church is called to be a community of hope.

In terms of pastoral care, the church needs to help its members keep in contact with the gospel of hope. We can encourage this through reminders, celebrations, and testimonies of experience. In terms of outreach into the world, Christians are wise to remember that hope is an attractive facet of the gospel in an age of despair. Biblical hope is neither a message of escape nor a hollow promise of avoiding all problems. It is the good news that for each day and for eternity, there is a future because a sovereign God is in it. Therefore, a victorious outcome is certain in Christ.

Colossians 1:24—2:5

Explaining the Apostle's Ministry

PREVIEW

Thoughts on ministry logically and naturally follow mention of the gospel that is for everyone. In 1:24—2:5 Paul elaborates on his calling to become *a servant of this gospel* (1:23). His comments are intensely personal. Note the pronouns, *I, me,* and *my,* fifteen of them in NRSV. Paul shares deeply of himself with believers that he has not met face to face (2:1).

This segment reveals why Paul so enthusiastically and energetically works at his commission. Note such words as *servant* (minister), *sufferings, mystery* (three of the four occurrences in Colossians), and *striving.* Verse 24 raises some difficult questions of interpretation. Verse 27, although relatively familiar, needs to be seen, understood, and appreciated in context.

OUTLINE

Serving in God's Strength, 1:24-29
1:24	Suffering
1:25-27	Secret
1:28	Strategy
1:29	Struggle

Pastoral Matters, 2:1-5
    2:1-3   Pastoral Goals
    2:4   Pastoral Concerns
    2:5   Pastoral Affirmations

EXPLANATORY NOTES
Serving in God's Strength   1:24-29

What does it mean to be a servant of the gospel and of the church? What sustains faithful ministry when it entails suffering? The concluding paragraph of chapter 1 is Paul's testimony of experience.

1:24 Suffering

Paul is in custody as he writes to the church at Colossae (4:18). The chains on his wrists are a constant reminder of the *suffering* associated with his ministry. At the end of the paragraph, and continuing into chapter 2, *toil and struggle* characterize his ministry. Yet the tone is not one of discouragement, but of *rejoicing in . . . sufferings.*

Verse 24 is difficult. One clause raises the most questions: *in my flesh I am completing what is lacking in Christ's afflictions.* The following interpretations represent various attempts to understand what it may mean. Evaluative comments appear in parentheses.

1. Something is lacking in Christ's sacrificial suffering. (The existence of a "treasury of merit," built up in part by the sufferings of saints for the benefit of others, was a traditional teaching of the Roman Catholic Church, dating back to the thirteenth century. This concept implies that Christ's work of redemption is not complete, or at least that it can be supplemented. Neither the OT nor the NT supports this view. The clear testimony of the Scriptures is that redemption through Christ's suffering and death is complete. Nothing can or should be added.)

2. *Christ's afflictions* can possibly mean afflictions for the sake of Christ. (In Acts 9:16, note the Lord's instructions to Ananias regarding Saul: "I myself will show him how much he must suffer for the sake of my name." But *completing* and *lacking* make little sense in connection with this meaning, and neither does *for the sake of . . . the church.*)

3. Christ's afflictions may mean sufferings which resemble those of Christ. (But this has the same weaknesses as option 2.)

4. The sufferings in view may be those resulting from the believers' mystical union with Christ. (Believers do identify with Christ in his suffering and death, but the benefit is for the believer rather than it being for the sake of others or the church. *Lacking* is not explained, unless perhaps in the sense of what is yet to be shared, with awareness that it is never completed before death.)

5. A concept of "the woes of the Messiah" developed out of Jewish expectations of the end-times. This focused on the travail out of which the messianic age was to be born, with limits set by God, but not yet reached. Paul's sufferings go toward making up the total and thus reduce suffering for the church. (The NT view is that the messianic age has already begun and tribulations are to be expected, especially near the end. The idea of needing a full number of martyrs could be implied in Rev. 6:11. However, Colossians does not give evidence of an apocalyptic perspective.)

6. The corporate personality concept may help to explain Paul's thought. Israel was to be God's suffering servant but failed in that task. Jesus was indeed God's suffering servant. By identifying with Christ, the people of God now share in that suffering-servant ministry. (The vicarious element of the suffering, *for the sake of*, fits with this interpretation, but *what is lacking* is not explained.)

7. A distinction may be made between suffering that saves and suffering that edifies. The work of redemption has been fully accomplished in Christ, but Christ's ongoing suffering to bring believers to perfection is shared by Christ's servants. As Paul applies the principle to himself, he suffers, not for his own benefit, but for the edifying benefit of others. (This distinction is not at all implied in this text, but it does respect the fact that the word used in 1:24 for Christ's *afflictions* is never used in the NT in explicit reference to Christ's redemptive suffering.)

8. Nothing is lacking in Christ's sufferings, but a deficiency in Paul's suffering is in view. Philippians 3:10 is a supporting text. (Paul does accept suffering and recognize value in it, but this explanation fails to include all the factors for an acceptable explanation.)

9. Sixteenth-century Anabaptists cited and alluded to Colossians 1:24 as they sought to understand their own sufferings. Conrad Grebel noted in a letter that many were putting their trust in leaders regarded as the learned, while few believed the Word of God. He went on to say, "And if you should have to suffer for it, you know that it cannot be otherwise. Christ must suffer still more in his members, but he will strengthen them and keep them steadfast to the end" (293).

A faithful interpretation must respect previous references in Colossians to the completed work of Christ (1:12-14, 20-21), and many other similar teachings of the NT. It must allow for something that is not yet complete, associated with *Christ's afflictions*. It must also understand the sufferings as being on behalf of the church, the church at Colossae in particular. Although there are elements of truth in several of the above interpretations, this commentator finds explanation 7 offering the most comprehensive point of view. (This explanation has been set forth and elaborated by Lightfoot and favored by scholars such as H. Moule, Schweizer, and Barclay.)

Paul senses purpose in his sufferings and therefore can rejoice in them. (A similar testimony is found in Rom. 5:3 and in 2 Cor. 12:9-10, although for a different purpose.) From the word order in Greek, it is clear that Paul has in mind suffering *in my [his own] flesh for the sake of his [Christ's] body, that is, the church* (EDM). Ephesians 3:1-13 is similar to this passage, with verse 13 also including a perspective on suffering grounded in purpose. Note that the rare word translated *completing* implies that Paul is contributing to the filling but not finishing it. *[Grammar, p. 290.]*

Key words in 1:24 (and its context) occur also in 2 Corinthians 1:3-11. Both passages use *sufferings* and *afflictions* with the same meanings and distinctions.

1:25-27 Secret

In 1:23 Paul identifies himself as a *servant* (*minister*) of the *gospel*. In 1:24-25 he writes of himself as a *servant* (*minister*) of the *church*. These are not two ministries, but one, the source of which is *God's commission*. The key word in Greek is *oikonomia* (from which *economy* is derived). In Luke 16:2-4 it means management or stewardship. In Paul's letters it has a double meaning, denoting God's plan and management of salvation and the universe (Eph. 1:10; 3:9) and Paul's commission (1 Cor. 9:17). Although the words *given to me* point to Paul's commission, the wording in verse 25 requires the first meaning to be included as well. This therefore is the sense of the text: *I became a minister according to God's plan, the execution of which has been assigned to me, for your benefit* (EDM).

God's plan and God's *mystery* are closely intertwined. (The words *oikonomia* and *mustērion* are often in close proximity.) Paul views his trusteeship as within God's larger purposes. Elsewhere Paul refers to his ministry as a "commission of God's grace" (Eph. 3:2) and wants believers to regard him as one of the "stewards of God's mysteries" (1 Cor. 4:1).

A key term in 1:24—2:5 is *mystery* (or *secret*). The prevalent translation is *mystery* (as in NRSV), a derivative of the Greek word *mustērion*. *Mystery* may suggest a puzzle that is difficult or impossible to solve, but such is not the meaning here. *Secret* may better convey the biblical sense—something once hidden but now revealed. (It could also be misleading if considered to be knowledge that a few keep to themselves, as in secret societies.) At the heart of Paul's ministry is a secret that is no longer a secret. Paul does not define the term when he first uses it in Colossians, or anywhere else, for that matter. The context reveals the meaning. First, some observations from verses 25b-27:

1. The secret is associated with *the word of God* (1:25), meaning the gospel message (as in 1 Thess. 2:13).

2. The secret was *hidden throughout the ages and generations*, known only to God, but now made known.

3. The secret *has now been revealed to his saints* (God's people) as an integral part of the revealed message of the new era of salvation history.

4. The secret has been disclosed because *God chose* to reveal it, unveiling his sovereign purposes.

5. The secret is described in terms of *the riches of [its] glory*, expressing how wonderful the revealed message is.

6. The secret is to be made known openly *among the Gentiles*, who are most directly affected by the revealed secret. This is the new dimension.

7. The secret is simply stated as *Christ in you*, and *you* refers to the Gentiles as full participants in God's purposes, with assurance of a glorious destiny in the age to come (1:5; 3:4).

Two features of the secret stand out in 1:25-27. One is the note of revelation, or the present openness of the secret. The other is the note of proclamation. The unveiled plan is to be proclaimed. Two words (in 1:26-27) associated with the secret are translated as *revealed* and *make known*.

The essence of the secret now disclosed is that in God's plan, Gentiles are also included; or more precisely, Jews and Gentiles are remade into one new body in Christ. *[Secret, p. 315.]* With this overarching meaning in mind, we need to read the phrase *Christ in you* (1:27) with special emphasis on *you*, meaning *you Gentiles*. Of course, *Christ* in you, and Christ *in* you are also important biblical themes, though not the ones emphasized here. In line with earlier references to the body of Christ as a corporate experience of Christ, *you* is plural in *Christ in you*, indicating that Christ is experienced in the community of response and not only individually.

1:28 Strategy

This verse crisply states how Paul carries out his ministry and to what end. By switching from *I* to *we*, Paul acknowledges that he is not God's only minister following this strategy. At least he needs to include Epaphras, since he himself has not taken the gospel to Colossae.

Four action words outline Paul's strategy: *proclaim, warning, teaching,* and *present.* The first three have to do with method and the last one with motive. Paul's primary thrust is proclaiming—even better expressed as announcing or broadcasting. (The tense here implies continuing action.) In this text Paul designates not what but who is being announced. Christ, at the center of the revealed secret, is Paul's message. The expression, proclaiming Christ, is also in Acts 17:3 and Philippians 1:17-18. In other texts we find church leaders proclaiming the Word of God (Acts 13:5, 46; 17:13) and proclaiming the gospel (1 Cor. 9:14). There are two other Greek words commonly used in the NT with meaning and usage similar to the one here translated proclaim: kērussō, rendered as proclaim (1:23) or preach; and euangelizō, from which we get our English word evangelize (proclaim/preach the gospel).

Paul identifies two activities supplementing his ministry of proclamation—warning and teaching. Warning, also translated as admonish (as in 3:16), has a somewhat negative connotation to it, having to do with cautioning about what not to do, correcting, and getting the mind in proper order. However, the intent is not punishment but the "cure of souls." (Other occurrences among the total of eight in the NT may be observed in Acts 20:31; Rom. 15:14; and 1 Cor. 4:14.)

The companion activity is teaching. Teaching has been a ministry of the church from its beginning (Acts 2:42). It has to do with understanding the Scriptures (the OT for the early church), understanding Jesus, and giving directions for living. The term occurs two other places in Colossians: in 2:7 with focus on the foundational teaching received, and in 3:16 associated with the word of Christ.

We make four observations about warning and teaching in 1:28:

1. Together they represent a balanced, supportive ministry. Only in Colossians do these particular terms occur together, although the balance is expressed in other ways in other places. Admonition is balanced with instruction, correction with building up, rebuke with encouragement.

2. Responsibility for warning and teaching rests not only with leaders (as in the example of Paul, and as found in the pastoral letters) but with all members in a ministry to each other (3:16; Rom. 15:14).

3. Repetition of everyone (plus a third time in the last phrase of the verse) indicates individual care of each person. It also emphasizes the inclusiveness of the gospel, likely in contrast to the exclusiveness of the teachings threatening the churches in the Lycus Valley.

4. In all wisdom qualifies how both warning and teaching are done. [Grammar, p. 290.] Warning and teaching done in a wise manner will focus on doing God's will (cf. comments on 1:9) rather than on speculative and privileged matters.

The motive part of Paul's ministry strategy, to present everyone mature in Christ, echoes the goal of God's reconciling action in 1:22. As noted there, a presentation at Christ's coming is likely in mind, but the same goal of maturity applies now. This here-and-now goal is stated in similar language in Ephesians 4:13: "Until we all reach unity in the faith and in the knowledge of the Son of God and become mature, attaining to the whole measure of the fullness of Christ" (NIV). The word translated *mature* describes a complete person, one who is spiritually adult. Colossians 4:12 adds the element of maturity of conviction regarding God's will. This practical goal in present human experience is achieved only in the undivided mind and heart, fully oriented to God and to Christ. *[Mature, p. 307.]*

1:29 Struggle

Paul returns again to his highly personal testimony, using *I* (cf. 1 Cor. 15:10). He uses vivid figures to express his intense investment of himself in ministry. The word *toil* denotes hard work, exertion, as with an athlete straining to the limits in training. *Struggle*, a word also used regarding an athletic contest, further describes the toil as a deeply intense effort to achieve a goal. The Greek word is the one from which the English word *agonize* is derived. *Agonizing* aptly conveys the meaning of the word in this verse (and in 2:1), expressing the rigorous demand on physical and emotional energy in Paul's expenditure of himself. The same term is commonly translated *fight* (as in 1 Tim. 6:12 and 2 Tim. 4:7), with connotations of contest and conflict. Forms of the two words, *toil* and *struggle,* also occur together in 1 Timothy 4:10.

The source for the enablement of Paul's intense ministry comes out in the final phrase of verse 29. The translation of the phrase can preserve a play on words: *agonizing with the energy he is powerfully causing to be energized in me* (EDM). The Greek word here (in two grammatical forms) is the one from which we get the word *energy.* It is always used in the NT to describe the supernatural. (Twice it refers to "evil-working.") It appears as "work" in Philippians 2:12-13, a text with a meaning obviously parallel to Colossians 1:29. Paul's testimony is that Christ's power within him fully matches his own expenditure of energy. The measure of God's energy is often expressed as the power to raise Jesus from the dead (Col. 2:12; Eph. 1:19-21).

In summary, along with the four concepts explored above (suffering, secret, strategy, and struggle), an understanding of ministry stands out. Paul sees his ministry as an assignment within God's arrangement of things. Translating the Greek work *diakonos* as *servant* (NRSV) appropriately conveys Paul's emphasis on function and style of ministry rather than on office. Paul can rejoice in his assignment even though it involves suffering and struggle.

Pastoral Matters 2:1-5

In chapter 2 the tone becomes even more pastoral. Imagine the impression such an intensely personal message from Paul would make on the believers at Colossae. Apparently few of them have met him face to face, and he himself, being in prison, might be expected to be wrapped up in his personal agenda. Yet his words show a deep concern for them and their welfare. Sensing the genuineness of his personal interest should dispose them to take seriously his warnings.

2:1-3 Pastoral Goals

The "disclosure form" at the beginning of verse 1, or the variation, "I do not want you to be unaware/uninformed," appear a number of times in Paul letters (e.g., Rom. 1:13; 11:25; 1 Cor. 10:1; 11:3; 12:1; 2 Cor. 1:8; 1 Thess. 4:13). The form was evidently a letter-writing convention of that time.

Paul emphasizes the greatness of his struggle (agony) on their behalf (1:29). Along with the hard work he does and the opposition he faces, his pastoral interest expresses itself inwardly as prayer and concern and outwardly as letters and other communications through various persons. He has in mind the Christians at Colossae and those at Laodicea, another city of the Lycus Valley, about ten miles northwest of Colossae. The additional phrase, *for all who have not seen me face to face*, may well mean all others of the Lycus Valley, such as those at Hierapolis (4:13). It is widely accepted that 2:1 means that Paul has not been to Colossae. (See the maps in the introduction to Colossians and the discussion of the possibility that Paul never visited the area.) The point of 2:1 seems to be that Paul's personal interest in Christians and churches is not limited to those he has founded, but also includes those he knows about but has not started or visited.

Paul is not asking for pity when he again mentions his agonizing. Rather, he directs his intense exertion toward specific goals affecting the Christians who read and hear his letter. Three pastoral goals stand out:

1. *Encouragement.* The key word here sometimes means console or comfort (as in 2 Cor. 1:3-7 and in 2 Thess. 2:17, where it is coupled with strengthen). Paul's goal was to ward off discouragement and despair (cf. 4:8).

2. *Unity in love.* To be united or knit together is one of two meanings of the word Paul uses. The other meaning is to instruct (as it is used in Acts 19:33 and 1 Cor. 2:16). Being instructed in love fits the flow of thought here, which moves to understanding and knowledge. However, Colossians 2:19 (and Eph. 4:16) employs the word in the imagery of the connectedness of muscles and tendons, a meaning that fits even better here (cf. Col. 3:14). The goal of community enabled by love is lost if the meaning is only instruction. This goal, then, guards against bickering and division among believers.

3. *Confident understanding.* In characteristic fashion Paul piles up words, four of them in this case, to convey the potential for which he seeks. They are translated as concepts on a par with each other: *wealth, full assurance, understanding,* and *true knowledge* (NASB). *All* modifies *wealth/riches,* a word that already means superabundance. The thought of full assurance is also found in 4:12 (cf. 1 Thess. 1:5). Confidence or assurance is linked with *understanding,* or discerning insight. The series climaxes with true *knowledge of God's mystery, that is, Christ himself.* Knowledge is not to be regarded as a collection of abstract facts, as noted in comments on 1:9-10, but as spiritual perception of God's truth experienced in participation in his will. The four synonyms in this series greatly elevate the potential of experience for those in Christ.

There are several explanations for the variations found in translations of the phrase, *of God's mystery, that is, Christ himself.* There are eight different readings of the phrase in the Greek text, and scholars do not all agree on which reading to use. *[Text, p. 319.]* In addition, the phrase calls for some interpretation. Many versions add words to make a meaning clearer. Four meanings are possible in the literal translation of the best-supported text, *of the secret (mystery) of God, of Christ* (EDM):

1. The secret of God, which is Christ (taking Christ as parallel to secret).
2. The secret of God, that is, of Christ (taking Christ as parallel to God).
3. The secret of the God of Christ (taking Christ as identifying God).
4. The secret of the God Christ (taking God as identifying Christ as divine—but without NT parallel).

The first one has the most merit; yet, compared with other passages referring to the secret (1:26-27, etc.), it is an oversimplification to say that the secret is Christ. Rather, the sense of the phrase in its context is that Christ is the revelation of the purpose and wisdom of God, a revelation both exclusively in Christ and fully unfolded in Christ.

Verse 3 complements verse 2, matching resources in Christ with pastoral goals. The person of Christ is the answer to the search for *wisdom and knowledge*. The word *all* emphasizes both the uniqueness and adequacy of the spiritual *treasures* stored up in Christ. Those treasures remain hidden for the unresponsive and disobedient, but the thrust of Paul's message is not on special insights for an elite few. Instead, the emphasis is on access to the treasures. All who truly seek may find. There is no need to look elsewhere. Christ *is the key that opens all the hidden treasures of God's wisdom and knowledge* (GNB). Cults, then and now, lay claim to special revelations. Paul says that it is all available in Christ. Romans 11:33 also couples wisdom and knowledge and identifies them as riches. (See Prov. 2:1-15 and Isa. 45:3 for similar words and expressions in the OT.)

Verses 2 and 3 shed light on the nature of the false teaching at Colossae. "Paul's insistence that Christ is God's mystery in whom are hidden all of the treasures of wisdom and knowledge makes the most sense, in the light of 2:4, when one supposes that the opposition was advocating a knowledge of God's mysteries for which Christ was not really necessary" (Bandstra: 340). The phrase *treasures of wisdom* has been surmised by some to echo Gnostic (or pre-Gnostic) expressions. Others suggest that it is an allusion to Hellenistic-Jewish concepts, but several clearer parallels are found in one of the Jewish books of the Pseudepigrapha (e.g., 2 Baruch 44:14; 54:13; plus reference to "mysteries" in 48:3). This evidence points to the opposition being of Jewish character (Bandstra: 343).

2:4 Pastoral Concerns

This is the first explicit reference to Paul's sense of a danger facing the Colossian believers. Elaborations of the excellencies of Christ in the first part of the letter grow out of a concern that the Lycus Valley Christians might become victims of devious and dangerous teaching.

The expression *I am saying this* is best taken to refer to the affirmations in verses 2 and 3. The first descriptive word, *deceive*, occurs only one other place in the NT in the sense of self-deception (James 1:22). Here it means convincing someone by misleading reasoning. The companion word, translated as *plausible arguments* (occurring only here in the NT), depicts the presentation as both persuasive and seductive. The believers should not be deceived, no matter how good the arguments sound. Teaching needs to be tested by standards of truth and not by the attractiveness of the way it is packaged. Paul's concern continues to be pertinent. Christian people who are not grounded in spiritual knowledge are in danger of being duped by fancy rhetoric. Paul addresses the issues at Colossae more directly in 2:8-23.

2:5 Pastoral Affirmations

Paul concludes a discussion of his ministry and its relevance for the readers with further words of encouragement. Although he is not able to go in person to the Lycus Valley because he is in prison, he assures them of his presence *in spirit*. This implies a sense of spiritual identity with them (as in 1 Cor. 5:3-5). Both authority of apostleship and vested interest in the outcome may well be included in Paul's thoughts at this point in the letter.

Paul's feel for the heartbeat at Colossae leads him to *rejoice*. Presence *in spirit* enables him to *see* two qualities he wants to affirm. *Morale* (*good discipline*, NASB) connotes orderliness. They are staying in line. The church has not been wrecked by strife and division. *Firmness of your faith in Christ* identifies the solidness of their beliefs and experience. *Firmness* is associated with foundation (2 Tim. 2:19) and with faith (Acts 16:5; 1 Pet. 5:9). Some other-than-biblical usage of the terms *morale* and *firmness* suggests that they were military terms. However, since much usage has no association with military descriptions, the meanings are determined by the context. The context here can be viewed as preparation for battle against perversions of the gospel. But the tone is affirmation of the basic health and soundness of the church. The new, false teaching has not yet had success in the valley, and Paul's deep desire is to keep it that way.

THE TEXT IN BIBLICAL CONTEXT
Colossians and Galatians, Two Different Approaches

These two letters illustrate vastly different styles of approach to a problem. In Colossians 2 it becomes clear that a dangerous religious influence threatens the future stability of the church. [*Problems, p. 310.*] Yet no indication of the nature of the problem shows up until thirty-seven verses into the letter. In Galatians, however, immediately after the greeting, Paul begins to directly confront a perversion of the true gospel. In Colossians 1 the tone is warmly positive and affirming. Most notable is the emphasis on the supremacy and sufficiency of

Christ. In Galatians 1 the terse style is highly charged with strong feelings. Readers find themselves in a combat zone. What accounts for the difference?

Paul has had previous personal contact with the churches of Galatia, but has not been to Colossae. However, discreet politeness can hardly explain the style of Colossians. Galatians is the response of an apostle under attack. Apparently his apostleship has not been challenged in Colossae, and that may account for some of the difference. The basic issue in Colossae is Christology. In Galatians, Paul vigorously defends his apostleship because the integrity of the gospel is at stake. In Colossians, particularly in the segment under discussion, he also includes his credentials, but in an indirect way. For example, as we look carefully at 1:24—2:5, we see that Paul says he is commissioned by God, working hard in God's power, suffering for the church, fully proclaiming the gospel message to all, and feeling personally responsible for their welfare. However, he does not marshal the evidence in a defensive way.

Another factor that may explain the difference is the degree to which the dangerous influence has progressed. In Galatians, we sense that the Judaizing influence is so far advanced that only a frontal attack has a chance of succeeding. In Colossians, we sense that a teaching that could do a lot of damage has not yet affected the church, at least not much. Therefore, Paul is led to review the excellencies of Christ, thereby undergirding the solid teaching they have already received. The approach is more preventive than remedial.

While the differences between Colossians and Galatians are real and not imagined, they are not absolute. Colossians 2:8-23 has an argumentative tone to it. On the other hand, Galatians not only points out what is wrong; it also stresses the excellencies of the gospel as a deterrent to turning away from it.

Careful Bible study requires paying attention to the tone and style of the material, looking for what accounts for the emotional tone and communication style.

God's Secret

It is crucial for us to have an adequate understanding of the term *secret* (or *mystery*) if we are to grasp Paul's message, method, and ministry. In addition to the three references to this secret-now-revealed in 1:24—2:5, Paul encapsulates his message as *the mystery of Christ* in 4:3. The inclusion of Gentiles may not seem as momentous in the twentieth century as it did in the NT era. Then it was a major adjustment for those of Jewish background and glorious good news for Gentiles who heard and responded to the gospel of Christ. The issue runs all the way through Acts and is a major theme in Romans and Galatians (and in many other texts). *[Secret, p. 315.]*

Paul's View of Ministry

By drawing on Colossians 1:24—2:5 and related texts, a composite picture comes into focus:

1. *How he describes it.* The predominant terms are *diakonos* (servant) and *diakonia* (ministry). He uses another word, *doulos* (slave), almost exclusively of his relationship to Jesus Christ, a word that emphasizes total allegiance. *Slave* is also used in the NT in the sense of human slavery. When the term *minister* is used instead of servant, we do well to remember that the focus is on attitude and style rather than on position or office. Ministry is described in a number of ways (EDM translations):

> "servants of God" (2 Cor. 6:4)
> "servant of Christ/Christ Jesus" (Col. 1:7; 1 Tim. 4:6)
> "servant of the gospel" (Col. 1:23)
> "servant of the church" (Col. 1:25)
> "ministry to the saints" (1 Cor. 16:15)
> "ministry of the Spirit" (2 Cor. 3:7-9)
> "ministry of the word" (Acts 6:4)
> "fellow servant" and "faithful minister" (Col. 1:7 and 4:7)

Paul uses *servant/minister* to refer to himself and others who had special functions in the church, but he does not limit ministry to those with a specialized role, especially not to clergy in the modern sense. All the saints are to be ministers. Ephesians 4:11-13 speaks of Christ's gifts to the church "to equip the saints for the work of ministry" (NRSV, leaving out that unfortunate comma in some translations). Romans 12:7 lists service as a gift of helping. The context emphasizes the use of gifts, and in a sense the exercise of all gifts is ministry (cf. 1 Pet. 4:10-11).

2. *How Paul came to be a minister.* Paul has not volunteered for the task. His call is an integral part of his conversion. He confesses that his ministry was given to him. Ministry as a gift of grace is further expanded in Ephesians 3:7-10 and Romans 15:15-16. Paul has not become the outstanding church leader of his day by climbing over whomever gets in his way. He calls himself an apostle, but the least of

the apostles because he has persecuted the church (1 Cor. 15:9). However, Paul does not hang his head apologetically; he considers ministry a privilege even more than an obligation.

3. *How Paul does ministry.* The way ministry action is described corresponds to the style of relating implied in the word *servant.* Paul writes of what he does "for the sake of," "in behalf of," or "for" believers and the church. He calls the relief offering taken to Jerusalem a ministry. Clearly Paul does ministry the way Jesus modeled and taught. As a disciple of Christ himself, Paul does not share the popular Greek attitude expressed in the statement, "How can a man be happy when he has to serve someone?" Paul's servanthood ministry meshes with what he writes about the mind of Christ Jesus in Philippians 2:5-11.

From Jesus we hear the words in Mark 10:42-45 about not coming to be served but to serve. In Luke 22:24-27 we hear Jesus say that the kingdom does not have to do with hierarchy but with suffering and death. Jesus spoke and acted in the suffering-servant style described in the servant songs of Isaiah 42-53. The message and the medium merge in Jesus; and they do also in Paul. How Paul does ministry reinforces his message, and his message is Jesus.

Mind as a Biblical Term

Words and activities associated with the mind are part of this section of Colossians. The word translated *warning* in 1:28 is part of a family of Greek words identified with the human mind. A biblical perspective on the mind helps in catching the meaning of this and other texts. [*Mind, p. 307.*]

The Hebrew view of the human person showed no interest in the psychological compartments of mind, spirit, and soul. Instead, the person was seen a whole. In Paul's use of the term, mind has to do with thinking, reasoning, reflecting, and purposing. As such the mind is a neutral human faculty. It is capable of being corrupted, blinded, and hardened (Rom. 1:21; 2 Cor. 3:14-16; Col. 2:18; 1 Tim. 6:5), and it is capable of being renewed (Rom. 12:2). The mind may be controlled by the flesh or controlled by the Spirit.

Paul recognizes the mind and thinking as an integral aspect of personhood. The mind is involved in conversion. One of the words translated *repent* means change of mind. The mind is also involved in growth toward maturity. To admonish is to try to adjust another's mind. Right thinking is needed for standing ground against false and distorted teaching. The Christian mind is the mind of Christ.

THE TEXT IN THE LIFE OF THE CHURCH
Insights for Evangelizing

From Colossians (and elsewhere) it becomes clear that Paul sees evangelism the same way it is expressed in Jesus' words in Matthew 28:19-20, making disciples. Obviously Paul is not a preacher who feels his job is completed when someone decides to accept Jesus. He does not see Christian experience as a once-for-all action of faith. Rather, his teaching and practice indicate that becoming a Christian means coming into relationship with Christ and the church and going on to maturity in faith and life.

So, when is evangelizing done, or when is a person "saved"? A biblical church will need to find a wholistic way to engage in the gospel mission in the world. Some evangelizing separates forgiveness and assurance of heaven from growth, morality, and mission, but that is not true to the gospel of Jesus Christ. The more comprehensive term *discipling* may help the church to avoid too narrow a view of the task. Yet it is a false division to make evangelism and nurture two separate enterprises of the church. The church needs to learn from Paul that the traditional doctrines of justification and sanctification are facets of a whole experience in Christ. Without a wholistic view, the church tries to help persons be "saved" but then leaves further response as somewhat optional, such as obedience in areas of ethics, peace, and justice. Instead, discipling continues for life in the mutual caring, supporting, restoring, and encouraging that should make up participation in the body of Christ.

Maturity in Christ

One wonders what Paul would say and do about the mediocre church members found in many congregations in our time. He did not consider acceptable the immaturity among Christians that has been called "chronic adolescence." Paul bared his heart when he said that maturity in individuals and churches was the goal of his servant calling. Several aspects of Christian maturity that have particular relevance for the church today can be gleaned from his comments.

What Paul meant by maturity in Christ needs to be clearly understood. *[Mature, p. 307.]* Even if we allow that absolute perfection describes only God or Christ and that human perfection and maturity is somewhat relative, we are faced with extremely high standards in Paul's statements. In Galatians 4:19 he writes of his travail until Christ be formed in those he calls his little children. This text makes maturity a matter of inward and relational experience in personal and congregational life, not a matter of external conformity. In Ephesians 4:13 he makes the stature of the fullness of Christ the measure of maturity. Yet he does not view such maturity as dreamy idealism, but as an attainable potential. Paul's words challenge any tendency to lower the goal because of "practical realism."

Who is to be mature in Christ? Paul gives no room for those who claim super wisdom, for the few who learn the secrets of the universe. By insisting that maturity is for all who are in Christ, Paul does not necessarily deny that there are degrees of maturity. But he does not affirm as acceptable several levels of spirituality in the church.

Why is maturity important? From Colossians 1:23; 2:4, 8-23 (and Eph. 4:14) we can see that maturity is an antidote to being vulnerable to damaging influences. The specifics may be different today from those in the Lycus Valley, but the need for Christians who are strong and secure is even more critical now. It requires mature Christians to remain faithful to Christ in a culture that is not only secular but increasingly pagan. To keep from getting drawn into an array of cults with their warped doctrines, Christians need to know what they believe and why.

How do believers become mature? As in the early church, leaders are important for building maturity. Feeding, encouraging, warning, and correcting are all necessary pastoral care functions. Yet even the best of pastoral care cannot guarantee maturity. These functions are to be shared as members care for each other. Also, individuals must maintain personal disciplines and remain open to the Spirit of Christ. An old legend illustrates Paul's approach in Colossians. With the sweetness of their songs, the sirens lured many sailors onto the rocky shores of their islands. Many had met their death there. Ulysses responded by putting wax in the ears of his men and having himself tied to the mast. Orpheus used a better method. He raised his voice in even louder song, praising his gods with charm that excelled the sirens' charms.

The Gospel and Human Intellect

Emphases change from time to time. During one era the emphasis may be on activism and justice. At another time the emphasis may be on piety or freedom in worship. During some eras the mood has been strongly anti-intellectual. In other times Christians have attempted to use the methods of scientific reason to prove a faith conviction that is under attack. The church needs to maintain a balanced perspective with respect to human intellect.

The gospel of Jesus Christ is not a matter of intellectual abstractions understandable by only the brilliant. Neither is it a matter of heart experience that excludes intellect from matters of faith. When Paul wrote his letters, he assumed intellect on the part of the recipients. The Bible affirms the mind as an integral part of human personhood. Human minds can be used by God and are being so used. For the gospel to touch and transform modern, sophisticated unbelievers, a conversion of the mind will need to take place. Denying human mental ability will not help. Minds shaped by the mind of Christ will need to present the gospel in ways intellectually respectable without making modern scientific thought structures the ultimate measure of reality.

Ministry That Fits the Gospel

Message and method must mesh. Methods will either reinforce the message or cancel it out. It is crucial that we mesh method and message together, particularly in an age when the church is tempted to compete with a sophisticated entertainment industry for the attention of people. Paul renounced ways that would deny or distort the gospel. The integrity of the gospel is sacrificed when preachers take advantage of hearers or manipulate them. Images of glamour and prosperity do not prepare disciples for suffering and death in the cause of Christ. Mixed messages confuse the hearer. The church cannot announce the gospel for all and then cater to the rich. Christ's ministers cannot proclaim Christ's power and then carry on in the power of the flesh. The message of Jesus will need to come through ministers who are servants. Both integrity and consistency are demonstrated in Paul as a servant of Christ, the gospel, and the church.

Colossians 2:6-23

Exposing Warped and Inferior Teachings

PREVIEW

"Warning: This product may be hazardous to your health." Health dangers need to be publicized, and many products carry the required warning labels. In a similar vein Paul exposes teachings that he considered hazardous to spiritual health. In Colossians 2:6-23, Paul confronts certain teachings that cause him to be concerned about the Lycus Valley believers.

A distinct change in the tone of the letter is noticeable in this segment. For the first time we find imperatives or directives. So far the letter has been concerned with what God has done and what the Colossian believers have experienced. Now we come to four specific injunctions (in 2:6, 8, 16, and 18).

Concern about a potential danger first surfaces in 2:4. An affirmation of the Colossians' stability follows immediately in 2:5. Both the concern and the affirmation are elaborated in 2:6-23. Although Paul does not fully label the threat that concerns him, he does leave a number of clues in this section that help to identify features of the problem. [Problems, p. 310.]

Especially noteworthy is how Paul goes about equipping the Lycus Valley believers to recognize and to be unaffected by the distorted teachings. Considerably more space is given to the positive elements than to the negative ones. In the text of verses 6-23 (NRSV), the positive and negative elements divide like this, with the number of words in parentheses:

218 Positive Words   **166 Negative Words**

As you therefore have received . . . (35)	
	See to it that no one . . . (31)
For in him . . . (143)	
	Therefore do not let anyone . . . (31)
but the substance . . . (6)	
	Do not let anyone . . . (33)
from whom . . . (22)	
If with Christ . . . (12)	
	why do you . . . (71)

Even if verses 6 and 7 were counted with the previous section (as they are in some translations) the positive words outnumber the negative ones. The positive blocks emphasize the superiority and adequacy of Christ. Except for the personal reference in verse 13, the second positive block (2:9-15) reads like another christological hymn, similar to 1:15-20. The threat that concerns Paul has its roots in a lowered view of Christ. Paul's response: With all that is yours in Christ, don't settle for something less.

OUTLINE

Admonition: Live As Taught, 2:6-7

First Warning: Don't Let Anyone Ensnare You, 2:8-15
    2:8   Nature and Source of the Threat
    2:9-15   Reasons to Avoid the Trap

Fullness in Christ 2:9-10
Union with Christ 2:11-12
Freedom Through God's Actions 2:13-15

Second Warning: Don't Let Anyone Control You, 2:16-17
    2:16   Specific Impositions
    2:17   Reasons Not to Regress

Third Warning: Don't Let Anyone Disqualify You, 2:18-19
    2:18   Description of the Attraction
    2:19   Reasons to Stay with Christ

Appeal: Why Submit to Useless Regulations? 2:20-23
    2:20a   Reminder of Freedom in Christ
    2:20b-23   Reasons to Discard Valueless Regulations

See the essay *[Literary Structure, p. 305]* for an analysis of the way the parts of this segment are related.

EXPLANATORY NOTES
Admonition: Live As Taught 2:6-7

Verses 6 and 7 serve as a prologue to the pointed teaching that follows. Here is the first directive in Colossians: *continue to live your lives in him.* The charge is framed with *as* and *just as—as you therefore have received Christ Jesus the Lord,* and *just as you were taught.* The imperative is based on an indicative, a statement of what they have already experienced. The word translated *received* is frequently associated with accepting a tradition handed down (see TBC). The word *taught* implies the content or object of the faith tradition being learned.

Here in the prologue the title or name for Christ is in the strongest possible form. This is the only occurrence in Colossians with this order and with articles: literally, *the Christ Jesus the Lord* (EDM). The full title communicates that Jesus is both the Christ and the Lord to the fullest extent of the words (cf. Acts 2:36). *[Titles, p. 323.]*

Living in Christ is to be integral with an experience of Christ. The admonition to *continue to live* (lit., *walk*) in Christ makes use of Paul's favorite imagery (cf. 1:10). In the NT view of Christian experience, belief and life are not merely casual acquaintances. How Christians live is to match what they say they believe.

Three expressions support the call to live as taught. All three are stated in a way that shows God's involvement; the continuing condition of believers is more than their own doing. *[Grammar, p. 291.]*

Rooted . . . in him, or more precisely, *having been rooted* (EDM), refers to previous action with continuing effect. The imagery is that of a securely rooted tree.

Built up in him implies *being constructed/reconstructed in him* (EDM). The metaphor of a building sometimes focuses on the foundation (e.g., 1 Cor. 3:12; Eph. 2:20). But by saying built up *in* him rather than *on* him, Paul calls attention to the sphere of growth and progress.

Established in the faith, or *being made firm in the faith* (EDM), has the sense of being reinforced or made stable, with imagery that may have come from the legal world (cf. 1 Cor. 1:8; 2 Cor. 1:21; Heb. 13:9). *The faith* likely has the same meaning as in 1:23, the apostolic gospel with Christ at the center of it.

Another of the letter's references to thanksgiving stands out like a familiar landmark in the text. *Abounding in thanksgiving* suggests an overflow of gratitude, outwardly expressed. For what? Thanks for a solid, growing experience in Christ is implied. *[Thanksgiving, p. 322.]*

Three warnings of dangers follow, with descriptions of the dangers and of the superior alternatives in the gospel of Christ.

First Warning: Don't Let Anyone Ensnare You 2:8-15

2:8 Nature and Source of the Threat

The words *see to it that no one* (or *beware lest anyone,* EDM) constitute a warning formula (1 Cor. 8:9; 10:12; Gal. 5:15). The readers are to open their eyes and see the dangers for what they are. By the way the warning is expressed *[Grammar, p. 290],* Paul intends that the believers look out for each other (cf. Heb. 12:15-16).

This first warning puts content into the concern raised in 2:4. *Take you captive* conveys the thought of a slave raider carrying off captives as booty. Paul sees the danger of such malicious kidnapping taking place through the means of *philosophy and empty deceit.* The term *philosophy* (used only here in the NT) is a relatively neutral word. However, the associated words identify a dangerous kind of philosophy. Philosophy may have been a favorite term with the troubling teachers. Paul calls their kind *empty* rhetoric, unable to fill (Eph. 5:6). Phillips paraphrases the thought as *high-sounding nonsense.* Paul further calls it *deceit* (cf. Mark 4:19; Eph. 4:22; 2 Thess. 2:10;

Heb. 3:13), a word that exposes the seductive nature of the perverse teachings and implies that the teachers were setting a snare with evil intent. In contrast, Colossians emphasizes *the word of the truth, the gospel* (1:5) and *the riches of the glory of this mystery* (1:27).

Three phrases follow that identify the source of the perverse, dangerous teachings. The word *according* reveals the outline.

According to human tradition. The human origin of the new teachings leaves it without the credentials of divine revelation. Jesus accused the Pharisees and scribes of rejecting the commandment of God and holding to human tradition (Mark 7:8).

According to the elemental spirits of the universe. The meaning of this term has intrigued scholars for centuries. The key word, *stoicheia*, translated *elemental spirits* (perhaps best rendered simply as *elements*), occurs seven times in the NT. Walter Wink, in an extensive treatment of the topic, contends that the word carries several meanings and that the context must determine what it means in a given text. (See *[Elements, p. 285.]* for a summary of Wink's research.) Wink concludes that in 2:8 the *elements* refer to "first or fundamental principles of the universe" (1986:130). The NRSV footnote, *the rudiments of the world*, expresses this understanding. The context has to do with human philosophy and tradition (2:8a) as the visible and invisible structures of the universe over which Christ is supreme.

Not according to Christ. This is the most telling appraisal. Since Christ is the touchstone of truth, whether a teaching is according to Christ or not is the ultimate test. The life and purpose of the Christian community must be determined by Christ and an understanding of who he is. The presuppositions behind the perverse teachings are both deficient and distorted. *[Problems, p. 310.]* Christ's uniqueness is being compromised and the Christian faith adulterated.

2:9-15 Reasons to Avoid the Trap

Verses 9-15 are tied together by the repeated phrase *in him* (and the variation *with him*), referring to Christ. *[In Christ, p. 299.]* When Paul becomes aware of warped and misleading systems of thought, he responds with an extended restatement of the greatness and sufficiency of Christ. Three affirmations about God's provision in Christ are reasons enough to avoid the deviant teachings:

1. *Fullness in Christ 2:9-10.* Note two references to *fullness.* First, with reference to Christ: *in him the whole fullness of deity dwells bodily.* Coupling the word *whole* with *fullness* amplifies the

claim, making it even stronger than the similar one in 1:19. *Deity* further explains what fullness Paul has in mind. *Deity* means divine essence, a stronger term than divine nature (Rom. 1:20). *Bodily* defines the manner of dwelling. Although it is true that the fullness of deity actually, not apparently or symbolically, dwells in Christ, *bodily* makes incarnation a crucial factor. This reference to the humanity of Christ coincides with the biblical understanding that deity is to be understood as a matter of activity as well as a matter of substance. God is God in what he does as much as in who he is. *Dwells* (in the present tense) emphasizes an ongoing, permanent reality.

This text declares Christ to be the embodiment of the entire completeness of the Godhead. He is in no sense a lower-level deity. All that makes God God, resides fully in Christ. We should not think of quantities here, or the entirety of deity being in Christ would mean that the Father ceases to exist. Yet the claim is no doubt intended to affirm that Christ is unique and does not stand as one of a number of intermediaries between God and human existence. In a practical and pastoral sense, the assertion of verse 9 means that as Christians see and appreciate all they have in Christ, they will not be distracted by teachings that pretend to offer more exciting things.

Fullness appears a second time: *you have come to fullness in him* speaks of the fullness of Christians in Christ, as in the rendering "and you are in him filled full" (H. Moule: 145). *[Grammar, p. 290.]* Christ's fullness has a direct effect on the experience of believers. The flow from verse 9 to verse 10 is like this:

Christ: fullness of deity (bodily)—> you, in him (his body): fullness

The word *fullness* ties the two parts together. *In him,* meaning in union with Christ in his body, provides the bridge in this extension of Christ's completeness to believers. Neither NRSV nor the Greek text states the content of the filling. Elsewhere we find that the filling is with the graces of joy and peace (Rom. 15:13), the Spirit (Eph. 5:18), fruits of righteousness (Phil. 1:11), and knowledge (Col. 1:9). Colossians conspicuously does not describe Christian experience in terms of the Holy Spirit (in contrast to Ephesians). Thus we do well to let the text stand on its own feet and refrain from reading into it other texts written from a different perspective. This text, then, emphasizes that in Christ, believers are given everything that matters. Paul seems to direct these words to those who have been told that fullness is beyond the grasp of ordinary people.

The wording of 2:10a implies that the fullness given to us in Christ is available and experienced in community. To be incorporated into Christ is to be integrated into the body of Christ. This factor provides the link between the focus of fullness in Colossians and the parallel focus in Ephesians (where the church is the fullness of Christ). [Fullness, p. 288.]

The supplemental clause, *who is the head of every ruler and authority*, recalls the claim of 1:16-18. The affirmation has relevance in two ways. Since Christ's lordship supersedes the powers, they need not be feared as a barrier to all that is available in Christ. Nor are these powers (still active in the world) any part of how one gets into the fullness God offers and intends. Nowhere does the NT suggest that these powers in the world constitute a body for Christ, the head. [Head, p. 293.] The church is Christ's body. Christ's triumph over these spiritual forces is already accomplished (2:15). Thus their power over believers is already broken, though the full manifestation of victory awaits the future consummation (1 Cor. 15:24-28). [Powers, p. 308.]

2. *Union with Christ 2:11-12* (EDM). How believers experience fullness is Paul's next point. Verses 11-12 are composed of three closely related components of being in union with Christ. Notice the sequence of *circumcised, buried,* and *raised* in verses 11-12. The words *in him* and *with him* continue to hold the passage together like a brightly colored thread.

In him also you were circumcised . . . 2:11. Three questions arise in trying to understand this verse.

a. Why is *circumcision* mentioned? A death-burial-resurrection motif occurs in Romans 6:3-5 and 1 Corinthians 15:3-4. More common is the shorter death-resurrection combination (2 Cor. 13:4). In this text we have an unusual sequence, circumcision-burial-resurrection. Although the teachings being countered seem to have some Jewish overtones, evidence is lacking that the proponents advocated circumcision. As used here, circumcision does not seem to mean what the Judaizers mean by it (Acts 15; Gal. 5:1-12). A spiritual circumcision (lit., *not hand done*, EDM) is elsewhere called a circumcision "of the heart" (Rom. 2:29) in contrast to an external rite. The circumcision to which Paul refers is experienced by the believers: *you were circumcised.*

b. To whom does *putting off the body of the flesh* refer? Is this describing Christ's death in words similar to 1:22, or the experience of believers in putting off the old nature, as in 3:9? Or is it more likely both? Several translations decide the issue with an interpretative rendering (e.g., NIV, *the putting off of the sinful nature*). [Text, p. 319.] The word translated *putting off* occurs only here, and was likely coined by Paul. It means to strip off completely.

c. What is *the circumcision of Christ?* Jesus being circumcized at eight days of age is not the point (Luke 2:21). But does the phrase have to do with Christ's death, or with the spiritual circumcision he gives?

Some interpretations of this passage are colored by the presupposition that Christian baptism is the counterpart of OT circumcision. Answers to all three questions must obviously mesh. An interpretation that commends itself as consistent understands *circumcision* to refer to death, both Christ's death and believers' spiritual death. The term thus fits the more common sequence of death-burial-resurrection. The grammatical construction indicates that *putting off the body of the flesh* refers primarily to the gruesomeness of Christ's death. Secondarily, it points to believers being enabled to die to the sinful self. *[Grammar, p. 291.] The circumcision of Christ*, then, is his death, and verse 11 as a whole speaks of the believers' identification with Christ in his death.

When you were buried with him in baptism, 2:12a. In a descriptive series, when burial follows death, burial confirms the fact of death. Here burial is linked to baptism. Romans 6 also links baptism and death. In the symbolism associated with baptism, the imagery of burial emphasizes the completeness of death—death to sin.

You were also raised with him . . . 2:12b. Resurrection is the counterpart to death. The believers' resurrection is expressed as already having taken place (cf. 3:1; Eph. 2:6). Romans 6:5-8 implies a raising in the future, although in the same context newness of life is expressed as a present experience. The difference is a matter of emphasis. Colossians does not say that all the resurrection there is going to be, has already taken place. Rather, the emphasis is on the present benefits of Christ's resurrection. God's power is supremely manifested in raising Jesus from the dead, and in Christ, believers are raised to newness of life.

Note the relationship of the three parts of verses 11-12, keeping in mind that *circumcision* refers to death. Leaving out the supplemental words and phrases, the sequence is as follows (EDM):

in whom . . . you were circumcised . . . in the circumcision of Christ,
   having been co-buried with him in baptism,
in whom . . . you were co-raised through faith.

Union with Christ in death, burial, and resurrection is the common factor in these verses. This spiritual identification is more important than any reference to sacrament or symbol that may be found here.

The implicit personal involvement does not assume infant baptism. Both repentance (voluntary death) and faith are vital to experiencing personal transformation.

3. *Freedom through God's Action 2:13-15*. Here Paul climaxes the first warning with three statements of God's action. Each of the three verses has essentially the same construction. *[Grammar, p. 291.]* In each case the middle line, a statement of God's action, is dominant and is flanked by supportive explanations. With some abbreviation, the text of these three triads flows like this (using NASB, which reflects well the Greek construction, emphases added):

13a. *when **you** were dead in your transgressions*
        and the uncircumcision of your flesh,
   b. *HE MADE **YOU** ALIVE TOGETHER WITH HIM,*
   c. *having forgiven **us** all our transgressions,*

14a. *having canceled out **the certificate of debt***
        consisting of decrees against us and which was hostile to us,
   b. *HE HAS TAKEN **IT** OUT OF THE WAY,*
   c. *having nailed **it** to the cross.*

15a. *When he had disarmed **the rulers and authorities**,*
   b. *HE MADE A PUBLIC DISPLAY OF **THEM**,*
   c. *having triumphed over **them** through him.*

The words in bold type reveal significant parallels. Observe that in verse 13 the focus is on *you/us*. (Note also the repetition of transgressions). In verse 14 the focus is on *it: the certificate of debt* (EDM). In verse 15 the focus is on *them: the rulers and authorities*. (Comments on verses 13-15 will refer to the NASB wording, quoted above, unless otherwise indicated.)

The structural details are a key to the thought sequence, but several difficult issues of interpretation remain:

a. God, rather than Christ, seems to be the implied subject of *made you alive together with him* (as is supplied by NRSV and NIV). But is God the subject through verse 15, or does the subject change to Christ in verse 15, or before?

b. What is the *certificate of debt* (EDM) that is canceled, in verse 14? More specifically, is it a reference to law of some sort? What kind of law?

c. What is the connection between *the rulers and authorities* (2:15), and what is against us and hostile to us (2:14)?

d. The same word translated *disarmed* (2:15) is rendered *putting off* in 2:11 (NRSV) and *stripped off* in 3:9 (NRSV). GNB renders the clause, *and on that cross Christ freed himself from the power of the spiritual rulers and authorities*. Who is divested of what?

e. Should the final phrase be *through him* (Christ) or *in it* (the cross), since the form of the word allows for either?

Before attempting to suggest a consistent interpretation of these and other factors, note the following: The word translated *made alive together with* is found only here and in Ephesians 2:5. It is a compound word with the same prefix as words in verse 12, *buried with* and *raised with*. Translating these words as *co-buried, co-raised,* and *co-quickened* (EDM) makes the similarity more apparent. The phrase *with Christ/with him* is found three more times in Colossians: 2:20; 3:3-4 (in Greek). *[In Christ, p. 299.]*

In the first triad (2:13) Paul gives special attention to what God has done about the believers' prior condition. He mentions two aspects of that condition. (1) Being *dead in your transgressions* (EDM). This expression obviously uses a different sense of *dead* than the result of dying in Christ (2:20). The word *transgressions* emphasizes sin as deliberate disobedience and unfaithfulness to God. Although the word translated *transgressions* is not the most common NT word for sin, the two words are nearly synonymous (cf. Rom. 5:20). (2) Being in *the uncircumcision of your flesh.* This factor may point to the hearers being Gentiles, those outside the old covenant. If so, it fits the beginning words, *and . . . you [Gentiles].* Often in the twenty occurrences of *uncircumcision* in the NT, the term means pagans (Rom. 3:30; Gal. 2:7; Eph. 2:11). A connection with verse 11 comes to mind. Although they are Gentiles (physically uncircumcised), their alienation from God has been removed by a spiritual circumcision (not made with hands). Uncircumcision may also be taken as a metaphor, descriptive of a continuing state of spiritual rebellion, for Jews and Gentiles alike.

The second line (2:13b) is the main statement of verse 13, focusing on God's action in spiritual resurrection. This is another example of the before—after contrast noted in 1:21-22. Nothing less than a resurrection experience could remedy the situation, and God has acted. The new life is life shared with Christ.

In the third line of verse 13, new life is associated with being forgiven. Two words in the Greek NT are translated *forgive.* The one used here, *charizomai,* emphasizes the element of grace in God's forgiveness (cf. Eph. 1:7, where the other word, *aphiēmi,* occurs in noun form, emphasizing forgiveness as remission of sins). *All* our transgressions indicates complete removal of the cause of spiritual death, effective as it is appropriated. The switch from *you* in the first two lines of the verse to *us* in this third line implies that Paul wants to include himself, and perhaps all Jewish believers, as also benefiting from what God has done.

The topic of verse 14 is *the certificate of debt* (EDM). This is the only place in the NT where this word is found. In extrabiblical usage the word identifies a document of indebtedness, a personally signed IOU. Philemon 19 is an illustration of the concept, although the word is not used there. Two features of this written obligation are mentioned. The certificate comes with *decrees* or regulations (a term also used in 2:20, with examples given in v. 21). The indebtedness in view rests on legal demands. The other feature is that the certificate is *against us* and *hostile to us*. The description goes beyond the fact of indebtedness to an active hostility (a term frequently used to describe an enemy).

An interpretation going back to the church fathers sees the certificate referring to Adam's debt to Satan in the Fall. However, support is lacking for that view. Another interpretation identifies the certificate as an indictment presented in the heavenly court, either out of God's records or the adversary's charges. However, neither way does this view do much with the sense of it being a signed acknowledgment.

Another line of thought keeps the concept related to both God's forgiveness (2:13) and the activity of the rulers and authorities (2:15). If the thought is of an autographed self-condemnation, for Jews the basis would be God's law. For Gentiles the indebtedness before God would arise out of a failure to live up to a sense of moral law (cf. Rom. 2:14-16). The culprit, then, is not the Mosaic Law as such, but a spirit of legalism. It would include both the genuine failures or sins which must be acknowledged before God and the indictments inflicted on the human spirit by hostile powers using imposed rules to gain and maintain control over humans (cf. Gal. 4:3).

Over against that description of human entrapment, what has God done? The central affirmation is, he permanently removed *it*, the troublesome IOU. *[Grammar, p. 291.]* Two phrases employing dramatic metaphors clinch the direct statement. In the search for precise meaning, we will not overlook the overt emotional tone of these lines. In the first line, *canceled out* connotes not only canceling the debt itself, but also obliterating the record, the opposite of entering a name or account in the ledger. The figure is that of wiping or smearing out writing, such as rubbing over writing in wax. The same Greek word is found in Isaiah 43:25 (LXX) and Acts 3:19 for blotting out sins.

The phrase *having nailed it to the cross* (EDM) is also graphic and makes the cross of Christ the key factor in God's decisive action. The expression carries a note of triumphant defiance. Jesus' death brought an end to the blackmail and bondage that plague humans. Verse 14 is not saying that God has reduced guilt by destroying the law codes. Rather, by forgiving transgressions and by exposing and breaking the power of an imposed system devoid of grace, God liberates from moral bankruptcy and entangling bondage. God has removed the certificate of debt out of sight, *taken it out of the way* (EDM), so that it is no longer a constant reminder.

Verse 15 turns the spotlight on the rulers and authorities again (as in 1:16; 2:10). *[Powers, p. 308.]* The middle line, *he made a public display of them* (EDM), is the primary statement. There is no explicit indication within verses 13-15 that the subject has changed. Thus we could assume that God is the one who has *disarmed, made a public display,* and *triumphed*. If we understand God to be the subject, the meaning of the first line is that God has stripped the powers of their power, either *disarmed* them (military imagery) or *divested* them of their dignity and authority (political imagery). The second and third lines assert that the humiliated powers stand exposed, their illusion of power exhibited for ridicule. It follows that since the powers have been stripped of their power, they need not be feared or worshiped, and they are not to be obeyed as though they were ultimate. God's victory has been accomplished through Christ.

An alternate way to understand the first line is that the action is a stripping off from himself and that the implied subject is Christ. *[Grammar, p. 290.]* This view construes the stripping off (2:15a) in the same way it is used in 3:9 (where the meaning is clearly reflexive). In this sense Christ accomplished the victory by refusing to give allegiance to the powers, rejecting their right to tyrannize, and remaining obedient to God even unto death. Through the cross (and resurrection), Christ stripped off the powers' claim to ultimacy.

Both interpretations are tenable. The first one, held by the majority of scholars, emphasizes the fact of the triumph. The second one, also supported by respectable exegetes, accents the strategy of victory.

The meaning and translation of the final line is also open to dispute. The only other NT occurrence of the word translated *triumphed* (in 2 Cor. 2:14) strongly suggests that the idea here is not so much the accomplishment of the victory itself as the celebration of the triumph, with the imagery of a victory procession.

The final words are such as to allow the translations *in him*, meaning Christ, or *in it*, meaning the cross. If the subject is understood to be Christ, then *in it* is preferred. If the subject is God, then either is possible. If we include the raising of Christ from the dead as an integral part of how God in Christ defeated the powers and exposed their powerlessness, then *in him* is the most likely way to understand this text.

By way of summary, in this lengthy first warning (2:8-15), the caution against becoming captives through deceptive philosophy is thoroughly supported with reasons. First, the source of the teachings is exposed (2:8). Two additional lines of reasoning follow: who Christ is and the superiority of what believers have in him (2:9-12); and what God has already done, emphasizing freedom (2:13-15):

> 1. Freedom from transgressions of the past (which result in death).
> 2. Freedom from the certificate of indebtedness hanging over us, both out of wrongs committed and the accusations of hostile cosmic powers.
> 3. Freedom from those powers themselves, powers that are already defeated so that they need not be allowed ultimately to control believers.

Falling for the seductive line of the false teachers would surely be a major step backward.

Second Warning: Don't Let Anyone Control You 2:16-17

(Comments that follow are based on the NRSV text.)

2:16 Specific Impositions

Paul's second warning in this section has to do with restrictions and requirements being thrust upon Christians. The style of the warning is similar to the first one (2:8). The word *therefore* denotes a connection with the teaching preceding this advice. That is, with all that God has made available in Christ, the believer need not and should not come under imposed restrictions that promise a spirituality they cannot produce.

Specifically, the warning is against letting anyone *condemn* in matters of food and special days of the religious calendar. The inappropriate behavior included the making and imposing of certain rules and then taking believers to task for not keeping them. The way the warning is expressed strongly suggests how it is to be understood: "Stop letting them do this to you." *[Grammar, p. 291.]*

We may do some surmising about the what and why of the regula-

tions that concern Paul. The *food* and *drink* regulations likely have to
do with forbidden things. The regulations with respect to *observing
festivals, new moons, or sabbaths* are likely about things being required. The categories are broad: yearly festivals, monthly new
moons, and weekly sabbaths. Some Jewish influence seems likely to
be mixed into the new teachings, but also pagan religions are known
to have promoted these kinds of regulations. *[Problems, p. 310.]* Although one must exercise caution in trying to reconstruct the content
of the false teachings from these few verses in Colossians, some features are reasonably sure.

The issue is bigger than whether the OT regulations still hold for
Christians. To be sure, references to the same special days are found
in the OT (e.g., 1 Chron. 23:31; Ezek. 45:17). In the NT, Galatians
4:10 shows Paul's concern about Christians reverting back to the old
ceremonies. Mark 7:19 speaks of Jesus setting aside the OT dietary
regulations. For the Jews, keeping their rules was evidence of obedience and identity. However, Colossians counters teachings that seem
to go beyond Jewish reasons for such regulations to include respect
for the powers perceived to be ruling the universe. This factor is what
makes the issue bigger than just legalism. In Christian understanding,
as wonderfully set forth in Colossians, Christ is in control. The cosmic
powers, the stars, the elements have no ultimate power and deserve
no honor. Christ is to be worshiped.

2:17 Reasons Not to Regress

Verse 17 cuts to the root of the matter. The first line states the critique, and the second line states the truth about Christ—the basis for
the contrast between shadow and reality. At best, dietary restrictions
and special days only prepare for the anticipated reality. The rendering of NIV in 17a, *shadow of the things that were to come* (cf. Heb.
8:5; 10:1), appropriately conveys the thought that the coming has already taken place. Christ and the new age of the kingdom have already come. Living in the shadow side of religion tends to produce
superstitions, fears, and inhibitions. Since *body* is the most common
translation of what is rendered here as *substance*, some commentators find this a reference to the church. That inference is not untrue,
but reading it into this text is questionable.

Paul's admonition is basically clear: "Don't settle for less than
what is all yours in Christ." As with the first warning, this second one
takes a positive approach in counteracting a danger of regression.

Third Warning: Don't Let Anyone Disqualify You 2:18-19

The third warning is similar to the other two in style and content. The general thrust of the warning is reasonably clear, but these two verses confront translators and interpreters with numerous problems. Words with several shades of meaning account for some differences in translations. We encounter some difficulties:

1. How does one determine the meaning of a word occurring only once in the NT (and only several times anywhere else)?
2. Does *worship of angels* mean worship directed to angels, or angel-like worship?
3. Which of several possible meanings should be adopted for the words *insisting on*?
4. How can we account for the *not* in the KJV rendering in verse 18, *which he hath not seen*?
5. What word should be supplied near the end of verse 19?

Several significant features stand out when the structure of the text is analyzed. *[Grammar, p. 291.]* This translation reflects the author's interpretative choices (EDM):

Let no one deprive you (of your prize),
(1)   *being taken up with (false) humility*
      and worship of angels,
(2)   *venturing into visions he has seen,*
(3)   *being inflated with empty conceit*
      by his human way of thinking,
(4)   *and not holding on to the head,*
      out of whom the whole body,
      by its joints and tendons
      being equipped and joined together
      grows according to the growth God supplies.

Observe the first three numbered descriptions of the one who seeks to keep believers from experiencing what is theirs in Christ: *being taken up with . . ., venturing into . . ., being inflated with. . .* (EDM).

In this warning Paul gives as his primary caution and prohibition, let no one *deprive* you. The root part of this compound Greek word was used for umpiring a game. Following that lead, the picture is of one who enforces the rules and makes decisions. When put in a negative light, it implies action to disqualify in the race or to deprive of the rightful prize. In the simplest language the warning is given: don't let anyone cheat you out of your spiritual privileges.

2:18 Description of the Attraction

The first of the descriptive lines, *being taken up with* (EDM), appears in other translations as *delighting in* (NASB) and *being bent on* (Berkeley). The renderings *insisting on* (NRSV) and *insists on* (GNB) are somewhat stronger than the literal sense: *willing in*. Yet the sense of imposing ideas on others is consistent with the tone of the descriptions. Humility is usually a virtue in the NT, and it is used that way in 3:12. Here and in 2:23 a negative meaning is required, denoting a false humility, either an advertised humility or a severe self-abasement. Later in the verse, pride is exposed. The boasted humility is not genuine.

The second part of what the "cheater" delights in and seeks to impose on others is closely associated with the emphasis on humility. It has to do with *worship* and *angels*. One possible meaning is worship which angels supposedly perform, as a model for "super-Christians" to try to emulate. Or, perhaps the reference has to do with joining with the angels of the heavenly court, without needing any mediator, as inferred by the Qumran Thanksgiving Hymns (1QH). References to angels in other Jewish apocalyptic and mystical literature also support this view. "The Ezra Apocalypse closely connects 'fasting' and related practices with the reception of revelation by means of visionary experience. In this regard it portrays a kind of 'humility' and 'heavenly entrance' so important in understanding Colossians 2:18" (Bandstra: 335).

Another proposed meaning is a cult of angel worship. The practice may reflect the perception of angels as among the forces to be feared (in Rom. 8:38, angels are listed along with other manifestations of the powers). Or, angels may be worshiped as another way to get beyond the elements of the world (Schweizer, 1988:455-468). Both Hellenistic Judaism and Greek philosophy had doctrines of angels (cf. TDNT, 1:74-87; Willoughby: 241-244). [*Religions, p. 313.*]

These suggested meanings of *worship of angels* have inconclusive merits. Whatever the aberrant practice was, it did not accord Christ his due as the *fullness* and as the true access to God in worship.

The meaning of the second descriptive line, rendered here as *venturing into visions he has seen* (EDM), is far from certain. NRSV has *dwelling on visions*, with a footnote that the meaning of the Greek is uncertain. [*Text, p. 319.*] Most interpretations see in the phrase evidence of a mystical emphasis in the new teachings threatening the churches of the Lycus Valley. Proponents of the new teachings may be showing an unusual interest in getting into visions or other mystical experiences, and claiming spiritual superiority because of what they have seen. In contrast, Paul, on another occasion, refuses to exploit his third-heaven experience, saying he is not allowed to talk about it (2 Cor. 12:4). Similar cultic practices were part of the assortment of mystery religions of the first century. These provide some ideas of what Paul may be referring to in this third warning. *[Religions, p. 313.]*

Whatever the precise nature of the religious experiences, they give people an unfounded sense of superiority. *Inflated with empty conceit* (EDM) describes a case of self-delusion, in contrast to the divine fullness available in Christ (2:10).

2:19 Reasons to Stay with Christ

The fourth descriptive line becomes the strongest critique, *not holding fast to the head*, that is, Christ (cf. 1:18). The boasted special piety and special religious experiences did not come from Christ. Those who willingly detach themselves from Christ put themselves out of touch with the source of life and truth. As a result, they slide into cultic religious practices and distortions.

As with the previous warnings, the third one ends on a positive note. Attention is turned to Christ as the head of the body. *[Grammar, p. 292.]* How do believers hold on to the head, Christ? They do so by being members of his body. The figurative language associated with the body analogy may not be precise in terms of physiology, but the inference is strong that to be separated from the head (Christ) results in being separated from the body (the church). Conversely, to be separated from the body results in being separated from the head. Christ is the one out of whom the whole body grows. Note the reference to *the one [whole] body* (cf. 3:15).

Everything in verse 19b points to the word *grows*. The last phrase of the verse is, literally, *grows the growth of God*. Most translations supply one or more words to further explain the meaning. *The growth of God* describes the nature or content of the growth, and thus a growth in godly qualities is primarily in view rather than numbers. Some commentators have taken *joints and tendons* (EDM) to refer to certain members or to officeholders in the church, but the terms are better taken as figurative expressions of the important interrelationships between all the members of the church.

Ephesians 4:16 is notably similar to Colossians 2:19, with eight key words in common. In both texts Christ as head is the source of nourishment, unity, and growth in the church, and he coordinates the functioning of the body. The false teachers are *inflated with empty conceit* (EDM), but those attached to Christ experience true growth. Without that connection the church becomes impoverished, fragmented, and stagnant. Again, note Paul's approach: with all you have in Christ, don't settle for the inferior package being offered.

Appeal: Why Submit to Useless Regulations? 2:20-23

This final segment of the larger section, 2:6-23, is a powerful appeal in the form of a question, backed up with further exposure of the seductive, perverse teachings threatening the church.

2:20-21 Reminder of Freedom in Christ

Verse 20 takes up a practical application of the thought of verse 11 (where circumcision carries the meaning of death). The condition, *if with Christ you died*, is assumed by Paul to be true (NIV has *since*). Usually in Paul's writings, dying is *to* something, such as dying to self, to sin, or to law; and here NRSV uses *died to*. But the word Paul uses carries a meaning that can be paraphrased as *escape out from under the control of* (EDM). The particular bondage in view is to *the elemental spirits of the universe* (world), an entity encountered in 2:8. *[Elements, p. 285.]* Here they are the outward symbols of religion, such as rituals, festivals, restrictions, and worship practices.

Although not reflected in all translations, verse 20 mentions *the world* twice. The worldliness in view is not simply being in the world, but living as if still in the clutches of the powers rampant in the world. Why, Paul asks, do you live as enslaved when you are free through death with Christ? Specifically, their unfitting behavior is in submitting themselves to regulations. A connection is implied between some sort of external forces and the imposing of regulations. The Greek grammar indicates that Paul does not consider the Colossian believers as helpless victims. Just as they submit themselves to the restrictions, they can also resist. *[Grammar, p. 292.]* Verse 20 is the strongest hint in the letter that the new false teachings are actually making inroads into the Christian community.

Next follow three examples of the regulations that rob believers of their freedom. These three stand as caricatures of the restrictive rules that are part of the new teachings. The quoted prohibitions do not state what is not to be handled, tasted, or touched. They are hardly absolute rules. Food and drink restrictions may be intended. The point of the argument is certainly not that all prohibitions are out of place for Christians. After all, many negatives and prohibitions are included in 3:5-9. Paul goes on to clarify his objection to the way rules are being used.

2:22-23 Reasons to Discard Valueless Regulations

The apostle makes three charges against the rules being thrust on free believers. (1) The rules in question deal with perishing things, not ultimate realities (cf. Rom. 14:17; 1 Cor. 6:13). (2) The taboos are of human origin. Paul states the indictment similarly in 2:8 (cf. Mark 7:7-8; Titus 1:13-14). (3) Despite their reputation for value, the regulations serve to indulge the flesh, not curb it.

Many regard verse 23 as hopelessly obscure. A number of versions (including NRSV, NIV, and NASB) give the distinct impression that the rules in question are ineffective against restraining the flesh. The NRSV note offers an attractive alternative that can be seen best by altering the punctuation (which was not part of the original text anyway) in verse 23:

> Which things lead—though having a reputation for wisdom in the matter of voluntary worship, humility, and severe treatment of the body, without any value whatsoever—to the gratification of the flesh. (EDM)

The system in question is counterproductive because it is a religion with self at the center. Notice in verse 23, *self-imposed piety* (NRSV), *self-abasement* (NASB), and self-punishment—expressed as *severe treatment of the body*. The self-centered approach feeds rather than starves the flesh.

The final block (2:16-23) elaborates the note of freedom through Christ. Paul exposes the fact that the new teachings, despite all the attractiveness and subtle appeal, can not give freedom from the world, freedom from law, or freedom from the flesh. It leaves its devotees still enslaved. True freedom is found in experiencing and obeying Christ as Lord of all of life. In retrospect, not only the extended christological passage (2:9-15) but the section as a whole makes a profound contribution to the theme of Christ's sufficiency.

THE TEXT IN BIBLICAL CONTEXT
Tradition Comes in Several Varieties

A frame of reference is needed for understanding the several statements about tradition in Colossians 2. In the Greek world, teaching
took place within a personal relationship between teacher and pupil.
In Judaism, what was taught, a body of material known as "the tradition," became more prominent than the way it was transmitted. From
a biblical perspective, a basic and useful definition of tradition is
"what is passed on." Tradition in this sense is to be distinguished from
"human traditions," often viewed negatively in Scripture (Isa. 29:13;
Mark 7:3-13).

Paul writes of his former zeal for "the traditions of my ancestors"
(Gal. 1:14). That designation had come to mean the Law (Torah) and
its oral interpretation, with emphasis on the latter. The rabbis could
trace the chain of tradition back to Moses: "Moses received Torah
from Sinai and delivered it to Joshua, and Joshua to the Elders, and
the Elders to the Prophets, and the Prophets delivered it to the men
of the Great Synagogue" (Mishnah Aboth 1:1).

The central core of apostolic teaching regarding Christ, the gospel, and right living emerged as a "tradition" to be "received" and
"delivered." The tradition shaping the early church rested squarely
on God's revelation in Christ, as shown by these examples:

> Luke 1:2, an eye-witness tradition; Rom. 6:17, a form of teaching entrust-
> ed to them; 1 Cor. 11:2, traditions handed on; 1 Cor. 11:23, what Paul re-
> ceived from the Lord and handed on; 1 Cor. 15:3, a confessional state-
> ment received and handed on; Phil. 4:9, things learned, received, heard,
> and seen; 2 Thess. 2:15, oral and written traditions; 2 Thess. 3:6, not liv-
> ing by the tradition received; 2 Pet. 2:21, holy commandments passed
> on; Jude 3, the faith once for all entrusted to the saints.

However, the brand of tradition that Paul warns about is clearly
human tradition (Col. 2:8, 22). Paul's language is similar to the words
of Jesus regarding the traditions of the Pharisees (Mark 7:8). The new
teachings alter, adulterate, and add to the truth as it is in Jesus. The
source of the tradition is always a crucial factor. These perverse
teachings are reputed to be the product of special revelation, an exclusive wisdom received in the rites and secrets of "the mysteries." To
counteract that attractive and seductive tradition, Paul focuses attention on Christ and the teaching tradition through which Christ has become known.

The Correlation Between Colossians 2 and Romans 6

Colossians 2:11-13 and Romans 6:3-8 are strikingly similar. One scholar goes so far as to say that the Colossians 2 passage (even though shorter) is Paul's commentary on the Romans 6 passage (G. Beasley-Murray, 1962:152). Observe the two passages set alongside each other (NRSV in both cases, with key words/phrases in bold type).

Colossians 2	*Romans 6*
11 In him also you were circumcised with a spiritual circumcision, by putting off the body of the flesh in the circumcision of Christ;	3 Do you not know that all of us who have been baptized into Christ Jesus were baptized into his death?
12 when you were **buried with him** in baptism, you were also **raised with him** through faith in the power of God, who raised him from the dead.	4 Therefore we have been **buried with him** by baptism into death, so that, just as Christ was raised from the dead by the glory of the Father, so we too might walk in newness of life.
13 And when you were dead in trespasses and the uncircumcision of your flesh, God **made you alive together with him**, when he forgave us all our trespasses.	5 For if we have been **united with him** in a death like his, we will certainly be **united with him** in a resurrection like his.
	6 We know that our old self was **crucified with him** . . . .
	8 But if we have **died with Christ**, we believe that we will also **live with him.**

Although christological concerns lie behind the teaching in Colossians 2 and ethical concerns lie behind Romans 6, several common elements stand out. Both passages use compound words that especially emphasize experience with Christ, although only one of them is common to both passages: *buried with him.* Both passages connect being united with Christ with a change in life. The death-resurrection motif dominates both passages. The faith factor is added in Colossians 2:12 (cf. Gal. 3:26-27; Eph. 2:5-6).

The Thrill of Victory

Colossians 2:13-15 sounds an unmistakable note of victory. This thrilling passage is not, however, an isolated text on the themes of triumph and freedom. A victory motif pervades the Scriptures. Although some of the concepts may be hard for the modern mind to grasp at first, undoubtedly they were part of understandings in the biblical era.

In the OT, we see the conflict between God and Pharaoh. Pharaoh lost. The refrain in Ezekiel, "Then they [or you] shall know that I am the Lord," echoes an anticipated vindication and triumph of God. Although Israel kept distrusting God's power to triumph, the prophets were given faith to see both God's certain victory and a method of triumph different from brute force.

In the Gospels we find the victory motif in Jesus. His conflict went beyond his encounters with the Pharisees and others of the religious establishment. He compared his expulsion of demons with a stronger man overpowering a strong man and plundering his house (Mark 3:22-27; Luke 11:14-23). When the seventy excitedly reported their successes, Jesus said, "I watched Satan fall" (Luke 10:17-19). A woman had an infirmity for eighteen years, and Jesus said she was bound by Satan (Luke 13:16). Shortly before his passion Jesus said, "Now is the judgment of this world; now the ruler of this world will be driven out" (John 12:31). He went on to speak of his death on a cross.

The early church affirmed that because God was with him, Jesus healed all who were oppressed by the devil (Acts 10:38). The emerging church soon found itself directly involved in conflict and opposition. The people of the fledgling church turned to the Sovereign Lord with their problem, asking for renewed boldness to minister in the name of Jesus (Acts 4:24-31).

The epistles contribute to the victory motif. Major features include a complete triumph in the end (1 Cor. 15:24-28) and a sharing in victory now (Rom. 8:35-39). Galatians 1:4 says that our Lord Jesus Christ "gave himself for our sins to set us free from the present evil age." Galatians 4:3-11 speaks of being "enslaved to the elemental spirits (or rudiments) of the world," "enslaved to beings that by nature are not gods." There Paul warns against turning back again as slaves to "the weak and beggarly elemental spirits (or rudiments)." The children of promise need not submit to such bondage: "for freedom Christ has set us free" (Gal. 5:1).

Ephesians 1:19-23 also assures of present as well as future victory. According to 2:14-16, the power of the cross ends hostility and brings peace between Jews and Gentiles. In 6:10-12, the letter identifies the nature of the powers against which Christians contend and the divine resources. God's triumph in Christ and the believers' participation in that triumph are clear in Ephesians.

In Revelation, victory is again linked with the cross. In *Triumph of the Lamb*, Ted Grimsrud says of Satan's defeat, "Satan is so easily defeated in the end because his real defeat came when Christ was crucified and rose from the dead" (177). Wesley J. Prieb quotes 5:13 and then comments, "John is making a promise—the Lamb will win. The Lamb has power, power to establish a kingdom of peace that will endure forever and ever. . . . Lamb power will win" (126-127). God's story ends in victory, a victory achieved through the Lamb.

Forgiveness comes into the victory scenario (Col. 1:13-14; 2:13; 3:13). If forgiveness is limited to absolving the guilt and erasing the record of wrongs, we miss the impact forgiveness has on the powers that enslave. Forgiveness, dealing as it does with the past, does not change the inner nature of the person. Transformation is also needed. Yet forgiveness does break the power of sin. The very possibility of God's forgiveness opens the way to release, not only from the guilt of sins, but also from the power of sin.

What then is the message in the biblical affirmation of victory in Christ? Christ's victory enables us as believers to appropriate a victory perspective and dethrone the spiritual forces without closing our eyes to their existence. We rely on the power of the Lamb in our spiritual warfare.

Christ Is Front and Center

Affirmations of the excellence of Christ give Colossians its special character. The section 2:6-23 exalts Christ as embodying the whole fullness of deity, as being the head of all rulers and authorities, as the substance in contrast to shadows, as the head (the source of life, nourishment, and growth) of the body (the church). These are indeed expressions of superiority.

Emphasis on the excellence of Christ in Colossians accords with the rest of the NT. Many texts come together to make up a symphony in praise of Christ, enhancing awareness of the glory of Christ as portrayed in Colossians. Alongside *fullness* and *substance* (or reality), Hebrews 1:1-4 claims ultimate revelation in Christ. Paul's concern about perversions of the message of Christ brings to mind his ada-

mant reactions in Galatians 1:6-9 when anyone tampers with the
gospel of Christ.

Expressed positively, Christ is at the heart of the gospel of truth
(Col. 1:5), "as truth is in Jesus" (Eph. 4:21). Colossians 3:4 declares
that Christ is our life; and 1 John 5:12 says frankly, "Whoever has the
Son has life; whoever does not have the Son of God does not have
life." Regarding Christ as the pattern for living, Colossians 2:6 (cf.
3:17) reminds one of Revelation 14:4. Those who "follow the Lamb
wherever he goes" in the next stage of eternal life continue to do
what they did on earth; they follow the Lamb.

Like a compass needle pointing to a magnetic pole, whatever elements of human existence or whatever perspective on reality one
chooses, they all point to Christ. As examples of Christ's supremacy
multiply and blend into a composite picture, one finds good reasons
to choose as a favorite text the same one with which Menno Simons
began or ended all his writings: "For no one can lay any foundation
other than the one that has been laid; that foundation is Jesus Christ"
(1 Cor. 3:11).

THE TEXT IN THE LIFE OF THE CHURCH
Is Baptism the Counterpart of Circumcision?

Colossians 2:11-12 crops up in the debate over infant baptism.
Those who advocate infant baptism, pedobaptists, have long identified baptism as the counterpart of circumcision, and take *the circumcision of Christ* (2:11) as referring to Christian baptism. Those rejecting infant baptism see this text differently. The challenge of biblical
interpretation is to be aware of the presuppositions and biases the interpreter brings to the text, and then to let the text speak its message
without imposing the prior views.

Pedobaptists point to indirect references in the NT and to possible
references to infant baptism in the church fathers as support for baptizing babies (cf. IDB, 1:352). The issue was hotly debated in the sixteenth century. Menno Simons, among others, rejected the common
practice of defending infant baptism as the Christian counterpart of
circumcision. He repeatedly referred to Colossians 2:11.

In challenging those who used this text to support infant baptism,
Menno Simons used several closely related arguments. The fact that
circumcision did not include females spoils the pedobaptist defense,
he said. If children share in the covenant of grace and should therefore be baptized, then Israel should have circumcised females as well

as males because females also shared in the covenant. They did not circumcise females because the command was only to circumcise males. But the command did not forbid the circumcising of females.

Although the advocates of infant baptism could not say the Scriptures command the baptizing of infants, they defended the practice on the ground that it is not prohibited in the Scriptures. Menno Simons asked where in the Word of God it is expressly forbidden to baptize bells. Of course, the answer is, nowhere. But, he argued, the absence of the prohibition does not make it just and right to baptize bells (263). Arguments from silence on the part of the pedobaptists, coupled with a faulty association of circumcision with baptism, brought forth many pages of reaction from Menno Simons.

Another challenge to the notion that baptism is the counterpart of circumcision comes out of the experience of the early church. The Jerusalem church required both circumcision and baptism. This indicates that baptism was not considered a replacement for circumcision. The supposition that Paul's reason for not imposing circumcision on Gentiles was that he saw baptism as a replacement for circumcision lacks support. Arguments based on the direct continuity between the old and new covenants fail to take into account the significant discontinuity between the covenants. (Cf. G. Beasley-Murray, 1962:152-162, 334-344, for a comprehensive review of the issue.)

The debate of infant baptism versus believers baptism goes on. Many Christians in denominations with a state church background have not stopped to question the assumptions on which the practice of infant baptism rests. However, voices out of the state church tradition are emerging to question the evidence and reasoning used to defend the practice.

Perversions of the Gospel Today

What would Paul have to say to the contemporary church? What perversions of the gospel would get his attention? What downscaling of Christ would trigger his reactions? We should assume that strategies for depriving Christ of his rightful place and for subverting the gospel are around at all times. The fact that they keep changing is reason for the church to remain alert.

Consider these teachings and movements that are especially dangerous because they appear not to be blatantly anti-Christian:

1. Paul would speak out against an array of Christianity-based cults seducing persons who are not deeply rooted in biblical faith.

Among a number of common features in such cults, one major mark is a defective Christology. In various ways Christ's uniqueness is compromised. Some quote the Bible profusely, but conveniently leave out reference to Christ's victory by way of the cross.

Ersatz religious movements pose a threat to the gospel of Christ: selected Christian values (such as simplicity, wholeness, and contemplation) mixed with a variety of religious views, mostly oriental (with features of mysticism, human-centered introspection, and inclusiveness). Without the kind of analysis and perspective Paul sent to the Lycus Valley, some Christians fail to see that they are being lured into a substitute for the gospel of Jesus Christ.

The New Age movement is a contemporary example of a mixture of borrowings from Eastern religions and humanism that, Paul would say, flagrantly compromises the uniqueness and supremacy of Christ. He would especially want to enlighten Christians who are being attracted to New Age ideas. In the biblical faith, "new age" or "age to come" can refer to God's coming kingdom (cf. Col. 1:26; Eph. 1:21; Mark 10:30. Also, emphases such as meditation, wholeness, and unity are important for those who honor Jesus as Lord. Yet the New Age movement is a dangerous perversion because it rests on a defective Christology.

2. A gospel of prosperity has attracted many followers, but it is a serious distortion of the gospel of Christ. They justify plush extravagance as God's intention for Christians. This does not fit with the Jesus of the Gospels or with the grim realities of life for Christians in third world countries. People of limited means may get a vicarious feeling of identification by sacrificing to support lavish lifestyles for a few at the top of religious empires. But is this according to the gospel of Christ?

3. Paul would be upset to discover a highly individualistic religion being presented as the gospel of Christ. He would say that encounters with the Lord are personal, but never purely private. Colossians again and again points to experience in the community of faith. Some limit an experience of Christ to getting saved so they can go to heaven at death. This distorts the gospel by leaving out matters of morality (public and private), justice, peace, reconciliation, and community.

4. Paul could be expected to react to folk religion or civil religion and to contrast it with the true gospel. Civil religion, with dominant cultural and nationalistic overtones, uses many religious words, but the trust-base is not Christ. Authentic Christianity is shaped to some extent by the cultural setting, but it dare not completely identify with

any culture. Nationalism reduces God to a tribal deity and ignores the fact that the church of Jesus Christ is a supranational church.

5. Paul would object to the perversions that come about with a human-centered emphasis. Christianity is a people religion, but a primary focus on inner psychic resources, human potentials, and self-fulfillment tends to obscure Paul's insistence that fullness and growth come only by being attached to Christ. A human-centered interpretation of Christian faith has a do-it-yourself appeal. But it is at the expense of soft pedaling or ignoring the hard sayings of Jesus and his call to take up the cross and follow him.

6. Paul could also be expected to speak to the way secularism moves on to paganism. Secularism, although giving prime time to things secular (life operated without God), does acknowledge the existence and validity of the sacred. Secularism not only separates the sacred and the secular; in practice it puts the secular in highest place. At best, Christ gets a nod. Eventually, as demonstrated in Western culture, secularism becomes full-scale paganism. A system without values or ultimate purpose becomes a religion of its own that is not Christian. The Christian church not only needs to resist the secularism and paganism that has been allowed to shape understandings of the gospel, but also needs to accept the challenge of genuinely confronting Western culture with Christ and the gospel (cf. Newbigin).

Paul could be expected to speak to distortions and perversions of the gospel that threaten the church today. He would no doubt address the church in positive ways, as in Colossians, calling believers to solid foundations, building them up in understanding and experience of Christ. He would contend that the best defense and preparation is to deepen and broaden life in Christ as members of the church.

Christ and a "Spirited Universe"

People who are the products of Western culture, including church people, find themselves in a strangely different belief system when they study the NT. Colossians is no exception. The NT presupposes a "spirited universe." Western culture, and to a large degree Western Christianity, generally denies and avoids the possibility of a spirit world. A highly rational, scientific outlook finds no place in its reality base for hostile spirits and powers. The net result is that the relevance of Christ and NT Christianity are not deeply appreciated. When the assumed power base is a coalition of facts, money, technology, and armaments, Christ is little appreciated as the power base for personal and church life.

We can learn from how mission churches encounter rampant spiritism in other parts of the world. These believers can raise our awareness of the significance of Christ being engaged in such conflicts of powers. In a cultural context of spiritism, the claim of Colossians that Christ is supreme over all powers takes on fresh meaning.

As an example, a Mennonite Brethren missionary in Brazil shows the relevance of Christianity according to Paul for the Christian missionaries' attempt to confront spiritism with the gospel of Christ:

> The very existence of the church, in which blacks, Indians, and whites, who previously acted according to the persuasion of the world, exist together in Christ's loving community, is itself a sign, a mystery, a message to the powers that their ruthless domination over humanity has come to an end. . . . In order for Jesus Christ to be presented relevantly and universally, he must be presented in terms of a power encounter. . . . The thrust of the gospel is that Christ is to be received in terms of a transfer of allegiance. . . . Any true conversion will involve a shift in power base. (Harms-Wiebe: 8-9)

North Americans are also part of a "spirited universe" even though the fact has been generally spurned and denied. A worldview shaped by the predominant scientific mentality has no place for "spooks." As a backlash to the materialistic outlook, many have a fascination with all kinds of supernatural phenomena. Interest in the occult arises to a large extent out of spiritual starvation. Missionary experience in Brazil and elsewhere can enable the church to discover the relevance of the gospel for confronting the powers in any culture. The church has the alternative to a deficient reality base and power base of an increasingly pagan society. Serious consideration of the NT view of the world (cosmology) and of Christ (Christology) will provide a base for confronting Western culture with the gospel of Christ.

For the church of Jesus Christ, the challenge of the day is to equip the saints with balanced teaching; provide pastoral care that delivers persons from spiritual bondage and frees them to grow in their life in Christ; proclaim the gospel of freedom, power, and victory; and resist and confront the spiritual powers that bind, oppress, and destroy those for whom Christ died and rose again.

Colossians 3:1-4

Living Oriented to the Exalted Christ

PREVIEW

"Keep your orientation clear" is Paul's advice. When Christians know who they are, which side is up, and where they are headed, they are not nearly as vulnerable to the side attractions and not so likely to take wrong roads.

The gospel is normally stated in indicatives (e.g., Christ died for our sins; he was raised from the dead). But the gospel also contains imperatives (e.g., be reconciled; be holy). The imperatives of the gospel of Christ grow out of the indicatives. Exhortations about life spring from the foundation of Christology. In Colossians we hear the call to become in daily experience what we are in Christ.

The section 3:1-4 serves as a launching pad for a trajectory into the ethical sections which follow. In these four verses (and in the following sections, 3:5-14; 3:15-17; 3:18-4:1; and 4:2-6), imperatives dominate the tone. They are similar in nature to the first imperative in Colossians, in 2:6. The warnings in 2:8, 16, and 18 are also imperatives, but 3:1—4:6 has a concentration of injunctions about how to live the new life in Christ.

At the same time the paragraph is a natural complement to the previous section. The opening phrase, *So if you have been raised with Christ*, is a counterpart to 2:20, *if with Christ you died*. (The outlines of some commentators follow this parallel, making the major break at 3:5 instead of 3:1.) This commentary regards 3:1-4 as a transitional paragraph. (See the block chart of Colossians, p. 28.)

Outlines of Colossians traditionally show a major shift from doctrinal to practical matters at 3:1. Indeed Colossians, along with Romans (12:1) and Ephesians (4:1), and unlike 1 Peter, has an identifiable point of transition (3:1). But labeling chapters 1—2 as doctrinal and 3—4 as practical greatly oversimplifies the flow of the letter. In typical Pauline style, theology and ethics are not neatly separated. Paul intends them to be as inseparable as the hardware and software of a computer. Watch for theological affirmations mingled with ethical instructions in chapters 3—4.

As you read and study the paragraph, pay attention to the connecting words, *so if, for, when,* and *then.* Notice also the expressions *with Christ* and *with him.*

Paul uses intentional, preventive measures in his attempt to steer the Colossian believers away from dangerous influences. The previous section of the letter exposes a tendency toward rigorous regulations. In 3:5-17, Paul addresses the opposite danger, indulgence of the flesh. His approach gives protection against slipping off either side of the road.

OUTLINE

Orientation: Seeking the Things Above, 3:1b-2

Basis: Co-raised with Christ, 3:1a, 3a, 4a

Security: Hidden with Christ in God, 3:3b

Anticipation: To Be Revealed with Christ, 3:4b

EXPLANATORY NOTES

Two imperatives set the direction and tone of 3:1-4. The first: *seek.* Seeking has to do with the orientation of the will. As an analogy, visualize a compass needle seeking the magnetic pole. Seeking does not have to do with hunting God, because he is not lost! Instead, it has to do with aims and ambitions. It goes beyond investigating to obtaining. The second imperative: *set your minds on.* The concept is stronger than *set affections on* (KJV). To keep thinking about, to concentrate on, and to be disposed toward—these convey the meaning and

support the overall theme of orientation. Paul uses the same imperative *(phroneite)* in Philippians 2:5 to focus on the attitude out of
which right behavior springs: "Your attitude should be the same as
that of Christ Jesus" (NIV).

Orientation: Seeking the Things Above 3:1b-2

Believers are to concentrate on the *things that are above.* Stated
negatively, they are not to be oriented to *things that are on earth.*
Paul even defines *above: where Christ is.* A comma is appropriate between *where Christ is* and *seated at the right hand of God* (as in
NRSV and NASB). The two clauses, although related, have separate
meanings.

The expression *seated at the right hand of God* is a figure of
speech conveying exaltation, a position of honor, and an active rule.
The one with whom believers are co-raised is the exalted Lord. The
interests of the exalted Christ must be the interests of believers. The
new orientation calls for the conduct of life in the realm of the Lord's
rule. Mention of *the right hand of God* is an allusion to Psalm 110:1.
(Psalm 110 is the OT passage most frequently cited in the NT, with
thirty-three quotations or allusions.) Other texts also speak of the as-
cended, exalted Lord (e.g., Eph. 1:20; 4:10; Phil. 2:9-11).

The *things that are above* are the things that belong to the as-
cended Christ, things ultimate, transcendent, and spiritual. The
things that are on earth (things below) are not the physical, material
things, for the Bible does not teach that material things are evil in
themselves. Rather, the expression speaks of the earthbound, the un-
spiritual, the things of the self-life (cf. Phil. 3:19). The terms *above*
and *on earth* have nothing to do with the geography of the universe;
instead, they contrast two orientations. The superstitions and rituals
implied in 2:8-23 are also part of the things below. Since it is impossible not to think at all of mundane things, the point of Paul's admonition is not to think about heaven all the time, but to let Christ and the
things of his realm set the values, priorities, and direction for living in
the here and now.

Basis: Co-raised with Christ 3:1a, 3a, 4a

Paul bases his appeal on three closely related indicatives. First, the
call to be oriented toward Christ rests on the prior experience of spiritual resurrection. Most translations begin 3:1 with *if.* However, *since*

(NIV) more nearly expresses a condition assumed to be true. The experience of being raised with Christ is essentially parallel with being born again. Believers are already *raised*, but, as we find in verse 4, they look forward to more, when Christ appears.

The second basis for this new orientation is that *you have died* (3:3). Paul builds on previous declarations in 2:11-12 (where death is indicated by circumcision and burial) and in 2:20. Here he again reminds the Colossian believers that in Christ they are dead to the old order, the things on earth. His point is that believers have died to sin and to the world, and therefore they do not need to be oriented to them or responsive to them (cf. Rom. 6:1-13; Gal. 6:14).

Paul also gives a third basis for the new orientation for living: *Christ who is your life. [Text, p. 319.]* To say that Christ *is* life for believers includes the sense that he is the source, the meaning, the purpose, the identity, and the destiny of life, both individually and corporately. Thus the exhortation to live in this orientation. Here *life* refers both to what is to be received in the age to come and to what believers already experience in Christ.

Parallel constructions in verses 3 and 4 reinforce the message. (Bold type highlights the parallel wording.)

3:3 *For you have died,*	3:4 *When Christ*
*and **your life***	*who is **your life** is revealed,*
*is hidden **with Christ***	*then you also will be revealed **with him***
***in** God.*	***in** glory.*

Security: Hidden with Christ in God   3b

The statement *your life is hidden with Christ in God* has several possible meanings. The hiddenness can not plausibly refer to the imagery of burial. Since verse 4 focuses on a future appearing or manifestation, some take the hiddenness to mean that the life in Christ is kept a secret from the unconverted and is not even now fully known to Christians themselves. We certainly agree that the full import of life in Christ is not yet fully revealed. Yet the wording implies an intentional action of hiding that points to a deeper meaning.

It is better to take the expression as a statement of security, as in this paraphrase: *Your life in Christ is securely tucked away* (EDM). The tense of the verb (perfect passive) means that your life has been hidden and stays that way. Ephesians 2:6 has a similar thought: "[God] raised us up with [Christ] and seated us with him in the heavenly places in Christ Jesus." The "sure and steadfast anchor of the soul" (Heb. 6:18-20) is yet another way to express the security of being in Christ.

Is hid translates one member of a family of words we may assume was used by the false teachers in the Lycus Valley. Barclay brings out this probable reference by proposing that Paul's meaning was something like this: "For you the treasures of wisdom are hidden in your secret books; for us Christ is the treasury of wisdom and we are hidden in him" (1975a:148).

The end of verse 3 has an unusual combination of words. The phrase *with Christ* is a favorite with Paul. *[In Christ, p. 299.]* The phrase *in God* occurs only two other places (in the opening verses of 1 and 2 Thess.). Putting the two together as they are here doubles the note of security: *with Christ in God.* As has been said, "No hellish burglar can break that combination." John Newton's hymn "Rejoice, Believer, in the Lord" affirms that "Your life is hid with Christ in God / Beyond the reach of harm."

Anticipation: To Be Revealed with Christ 3:4

Verse 4 has the only reference in Colossians to Christ's second coming. The certainty of the event is emphasized. The only variable in the declaration is *when.* Three words are used in the NT for the anticipated return or second coming of Christ: coming (*parousia*), revelation (*apokalupsis*), and appearing/manifestation (*epiphaneia*). Here a closely related verb form of the latter is used: *phanēroō*, translated as *revealed.* (See 1 Pet. 5:4; 1 John 2:28; 3:2 for the only other NT uses of this verb to refer to Christ's future coming.) The three words for Christ's coming again are sometimes used interchangeably.

Paul's teaching moves from the certainty of Christ's being *revealed* to the equal certainty of believers being *revealed.* The believers' destiny is expressed as being *in glory.* (Cf. earlier references to *glory* in Col. 1:11 and 1:27.) On a number of occasions, Jesus spoke of the glory associated with his coming (e.g., Matt. 19:28; 24:30; 25:31; Mark 8:38).

In keeping with the emphasis on Christ in Colossians, we find the name *Christ* included four times in as many verses (3:1-4), plus an additional reference to *with him.* Clearly the focus of this new orientation, search, and meditation is not inward but upward. In such a Christward orientation lies the secret of moral living.

THE TEXT IN BIBLICAL CONTEXT

Things Above Versus Things on Earth

The *above* metaphor, set over against *earth* in Colossians 3:2, is sometimes contrasted with *below*. These terms do not usually have a literal *up* and *down* meaning. They do not refer to locations in the universe, but rather have a religious or moral sense. *Above* translates the word *anō*, found also in Jesus' words in John 8:23, "You are from below, I am from above" (*see* also Gal. 4:26; Phil. 3:14). As usage indicates, *above* also points to the new era of the kingdom of Christ.

Such spatial imagery is found in the OT as well (e.g., Gen. 11:5; Exod. 19:20; Ps. 14:2; Ezek. 1:26; Dan. 7:13). Isaiah 57:15 illustrates transcendence in the language of metaphor, "For thus says the high and lofty one who inhabits eternity, whose name is Holy: I dwell in the high and holy place, and also with those who are contrite and humble in spirit." Similar examples occur in the literature of Greek-speaking Judaism and in the writings of the rabbis.

In Greek philosophy, *above* carries meanings foreign to the NT. Concepts that underlie Gnostic views include an upper and lower world, a pure ether world of ideas as the ideal into which the true self ascends, and the mundane material world from which the soul seeks to escape. From this perspective the idea of incarnation is unthinkable. From biblical Hebrew and Christian perspectives, the created world is viewed positively rather than negatively. Seeking things above does not mean being removed from the earth/world. Christ can be honored in human bodies. Paul calls Christians to be caught up in Christ's concerns and values without being literally detached from the world of space and time.

Paul's contrast of Spirit and flesh (Rom. 8 and Gal. 3—5) bears on his metaphor of *above* and *below*. In Romans 8:5-6 he says that believers "set the mind on" the Spirit, not the flesh (using *phroneō*, the same verb as in Col. 3:2). Yet another parallel imagery is that of the heavenly and the earthly (John 3:12; cf. James 3:15-17). Philippians 3:18-20 contrasts the orientation and behavior of those whose minds are set on earthly things, with that of those whose citizenship is in heaven.

Imperatives and Indicatives—"Be What You Are!"

The sequence, "You are . . . therefore, you ought . . ." echoes through the NT, especially in Paul's letters. Calls to response and action are linked to statements of what already is as a result of God's action. Exhortations (imperatives) rest on theological foundations (indicatives).

In Colossians the pattern emerges already in 1:9-14. An explicit indicative-imperative form of this pattern first appears in 2:6: *As you therefore have received Christ Jesus the Lord, continue to live your lives in him.* The combination is implied in 2:20. In 3:1 the sequence stands in classic form.

Jesus' first preaching follows this style, pronouncement followed by command: "The time is fulfilled, and the kingdom of God has come near; repent, and believe in the good news" (Mark 1:15). A number of passages in Paul's letters serve as examples of indicative-imperative teaching (e.g., Rom. 6:12-13, with the imperatives following and arising out of the indicatives in 6:3-11; Rom. 12:1-2, with God's mercies being set forth in chapters 1-11; 1 Cor. 5:7; Gal. 5:25; Eph. 4:1-3). The interaction of the indicative and the imperative occurs also in 1 John 4:11: "Since God loved us so much, we also ought to love one another."

Here are several pertinent observations:

1. The indicatives review the acts of God, with primary focus on what God has done in Christ.

2. The imperatives do not hold up abstract virtues as ideals (as Greek philosophy does), but have to do with attitudes and actions, works and fruits (yet without falling into Jewish legalism).

3. No clean-cut division exists between the indicative and imperative sections. When the emphasis is on proclamation, short exhortations appear here and there, as in Colossians 1—2. When the primary emphasis is on exhortation, reminders of what is true in Christ are thrown in. This kind of mixing is found in 3:5-17.

4. The order is crucial. Never are the imperatives a prerequisite for receiving God's grace in Christ. Grace and salvation come before the demands. This is always God's way. Sinai and the law came after the Exodus from Egypt (note the indicative-imperative relation in Exod. 19:3-8 and 20:2-17).

5. The imperatives are not of the nature of legal demands. Instead, they are characterized by an appeal: Do what is fitting in light of what you have experienced in Christ.

6. The imperatives, as well as the indicatives, are a form of the gospel. The fact that they are there at all implies that believers are set free and enabled to do God's will, and that is good news. Rather than think of the imperatives as the dark side of the gospel, we should see them as open gateways into the potentials of life in Christ.

The command, Be what you are, is paradoxical. It is illogical. But it expresses the creative tension in which Christians find themselves. The biblical integration of the indicative and the imperative is profoundly important. The indicatives of theology and Christology may not be proclaimed or discussed as if they have nothing to do with the issues of behavior. Likewise, ethical imperatives may not be separated from the message of what God has done in Christ. The gospel call is to *be* in daily practice what we *are* potentially in Christ.

Failure to come to terms with this inevitable tension between the indicative and the imperative may cause people either to suffer a chronic feeling of guilt or to dismiss the call to new life as impossible idealism. Neither of these reactions is intended by the biblical tension. Instead, the biblical texts maintain a creative tension that enables Christians to be relaxed while at the same time taking seriously the upward call to holy living. The gift of grace is offered before demands are made. Mountain climbing offers an apt analogy: "The indicative precedes the imperative as surely as the rope is made fast round a firm piece of rock for the climber's security before he has to apply himself to the struggle" (C. Moule, 1973:482).

Already Raised and Shall Be Raised

Only in Colossians 2:12; 3:1; and Ephesians 2:5-6 is being raised with Christ spoken of as a past event. In all other texts, being raised with Christ is stated as a future anticipation. In Romans 6:5-8 we read, "We will certainly be united with him in a resurrection like his. . . . We will also live with him." Second Corinthians 4:14 is another example of numerous texts that express anticipation of being raised with Christ in the future. How shall we understand this difference?

Two things need to be said. One is that both affirmations are true. Those who are identified with Christ have been raised with him and they shall be raised with him. Yes, believers have already experienced resurrection, but that does not mean that the Lord has come and the final day is past. Hymenaeus and Philetus "swerved from the truth by claiming that the resurrection has already taken place" (2 Tim. 2:18). Instead, being raised with Christ means that believers are already sharing in the effects of Christ's resurrection, as *co-raised* implies.

In several texts that anticipate being raised with Christ in the future, the contexts imply a present benefit of resurrection. Romans 6:4 speaks of walking "in newness of life," verse 11 of being "alive to

God," and verse 13 enjoins behaving as though "brought from death to life." It is in present experience that "the life of Jesus may also be made visible in our bodies" (2 Cor. 4:10). These texts do not assume that resurrection is totally a future event, but that believers are sharing in resurrection life now.

The other point is that Romans and Colossians were written to different situations. Romans 6 stresses that believers are dead to sin and should not presume on God's grace. Colossians asserts completeness in Christ, that neither a new philosophy nor ascetic practices are needed to come into *fullness in him* (2:10). The differences in the author's purposes account for the differences in emphasis.

THE TEXT IN THE LIFE OF THE CHURCH
Spiritual Resurrection

"The Spiritual Resurrection" is the first booklet by Menno Simons after he renounced the Roman church, of which he was a priest. In about 1536 he wrote this:

> The Scriptures teach two resurrections, namely, a bodily resurrection from the dead at the last day, and a spiritual resurrection from sin and death to a new life and a change of heart. That a man should mortify and bury the body of sin and rise again to a life of righteousness in God is plainly taught in all of the Scriptures. (53)

Menno identified the spiritual resurrection, or new birth, with the first resurrection mentioned in Revelation 20:6. Near the end of the tract, he gives a benediction:

> May the God of all grace who will in the last resurrection gather the elect into his eternal kingdom grant us such hearts, minds, and dispositions that we, through true faith, and denial of self, may so deny and renounce ourselves that we may have part in the first resurrection of which we have spoken. . . ." (61)

A Radical Transformation of Values

When we think of the church as a subculture in the larger culture, we may have the impression that Christian values are simply options to be added to the generally accepted values in society. On that assumption Christians may conclude that life in Christ is a matter of a few modifications and several additions to an otherwise respectable life. Of course, certain glaring social sins must go. But the assumption is that coming into the stream of Christian faith leaves much of society's values intact.

However, if we accept the church as a counterculture, this brings a new perspective. Rather than beginning with the culture and adding on a few religious principles, we begin with the gospel of Jesus Christ and construct a life and values out of an orientation to Christ (the things above). Orientation is the key factor. The point is not that Christ's people size up the world's values and then choose an inverted set of values. Instead, they begin with Christ and his values, and if they are in contrast with this world's norm, so be it. A radical difference in values is to be expected, even though they are not different at all points. If new life in Christ is seen as a way to make a comfortable life in this world a little better, then somehow the component of dying with Christ has been skipped.

If with Christ we have died to the world (Col. 2:20; cf. Gal. 6:14) and have been raised with him, this will affect perspective, purpose, and priorities. The new orientation will mean that "what we can taste, touch, and tabulate can never be our satisfaction" (Ogilvie: 97).

The song writer, Helen Lemmel, identifies this correlation:

> Turn your eyes upon Jesus,
>   Look full in his wonderful face,
> And the things of earth will grow strangely dim
>   In the light of his glory and grace.

Since the things of earth have not grown dim for many professed Christians, is not the church rightly concerned that they may not be turning their eyes upon Jesus? Terminally ill persons frequently testify to a major rearrangement of values and priorities. The church needs to hear their testimonies and learn from them.

Life After Death

> "Where can I find the road to life?" you ask;
> "How can I fill the void that haunts my soul?"
> My friend, I know that path to life you seek;
> You need not suffer life that's bland and droll.

> The Good News is, abundant life's in Christ—
> The antidote to life that goes askew.
> You can escape the futile fling you're on;
> With Christ, you can be raised to life anew.

Before you try to sweeten life with Christ
By thinking he's like frosting on your cake,
I must make sure you clearly understand
The entrance gate that you must take.

Before there's life that's really life, there's death.
"Not death," you say, "I want to live, not die."
I know, but easy shortcuts will not work;
The life you seek will come when first you die.

It's self that needs to die, the ingrown self.
When you with Christ are dead to self each day,
And to the world of lusts that lure and trap,
Then you can know abundant life today.

—EDM

Colossians 3:1-4 speaks to the human spirit's search for life (cf. Col. 2:20; Luke 9:23; John 10:10; Gal. 6:14).

Christ, Who Is Our Life

Whoever says with integrity, Christ is my life, chooses an orientation of life that is alien to the value system of North American culture. Time and energies become absorbed in many substitutes for Christ. The church needs to keep sounding the reminder that the followers of Christ are in another value system.

The dominant North American culture has put strange price tags on human worth. The *American Almanac of Jobs and Salaries* gives detailed listings of who receives what kind of remuneration, who gets a million dollars or more a year, and for what. Topping the list are corporate executives. Next are professional athletes, entertainers, actors, actresses, and other TV celebrities. The values of our society are reflected in the gross disparity in salaries and especially in what kinds of jobs receive the highest remuneration.

One of the perils of professionalism that has been uncovered is the greater tendency to identify personal selfhood with one's job/profession. After retirement those in the professions tend to introduce themselves as what they used to be. Perhaps non-professional people are less inclined to identify themselves with their work because their work has not been as exciting or fulfilling. Non-professional people who have been highly work oriented also often find meaning in their jobs. Then, when for reasons of age or disability they can no longer produce, they think of themselves as worthless. The church needs to keep reminding all people that ultimate worth and identity is in Christ, even more than in what Christ has enabled them to do.

Making Heaven's Agenda Our Agenda

The directive to seek the things above comes to the church on earth where the things of earth have their "gravitational pull" on the resurrection community. Jesus makes it clear that the church is in the world by divine design (John 17:14-18). The mission of the church is to be intentional and proactive, not merely defensive and reactive. By focusing on what we can know about heaven's agenda, the church can find help in discovering its own intended agenda. Awareness that we are in the world as Jesus is in the world (1 John 4:17) will put us on the right track. Being heavenly minded will have to do with being about heaven's business on earth.

Colossians 3:5-14

Putting Off and Putting On

PREVIEW

Christian identity must be reflected in appropriate living. Evangeline Booth was coming into her teens when her father began the Salvation Army movement. Caught up in its fervor, Evangeline made a complete Salvation Army Lassie uniform to fit her playful pet monkey. Expecting praise for her enthusiasm and creativity, she called her mother to come and see. Her mother promptly removed the clothes. In response to Evangeline's protest, she said, "You can't wear this uniform unless you live the life."

From the more general teaching about Christ-oriented living (3:1-4), we now come to a longer section of specific instructions about death-and-resurrection living. The section includes two vice lists of five items each and one virtue list also of five items. Having repudiated rules and regulations (Col. 2) as being of any help in pleasing the Lord, Paul went on (Col. 3) to incorporate specific morality codes into his teaching. How is this ethical teaching different from the kind he criticized in chapter 2?

This wave of teaching, 3:5-17, washes up on shore a plethora of interesting and relevant matters for Bible students to explore. The range of interrelated topics encountered here makes the study an exercise in theological integration.

Many of the words in the vice and virtue lists in Colossians are also found in the corresponding section of Ephesians. Similarities with other NT passages have led scholars to the thesis that a traditional body of new-believer instructional material may lie behind the particularized teaching found in various NT letters. *[Ethical Lists, p. 287.]*

In preview, note yet that the specific negative and positive qualities in the lists have much to do with relationships. The negative ones spoil relationships, and the positive ones enable community. The focus is not on private piety, but on the community of faith in which new life in Christ is experienced and expressed.

OUTLINE

Anyone who has split firewood has discovered that some kinds of wood split cleanly and easily while other kinds have the fibers so interwoven that it is difficult or virtually impossible to split them without a power splitter that rips them apart. Similarly, biblical material may or may not allow for neat outline divisions. Colossians 3:5-17 resists outlining. For example, verses 9-11 include both putting off and putting on. These verses provide a connection between the vice and virtue lists, yet cannot be neatly included in either what is before or what is after. In the following outline, analytical subheadings show how the topics are developed.

Putting Off the Old Ways, 3:5-8
3:5a	Directive: Put to Death What Is Earthly In You
3:5b	First Vice List
3:6-7	Incentives
3:8a	Directive: Get Rid of All Such Things
3:8b	Second Vice List

New People—New Community, 3:9-11
3:9a	Directive: Do Not Lie to One Another
3:9b-10a	Incentives
3:10b-11	Description

Putting On the New Ways, 3:12-14
3:12a	Incentive
3:12b	Directive: Clothe Yourselves
3:12c	Virtue List
3:13a	Explanation
3:13b	Incentive
3:14	Directive: Clothe Yourselves with Love

EXPLANATORY NOTES
Putting Off the Old Ways   3:5-8

In the structural arrangement below, observe how the text flows functionally, according to the analysis on the left side. The imperatives are indicated with bold type. Words in brackets are alternate (EDM) translations.

Analysis	*NRSV Text of 3:5-8*

First
Directive   (5) **Put to death,** *therefore, whatever in you is earthly:*
Vice List   *fornication [illicit sex],*
                       impurity [indecency],
                       passion [lustfulness],
                       evil desire [corrupt craving], and
                       greed [covetousness]
                       (which is idolatry).
Incentives   (6) *On account of these the wrath of God is coming*
                 on those who are disobedient.
             (7) *These are the ways you also once followed,*
                 when you were living that life.
Second
Directive   (8) *But now you must **get rid of** all such things—*
Vice List   *anger [seething anger],*
                    wrath [outbursts of temper],
                    malice [spitefulness],
                    slander [abusive language], and
                    abusive language [obscenities]
                       from your mouth.

3:5a Directive: Put to Death

Verse 5 abruptly confronts the reader with the ethical demands of the gospel. The nature of this first directive, *put to death*, makes one scurry for an explanation of a paradox. Verse 3 (also 2:20) declares, *you have died*, and now the charge comes, *put to death, therefore, whatever in you is earthly.* Why must believers put to death what has already died in Christ? Eduard Schweizer may be on the right track with his comments: "In baptism the old Adam is indeed drowned; but the scoundrel can still swim!" (1976:202). Essentially the same paradox appears in other texts. In Romans 6 "if we have died with Christ" (6:8) is followed by "consider yourselves dead to sin. . . . Do not let sin exercise dominion in your mortal bodies. . ." (6:11-12). Note the NASB rendering of Colossians 3:5: *Consider the members of your earthly body as dead to. . . .* Also, *Put to death . . . whatever in you is earthly* (3:5) is closely paralleled in Romans 8:13: "Put to death the deeds of the body" (this text has a different but synonymous word for death).

What is to be put to death? In literal translation, *the members [limbs or parts] on the earth* (EDM), with the human body in mind. According to some Jewish rabbis, there are as many commands and prohibitions in the law as there are members of the human body. However, the list that follows is not made up of eyes, hands, stomach, and so on, but is a list of practices and inner passions. What is to be killed off and eliminated is the use of the body and its drives for earthly or sensate purposes. The word *mortify* (KJV) has come to mean "cause to be embarrassed," and it is not strong enough to convey the meaning of this radical ethical demand.

The tense of the imperative, *put to death*, calls for decisive action, yet that action may need to be repeated. *[Grammar, p. 290.]* (The grammar of Romans 6:11 implies that we must continue to consider ourselves dead to sin.) The text at hand seems to resonate with the severe discipline that Jesus called for when he used the vivid imagery of tearing out eyes and cutting off hands that cause one to sin (Matt. 5:29-30). In both texts inner passions are the root problem, not physical members.

3:5b First Vice List

Ethical imperatives in the NT, and the vice lists in particular, are direct and to the point. Paul Scherer observes:

> It has to be borne in mind that the gospel does not traffic in advice. Nor did Jesus. Nowhere is it recorded that he spent much time saying "Please." Or "It would be very good for you indeed if you would." The wind never tips its hat. It sends you scurrying after your own. So does the New Testament. (60)

Four of the five vices in this first list are sexual (although all but the first one also have a more general meaning in some NT occurrences). It would not be true to Paul and the NT to construe Colossians 3:5 to imply that the human body and sexuality are evil and must be denied.

Instead, this first directive demands that sensual and sexual misuse and excess be stricken from the new life.

Fornication includes the full range of unrestrained sexual behavior; its meaning is not to be limited to a narrow definition of the word. Barclay notes, "Chastity was the one completely new virtue which Christianity brought into the world" (1975a:150). The meaning of *impurity* is caught by the Phillips paraphrase: *dirty-mindedness. Passion* connotes being dominated by sexual feelings and drives. Desire can have a positive sense (Luke 22:15; Heb. 6:11), but here it is qualified as *evil desire*, a craving for the wrong things.

Greed can also apply to sexual lust, but a broader *desire for more* (EDM) should be included in the scope of meaning. The word describes an insatiable desire for more without regard to the rights or needs of others. When we do not seek the things above, we are prone to seek the things below. Greed is *idolatry* because it leads to making gods out of things other than God. (See TBC for a chart of vices in Col. 3:5, 8, and their occurrence in other vice lists of the NT.)

3:6-7 Incentives

Christians seem to need inducements to obedience. Even if we know what is expected, that is often not enough to produce compliance. NT writers regularly supply stimuli along with moral imperatives. Two incentives support the exclusion of the sins just listed.

The first incentive is that such practices incur *the wrath of God*. The term requires careful definition. On the one hand the concept is made too impersonal if it is reduced to a matter of simple cause and effect in a moral universe, even though the principle of cause and effect seems to explain many negative consequences. On the other hand, we should not think of God's wrath in terms of vindictive human fury. Instead, *wrath* speaks of God's profound displeasure with evil, both as revealed in the present (Rom. 1:18-32) and in the consummation (1 Thess. 1:10). Mention of *the wrath of God* does not constitute a threat, but it casts the attitudes and behaviors of believers in the light of what is pleasing (and displeasing) to the Lord (1:10). (See TBC on *The Wrath of God*.) The phrase *on those who are disobedient* (or an equivalent) appears in the footnotes or not at all in most major translations. *[Text, p. 319.]*

The second incentive (3:7) is a reminder of what the Colossian believers had been changed from. Such vices had been part of their pagan past. This third comparison of *then and now* in Colossians

(1:21-22; 2:13) serves as another plea not to regress back into the old ways. The approach is similar to that in 2:20, with the focus here on moral behavior rather than on regulations.

3:8a   Directive: Get Rid of All Such Things

Now stands over against once, in verse 7. [Before—After, p. 282.] What follows is not a statement about the transformed life in contrast to the former ways, which might be expected. Instead, now introduces a new imperative and an additional list of vices. A reminder of the reality of the transformed life leads to a call for further discipline.

This directive is couched in a clothing metaphor. Like discarding soiled clothes, those in Christ are to divest themselves of certain things. All such things looks forward to the second vice list.

3:8b   Second Vice List

This second list focuses on sins of speech, as differentiated from the first list which is predominately sexual sins. We wonder why these lists each have five items. The ethical tradition from which they are drawn may have used this pattern of grouping, or Paul may be responsible for this rhetorical style. Paul no doubt chooses these vices out of a longer list. The choice of ten specifics possibly echoes the Ten Commandments. The vices that make up this second group are especially detrimental to Christian community.

First on the list is anger—the same word attributed to God in verse 6 (there translated wrath). NT usage does not support a rigid distinction between two words here translated anger (orgē) and wrath (thumos). Yet the first may be thought of as an inner elevation of emotional temperature and the second as outward eruptions of those feelings. Both words also occur in Ephesians 4:31. Malice implies a viciousness of mind. Such animosity leads to slander, language that attacks and defames the targeted person. The word is commonly translated "blaspheme" when directed to God. Employing this same word, Christians are commanded in Titus 3:2 to "speak evil of no one." The last vice of this list, abusive language, denotes the spreading of gossip as well as vulgar obscenities. The phrase from your mouth may apply to more than the fifth vice of this list and thus may indicate that this catalog focuses on speech sins.

•

New People—New Community 3:9-11

Note the flow of this segment. Words in parentheses are added to clarify the meaning, and words in brackets designate alternate translations. The imperative is in bold type.

Analysis   *NRSV Text of 3:9-11*

Summary Directive	(9)	***Do not lie to one another***
Incentives		*seeing that you have stripped off the*
		old self with its practices
	(10)	*and have clothed yourself with the new*
Description:		*self, which is being renewed*
New Individuals		*in (full) knowledge*
		according to the image of its creator.
New Community	(11)	*In that renewal there is no longer*
		(distinctions of) Greek and Jew,
		circumcised and uncircumcised,
		barbarian [foreigner],
		Scythian [uncivilized],
		slave and free;
		but Christ is all (that matters) and (is) in all!

3:9a Directive: Do Not Lie to One Another

Why, we may ask, does Paul single out lying for special treatment? Could he include it as the sixth practice to get rid of, along with other speech sins? On first thought, it may seem anticlimactic. Yet several features of the text mark this as a highly intentional moral directive. The present-tense prohibition implies, *Don't lie anymore* (EDM), as if various kinds of lying are common in the surrounding pagan society. *[Grammar, 3:9, p. 292.]* Deeply ingrained habits resist change. Furthermore, this is a direct command, without the metaphor of shedding a garment.

Upon further reflection, truthfulness is a crucial ingredient of Christian community. Lies and pretense destroy the fabric of trust essential for community, even more so than the other vices listed here. Ephesians 4:25 (in context) also stresses the profound importance of ridding the community of falsehood. Note the inclusion of *one another* in both texts. God's drastic action against Ananias and Sapphira (Acts 5) points to the devastating effect of pretense and outright falsehood in the emerging Christian community.

3:9b-10a Incentives

The participles in these phrases are translated as *have stripped off* and *have clothed yourselves with*. Some scholars take them as imperatives or commands, along with the other directives of the passage. Understood that way, these phrases are parallel with those in 3:8a and 12a, and similar to Ephesians 4:22-24. However, it is better to treat these phrases as describing a prior life-changing event that becomes the basis for fully abandoning the former ways. This is in keeping with what we have found earlier in Colossians. *[Grammar, 3:9-10a, p. 292.]* The fundamental change has been made in the identification with the crucified and risen Christ and with his body, a change signified and sealed in baptism (Gal. 3:27). That reality is offered as an incentive for changed persons becoming what they are in Christ.

The terms *old self* and *new self* call for further exploration. What is put off and what is put on? The exchange goes deeper than quitting a few bad habits and trying harder to be nice. It involves a change of character, not only a change in status before God. This implies an inner regeneration that is then to result in changed outward behaviors. Notions of self-reformation fade away when the change is thought of as putting on Christ. (Cf. Rom. 13:14, "Instead, put on the Lord Jesus Christ, and make no provision for the flesh, to gratify its desires.")

In this text many students see a reference to an individual's experience of change. But there is more here. The terms *old self* and *new self* could just as well be rendered "old humanity" and "new humanity." In this way we would be faithful to the corporate association which needs to be included in an understanding of these terms in context. A change in identity and a new order of existence go beyond individual reformation. This facet of gospel experience may also be expressed as no longer sharing in the "old Adam," but now sharing in the "new Adam," Christ (Rom. 5:12-21).

3:10b-11 Description

After reminding his readers of their new identity in Christ, Paul describes the results in terms of new individuals and a new community. What is *being renewed* is not the *old self*, but the *new self*. The process as described is not a matter of gradually changing the old into something better, but of progressively actualizing the already-existing new creation. The old self/humanity has to be put to death continually. The new self/humanity is always under construction. The renewing process referred to here does not assume a regaining of lost ground because of slipping back. Instead, it looks forward to being more and more like the original intent as revealed and demonstrated in Christ.

In the phrase *in knowledge*, it may be better to render the preposition as "into" or "unto," indicating the purpose or result of the renewal rather than the sphere. But in what sense is *knowledge* the goal of the renewal? C. F. D. Moule considers all of the occurrences of the word translated *knowledge [Know, p. 304]* and concludes, "It is clear that it is closely concerned with *the knowledge of Christ and conformity to his likeness*, which, in turn, is the substance of *God's self-revelation*" (1957:161, italics his).

This progressive renewing of the new self has as its archetype *the image of its creator. [Image, p. 298.]* A parallel text has "the new self, created according to the likeness of God in true righteousness and holiness" (Eph. 4:24). Consistent with other NT texts, God is the creator and the re-creator, and the re-creating follows the pattern of Christ, who is God's image (1:15). Earlier in Colossians, entrance into the new life is expressed as dying and rising again (2:20; 3:1-3). By designating the actualized renewal process as a re-creation, recalling the original work of the creator, the writer emphasizes how radical the transformation needs to be. It also becomes clear that this renewing after the image of God is God's work in the believers, with their cooperation, and not a matter of self-reformation or self-actualization.

With the phrase *in that renewal* (3:11), the new creation now leads to a new people, a new humanity, the church. Eight categories of the human race illustrate the barriers that Christianity breaks down. *Greek* stands for Gentiles as a whole. *Jew* represents an exclusive ethnic grouping with barriers challenged by the gospel. The second pair reverses the order of the first: *circumcised* (Jew) comes before *uncircumcised* (non-Jew). *Barbarian* designates the foreigner, one with a strange language, perceived as gibberish. *Scythian* is a derogatory term for the least civilized. A *slave* has no dignity or rights and is considered as impersonal property. *Free* connotes a social and political status of privilege. These categories illustrate the broad range of distinctions with superior-inferior implications that the gospel confronted in the days of the early church.

Perhaps people with all these backgrounds were in the church at Colossae. The apostolic congregations apparently were a cross-section of the population of their respective cities. The Christian congregations seem to have been more inclusive than the pagan social groupings of that time, showing that the gospel was breaking down old barriers as well as old attitudes and practices. The implications for Philemon and Onesimus were no doubt obvious.

The tunnel vision of individualism should not be allowed to block out vision of the new community implicit in this section of Colossians. As already noted, the vices to be put off assume a context of community relationships as well as individual behaviors. Verse 11 focuses specifically on racial, social, and cultural stratifications, for which there is no room in the Christian community. Verse 12 addresses the readers in the terminology of the new Israel, a corporate entity, about qualities relevant to relational living. Three occurrences of *one another/each other* in verses 13-17 further reinforce the intended application for the corporate realm of the new humanity. Clearly the gospel of Christ cuts across the all-too-common class distinctions of society. The point is not that all individual differences disappear when diverse people become Christians. Instead, this teaching affirms the common ground and unity in Christ for all believers.

By way of contrast to various labels put on people in the world, and as a concluding statement to the negative part of these ethical instructions, Paul directs attention to Christ. The meaning of the pronouncement, *Christ is all and in all*, is caught in the interpretive paraphrase, *Christ is all that matters and he is in all of you (us)* (EDM). The context of this exclamation of the excellence of Christ is the call to put off the old ways and to put on the ways of the new creation.

Putting On the New Ways   3:12-14

The text is included again with analysis of the flow of thought. Words in brackets are alternate translations. The word in parentheses is added to clarify the meaning. The imperatives are in bold type.

Analysis	*NRSV Text of 3:12-14*
Incentive	(12) *As God's chosen ones, holy and beloved,*
Directive	**clothe yourselves** *with*

Virtue List	*(heartfelt) compassion,*
	kindness [generosity],
	humility [modesty],
	meekness [submission], and
	patience [long-suffering],
Explanation	(13) *Bear with one another and,*
	if anyone has a complaint against another,
	forgive each other;
Incentive	*just as the Lord has forgiven you,*
	so you also must forgive.
Directive	(14) *Above all,* **clothe yourselves** *with love,*
	which binds everything together
	in perfect harmony.

3:12a Incentive

The apostle's summons is based on a powerful threefold designation for the new community, *God's chosen ones, holy and beloved.* Two important observations about these terms need to be noted:

1. These are characteristic titles for Old Covenant Israel (Deut. 4:37; 7:6-8; Ps. 105:43; Jer. 2:3; 11:15) that are carried over and used of the new Israel, the church (Rom. 8:33; 1 Thess. 1:4; 2 Thess. 2:13; 2 Tim. 2:10; Tit. 1:1; 1 Pet. 2:9; Jude 1). The point is not that Gentiles are to become Jews, but that the new Israel completes God's intent for the old Israel.

2. These terms are also used with reference to Christ. (Christ as the chosen one: Luke 9:35; 1 Pet. 2:4, 6; Christ as the holy one: Mark 1:24; John 6:69; Acts 4:27, 30; Christ as the beloved: Eph. 1:6.) The imperative of the gospel for believers to become who they are, as in 3:1-14, meshes beautifully with the affirmation of Galatians 3:27, "As many of you as were baptized into Christ have clothed yourselves with Christ."

Chosen or "elect" in Pauline usage is parallel with "called." *Holy* is sometimes rendered "saints" and means set apart. *Beloved* is equivalent to a related word in Matthew 12:18; 17:5; and Romans 1:7, also translated "beloved." Together these terms constitute the identity of the new people of God. The incentive of 3:12a is, let who you are determine how you "get dressed" to live as Christians.

3:12b   Directive: Clothe Yourselves

The purpose of putting off is not to create a vacuum. Nor is there any suggestion that putting off certain vices makes one all right. Putting off makes room for putting on. The clothing imagery could suggest purely external changes. But the figure implies more than cosmetic put-ons, as is also evident from the virtue list.

The clothing metaphor, in the grammatical form used here, is a strong figure. *[Grammar, 3:10, 12, p. 292.]* It carries the sense of submitting oneself to the ownership and control of another, conforming to the other (in this case, Christ). This human action is in response to God's call and love. It means putting on the practices of the new self in contrast to the practices of the old self (3:10).

3:12c   Virtue List

One virtue list of five items follows the two vice lists. The virtues are not counterparts to the vices, however. These qualities, plus those in verses 13 and 14, are all distinctly relational, with the Christian community in mind. In a practical sense they all serve to reduce friction in the congregation. Significant as that may be, the reason for including them here is that they are family characteristics of the people of God. They are all used to describe God and Christ. They therefore give substantive meaning to the *image* of verse 10. It is not that Christians put these on in order to be like Christ, but that being like Christ will need to result in these demonstrated qualities.

Distinctively Christian virtues make up the composite picture of those who are becoming Christlike. The four cardinal virtues of the Greek world were temperance, prudence, justice, and fortitude. What a contrast with the description here!

Compassion translates two Greek words. The first means the viscera, inner parts, which in NT times were thought to be the seat of emotions. As used here it points to deep feelings. (Cf. Luke 15:20; Phil. 1:8.) The second of the two is, in Greek usage, essentially synonymous with the word commonly translated as "mercy." Here it stands for compassion and sympathy that is acted out. The same words are found in Philippians 2:1 with an "and" between, translated "compassion and sympathy." (See also Rom. 12:1 and James 5:11.) Barclay observes: "Christianity brought mercy into the world. It is not too much to say that everything that has been done for the aged, the sick, the weak in body and in mind, the animal, the child, the woman has been done under the inspiration of Christianity" (1975a:157).

Kindness describes the kind of person we all like to be around. Synonyms for this quality include graciousness, courtesy, ability to listen and respond, goodness, empathy, respect for the other's feelings, and generosity. In the LXX *[Septuagint, p. 316.]*, kindness is a favorite word for describing God's gentle, caring ways (as in Ps. 25:7; 31:19; Jer. 33:11). The word is used as a quality of God with a different twist in Romans 2:4, "Do you not realize that God's kindness is meant to lead you to repentance?" (Cf. also Rom. 11:22; Eph. 2:7; Tit. 3:4.) The same Greek word is in Jesus' statement, "My yoke is easy (gentle)" (Matt. 11:30). Paul applies it to himself (2 Cor. 6:6) and makes it a required Christian quality (Eph. 4:32).

Humility was not highly regarded in the ancient Greek world. But it is a quality that Jesus attributed to himself (Matt. 11:29) and one that stands out in the verbal portrait of Christ in Philippians 2:5-11. Earlier in Colossians (2:18, 23), the word is found twice, with the contextual meaning of false humility. In clear contrast, those with true humility are unassuming, yet not needing to put themselves down before others. Humility connotes modesty, and it is the opposite of arrogance and conceit. Among the parallel concepts in Philippians 2:3-4 is the capacity to look to the interests of others rather than the wishes of the ingrown self.

Meekness is also a characteristic of Christ. He spoke of himself as being meek (Matt. 11:29). Using the messianic reference in Zechariah 9:9, Matthew's account of Jesus riding into Jerusalem describes this nonviolent King as meek. In 2 Corinthians 10:1, Paul makes his appeal through "the meekness and gentleness of Christ." Meekness is not even remotely related to weakness, although that identification is a common perception today, as it was in the NT world. John W. Miller's comment is helpful: "In the Greek language a donkey, broken and trained, can be spoken of as a meek animal" (30). This analogy depicts meekness as submission, first of all to the Lord, which then results in behavior that is disciplined and controlled through brokenness and the Lord's training.

Contrasting behaviors help to define the concept in 1 Corinthians 4:21 and 2 Timothy 2:24-25. (Note also how meekness, sometimes translated "gentleness," is employed in Gal. 6:1; Eph. 4:2; Tit. 3:2; James 1:21; 3:13; and 1 Pet. 3:15-16.)

Patience is a quality of behavior also grounded in the character of God and of Christ. God proclaimed his patience in Exodus 34:6 as being "slow to anger." God's patience stands out in texts such as Romans 2:4; 9:22; and 2 Peter 3:15. Paul sees the patience of Jesus

Christ in his own pilgrimage into faith (1 Tim. 1:16). Synonyms include longsuffering and tolerance. Said another way, patience is the
capacity to put up with aggravating behaviors in others without re-
sorting to retaliation. Colossians 1:11 is one of a number of instances
where *patience* is coupled with endurance. *[Endurance, Patience,
p. 286.]*

3:13a Explanation

The virtues, listed as nouns, are followed by two action words that
tell us how these qualities work in daily interaction with people.
[Grammar, p. 292.] Relationships with other Christians are primarily
in view, as indicated by *one another* and *each other*.

Bear with conveys the idea of putting up with, tolerating. Jesus
said to his exasperatingly dull disciples (Matt. 17:17), "How much
longer must I put up with you?" The word is used in 2 Thessalonians
1:4 of enduring affliction. Here in 3:13 it has to do with interpersonal
tensions. The forbearing called for is different from the intent of
"Please bear with me," which seems to mean, "You will need to ac-
commodate to me and my ways."

Forgive, as noted in comments on 2:13, can be expressed by two
different Greek words. The one Paul uses in Colossians is based on
the word for "grace." Here it conveys a gracious manner of pardon-
ing, that is, not grudgingly or condescendingly.

Both *bear with* and *forgive* are in a form that implies continued
action. *[Grammar, p. 290.]* Both assume a community context.
(Some older commentaries make a distinction between the words
translated *one another* and *each other*, but later research indicates
that the difference is only a matter of literary style.)

The conditional clause, *if anyone has a complaint against
another*, should likely be taken as setting the scene for both bearing
with and forgiving (although some translations seem to connect it
only to forgiving). The way Paul states the teaching does not suggest
that he is aware of a particular problem, but that he recognizes that
believers can become vexed with each other in the congregation.
Here we have something of a grievance procedure for the church. To
bear with is primarily nonaction, or better, nonreaction. It means re-
fraining from responding in kind to provocations. Forgiving, however, is a gracious positive action that goes beyond tolerating to wiping
one's own heart clean of resentment and canceling out the offense.

3:13b Incentive

Experience of the Lord's forgiveness is abundant reason for forgiving others. Ephesians 4:32 is a parallel text. *[Text, p. 319.]* Jesus had made the same point with his parable of the unforgiving servant (Matt. 18:23-35; see Rom. 15:7 for a similar kind of appeal).

3:14 Directive: Clothe Yourselves with Love

Paul sums up the "put on" teaching with the key virtue, *love*. All of these virtues are characteristics of God/Christ, and so it is not surprising that Paul includes the primary characteristic. (Recall the designation *beloved* in verse 12.) Verse 14 begins with *above all* (*beyond all these things*, NASB; *over all*, NIV). If the clothing metaphor is still in mind, the phrase may suggest that love needs to be added to tie all these behaviors together. Certainly the NT holds up love as a supreme and indispensable factor (e.g., Matt. 22:37-40; Rom. 13:8-10; 1 Cor. 13; Gal. 5:14, 22; 1 John 4:11-21). There is good reason to consider love as a *sine qua non* (without which there is nothing).

But, in the context of Colossians 3:5-14, what is being held together by love is more likely the people of the Christian fellowship rather than the virtues. The last line of the verse could be rendered, *the bond which produces perfection/wholeness/unity* (EDM). *[Mature, p. 307.]* That is, love is what keeps the fellowship from flying apart. In Ephesians 4:3, peace is the bond of unity. *[Col. & Eph., p. 284.]* In Colossians 3, Paul's next thought is *the peace of Christ* (Col. 3:15).

Five of the virtues in 3:12-14 are listed as the fruit of the Spirit (Gal. 5:22-23). In the only direct reference to the Spirit in Colossians (1:8), we find *your love in the Spirit*. Five of these virtues are also included in the description of the life that is worthy of the Lord's calling in Ephesians 4:2.

THE TEXT IN BIBLICAL CONTEXT
Christological Ethics

Colossians calls Christians to think of ethics christologically. What we know of Christ should inform our ethical decisions and moral behavior. How does Colossians match the NT perspective on ethics, and does the composite picture justify the assertion that Jesus is the norm for ethics?

This assertion is not accepted by all Christians. Jesus is dismissed

as irrelevant for ethics by (1) those who consider Jesus to be historically distanced from twentieth-century issues, (2) those who suppose
Jesus to be too idealistic for the tough realities of life, (3) those who
postpone much of Jesus' teaching to a future age, and (4) those who
see Jesus only in terms of his substitutionary atonement. But the NT
does testify to a direct link between Jesus, the whole word of Christ,
and ethics.

Before we come to specific texts on ethics, we note five general
factors about Christ and ethics in the NT:

1. The incarnation of Christ is the key to christological ethics and
the base for them. Since Jesus was human as well as divine, we must
take him seriously in matters of ethics. Neither his teaching nor his
example can be discarded as irrelevant to the human scene.

2. The concept of "image" adds a crucial piece. The NT testifies
that Christ is the image of God (1:15) and that those in Christ are being made into his image (2 Cor. 3:18).

3. The concept of the kingdom of Christ (John 18:36), of being
transferred into the kingdom of the Son (1:13), implies a value system shaped by Christ.

4. The teachings of Jesus stand as foundational to any system of
Christian ethics. The ethical instructions of the NT have the distinct
flavor of the sayings of Jesus.

5. The example of Christ provides a vivid demonstration of a
christological ethical framework. For instance, Jesus' example not
only encourages us to do the right, it also shows us the right way to
confront and respond to evil.

Many texts illustrate the unmistakable connection made between
Jesus and ethical values and behavior:

- Jesus called his disciples to a servant posture because he came to
serve (Mark 10:42-45).
- Jesus commanded his disciples to love as he loved them (John
15:12).
- We are to please our neighbor because Christ did not please himself
(Rom. 15:2-3).
- Paul's appeal is (in an ethical context), "Be imitators of me, as I am
of Christ" (1 Cor. 11:1).
- Appeal is based on the meekness and gentleness of Christ (2 Cor.
10:1).
- In contrast to common pagan ways, the rejoinder comes, "That is
not the way you learned Christ! For surely you have heard about him and
were taught in him, as truth is in Jesus" (Eph. 4:20-21).
- Christ's attitude in obediently taking the way of the cross is to be the
Christians' attitude (Phil. 2:5).

- Paul commends believers, "You became imitators of us and of the Lord" (1 Thess. 1:6).
  - Mistreatment is to be endured: "For to this you have been called, because Christ also suffered for you, leaving you an example, so that you should follow in his steps" (1 Pet. 2:21-23).
  - The experience of knowing Christ must result in consistent behavior: "Whoever says, 'I abide in him,' ought to walk just as he walked" (1 John 2:6).
  - In a context emphasizing love, we find, "As he [Christ] is, so are we in this world" (1 John 4:17).

This sampling accords with Colossian texts pertaining to christological ethics:

1:13, *kingdom of his beloved Son*
1:28, present everyone *mature in Christ*
3:1-3, life shaped by orientation to Christ
3:10, *renewed . . . according to the image of its creator*
3:12, virtues also attributed to Jesus
3:13, forgiving *as the Lord has forgiven*
3:15-17, *peace of Christ, . . . word of Christ, . . . name of the Lord Jesus*

These teachings constitute an inescapable call to make the ethics of the Savior the ethics of the saved.

Metaphors of Radical Change

Paul made use of four different Greek words in Colossians 3 to describe the process of the believers' transformation as viewed from the human side:

1. *Put to death* (3:5). This is the only NT use of the word in an active sense. Twice it appears in a passive sense, with the hyperbole meaning "considered . . . as good as dead" (Rom. 4:19; Heb. 11:12). NASB gives the word this meaning in 3:5, "Consider . . . as dead." A parallel text, Romans 8:13, employs a synonym (also in an active sense). J. B. Phillips offers a variation on the metaphor with the paraphrase in Romans 8:13, "Cut the nerve of your instinctive actions." Retaining the active meaning in 3:5 gives weight to the need for aggressive action to shut down self-centeredness.

2. *Stripped off*, or *put off* (3:9). Here and in 2:15 are the only NT occurrences of a double compound word that stresses complete removal. (The noun form appears once, in 2:11.) The word carries the sense "strip off clean." This word is the literal antonym of *clothe yourselves with*, or *put on*, in 3:10, 12 (see 4, below).

3. *Get rid of* (3:8). The word is used in a literal sense in Acts 7:58, taking off garments. It occurs often as the negative side of a metaphor for changing attitudes and behaviors (Rom. 13:12; Eph. 4:22, 25; Heb. 12:1; James 1:21; 1 Pet. 2:1; and Col. 3:8). This word is variously translated as "put away," "put off," "cast off," and "lay aside." The figure is that of removing and throwing away the old ways as one gets rid of an old garment.

4. *Clothe yourselves with*, or *put on* (3:10, 12). In the NT the word occurs in a literal sense (e.g., Matt. 6:25) and also as the positive side of the clothing metaphor. It stands as the explicit counterpart of put off (Rom. 13:12, 14; Eph. 4:24; Col. 3:10, 12). Putting on certain attitudes and behaviors (such as the virtues in Col. 3:12) is an integral part of putting on Christ. Being clothed with Christ means belonging to Christ, yielding to his control, and opening oneself to being transformed into Christlikeness.

The clothing metaphor is common in Greek and Hebrew writings, but not in the sense of changing natures, old for new. The NT knows nothing of the Greek notion of getting rid of the body as the source of evil in order to attain the pure life of the spirit. Some commentators see in the metaphor a reference to baptism: believers being baptized symbolize their change in life by discarding their old clothes and putting on new ones. The tense of the imperatives in Colossians 3:5-14 implies decisive action, not just gradually trying to do better.

These associated words emphasize the resolute and radical nature of the moral directives which prescribe human responsibility in the transforming work of Christ. Residual human nature prefers much less radical corrective changes.

Vice Lists in the NT: A Comparison

The construction of the ethical lists in Colossians (two vice lists and one virtue list, each with five items) suggests a deliberate choice of what is included. How do these lists compare with similar NT lists? The chart below shows the vices (NRSV translation) as they appear in Colossians 3:5-9, with indications of where the same (or closely related) Greek word is found in six other ethical lists. Since corresponding virtue lists appear only in Galatians and Ephesians, the virtues are not included in the chart.

Tracking the Vices of Colossians 3:5-9

Col. 3:5-9	Rom. 1	Gal. 5	Eph. 4-5	1 Cor. 5	1 Cor. 6	1 Pet. 3	Rev. 21
fornication	•	•	•	•			•
impurity	•	•	•				
passion	•	(•)					
evil desire	•	(•)	(•)			(•)	
greed	•		•	•	•		
(idolatry)		•	•	•	•	•	•
anger			•				
wrath	•		•				
malice	•		•				
slander			•				
abusive (filthy) language			•				
(lie not)	(•)		•				•

Those in parentheses (•) are similar but not identical. The essay *[Ethical Lists, p. 287]* offers more on NT vice (put off) and virtue (put on) catalogs, including references to Jesus' teaching and Mark 7:21-23.

The Wrath of God

This bold expression, which appears in 3:6 as an incentive for putting certain practices to death, has given rise to some misconceptions. It does pose some perplexing questions. Instead of projecting human angry emotions onto God, we need to let biblical usage shape our understandings of God's wrath.

How, then, is the term used in biblical context? It occurs in both Testaments. In the OT and in Revelation, God's absolute sovereignty results in wrath toward arrogant nations. However, the dominant occasions for the exercise of God's wrath, in both Testaments, is covenant violation. That is, wrath arises out of wounded love. When people do not return love to God, they turn to other gods, and God's response is jealousy and wrath (as in Exod. 20:5; Deut. 32:16; Ps. 78:58-62; and Ezek. 16:23-43.) Frequently God's wrath is set in relationship with his saving work, with gospel, repentance, righteousness, and kingdom (e.g., Matt. 3:2, 7-12; John 3:36; Rom. 1:16-18). Jesus' anger was a reaction to his mercy being despised.

Saying No to Jesus, who is God's word of love, results in God's No in the expression of wrath. The NT in no way scales down God's wrath. It actually presents a graver view of God's wrath than the OT does, while also announcing deliverance from the wrath to come through Jesus Christ (Rom. 5:9; 1 Thess. 1:10; 5:9-10).

Too often it is assumed that love and wrath are mutually exclusive. So some ask, "If God is love, how can wrath also belong to God?" But in reality, God's wrath is the other side of his love, although the Bible does not speak of wrath in terms of God's essence, as it speaks of love. As C. E. B. Cranfield has pointed out, we should see evidence of the goodness of God in the way he reacts to evil with wrath. As a human illustration, he observes that a person who knows about racial injustice and is not angry at such evil cannot be a thoroughly good person (109). It follows that lack of wrath is a failure to love. That is true of God as well as humans.

These understandings cast a different light on the wrath of God as a moral incentive. The biblical view stands in sharp contrast to the perceptions in the Greco-Roman world. Anger was a prominent characteristic of the Greek gods, an anger provoked by broken laws. The wrath of the Roman gods was also understood as punitive judgment on the guilty. They arrived at such ideas by projecting human emotions of anger onto their gods.

Associations of wrath with the biblical term translated "vengeance" have not been helpful in understanding the meaning of wrath. Biblical usage of *vengeance* (when attributed to God) connects the term with deliverance, vindication, and salvation of his people, not with retribution, revenge, and vindictiveness. Human reactions are often read into the texts. Fear of punishment undoubtedly has a deterring effect on evil behavior, but a right understanding of the wrath of God provides an even greater incentive for moral living.

We do not do justice to the biblical concept of the wrath of God by equating it with an impersonal law of cause and effect. This is not to deny that ours is a moral universe and that, as sometimes said, those who go against the grain get splinters. Sin has its own consequences in God's universe. God's wrath includes that and is more than that.

God's wrath is not anger in the common sense. It is not identical with the consequences of sin in a moral universe, and it is rightfully disassociated from an intent on God's part to get even or to inflict punishment. Nevertheless, it is a biblical concept (cf. Heb. 10:30-31). It is a present reality (Rom. 1:18-32; Eph. 2:3; 1 Thess. 2:16) and a future, eschatological certainty (Rom. 2:5; 1 Thess. 1:10). "Certainly the elimination of the punitive meaning in no way reduces the gravity or severity of the warning. Indeed, it deepens it, for it is infinitely more terrible to flout love than to defy anger" (C. Moule, 1973:488).

Greed and Idolatry

The identification of greed with idolatry (3:5) is expressed almost the same way in Ephesians 5:5: "No fornicator or impure person, or one who is greedy (that is, an idolater), has any inheritance in the kingdom of Christ and of God." These sins appear close together also in two other texts, 1 Cor. 5:10-11 and 6:9-10, where the terms are included in lists of vices, without any editorial comment about the idolatrous nature of greed. However, we may deduce that labeling greed as idolatry (1) warns against coveting the things of earth, especially at the expense of others, and (2) underscores that sins against the neighbor are sins against God.

Jesus' teachings, "Where your treasure is, there your heart will be also," and "You cannot serve God and wealth," are obviously in the same vein. Other warnings against both greed/covetousness and idolatry in the NT take on additional meaning when the connection between the two is kept in mind.

New Community As Well As New Individuals

In 3:10-11 the new creation shifts abruptly from new persons to the new community where racial and social differences no longer matter. The new creation has that meaning elsewhere as well. Galatians 6:15 affirms, "For neither circumcision nor uncircumcision is anything; but a new creation is everything!" In the next verse Paul is talking about "the Israel of God." Earlier in Galatians, Paul labels as no gospel at all the "gospel" that denies in theory and practice the creation of the new community in Christ. Ephesians 2:15 speaks in a similar way of the new humanity created out of the old entities, Jews and Gentiles.

Second Corinthians 5:17 is a text often quoted as teaching personal regeneration: "So if anyone is in Christ, there is a new creation." Many versions supply the words "there is" or "he is" (as indicated by italics in KJV and NASB). The word often translated "creature," but preferably "creation," nowhere else in the NT is used to refer to an individual person. It more often refers to the act of creating than to what is created. The "new creation" is the new community. (Cf. J. Yoder, 1972:226-228.) These texts do not deny the miracle of personal newness; instead, they lay special emphasis on the new fellowship of believers in Christ.

Parallel Texts About Equality in Christ

One cannot miss seeing the similarity between Colossians 3:11 and Galatians 3:28. The same point is made in 1 Corinthians 12:13, using some of the same words. The text from Galatians affirms that all who are in Christ are of equal status, with the inclusion of Gentiles (Greeks) as a primary issue. A unique feature is that "male" and "female" appear in the list. The text from 1 Corinthians emphasizes the unity of believers in one body. The text from Colossians includes two pairs of cultural contrasts not included in the other lists. A need to put away all notions of inferiority and superiority because of cultural differences seems to be the primary concern in Colossians.

None of these texts should be made to say that the gospel obliterates all differences of race, color, ethnicity, gender, language, or socioeconomic circumstances. The point is not sameness but equality of worth and unity in a context of diversity. Commonality in Christ is to overcome the world's tendency to stratify people.

THE TEXT IN THE LIFE OF THE CHURCH

Does Ethical Teaching Belong to the Gospel?

Colossians relates to the question of whether salvation and ethics can or cannot be separated in presenting the good news in Jesus. In practice, discipling is often separated from evangelizing. A minimal gospel is presented with the assumption that teaching will follow. Although proclamation (*kērugma*) and teaching (*didachē*) can be distinguished by definition, the line between them is blurred in both the Gospels and the Epistles.

Obviously new believers are not instantly mature. Ongoing nurture is essential for normal growth. But it is not fair to the gospel to say, Accept Jesus today and be saved; tomorrow we will talk about what that will mean in your life and relationships.

Several kinds of NT examples shed light on the question. Time and again Jesus placed heavy ethical demands on persons when he invited them to follow him. The syntax of Matthew 28:19-20 indicates that "baptizing" and "teaching" are to be seen as describing what it means to "make disciples" (the main verb). David J. Bosch comments: "A disciple is somebody who has been incorporated into the community of believers and who keeps Jesus' commandments" (233). Peter's exhortation had ethical implications: "Save yourselves from this corrupt generation" (Acts 2:40). As observed in Colossians, the indicatives and imperatives of the gospel are woven together tightly. The christological hymns and the "faithful sayings" of the pastoral epistles are the ground for moral exhortations. Obedience and belief are not separated in the NT.

A limited forensic view of salvation focuses almost exclusively on God's action to change the individual's status from condemned to justified. This feeds into the distortion of the gospel that occurs when ethics and evangelism are divorced. Perry Yoder highlights the relevance of Colossians 3:

> The inward, subjective aspect of the atonement, and the outward social, objective aspect of the atonement are also connected in Colossians 3:10-11. . . . The new nature which comes from our transformation, from the love of Christ controlling us, automatically results in a new way in human relations. Again, the old social divisions cannot any longer count among us. The NT does not here separate the personal aspects of the atonement—putting on the new nature and laying off the old—from the corporate aspects—the reconciliation of the old enemies into one new society. To neglect either aspect of the atonement is to proclaim less than what Christ died to accomplish. (68)

José Gallardo points out that both liberation and state church theologies neglect christologically based ethics. Drawing on his experiences in Belgium, Uruguay, Argentina, Bolivia, Switzerland, and Spain, he challenges the church to keep peace and justice in the mission message because they are an integral part of a holistic gospel (153-157).

Moral Teaching That Doesn't Go Out of Date

A study group readily observes that the put-off, put-on passages, and the vice and virtue lists in particular, are amazingly relevant for life today. Differences in the lists indicate that the particular items are selected to match the needs of the recipients of the letters. However, for the most part the items are generic in nature rather than culturally specific. For example, one finds reference to impurity rather than to length of skirts, and to greed rather than to how much one should spend for automobiles.

When the church has addressed matters of morality and nonconformity, the effort has often produced dated rules. The church needs to grapple with what the specific biblical directives mean for a given time and place, but we should not lose sight of the broader, underlying principles. Otherwise, when changes are made in specific applications of faithfulness in response to the current culture, some of those changes may be construed as a loss of ground to the world.

The biblical injunctions specify internal factors as much or more than external actions. The new life, described both negatively and positively in the ethical teachings, really cannot be faked. It is the out-working of an inner change. In contrast, the externals that enable one to "belong" to a social tradition—things like diet, dress, and other customs—can be adopted without an inner change.

The directive to put off greed seems especially relevant in a culture that idolizes affluence. Greed is not the same as the profit motive. Rather, greed is the hankering to get and to have more and more. Obviously, the problem is not limited to multimillionaires. Christians need to be highly intentional about the values of the kingdom of Christ when they are surrounded by a culture that not only approves of greed but encourages and rewards it. The experience of Zacchaeus illustrates how greed fares in an encounter with Christ.

Sexual Morality Without Denying Sexuality

It is hardly surprising that sexual sins appear in the vice lists of the NT. Excesses and misuses of sex were prevalent in the pagan society of the early church. Sexual morality needed to be addressed and delineated for the emerging Christian community. Since the church, as a counterculture, always needs to speak to sexual morality, we need to look at the NT standards carefully.

Greek thought viewed the human body negatively. The NT continues the OT (Hebrew) attitude of affirming the human body and sexuality (and sex) as gifts of God. The church does not regard the human body as evil, even though certain sexual attitudes and practices are identified as contrary to Christian morality.

A distinction between sexuality and sex is helpful. Sexuality refers to all that makes us either male or female. Every person is always a sexual being. Sexuality is an integral part of personhood in all dimensions, emotional and psychic as well as biological. To deny sexuality is to deny humanness. Sex refers to sexual expressions, mental and physical, having to do with genital activity. Humans can do without sex, but they cannot cease to be sexual. Morality enters the picture because sexuality comes with certain specifications as to what are healthy and what are sick sexual expressions. The Creator has set boundaries that require control over sexual feelings and drives. Genital sex, in God's design, is right and good, but only within the covenant marriage of one man and one woman.

Especially in cultures saturated with sex and in times of sexual revolution, the church must speak clearly about sexual morality and help people understand and accept their sexuality. NT teachings provide the basic framework for applying sexual morality to the specifics of the day. The negatives must be set in the context of the positives about human sexuality.

The Gospel Does Away with Walls—Or Does It?

The gospel of Jesus Christ cuts across the many natural and artificial barriers that separate people in the world. The impact of such a gospel on the pagan world of the early church can hardly be overestimated. Breaking down the old walls of prejudice was both scandalous and attractive.

The social world of early Christianity was rigidly stratified. In addition to the major wall between Jews and Gentiles and the massive cleavage between slaves and free citizens, other political, economic, and cultural factors determined relatively fixed social boundaries. However, being reconciled to God includes coming into a community where people are reconciled to each other. Here essential identity is in Christ rather than in race, nationality, culture, social class, or gender. The differences are not eliminated, but they no longer act as barriers or a basis of worth. Such is the potential when Christ, the leveler and unifier, builds his church.

However, the church's overall record falls short. Instead of racism being eradicated in the church, the Sunday morning worship hour continues to carry the stigma of being the most segregated hour of the week. Manifestations of sexism continue to blight the testimony of the church as females experience overt and subtle discrimination. Racism and sexism both survive, arising from the perversity of human nature to feel superior to and exercise power over others. The church also struggles with ethnicity. As with other differences, the solution is not in acting like the facts of difference do not exist. Everyone is ethnic. The gospel does not ask people to despise their own or others' background. The problems come when the gospel is identified with a particular ethnic culture and it is assumed that new adherents must be assimilated into the dominant ethnic mold.

In order to be faithful in the stewardship of the gospel, the church must proclaim the gospel to all people and accept persons without partiality. Failure to confront the world's social barriers is a denial and subversion of the power of the reconciling gospel.

Colossians 3:15-17

Incorporating the New Life

PREVIEW

This brief section is much like an artistic musical composition. It is made up of three movements. Each movement develops a theme reflecting the common motif of the piece and also incorporates a repeated subtheme, with individualized variations. Every segment of this summary trilogy picks up a particular attribute of the central motif, that is, of Christ/Lord Jesus, and relates that quality to the new life. The subtheme will be recognized as thanksgiving.

These three verses comprise a succinct and unique message to the church. The message deals with (1) the internal life and experience of the congregation; (2) the intermeshing of instruction, mutual care, and worship; and (3) experiencing all of life in the scattered experience of the church as shaped and hallowed by the one whose name Christians bear.

OUTLINE

The Peace of Christ, 3:15

The Word of Christ, 3:16

The Name of the Lord Jesus, 3:17

EXPLANATORY NOTES

Observe in this marked text (NRSV) things similar and things repeat-ed. Each verse has a primary imperative or directive. The one in verse 17 needs to be supplied in English translation, since it is implied rath-er than stated in the Greek text. An added imperative in verse 15 in-troduces the thanksgiving subtheme that is also part of the other two sections. Note the words that call attention to the relevance of these admonitions for the corporate life of Christians.

> (15) And let *the peace of Christ* rule in *your* hearts,
>> to which indeed *you* were called in the *one body*.
> And be **thankful**.

> (16) Let *the word of Christ* dwell in *you* richly;
>> teach and admonish *one another*
>> in all wisdom;
> and with **gratitude** in *your* hearts
> sing psalms, hymns, and spiritual songs to God.

> (17) And whatever *you* do, in word or deed,
>> do everything in *the name of the Lord Jesus*
>> **giving thanks** to God the Father through him.

The Peace of Christ   3:15

A phrase echoing Jesus' words in John 14:27 focuses the attribute of Christ that shapes the first charge to the church. *The peace of Christ* embraces the good news that Christ both is our peace (Eph. 2:14) and gives peace (2 Thess. 3:16). As noted in connection with 1:2, 20, *peace* is a good deal more than the absence of open conflict. As with the Hebrew term *shalom, peace* is concerned with wholeness in per-sonhood and relationships.

The word translated *rule* brings with it the imagery of serving as umpire or arbitrator. (A compound form of this same word is in 2:18.) This kind of action, Paul says, is to take place *in your hearts*. The heart is viewed as the center of a person. The goal of this directive is that with the peace of Christ calling the decisions in each of the be-lievers, they will be equipped as a community to deal with the differ-ences and frictions that disrupt shalom.

Although peace in individual hearts is appropriately included in the meaning here, the second line of this directive focuses on life in the *one body* into which all believers are *called*. In the NT view, this call is not a subsequent or optional call separated from the call into

Christ. Being called into one body does not have a meaning different from the metaphor of being transferred into the kingdom of God's beloved Son (1:13). The body of Christ is one body, but a general reference to that larger body does not have much meaning if it is not experienced in a local fellowship. A feeling of oneness with all God's people is not a substitute for dealing with a strained relationship with a particular brother or sister.

The body imagery emphasizes elements of harmony, cooperation, and interdependence. Note the similar wording in Ephesians 4:1-3: "Called . . . making every effort to maintain the unity of the Spirit in the bond of peace."

And be thankful. This is the fourth of the seven references to thanksgiving in Colossians. *[Thanksgiving, p. 322.]* Can gratitude be commanded? A more precise translation is *become thankful*, or *be those who give thanks* (EDM). The word translated *thankful* is part of a word family that implies more than an attitude or disposition. It includes the expression of thanks, in this case probably in the assembly as well as privately. The context suggests giving thanks for the privileges of belonging to the body of Christ and for his mediating presence.

The Word of Christ 3:16

Nowhere else in the NT do we find the phrase *the word of Christ.* Elsewhere in Colossians we have *the word of the truth, the gospel* (1:5), *the word of God* (1:25), and *the word* (4:3). If we could ask Paul whether he means the word/message about Christ (the story that underlies the Gospels), or the word Christ spoke/taught (the sayings of Jesus), he might well answer, Both.

Striking similarities between verse 16 and Ephesians 5:18-19 open another window of understanding. There we read, "Be filled with the Spirit, as you sing psalms and hymns and spiritual songs among yourselves, singing and making melody to the Lord in your hearts." The similarities lead to the comment, "The coming of the Word of God in the gospel is the coming of the Spirit, and the coming of the Spirit is the coming of the living and abiding Word of God" (Lucas: 154). As noted earlier, Colossians makes little direct reference to the Spirit, compared with Ephesians. We may well ponder the meaning of believers being filled with the Spirit, and whether that is equivalent to them having the word of Christ dwelling in them richly.

As already illustrated in Colossians, Paul is concerned to have right doctrine about Christ. But here, with the wording *dwell in you*, his burden is not to hold correct formulations of truth but to have the word of Christ fully at home in the being and experience of persons and in the believing community. The context keeps our attention directed to the church's corporate experience. Paul uses the word *dwell* to convey this idea, whereas John employs *abide*, as in John 15:7, "And my words abide in you."

A comparison of versions and commentaries shows that it is not easy to understand the rest of verse 16, with its several clauses and phrases. Some translations use four imperatives in verse 16. *[Grammar, 3:9b-10a, p. 292.]* Several more matters for interpretation come up. The phrase *in all wisdom* can be construed with *dwell* (KJV) or with *teaching and admonishing* (NRSV, NIV, NASB). Other references to *wisdom* in Colossians support the NRSV construction of the text. A prime example is 1:28, which also associates *wisdom* with *warning* (admonishing) and *teaching*.

The relationship of singing to teaching and admonishing raises a question. Are we to understand singing as the means for teaching and admonishing (KJV, NASB, and see Eph. 5:19) or as parallel with teaching and admonishing (NRSV, NIV, and many others)? All three terms are in the same grammatical form. *[Grammar, p. 292.]* All three should likely be seen as means by which the word of Christ dwells in believers. Teaching implies instruction, admonishing connotes an exercised concern, and singing adds the element of celebrative worship. Attempts to make clear distinctions between *psalms, hymns*, and *songs* are not convincing. (Perhaps *spiritual* is best taken to modify all three.) Together these terms portray "the full range of singing which the Spirit prompts" (Lohse: 151).

Setting words to music unquestionably enhances communication potential, as the advertising industry knows. Interest and retention are heightened with the addition of colorful music. Didactic hymns and scriptural songs are powerful means of passing on the faith. But such a function of singing in the church does not exhaust Paul's vision in this directive. Hymnody may be a more significant vehicle of theology than sermons are, but here the focus is on singing to God, not to one another. An important thrust of this text is captured in these lines:

Sing till we feel our hearts
Ascending with our tongues;
Sing till the love of sin departs,
And grace inspires our songs. (H. Moule: 228)

The phrase *in your hearts* does not specify silent worship, but an involvement of the whole being. This fifth reference to thanksgiving in Colossians identifies *gratitude* as the mainspring for singing. *[Thanksgiving, p. 322.]* Paul expresses the idea of thanksgiving differently here. Although grace is part of the word commonly translated thanksgiving (*eucharistia*), here the word grace itself (*charis*) carries the meaning of gratitude. A literal rendering is *with [or in] the grace singing in your hearts to God* (EDM, following well-attested texts including *the*). These details imply that grateful singing arises out of awareness of being in the realm of God's grace (1:6), and that Spirit-inspired singing is the lyrical expression of the devout soul. In the previous line, *with gratitude* is structurally parallel with *in all wisdom.*

Note the element of mutuality in the words *teach and admonish one another.* Paul does not thereby negate the place of teachers in the church. Rather, he envisions that in healthy body life members are equipped to minister to each other in what may be called "peer counseling" (cf. Rom. 15:14).

The Name of the Lord Jesus 3:17

Paul sums up this block of ethical teaching, not with a detailed listing of rules, but with an intensely practical principle. The principle is expressed even more comprehensively than the similar one in 1 Corinthians 10:31. Note the wording: *whatever . . . everything.* The imperative verb is not part of the Greek text, but *do* (at the beginning of line 2) is obviously implied. *In word or deed* explains the inclusive word *whatever.* Both talk and action are to be brought under the umbrella of *the name of the Lord Jesus.* The word translated *deed* is the primary word for "work." A theology of work and an orientation for all of life emerges in this summary directive. Paul's principle eliminates the notion of "secular" from the common dichotomy of "sacred and secular." This is the only mention of *the name* of Christ in Colossians, although the Bible has abundant references to the name of God and the name of Christ.

When faced with moral issues and other life decisions to which the Bible does not speak explicitly, Christians find guidance in reflecting on the principle: can this action be taken in the name of the Lord Jesus? His reputation is affected by the behavior of those who bear his name.

We come to yet another call to thanksgiving. *[Thanksgiving, p. 322.]* When everything is done in *the name of the Lord Jesus*, all of life is worship. Coupled, as it is, with a whole-life orientation to Jesus, thanksgiving is not a dutiful drudgery but a celebration of the freedom to live, worship, and work with Jesus as Lord. Thankfulness to God the Father blossoms out of the soil of dependence and humility. In contrast, an attitude of self-sufficiency often results in scorn of others, and self-pity feeds resentment and bitterness. The reminder that thanksgiving to God the Father is *through him* (the Lord Jesus) fits naturally in this letter that places much emphasis on Christ.

Three terms, *the peace of Christ, the word of Christ,* and *the name of the Lord Jesus,* are more profound than their simple wording may convey at first. They give verses 15-17 an aura of specialness for Christians. Furthermore, seeing them tied together with the triple strand of thanksgiving makes this summary an appealing trilogy with timeless relevance.

THE TEXT IN BIBLICAL CONTEXT
The Peace of Christ

This expression is unique in the NT, although Jesus' words in John 14:27, "My peace I give to you," convey the same concept. Colossians 1:20 puts the peacemaking of the blood of Christ's cross at the heart of God's reconciling enterprise. God in Christ reconciles to himself estranged and hostile individuals (1:21-22). Christ's peacemaking also results in the *mystery* of the gospel, the inclusion of Gentiles (1:26-27). The effects of Christ's peace are broadened even more in 3:11, as in Christ all sorts of barriers to fellowship are overcome.

Related expressions include "the Lord of peace" (2 Thess. 3:16, taking Lord to refer to Christ), and "he [Christ] is our peace" (Eph. 2:14). The *peace of Christ* concept also flavors the meaning of the several occurrences of "the peace of God," "the God of peace," and "the gospel of peace" (Rom. 15:33; 16:20; 2 Cor. 13:11; Eph. 6:15; Phil. 4:7, 9; 1 Thess. 5:23; Heb. 13:20).

Several parallel texts should be noted. Ephesians 2:11-22 explicitly brings together peace through the blood of Christ and reconciliation of Jews and Gentiles in the one new body. Key words in Colossians 3:14-15 also appear in Ephesians 4:1-4 (love, harmony/unity, peace, one body). The correlation of love and peace is especially evident in these similar texts. *[Col. and Eph., p. 284.]*

The peace of Christ provides the potential for "making things as they ought to be" (P. Yoder: 21). This resource is meant to apply to evangelism, ethics, and Christian community. A highly practical application of God's concern for peace is found in 1 Corinthians 7:15, where the options for a mixed marriage (believer and unbeliever) are weighed.

Hymnody and Music in the Early Church

In addition to Colossians 3:16 and similar wording in Ephesians 5:19, several other references indicate that singing was part of the life of the NT church. Jesus and his disciples sang a hymn before leaving the upper room (Matt. 26:30). If Jesus followed the traditional Passover service, the final hymn was Psalm 136. The account of Paul and Silas singing hymns to God in the middle of the night while in maximum security (Acts 16:25) includes nothing about what they sang. We may speculate that they supplemented the Hebrew Psalter with references to Christ. Singing and hymns are mentioned as part of Christian worship in 1 Corinthians 14:15. James 5:13 says singing praise is an appropriate activity of the cheerful heart.

Although the three terms in Colossians and Ephesians (*psalms, hymns,* and *spiritual songs*) cannot be defined as distinctly different kinds of musical expression, the appearance of the three suggests both variety and prevalence of singing in Christian assemblies. Further evidence of a positive regard for music is found in references to various musical instruments and in references to praise that possibly involved singing.

One generally accepted assessment is that "the Christian Church was born in song" (Martin, 1964b:39). As to what was sung, the evidence is less specific. Likely Christian assemblies drew on Jewish patterns of worship. The Jews sang the Psalms in their synagogues and temple. But Christians also had something new to sing about. William Smith says:

> It is very difficult to conceive of the life and worship of the early church in which the Lord Jesus Christ occupied such a central place and suppose that the first Christians did not sing about His person and His work using words which they had composed just for that purpose. (72)

A number of lyrical passages in the NT (mentioned in connection with Col. 1:15-20) have a liturgical, confessional quality about them, and it seems likely that they were sung.

The second-century Roman historian Pliny the Younger wrote of Christians in Bithynia who sang a hymn to Christ as to God. Second- and third-century writings refer to psalms being sung at Christian meals. Out of that same era came a vigorous opposition to pagan customs being brought into the church, especially the use of instruments. However, a distinction was made between pagan frivolities and acceptable art forms. In the fourth and fifth centuries musical aspects of worship involved soloists and congregation in various responsorial and antiphonal patterns (McKinnon).

The Name

The summary directive, *do everything in the name of the Lord Jesus*, fits into a NT pattern of employing "the name." In the OT "the name" is used many times in references to Yahweh, and in some NT occurrences "the name of the Lord" also refers to Yahweh. More than seventy-five occurrences of "name" in the NT, however, are associated with Jesus. In addition to Jesus speaking of "my name," we find a variety of prepositions introducing "the name" (e.g., in, into, on, by, through, for the sake of, for, because of). *In the name* means in the authority of, in the character of, and in the presence and power of. "The name of Jesus takes on the significance that it embraces the whole content of the saving acts revealed in Jesus" (TDNT, 5:273).

The following examples illustrate the wide range of associations with "the name":

```
baptism—Matt. 28:19; Acts 10:48
salvation—Acts 4:12; 1 Cor. 6:11
believing—John 1:12; 2:23; 3:18; 1 John 3:23
forgiveness—Acts 10:43; 1 John 2:12
eternal life—John 20:31; 1 John 5:13
giving of the Spirit—John 14:26
offering thanks—Eph. 5:20
miracles/healing—Mark 9:38-41; Acts 3:6, 16
expelling demons—Luke 10:17; Acts 16:18
admonition—1 Cor. 1:10; 2 Thess. 3:6
prayer—John 14:13-14; 15:16; 16:23, 26
confession—Phil. 2:10-11; Heb. 13:15; Rev. 2:13; 3:8
proclamation—Luke 24:47; Acts 8:12; 3 John 7
suffering—Matt. 19:29; John 15:21; Acts 9:16; 15:26
```

Note the designation *Lord Jesus* in Colossians 3:17 and in many of the references above (in Acts and the epistles). *[Titles, p. 323.]* The early church came to refer to Christ as *the/our Lord Jesus*, consistent with the confession "Jesus is Lord" (1 Cor. 12:3). When Jesus is acknowledged and served as Lord of all of life, work and worship and everything else needs to stand under the name of the Lord Jesus.

THE TEXT IN THE LIFE OF THE CHURCH

The Peace of Christ in and Through the Church

The peace of Christ functions in three interconnected relational arenas. The primary concern of Colossians 3:15 is peace in the body of believers. Since peace and reconciliation are related like twins, peace/reconciliation with God and the behavior of the children of peace in the world are equally significant arenas. The interrelationship of these three arenas may be thought of like this:

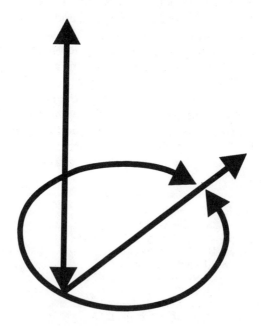

As important as personal peace with God is, it is not fair to Colossians (or the NT as a whole) to minimize or ignore what the peace of Christ means for the church and for life in this world.

The peace of Christ is to be the controlling factor for the in-house matters of the church. Members are to put off attitudes and practices that disrupt peace and put on the ways that make for unity and harmony. The peace of Christ is to umpire over the community's stresses and strains caused by eruptions of self-interest. Failure to *let the peace of Christ rule* is evident in the skeletons in the closets of church splits and in the stream of church alumni who have been turned off by the power struggles and petty bickerings of church people. Conversely, prospective members find the church attractive when they see peace in the fellowship, not because problems are swept under the rug, but because the peace of Christ is allowed to operate.

Life in the world is also radically altered when the peace of Christ is controlling the hearts of believers. Around 1552 Menno Simons wrote a "Reply to False Accusations" as an attempt to reduce persecution. His words were not abstract ideals, but insights and convictions held in the midst of religious and political turmoil. Several selections illustrate an Anabaptist understanding of the peace of Christ:

> The Scriptures teach that there are two opposing princes and two opposing kingdoms: the one is the Prince of peace; the other the prince of strife. Each of these princes has his particular kingdom and as the prince is so is also the kingdom. The Prince of peace is Christ Jesus; His kingdom is the kingdom of peace, which is His church; His messengers are the messengers of peace; His Word is the word of peace; His body is the body of peace; His children are the seed of peace; and His inheritance and reward are the inheritance and reward of peace. In short, with this King, and in His kingdom and reign, it is nothing but peace. Everything that is seen, heard, and done is peace.
>
> True Christians do not know vengeance, no matter how they are mistreated. In patience they possess their souls. Luke 21:18. And they do not break their peace, even if they should be tempted by bondage, torture, poverty, and besides, by the sword and fire. They do not cry, Vengeance, vengeance, as does the world; but with Christ they supplicate and pray: Father, forgive them; for they know not what they do. Luke 23:34; Acts 7:60.
>
> They do not seek your money, goods, injury, nor blood, but they seek the honor and praise of God and the salvation of your souls. They are the children of peace; their hearts overflow with peace; their mouths speak peace, and they walk in the way of peace; they are full of peace. They seek, desire, and know nothing but peace; and are prepared to forsake country, goods, life, and all for the sake of peace. For they are the kingdom, people, congregation, city, property, and body of peace, as has been heard. (554-556)

In contrast to the world's views of peace, the peace of Christ aims for a higher goal and employs greatly different means. In the world's view, peace is the absence of war and open hostilities. Pacification and peacekeeping are accomplished by eliminating the enemy or by flexing superior military power. From this perspective the atomic destruction of Hiroshima and Nagasaki were justified because that action hastened the end of the war, thus saving lives.

The assumption is that threatening forces must be confronted and defeated with superior power. In a sense this assumption is valid. The question is, What is the superior power? God's way of peacemaking and reconciliation is to offer the superior power of the blood of Christ's cross. The way of peace is not powerless acquiescence, as it may seem. "When the Christian whom God has disarmed lays aside carnal weapons it is not, in the last analysis, because those weapons are too strong, but because they are too weak" (J. Yoder, 1985:29).

A People in Which "The Word of Christ" Is at Home

How do congregations get to the place where it can be said that the word of Christ indwells them richly? Can it be argued that since we now have the NT and our own private copies of it, we do not need the church as a residence or repository of the word of Christ? Having the NT is not the same as the word of Christ *being at home* in the church. Colossians 3:16 calls for the whole message of Christ to pervade and shape the believers' collective life. Possession of a book and familiarity with it, significant as they are, do not begin to approach the apostle's vision for a congregation.

This vision may entail the use of structured programs and curricula. However, the text from Colossians points to more informal activities as the means into the vision—teaching, admonishing, and singing. The element of mutuality is noteworthy. Those in Christ are to teach and admonish each other. This implies informal settings rather than Sunday school classes in which everybody is expected to take his or her turn as teacher. Group participation in singing as well as the content of the lyrics support the vision.

The world does its molding and influencing in subtle, though highly intentional, informal ways. Without straying into devious, manipulative ways, the church needs to pay more attention to the many subliminal nonverbal factors that make up the dynamics of life in the family of God and engage them in the formation of believers around the word of Christ.

Colossians 3:18—4:1

Applying the Gospel in Domestic Relationships

PREVIEW

Rhetoric about an amazing new product may sound good, but the test comes when we get the item home. Similarly, we may properly ask, How does the gospel work when we get it home? In 3:18—4:1 we have the gospel applied in basic household relationships.

This highly structured segment injects a major change of subject and style. The verses are not explicitly tied to or obviously dependent on what is before or after. Observe that 4:2-6 connects well with 3:17. This strongly suggests that 3:18—4:1 is an independent unit of teaching. The same pattern, with its three pairs of admonitions, appears in Ephesians 5:21—6:9. A similar form of admonitions appears in 1 Peter 2:13—3:7, except that it includes reference to government instead of reference to children and parents.

Since the time of Martin Luther's translation, these passages have been given the label *Haustafeln*, from the German word meaning "house tables." Because these rules are addressed to persons in their station in life, the term "station codes" can also serve to identify this early Christian teaching. Three aspects of average household life receive attention. The term Domestic Codes will be used here.

Note that considerably more words are devoted to *slaves* than to any of the other five groups. This may well suggest that the basic core of instruction was elaborated to match the situation at Colossae, as reflected in Philemon.

Much debate has been generated about whether these codes have been borrowed and from whom, how much they have been "Christianized," and what relevance they have for centuries other than the first. Believers church perspectives and scholarship bring significant insights to the discussions about the meaning and import of this and related passages (e.g., the contributions of David Schroeder, John H. Yoder, and Willard M. Swartley).

OUTLINE

Marriage, 3:18-19
| 3:18 | Wives |
| 3:19 | Husbands |

Family, 3:20-21
| 3:20 | Children |
| 3:21 | Fathers |

Slavery, 3:22—4:1
| 3:22-25 | Slaves |
| 4:1 | Masters |

EXPLANATORY NOTES

Four parts make up the pattern of these household rules: who (both who is addressed and to whom related), what (the basic command), how (elaboration of meaning, negatively and positively), and why (reason or motive). Observe these stylistic features:

1. Counterpart classes are given reciprocal duties.
2. In each case, the least powerful class is addressed first.
3. All but one of the six have at least one motivation attached.
4. The instructions, except for slaves, are brief and pointed.
5. There are six references to *the Lord*.
6. The three pairs are not on a par with each other.
7. All of the specific imperatives call for ongoing action.
8. The directives are all in the context of relationships.

Marriage 3:18-19

3:18 Wives

The first aspect of domestic life to which Paul speaks is the primary relationship, the one between wives and husbands. He addresses *wives* in a manner that implies "You wives." (The same is true for the other five designated groupings.) *[Grammar, p. 293.] Wives*, who had few if any rights in the male-dominated social order of that time, are addressed as free, responsible persons. It is not up to the husbands to keep their wives in line!

The injunctions to wives, *Be subject to your husbands*, indicates the specific relationship in view, and what the nature of that relationship is to be. English translations of the imperative *[Grammar, p. 290.]* vary considerably, indicating the difficulty of finding an exact equivalent. For example, NRSV, NASB, and NEB: *be subject to*; NIV: *submit to*; KJV: *submit yourselves unto*; GNB: *submit yourselves to*; Goodspeed: *subordinate yourselves to*. As used here, the injunction is for wives to accept a lower position with respect to their husbands. This is not as an acknowledgment of their inferiority, but as a willing choice to defer to their husbands, in line with the prevailing social order.

A Christian motivation is attached. *As is fitting* sounds much like a phrase out of Greek Stoicism, but *in the Lord* establishes the criterion for what is proper. Some see here a Christian blessing on the hierarchical view of marriage. Others see voluntary subordination as expressive of being in the Lord, an ethic patterned after Jesus' own conduct.

Several questions beg for answers. Why did wives (and children and slaves, as we will see) need to be told to be subordinate? Where would they have gotten the idea that it could be any other way than what they had always known in that culture? Something must have suggested the possibility of relationships of a different kind.

3:19 Husbands

Husbands are handed a two-sided rule for their part in marriage. There is a positive side: *Love your wives.* The strong word for *love* (*agapē*), adopted by the Christian movement, means acting for the welfare of the other. The negative side is in stark contrast to love: *Never treat them harshly* (*pikrainesthe*). This term, stating what is prohibited, includes the meanings of becoming bitter, resentful, and incensed, and expressing these feelings in hurtful jabs. The text does not say whether these injunctions speak to besetting sins of husbands generally, or if Christian husbands were resenting the implications of their wives being persons, with minds and feelings of their own. As noted above, the grammatical details imply continuing action and thus the rule, "Keep on loving them, and stop being harsh with them" (EDM). (Cf. Eph. 5:25-33, which has a christological reason attached.) The rightness of *agapē* love hardly needs further proof. Love and harshness simply do not grow together. "The rule of love is always better than the love of rule" (Baggott: 121).

Family 3:20-21

3:20 Children

The term *children* refers to origin rather than to age, and it can be used of grown offspring. Here it likely means those growing up in their parental home. Again, the ones honored least in the relationship by the prevailing culture are addressed first. We may assume that the parents are Christians, although that is not said. This text does not apply to the situation where parental orders are contrary to faithfulness to Christ.

For children, the rule is, *Obey your parents in everything.* To obey (in a biblical sense) is to hear, as from a lower position, and to translate what is heard into action. Romans 6 argues that obeying sin makes one a slave of sin, and that obeying the gospel sets one free to be a slave of righteousness. Obedience also describes the expected response to the gospel, as in the language of "those who obey not the gospel" and "the obedience of faith." *Obey* is not identical to or interchangeable with the command to wives, *Be subject to.* Yet the latter verb occurs in Luke 2:51 and is often translated to say that Jesus was obedient to his parents. Obedience is the stronger concept. One may disobey a specific law of government out of a desire to obey God while being subject to governmental authority and accepting the consequences (Acts 5:29; Rom. 13:1). The stipulation *in everything* adds to the absolute nature of the command to children.

There is an attached reason for obeying parents: *For this is your acceptable duty in the Lord.* Literally, it means *For this is well pleasing in [the] Lord* (EDM). Conduct that pleases the Lord is the Christian rule for all of life (cf. Rom. 12:1-2; 14:18; 2 Cor. 5:9; Eph. 5:10; Col. 1:10). The phrase *in the Lord* has several possible meanings. The most likely sense maintains the parallel with the end of verse 18, emphasizing what is in line with the Lord's desires in the new community where Christ is Lord. Thus the appeal is to a higher motive than following social conventions.

3:21 Fathers

The expected counterpart to children would be parents, but the word is *Fathers*. Although in Hebrews 11:23 the same word obviously means parents (and is translated that way), fathers may well have been intentionally singled out in this domestic code (cf. Eph. 6:4), because of the almost unlimited power fathers had in the contemporary culture. Even though Roman fathers had absolute authority over their children, including power to sell them as slaves, we should not conclude that there were no kind, loving fathers among the pagans or the Jews.

The command to fathers here says only what they are not to do (cf. Eph. 6:4). The Greek word for *provoke* occurs only twice in the NT. In 2 Corinthians 9:2 it is used in a positive sense: to encourage, to stir to action. Here it has the negative sense of continually criticizing and nagging. As a counterpart of his command to children, Paul gives a word to fathers: *Act in a way that makes obedience easy* (EDM). He adds a specific reason: *or they may lose heart,* that is, so they do not become discouraged or dispirited. By implication, the Christian element in this pair of commands is to treat children as persons.

Slavery 3:22-4:1

3:22-25 Slaves

Paul assumes that slaves are an integral part of the household. Slavery as an institution is not discussed here or in parallel references. However, we cannot avoid the issue of Christianity and slavery in Colossians or in Philemon. *[Slavery, p. 317.]* Yet we need to begin study of this issue with what the text says to Christian slaves and masters rather than with the institution itself.

Christian *slaves* are addressed regarding their relationship with their masters, probably both Christian and non-Christian masters. The fact that they are addressed at all, and first, implies (1) their participation in the new community of faith and (2) a newfound freedom in Christ that accords them personhood and choice. Much more is said to slaves than to masters. This may reflect the relative numbers in the church or, more likely, the intensity of the questions being raised as slaves become fellow believers in Christ. Paul recognizes that the tension between freedom in Christ and the continuing reality of slavery deserves attention. This is new territory, not addressed in society's rules.

The same word, *kurios*, is used in Greek for Lord and for slave master/owner, and the word occurs frequently in 3:22—4:1. The designation *earthly masters* makes the reference clear and stands as a reminder that an earthly master is not the only "Master."

The fundamental rule is the same as the one to children (3:20): *Obey . . . in everything.* Paul's message to slaves is not to protest, strike, or revolt, but to obey. That by itself probably was not the expected or satisfying answer to the urgent questions of Christian slaves.

Next Paul expands how the Christian rule translates into daily life, negatively and positively. Full obedience will preclude obeying *only while being watched* and doing only what can be seen. Full obedience also precludes acting merely *in order to please them* (masters), or only calculated to gain approval and favor from the human master. Stated positively, *wholeheartedly* means without mixed motives, with simplicity, conscientiously, out of pure inward springs of behavior. (See 2 Cor. 11:3; Matt. 6:22-23, Jesus' words about the single eye.)

The phrase *fearing the Lord* is subject to misunderstanding. *Lord* in this instance most likely refers to Christ. "The fear of Yahweh" is a common expression in the OT, connotating awe and reverence rather than being afraid of Yahweh. Along with many occurrences of "Fear not" in the NT, the same attitude of reverence and respect toward God and toward Christ comes through (Acts 9:31; 2 Cor. 7:1; Eph. 5:21; 1 Pet. 1:17). The injunction to slaves is not simply to shift the locus of their dread of the consequences of disobedience from their human masters to Christ, even though future reward and judgment are factors (3:24-25). The primary incentive for obedient service is to be the life-motive of reverencing Christ.

Another command comes into the rule for slaves. This one takes the general statement in 3:17, *whatever you do*, and applies it specifically to slaves, *Whatever your task.* . . . The imperative is, *put yourself into it,* literally, *work out of [your] soul* (EDM). Somewhat like the concept "soul music," this expression speaks of "soul work." The wording lifts work from compulsory duty to enthusiastic service.

How is that possible? A new center of reference is offered, working as for the Lord, *as done for the Lord and not for your masters.* The work being done is still for humans, but this directive sheds new light on all work by Christians.

A supporting reason draws on previous teaching. To work as serving the Lord makes sense since the Lord is the one who is in charge of ultimate compensation and reward. Reward, rather than retribution, seems to be in view, although not as explicitly stated as in Ephesians 6:8. The recompense to come is further defined as *the inheritance*, recalling the words of 1:12. According to Roman law, slaves could not inherit anything and had no reason to expect any compensation. Thus it must boggle the minds of Christian slaves to hear that they will receive an inheritance as a reward from the Lord. In Christ there is indeed a whole new world!

The last statement in verse 24 requires interpretation: the same verb form can be indicative, *you serve the Lord Christ*, or imperative, "You are to be serving the Lord Christ." Many scholars favor the imperative, but the major translations have chosen the indicative. Although both are acceptable in context, it makes most sense to take it as an affirmation, in the indicative. A significant play on words is obscured by most translations. The word translated *serving* is the verb form of the noun translated *slave*; and *Lord* and *master* translate the same word. Thus we may read, *Slaves . . . you are slaves of your true Master, Christ"* (EDM). See Romans 16:18 for another example of the rare combination *the Lord Christ*.

Verse 25 also presents a problem. Is the warning, *the wrongdoer will be paid back*, addressed to slaves or masters? If it is for masters, it anticipates what follows, because they are not formally addressed until 4:1. If it is about slaves, it is the negative side of the future recompense (3:24). The principle is clear: those acting unjustly will receive back in kind from God, and this warning is applicable to both slaves and masters. Another complication: the statement about there being *no partiality* is attached to the part for masters in Ephesians 6:9, while here it is in the part for slaves. Perhaps the ambiguity is intentional. Another possible interpretation is that it is spoken to slaves about masters. From this angle it is a reminder that injustice is God's prerogative to deal with, and God decides fairly. This knowledge of God's certain justice enables the slaves to serve wholeheartedly, as to the Lord Christ, even when abused by earthly masters.

4:1 Masters

Paul's command to *masters* is brief but loaded. He does not tell them to free their slaves, but to treat them *justly and fairly*. His appeal is not for mercy or pity but for humane treatment. Masters are enjoined to do what is right and fair for those who have no legal rights. They have a moral obligation to see that equity, which goes beyond justice, is measured out to their slaves. Masters are the stronger party and thus responsible to look out for the rights of the weaker party.

As a motivational base, masters are reminded that they know they *also have a Master in heaven*. Christian masters cannot say, How I handle my slaves is my business, for it is the Lord's business. Both Christian slaves and masters are pointed to their Master, Christ. Loyalty and obedience to the same Lord must shape this as well as the other reciprocal human relationships.

The Domestic Codes do not answer all the questions we have about these several relationships. They are amazingly brief. Yet these directives are powerful examples of applied christological ethics. The picture of what the gospel looks like when we take it home has become clear. (Other NT references to slaves and masters are noted in the comments on Philemon.)

THE TEXT IN BIBLICAL CONTEXT
The Domestic Codes of the NT

The primary examples of the type of ethical teaching called *Haustafeln* (Domestic Codes) appear in Colossians, Ephesians, and 1 Peter. Comparing these texts, we find the following outlines:

Colossians 3:18—4:1	*Ephesians 5:21—6:9*	*1 Peter 2:13—3:7*
wives—husbands	wives—husbands	(Christian citizens)—
children—fathers	children—fathers	House servants—
slaves—masters	slaves—masters	wives—husbands

It can easily be seen that the version in 1 Peter is much different. The first part is for citizens, although they are not addressed as such, and no instructions are given to the government side of the pair. House servants instead of slaves are addressed, without a reciprocal word to householders. The Colossian and Ephesian texts are similar but far from identical. By comparing the texts, we may observe other similarities and differences. The version in Colossians seems to be the closest to the traditional core of the teaching, although the part to slaves is probably expanded. *[Ethical Lists, p. 287.]*

The form of the Domestic Codes is similar to OT laws, particularly a type known as "apodictic (categorical) laws." Their setting (*Sitz im Leben*) is the church in the first-century culture, a church that found new life and freedom in Christ. The faith supposition behind them is "Jesus is Lord." Several unique features need to be underscored. The fact that the "subordinates" are addressed at all and that they are addressed first is more than unusual; it is revolutionary. Wives, children, and slaves are addressed as persons, moral persons with choices.

Equally significant is the fact that the counterparts (husbands, fathers, and masters) also receive admonitions that bear directly on the relationships. Together the pairs of instructions function like a suspension bridge. The admonitions complement each other, and neither half is to be maintained in isolation from the other. To do so is to have half a bridge. Wives, children, and slaves are told to be subordinate or obedient, but those orders stand in a radically different light when seen as the complement of the exhortations to husbands, fathers, and masters.

Failure to appreciate the reciprocal nature of these teachings leads to unwarranted conclusions. Thus an injunction to one party does not excuse the other party from the same responsibility. Telling husbands to love their wives does not mean that wives need not love their husbands (cf. Titus 2:4). Likewise, the admonition to wives to be subordinate to their husbands should not be taken to mean that husbands therefore have no obligation to be subordinate to their wives (cf. Eph. 5:21; 1 Cor. 7:1-5).

The motivational factor is another feature that stands in sharp contrast to the social rules of that day. Stoics appealed to reason, the natural order, and self-interest. Christians are directed to their relationship with the Lord Jesus, in which respect for others, the teaching and example of Christ, Christian community, and imperatives are normative. The NT Domestic Codes are clearly on a different track.

(On the *Haustafeln* as part of the larger ethical teaching of the NT, see Essays *[Ethical Lists, p. 287.]*; Schroeder, IDB, Supp., "Lists, Ethical" and "Parenesis"; J. Yoder, *Politics of Jesus*, chapter 9, using two unpublished studies by Schroeder; and O'Brien, 1982:179-181, 214-18.)

In Search of an Equivalent Translation

A review of a dozen or so English translations reveals the difficulty in finding a serviceable rendering of the Greek word *hupotassō*. In 3:18, the NRSV renders this verb as *be subject to* (middle imperative form, *hupotassesthe*).

In its several grammatical forms, this word means the following: to place under, to subordinate, to subject oneself (voluntarily), to be subservient, to surrender one's own will and rights, to be subject. The word occurs thirty-one times in the LXX *[Septuagint, p. 316]* as a translation of ten different Hebrew words. In the NT, in thirty-eight occurrences, it also has a considerable range of meanings (as in Luke

2:51; 10:17-20; Rom. 8:20; 1 Cor. 14:32; 15:27-28; 16:16; Heb. 2:5-9 [quoting Ps. 8]; 12:9; James 4:7; 1 Pet. 5:5; plus texts including the codes surveyed above). Sometimes it refers to hierarchical order (1 Pet. 3:22) and sometimes to mutual submission (Eph. 5:21). It may reflect a compulsory arrangement or a voluntary one.

After we note illustrations of biblical usage, we still must find an appropriate English translation for the term in the Domestic Codes. Obedience may be involved, but "to obey" does not give the right sense. The most commonly used English words (*subject, submit, subordinate*) carry connotations that present communication problems. *Subjection* may suggest that someone is being put down. *Submission* may imply more passivity than it should. *Subordination* may suggest a higher and lower order of importance.

If we see the injunctions as calling for a voluntary stance of relationship, that does greatly modify any rigidity or harshness that the words may connote. The rendering of *The Jerusalem Bible*, "give way to," and the Bruce paraphrase, "defer to" (1965:257), offer several alternatives that may be strong enough, but not too strong. Unfortunately, preferences for one translation or another tend to be affected by what we want the text to say.

THE TEXT IN THE LIFE OF THE CHURCH
How Can the Same Text Support Opposing Views?

When we study Colossians 3:18—4:1, we soon encounter a perplexing fact. Some people use this and related texts to support a thoroughly hierarchical view of order in marriage, while others cite the same texts in support of an egalitarian view of marriage. This phenomenon is not limited to interpretations of what the Bible says about men and women. (See Swartley: 1983, for an analysis of the use of the Bible to defend opposing views on four social issues.)

Looking at this question from another angle, some see Paul as defending the status quo, while others point to revolutionary elements in the teaching. Further, some who understand Paul to be blessing the social order of the day sharply criticize him for failing to see and apply the implications of the gospel. Others find Paul simply being true to God's order for things, an order that goes back to creation.

Clearly, the issue is how the Bible is interpreted and used. Those who claim to expound what it says do not all have the same stance toward the Bible or employ the same methods for discerning its message. A primary factor is acceptance of the authority and integrity of the Bible. That will rule out a pick-and-choose approach. We must also challenge the assumption that the Bible is a flat book from Genesis to Revelation from which centuries later one can pluck selected texts and apply them as ready-made answers to all questions.

Authentic and faithful biblical interpretation results from following a number of important principles and guides. Some that are especially pertinent to the issue at hand are these:

1. Avoid selective use of the biblical witness. This means giving due emphasis and weight to all relevant texts. (For example, in the discussion of mutuality versus hierarchy in marriage and the meaning of Col. 3:18 for wives, it is important to consider 1 Cor. 7:1-6 and Eph. 5:21 alongside 1 Cor. 11:2-16 and Eph. 5:22-24.)

2. Be on guard against reading into the text what the interpreter wants it to say. This means hearing out the Bible as objectively as humanly possible even where it challenges cultural patterns or power positions.

3. Recognize tensions between some biblical texts as well as the basic unity of the whole. We can acknowledge diversity within the canon without sacrificing a high view of Scripture. It is better to work honestly with texts that do not seem to agree than to deny the possibility of tension or ignore it.

4. Look for the main emphasis of each text and section, and give priority to basic moral teaching and to theological principles. (Thus the wisdom of noting the reciprocal nature of each pair in the Domestic Codes, which points to treating others as persons rather than building a case from one of the commands.)

5. Respect the time and cultural gap between the text and the interpreter. This means not reading current meanings into the words of the Bible. It also means that when we say the Bible is historical revelation, we affirm both that it is historical and that it is revelation.

6. Keep in mind the missionary factor in the Bible. As we see the unfolding of the gospel of Christ in the context of changing cultures, we gain insight for participating as the gospel encounters varied cultures today.

7. Be accountable to the community of faith in the ongoing task of interpretation. Consistent with the emphasis on community that is explicit in Colossians, we should not regard interpretation as a private enterprise. Community discernment needs to include recognition of past understandings as tested by experience, the contribution of non-Western insights into the meaning of Christ and his people in the world, and the interpreter's own faith community setting.

(For further elaboration of issues and methods of interpretation, see Swartley, 1983:183-249; 256-269).

How Do First-Century Rules Apply Today?

The admonitions of the Domestic Codes are addressed to first-century settings, and they are somewhat shaped by local circumstances. Thus we cannot avoid the question, What relevance do these dated instructions have for us? The question becomes more complex when we recognize that marriage and family are part of the natural order of things, but slavery is now viewed as an imposed social order, even though it was assumed to be part of the natural order then. We now see the admonitions to slaves and masters relative to an existing social order in which slavery was taken for granted. By what rules of interpretation, then, do we consciously or unconsciously absolutize the codes having to do with marriage and family?

The way out of this woods is to emphasize *how* the early church addressed the issues of life in the world rather than the literal specifics of the various injunctions we find in the NT. If we work from the same christological base, we can both respect these texts in their historical setting and find direction in them for faithful living today.

The Gospel and Parenting

Parenting is an exercise in practical theology. This does not mean that parenting always reflects the parents' stated theology, but that an implicit theology is reflected in the way parenting is carried out. What shape will parenting take if the gospel truly shapes what parents do and do not do? The NT does not have much to say explicitly about parenting. The primary texts are in letters written to churches, a fact which implies the priority of the spiritual family over the biological family.

In the Domestic Codes of Colossians and Ephesians, we see the gospel intersecting with parenting. Colossians 3:21 in context opens a window on the issues of parenting. By way of review, the landscape includes (1) children being treated as persons, (2) reciprocal directives which call for parents who can be respected and obeyed without exasperation, (3) ethical teaching with roots in Christ's words and actions, and (4) the family imagery of the church.

Several issues arise if the gospel is to inform parenting. First, what is the gospel view of children? In contrast to the notion that human nature is essentially good, a widely held view that goes back to Augustine (A.D. 354-430) says that children inherit an evil and sinful nature and are damned unless they are baptized. A related view holds that little children are lost unless they confess their sins and ask Jesus to forgive them and come into their heart. The believers church perspective introduces a third category for children prior to an age of discretion and accountability: innocence. In this view children are "safe" in Christ's work and need neither baptism nor conversion. However, they do need to have their religious needs honored—needs for belonging, love, forgiveness, and worship.

Jesus' view of children should carry much weight for those who seek to apply the gospel to parenting. The occasions of Jesus blessing children (Mark 10:13-16) and of using a child as an example (Matt. 18:1-5) can tell us much about how Jesus viewed children.

The gospel is also relevant in the areas of discipline and punishment. Unfortunately, in common parlance discipline is considered a synonym of punishment. In biblical usage discipline includes some corrective actions, but it is basically a positive term, having to do with guiding, training, and encouraging. Thus the admonition to fathers is not to treat their children in ways that will be counterproductive in terms of the goals of Christian parenting. The views and practice of punishment need to be informed by a biblical understanding of God's ways. Christians who generally espouse nonviolence are sometimes inconsistent in their views of retributive punishment.

Children of Christian parents have a right to see integrity and consistency in their parents. As parents follow Christ faithfully, they can be the kind of models their children need. Martin Luther was not the only person to have difficulty addressing God as "Father" because of a bad experience with a human father. At the other end is the story of the twelve-year-old boy filling out a school questionnaire. He put his father's name on the line marked "father or guardian." On the next line asking for "relationship" he put "very good." When Christian parenting is kept in the context of the church, the spiritual family should provide models for children as well as parents.

Understandings and experience of the gospel of Christ will impact parenting, if the association is recognized. (For more on parenting, see Osborne: 1989; M. Yoder: 1984.)

The Early Church and Slavery

Christian writings following the NT (Apostolic Fathers) also call for

slaves to be obedient to their masters, and for masters to treat their
slaves with respect and fairness (Didache 4:10-11; Ignatius to
Polycarp 4:3; Ep. of Barnabas 19:7). Later, Chrysostom (347-407),
Augustine (354-430), and other church leaders critiqued the institution of slavery as arising out of sin. They urged the freeing of slaves
(McHugh: 855). (You will find further discussion of the church and
slavery in the Philemon section of this commentary.)

The Gospel in the Workplace

In much of the world, slaves and slave masters are not part of the social fabric as was the case in the first-century Graeco-Roman world.
However, slavery has been a social reality through the centuries in
various forms, and still is. De facto ownership of human bodies for
purposes of power and profit is far from absent in the modern world.
The church's response to institutionalized "slavery" will be discussed
more in connection with Philemon. The focus here is on the dehu-
manizing elements in society, particularly in the workplace.

Can we simply replace the words "slaves" and "masters" in the
Domestic Codes with the words "employee" and "employer"? In
some respects this seems like a natural way to contemporize these
texts. If both employees and employers function as if Christ is their
Employer, they would effectively apply the gospel to the workplace
relationships. Working honestly and wholeheartedly and treating
workers as persons in ways that are right and fair—this is consistent
with naming Jesus as Lord. There are many other motivating forces,
such as success, recognition, more money, ladder-climbing, and job
security exerting their pressures. Thus it is fitting that servants of the
Lord keep asking themselves, Why am I doing what I am doing?

Yet some may argue that this Christian idealism won't work in the
real world. Before we note how our world is different, we need to
recognize that the first-century world was also a real world. Admitted-
ly, the modern industrial society poses some tough questions for
Christian faithfulness. For instance, what is the Christian employee to
do when a slowdown is ordered by the union to which one must belong in order to work in that plant? What is the Christian employer to
do when facing competition, profits, and policies that stretch ethical
limits? Can systemic evil be confronted from within the system without compromising one's own standards? Where can either employees or employers go for help when facing difficult decisions in the
workplace?

In Colossians (and similarly in Ephesians) slaves and masters are both addressed in the context of *the saints and faithful brothers and sisters in Christ in Colossae.* Equal participation in the body of Christ brings with it a leveling effect. The community shaped around service to a common Lord should provide a safe place to talk, pray, and discern. Even then entrepreneurs and blue-collar workers will need to cultivate their common ground in Christ if they are to be of help to each other. Christians together need to flesh out what it means for Christ to be in Christ's people in the workplace.

Jim Halteman discusses the tension between the Christian and non-Christian value systems in economic matters. He points to the resources of the community of faith for facing the dilemmas in which Christians find themselves in their life and witness in the world. In Halteman's model the church is the basic unit for economic decisions. After illustrating the model with his own experience, he names four types of experience that express a strong conviction:

A congregation that believes in the dangers of materialism, a renewed joy in giving that comes from work on stewardship goals at the denominational level, a small group that attempts to practice the model I have described, and occasional involvement in inner-city churches in Chicago have convinced me that a believer must continue to swim upstream against the materialistic current of our time. It is not easy but it can be a joy, not a burden. The process is slow and uncertain, but somewhere behind it all is an awareness that life style and business practice are important areas of concern for the church in twentieth-century America. (91)

Colossians 4:2-6

Calling to Prayer and Witness

PREVIEW

A short paragraph of admonitions concludes the teaching part of the epistle. The Domestic Codes (3:18—4:1) are addressed to specific classes of persons within the church. These further words are for everyone in the church. A similar kind of teaching appears in several other Pauline letters (cf. Gal. 5:25—6:10; Eph. 6:18-20; Phil. 4:4-9; 1 Thess. 5:12-22).

The bottom line of Paul's admonition to this Lycus Valley church can be put in two words, pray and witness. These five verses distinctly direct the church to its mission outside of itself, with that mission based in prayer. Paul weaves together the practice of prayer and the practice of witness around his own immediate mission. These admonitions remind us of other parts of Colossians and of other texts of the NT. The structure of these verses is similar to the formulations of previous sections of teaching in Colossians.

OUTLINE

Prayer—Speaking to God About People, 4:2-4
    4:2   Urgency of Prayer
    4:3-4   Request for Prayer

Witness—Speaking to People About God, 4:5-6
    4:5   Lived Witness
    4:6   Verbal Witness

EXPLANATORY NOTES

Colossians 4:2-6 is an intricately constructed and highly unified composition. The details are significant. *[Grammar, p. 293.]*

Prayer—Speaking to God About People   4:2-4

4:2 Urgency of Prayer

The apostle's explicit command to the church is not simply to pray
but to *devote yourselves* to prayer. Prayer is assumed. The call is to
perseverance and constancy in prayer. Nearly identical wording is
found in Romans 12:12 and in Acts 1:14—the description of the believers after the ascension of Jesus. The same word for continuing
perseverance is used of the apostles' commitment to prayer and the
ministry of the word, in Acts 6:4. In contrast to fixed hours and set
patterns for prayer in Jewish and other religious traditions, prayer for
Christians is marked by devotion, resolve, and perseverance.

Two specifications for persistent prayer are *keeping alert in it* and
that it be *with thanksgiving*. Spiritual alertness fits with the overall
stance of the children of light. "Watch" is even one of the elements of
the instruction for new believers that we may identify in the NT. *[Ethi-
cal Lists, p. 287.]* "Watch and pray" were the words of Jesus to his
disciples. Watchfulness is frequently urged in view of the coming day
of the Lord. A sense of eschatological urgency may color the admonition here, even though it is not explicit. Much more than a reminder
not to fall asleep while praying, the call is to be intentional and vigilant about prayer. Prayer dare not become haphazard or perfunctory.

One more time, the seventh time, we hear the note of *thanksgiving* in Colossians. *[Thanksgiving, p. 322.]* This repeated emphasis indicates that for Paul thanksgiving was an essential component of
prayer. The letter itself (and the same is true of most of his other letters) begins with thanksgiving to God and then moves to intercession
on behalf of the Colossian believers. However, thanksgiving is not to
be thought of as proper etiquette, in which one should be careful to
show gratitude before asking another favor. Thanksgiving, in its own
right, is as much a part of Christian prayer as petition.

4:3-4 Request for Prayer

Verse 3 focuses on the intercessory aspect of prayer: *at the same time pray for us as well. [Grammar, p. 293.]* The words *prayer* (4:2) and *pray* are forms of the most frequently used word for prayer in the NT. Sometimes the meaning is narrowed to petition, and other times it conveys a general sense of prayer. (See TBC, "Synonyms for Prayer.") Paul asks that he and his associates (chiefly Timothy and Epaphras at that time) be included in the prayers of the saints at Colossae. Paul prays for others and asks for their prayer support.

Paul has precise prayer requests. Two purpose clauses, introduced with the word *that*, show Paul's priority of concerns at the time. Verbal proclamation of the gospel tops the apostle's agenda. Pray, Paul asks, that God may open a door of access for the word being spoken through human channels. Note that Paul does not see prayer as asking God to save lost people, but to facilitate witness. Even more than concern to make use of opportunities, Paul expresses his desire that God would make new opportunities. (Cf. Acts 14:27; 1 Cor. 16:9; 2 Cor. 2:12, and Rev. 3:8 for affirmations that God does indeed open doors for witness.)

Is Paul asking for prayer for him to be released from custody? It is not clear whether his circumstances are different from what we may gather from Acts 28:30-31 and Philippians 1:12-14. In general, Paul seems more inclined to use circumstances than to ask that they be changed, although he does refer to hindrances to his plans (Rom. 1:13; 15:22). His prayer request here is not explicitly in terms of his freedom or of any personal benefit.

Paul's stated mission is to *declare the mystery of Christ.* The term *mystery* in 1:26-27 and 2:2 is associated with God's word and Paul's ministry. *The mystery* (or secret) stands for what was previously hidden but now is out in the open. The heart of the revealed secret is that in Christ, Jews and Gentiles come together with equal access to the blessings of God (cf. "mystery of Christ," Eph. 3:4; "the mystery of the gospel," Eph. 6:19). Even though this central focus of Paul's message has resulted in his imprisonment, he continues to identify his message and ministry in these terms. *[Secret, p. 315.]*

In the first part of verse 3, Paul speaks for himself and his associates, *for us, to us,* but at the end of verse 3 and in verse 4 he speaks for himself only. (Observe the three occurrences of *I.*) He is probably the only one of them who is in prison. Where he is in prison is nowhere stated. (On the place of writing, see the Introduction.)

The second part of Paul's request is concerned with clarity in presenting the gospel of Christ. *It* refers to *the word* and *the mystery* all wrapped into one. God has revealed his mystery (implied in 1:26-27), but Paul keenly senses that God accomplishes that revelation through the medium of human preaching and teaching, and through himself in particular. Thus he asks for prayer that he might clearly and effectively speak the message. The word translated *declare*, verse 3 (repeated in Greek at the end of 4:4), conveys the thought of intelligible speech. "Articulate" is a useful equivalent if one does not focus on the mechanics of distinct pronunciation.

As I should (lit., *as it is necessary for me to speak*, EDM) reflects the obligation Paul senses. It could perhaps refer to Paul's binding commission to proclaim the message (Acts 23:11; Rom. 1:14-15; 1 Cor. 9:16). However, the wording here indicates concern about the manner of speaking. Such is a communicator's perennial concern—how to speak to be understood *clearly*.

By rallying the church at Colossae to pray for him, Paul calls the believers to share in the responsibility of an effective ministry of the word of Christ. As they support him in prayer, they participate in his ministry. Paul's thanks to the saints at Philippi for their "sharing in the gospel" (Phil. 1:5) has the same thought.

Witness—Speaking to People About God 4:4-6

4:5 Lived Witness

Paul has already been thinking about his own witness. With verse 5 the apostle's concern turns to the witness of the Colossian believers. The first level of witness is the witness of lives—lives lived before *outsiders*. The term *outsiders* reflects a Jewish way of speaking. When we ask, Outside of what? the answer seems to be, Outside the kingdom of Christ or outside the Christian community. It is another way of identifying unbelievers.

This is the fourth time we have come across the "walk" metaphor, variously translated as *lead lives* (1:10), *live your lives* (2:6), *living* (3:7), and now *conduct yourselves*. *Wisely* (lit., *with wisdom*) describes how Christians should behave toward non-Christians. *Wisdom* also occurs earlier in Colossians (1:9, 28; 2:3; 3:16). The wisdom to which Paul points stands in sharp contrast to what the false teachers boast of having, which, he charges, has only *an appearance of wisdom* (2:23). True spiritual wisdom is the application of a working knowledge of God's will in Christ. It is aptly connected with conduct here in 4:5 and in Ephesians 5:15: "Be careful then how you live, not as unwise people but as wise."

Making the most of the time translates three words with a literal meaning: *buying up the time* (EDM). The same three words, in a different order, occur also in Ephesians 5:16. The imagery of buying rests on commercial language. Possibly the slave-market action is in mind, in the sense of redeeming time and opportunity from the control of evil. This connotation fits with the added words in Ephesians, "because the days are evil." However, the more probable meaning here draws on the marketplace in general, in the sense of buying out the whole stock, or metaphorically, gobbling up every available opportunity. This word for time (*kairos*) carries the meaning of moment or opportunity, in distinction from another word (*chronos*) which indicates time as measured by clocks and calendars.

What connection is there between wise conduct toward outsiders and *making the most of the time*? A tension exists between wisdom (acting at the right time and in the right way) and urgency (seizing the moment because time and opportunities are not unlimited). Caution and enthusiasm need each other. So much is at stake that Christ's witnesses dare not slide off the road on either side.

4:6 Verbal Witness

Walk comes before talk, but talk needs to follow, and the two must give the same message. Verse 6 zeroes in on verbal witness as the corollary of visible witness. *Speech* translates the same Greek term as *word* does in verse 3. Here it has the broad sense of "what is spoken," including conversation as well as formal address. Paul notes two attributes of Christian speech. First, it is to be *gracious* (lit., *with grace*). Grace is a word with several meanings to be considered. In 3:16 the same phrase is commonly rendered *with gratitude/thanksgiving*. Awareness of God's grace may be intended here, but context and idiomatic usage at that time favor the sense of graciousness. Gracious speech replaces the speech sins of the second vice list (3:8; cf. Eph. 4:29). Paul specifies that speech should *always* be gracious: genuinely courteous, polite, and amiable, not put on as a congenial front when wanting to appear attractive. [Grammar, p. 293.]

Second, speech is to be *seasoned with salt*. The meaning of the figure is not immediately obvious. Pagan writers referred to salt in speech as wit. The speech of Christians no doubt should be interesting and compelling, but words like *clever, spicy, cutting,* or *coarse* go far beyond the intended meaning of salty. Evidence appears in rabbinic writings and in the church fathers of wisdom being associated with salt (Nauck: 165-178). This interpretation is attractive in that it matches wisdom with grace, parallels the reference to wisdom in regard to conduct, and leads into the last part of verse 6. The implication is that speech can be both gracious and salty.

Wisdom is of paramount importance in knowing *how . . . to answer everyone*. Relationships with outsiders continue to be in view. Paul seems to assume that Christian conduct and speech will result in questions being asked.

Paul's choice of words is well conveyed by NASB, *how you should respond to each person*. This indicates the necessity for personalized responses. People are searching for better answers, and they deserve answers that fit their questions. Lightfoot's rephrasing of Paul's teaching is worth quoting: "Not only must your conversation be opportune as regards the time; it must also be appropriate as regards the person" (233). Peter's admonition voices a similar concern: "Always be ready to make your defense to anyone who demands from you an accounting for the hope that is in you; yet do it with gentleness and reverence" (1 Pet. 3:15; cf. Matt. 10:19 and parallels).

Summary

Prayer and witness are basic to the existence and purpose of the church. These basics converge in the finale of Paul's message to the church at Colossae. Three entities interact in the process by which nonbelievers are confronted with the gospel. The three are intercessors (those who pray), God, and communicators (those who witness by life and word). How do these pieces of the action come together? Diagramed as a flow chart, it looks like this:

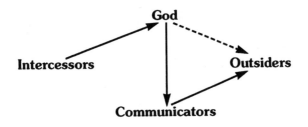

According to Colossians, responsibilities are distributed as follows:

Intercessors: be constant, alert, thankful
God: provide opportunities, enable communicators
Communicators: declare the word, be clear, act and speak wisely, seize the opportunities, be gracious, suit the message to the recipients.

These principles transfer into any time and place. The efforts of verbal communicators are futile if they do not:

1. Wisely answer the questions of seekers, rather than give canned speeches;
2. Have a matching, consistent life witness (their own and that of a visible community of faith);
3. Fully depend on and cooperate with God; and
4. Have the backing of faithful, vigilant intercessors.

THE TEXT IN BIBLICAL CONTEXT
Synonyms for Prayer

Five Greek words in the NT are translated (NRSV) as pray/prayer. In 4:2 Paul uses the one occurring most often (*proseuchomai/proseuchē*). It has the broadest generic meaning, although it is limited to prayer to God and sometimes signifies petition. It is also the most commonly used word for prayer in the LXX *[Septuagint, p. 316.]*, in which it almost always translates the most common of a dozen words for prayer in Hebrew. Only this one of the five is found in Colossians.

The second most-used word for prayer (*deomai/deēsis*) primarily refers to asking for benefits, but it is not limited to petitions to God. (See Luke 21:36; Acts 4:31; 2 Cor. 1:11; 1 Thess. 3:10.)

The other three words also do not carry sharply defined differences. *Entunchanō/enteuxis* is translated as prayer (1 Tim. 4:5) and as intercession (Rom. 8:27, 34; 1 Tim. 2:1; Heb. 7:25). *Erōtaō* (only the verb form appears in the NT) is mostly translated as ask. *Euchomai/euchē* is translated as pray/prayer (2 Cor. 13:7; James 5:15-16). The several words for prayer do not so much represent different kinds of prayer as prayer viewed from somewhat different perspectives.

Six additional words associated with prayer round out the vocabulary of the NT regarding prayer. Praying/prayer is viewed (with sample references) as giving thanks (Col. 1:3), invoking (1 Pet. 1:17), asking (John 14:13-14), appealing (2 Cor. 12:8), blessing (Matt. 26:26), and supplication (Heb. 5:7).

These synonyms and related words convey the prominence, breadth, and depth of prayer in the NT examples and teachings about prayer. Belief in and practice of prayer pervades the NT.

Pray, Watch and Pray, Pray for Us

The strong emphasis on prayer in 4:2-4 is much at home with the NT as a whole. Three comparisons are worthy of note: the call to pray, the combination of watch and pray, and specific requests for prayer.

Jesus commanded his disciples to pray for themselves and for others, notably persecutors (Matt. 5:44; 6:6; 24:20; Luke 18:1; 21:36). Paul also calls believers to pray (Rom. 12:12; Eph. 6:18; Phil. 4:6; 1 Thess. 5:17; 1 Tim. 2:1).

The combination of watchfulness and prayer is reminiscent of Jesus' words in the discourse about the future (Luke 21:36) and in the exhortation to his disciples in Gethsemane (Matt. 26:41). These two injunctions also appear together in Ephesians 6:18-20; 1 Peter 4:7; and 5:8. These and other references to watchfulness reflect one of the themes included in instructional materials. *[Ethical Lists, p. 287.]*

Along with repeated mention of his prayer for the churches, Paul again and again asks for prayer on his behalf, with a variety of specific requests. He greatly values the prayer support of the saints (Rom. 15:30-32; 2 Cor. 1:11; Eph. 6:19-20; Phil. 1:19; 1 Thess. 5:25; 2 Thess. 3:1-2; Philem. 22).

Insiders and Outsiders

The vocabulary of insiders and outsiders parallels a Jewish way of thinking and speaking. The outsiders, figuratively speaking, are foreigners, those banished and not recognized by the synagogue, or simply Gentiles. Jesus used the term with respect to those outside the kingdom (Mark 4:11). Paul uses these terms (1 Cor. 5:12-13; 1 Thess. 4:12; 1 Tim. 3:7), not in a derogatory sense, but as an honest and straightforward recognition of a basic division between unbelievers and believers. If we ask, Inside and outside of what? the answer from Colossians is, The kingdom of God's dear Son (1:13). Being "not far from the kingdom" is still outside. In God's eyes, the boundaries are clean.

Sadly, the boundary between insiders and outsiders has not always been defined in terms of faith and obedience and the kingdom of Christ. The designation "one of us" too often reflects ethnic and cultural identity, with overtones of superiority. White Western Christians especially have been guilty of such narrow, egotistical self-identity. Yet it is precisely this misuse of ethnicity that melts away when Christ is all and in all (3:11).

Several additional texts also emphasize the importance of faithful living on the part of insiders, because of the message which their behavior gives to outsiders (e.g., Phil. 2:14-15; 1 Tim. 6:1; Tit. 2:8; 1 Pet. 3:1-2; 3:16). Of particular concern is that God's name not be dishonored and that no stumbling block keep others from believing. The credibility of the Christian message depends on the behavior of those called Christians.

Colossians 4:2-6 and Ephesians 6:18-20; 5:15-16

Placing these texts side by side reveals amazing parallels and subtle differences:

Colossians	Ephesians	Unique Features
prayer	prayer	**Colossians**
devote yourselves to	always persevere	thanksgiving
pray	pray	God opening doors
keeping alert	keep alert	clarity of speech
for us	for me	outsiders
that	that	gracious, seasoned
open to us a door	open my mouth (lit.)	know how to answer
mystery of Christ	mystery of the gospel	
		Ephesians
in prison	in chains	supplication
as I should	as I must speak	all the saints
conduct yourselves	live	Spirit
wisely	as wise	boldness
making the most	making the most	ambassador
of the time	of the time	days are evil

Initial impressions point to much the same thought content being expressed in some of the same words, but each being modified by differences in time or circumstances (those of writer or recipients or both). More on the similarities and differences between Colossians and Ephesians, and the implications for authorship, can be found in the Essays. [Col. & Eph., p. 284.]

THE TEXT IN THE LIFE OF THE CHURCH
Witness as Walk and Talk

Like two rivers merging, faithful witness requires a confluence of walk and talk. Life witness (including both being and doing) and verbal witness are both necessary, and they must agree.

The prototype for authentic witness is Jesus Christ himself. In Jesus we find the epitome of the convergence of word and deed. He is the pattern for Christian witnesses. Particularly impressive is the way Jesus lived out and demonstrated what he announced and taught. He taught that people of the kingdom love and pray for their enemies, and he did just that. He taught compassion for the poor and oppressed, and he reached out to the outcasts of that day. If we begin with his words or with his life, we arrive at the same place, for they come together.

Both streams are necessary. Words about the gospel without demonstration in life can be tossed aside as empty rhetoric. Demonstration of kingdom living alone can serve to get attention and to raise questions, but by itself it does not explain that the source of the behavior is Christ in individuals-in-community.

Consistency of walk and talk is crucial. Conflicting signals are not only confusing, they also result in the gospel being discredited. Outsiders are quick to spot hypocrites in the church. They do not require perfection in Christians, but they do usually respect integrity. The blameless lives of Anabaptists presented a striking characteristic in the sixteenth century, recognized and confirmed by their critics and enemies. They were committed to living out the principles of the gospel in everyday life, and it showed. In 1582, a Catholic theologian commented:

> Among the existing heretical sects there is none which in appearance leads a more modest, better, or more pious life than the Anabaptists. As concerns their outward public life they are irreproachable. No lying, deception, swearing, strife, harsh language, no intemperate eating and drinking, no outward personal display, is found or discernable among them, but humility, patience, uprightness, neatness, honesty, temperance, straightforwardness in such measure that one would suppose that they have the Holy Spirit of God. (Franz Agricola, quoted by Horsch: 295-296)

In an essay entitled "The Missionary Vision and Activity of the Anabaptist Laity," Wolfgang Schäufele comments on the impact of the holy lives of "ordinary" members:

There is no doubt that the exemplary behavior of many Anabaptists gave a strong emphasis to their word-of-mouth appeals, and preached more loudly than the exegetically and theologically correct sermons of many a pastor who could not point to any "saints" in his church. (109)

Both Jesus' demonstration of witness and Paul's words in Colossians 4:2-6 underscore the need for articulate verbal witness. Knowing how to respond to seekers in their own life context, how to contextualize the gospel without compromising the message, how to communicate the good news of Christ clearly, and how to keep methods consistent with the message—these are essential ingredients for faithful witness.

An Example of Knowing How to Respond

About the middle of the sixteenth century, in Leeuwarden, then the capital of the Dutch province of Friesland, a boy of fifteen by the name of Jacques Dosie was imprisoned for his faith. On one occasion the lord and lady of Friesland had the boy brought before them so they could talk with him. When the lord needed to attend to other matters, the lady continued the conversation,

asking him why he, who was still so young, was thus severely imprisoned and bound.

Jacques answered: "This was done only because I believe in Christ, adhere to Him alone, and will in no wise forsake Him."

The lady asked him: "Do you not belong to the people who rebaptize themselves, perpetrate so much evil in our country, make rebellion, run together, and say that they are dispersed on account of the faith, and boast of being the church of God, although they are a wicked set, and cause great commotion among the people?"

Jacques. "My lady, I do not know any rebellious people, nor am I one of their number; but we would much rather, according to the teachings of the Scriptures, assist also our enemies, satisfy them, if they hunger and thirst, with food and drink, and resist them in no wise with revenge or violence. . . ."

Lady. "I consider this the worst thing in you, that you will not have the children baptized; for all Germany and every kingdom regards your doings as heresy."

Jacques. "My lady, it is indeed true that we are everywhere despised, and, like the apostolical band, evil spoken of in all the world; but do not think that such shall therefore perish at the last day."

Lady. My dear child, behold, I pray thee, come over to our side, and repent, and you shall get out of this trouble, and I promise to procure your release."

Jacques. "My lady, I thank you very much for your affection and favor towards me; but I will not change my faith, to please mortal man; unless it be proved to me with the Scriptures, that I err; for I have given myself entirely to God, to be His friend, and herein I hope to live and die."

The account concludes with these words:

> In this manner she had him brought before her many times; but as he, young in years, but old in the knowledge of Jesus Christ, had built his foundation upon the rock Jesus Christ, he valiantly repelled all the subtle devices of Satan—whether consisting in many severe threats, or in fair promises of the kingdom of this world—with the sword of the Spirit, which is the Word of God; and as nothing could move him to forsake Christ, he was condemned to death by the rulers of the darkness of this world, and thus testified and confirmed the true faith of the truth with his death and blood, and, through grace, obtained the crown of everlasting glory. (*Martyrs Mirror:* 498-500, Scripture references omitted)

Believers Church and Mission

The elements of witness, evangelism, and mission outreach are not prominent in Colossians. One could see 4:2-6 almost as an oh-by-the-way appendage. But we must remember that the incendiary nature of the gospel movement in the early church did not need a lot of motivational promotion. First-generation Christians do not need to be told to witness. They are keenly aware of the here and now of their experience (1:21-22; 2:12; 3:7), and they have a story to tell.

The sixteenth-century believers church movement gives evidence of a similar dynamic. The state church system, retained by the Protestant reformers, is not inherently missionary, except in claiming new territory for the state church. The Anabaptists, in contrast, were intensely missionary. They also were uniquely first-generation believers. Faith determined insiders and outsiders, not ethnic or institutional factors. Although they commissioned traveling missionaries, the movement spread largely because all members were internally motivated to share and spread the faith.

In *The Believers' Church*, Donald Durnbaugh deals with mission and evangelism:

> In the duchy of Württemberg in the sixteenth century, all of the Anabaptist men were expelled or executed. The government allowed only women with small children to remain at home. These they chained, however, to keep them from going to their relatives and their neighbors to witness to their faith, as the government had learned by experience was their custom. The Anabaptist women were considered to be as dangerous in spreading the illicit faith as their menfolk. (231-232)

Robert Ramseyer has made a strong case for mission being the only way to recover the Anabaptist vision. He proposes that the way to do that is to be so vigorously engaged in mission that first-generation believers are always a large proportion of the church.

> Thus the Anabaptist vision, the New Testament vision, can be recovered only in a group whose conscious orientation is to the first generation, to those who have made the radical step from the world to the people of God, to those whose allegiance has shifted from allegiance to the institutions of human society to faithfulness to Jesus Christ. Such a group is truly a people, the people of God; but the only marks of its peoplehood, the only cultural traits which its members have in common and which distinguish them from those who are not part of this people, are the marks which come directly from following Christ. (1984:182)

Prayer Linkages

Paul obviously takes prayer seriously. As we read Colossians 4:2-4, and similar requests for prayer in other letters to churches, it becomes clear that Paul is soliciting a network of prayer. He testifies that God has given him his ministry and that God is faithful. Yet he requests intercessory prayer, even from churches he has not visited. According to his letters, Paul also is seriously practicing prayer on behalf of all the churches.

Dare churches today take prayer any less seriously? Within congregations, prayer linkages support awareness of believers being a community while scattered in the world as well as when gathered. Prayer chains and hot lines help to facilitate prayer linkages. In the larger church setting, dedicated prayer partners undergird ministries around the world. Widely distributed prayer requests, with names and specific suggestions, help to facilitate an active prayer network. Yet if the church took prayer as seriously as Paul did, how much more this resource would be utilized. It is at least as important as monetary support. And, Paul would add, don't forget to give thanks!

Colossians 4:7-18

Maintaining Connections

PREVIEW

In characteristic fashion Paul ends the letter with references to a number of persons. He mentions both those with him at the time of writing and persons in the churches at Colossae and neighboring towns. Only Romans has a longer list of names. Although Paul has limited contact with the Lycus Valley, personal relationships are an important pastoral connection with the churches.

Paul includes personal greetings in his letters in a natural way. However, in addition to being friendly gestures, these personal notes have a preventive maintenance purpose in them, similar to routinely checking the hoses and wires under the hood of a car before there are known problems. The affirmations and two-way linkages suggest a strategy of intentional Christian networking.

This concluding section provides hard evidence that Colossians is written to an actual historical situation. The details supply valuable historical and biographical data. Although this section is about twelve persons out of the remote past, they are the characters in the real-life story of the spreading Christian movement about thirty years after Christ's ascension. This collage of clips from the story provides the modern reader with human linkages to the struggles and triumphs of the early church. Paul's reminder that the church is people with names has perennial value in itself. The pointers for co-worker relationships in the church are also of ongoing worth.

OUTLINE

Carriers of the Letter, 4:7-9

Greetings from Associates, 4:10-14

Personal Greetings and Instructions, 4:15-17

Autographic Conclusion, 4:18

EXPLANATORY NOTES

Carriers of the Letter   4:7-9

The two persons traveling to the Lycus Valley are not only to deliver the written correspondence but also to give an oral report of *all the news about* Paul. The letter of Colossians says little about Paul's circumstances, except that he is in custody. Once in each of these three verses, Paul mentions the oral update the messengers would bring (cf. Eph. 6:21, 22).

Tychicus, the primary messenger, is a native of the province of Asia (Acts 20:4), where, according to inscriptions, the name was common. As part of the third campaign, Tychicus was with Paul in Greece and preceded him to Troas. Acts does not say whether he was part of the entourage to Jerusalem. Paul sent Tychicus to Ephesus (2 Tim. 4:12), and he may have sent him also to Crete (Tit. 3:12).

Three affirmations serve to introduce Tychicus. (1) *A beloved brother* is an oft-used expression in the NT (Eph. 6:21; Col. 4:9; Philem. 16; 2 Pet. 3:15. Plural: 1 Cor. 15:58; Phil. 4:1; James 1:16, 19; 2:5). The connotation of spiritual family and the expression of warm affection is unmistakable. (2) *Faithful minister* is the same designation attributed to Epaphras in 1:7, with focus on function rather than a specific office in the church. (3) *Fellow servant (slave)* also describes Epaphras in 1:7, with the idea repeated in 4:12. The added phrase, *in the Lord [Titles, p. 323]* should probably be taken to modify *brother* and *minister* as well as *fellow servant*. All these designations have their source in the common experience of Christ. *[In Christ, p. 299.]*

A twofold purpose prompted the sending of Tychicus, beside delivering the letter or letters. One side of the purpose was telling them how things were with Paul. The other side was that he might *encourage* them. Fresh, direct news from Paul would reduce their anxieties. Even more, Tychicus would become part of the answer to the concern expressed in 2:2 that hearts be encouraged and united in love. Tychicus will encourage *(parakaleō)* and be the means for the Holy Spirit's strengthening (cf. Eph. 3:16).

Onesimus, although a common name especially for slaves, probably refers to the same person with this name in Philemon. However, no mention is made here of his being a runaway slave. The comment that Onesimus *is one of you* implies at a minimum that he is a native of Colossae. Since Paul says the same about Epaphras (4:12), likely a relationship with the church is implied. The further word about him echoes part of what Paul said of Tychicus. He is *the faithful and beloved brother.* Although going to the Lycus Valley for different reasons, these Christian brothers will both be welcomed bearers of news from and about Paul.

Greeting from Associates 4:10-14

Six persons (three Jewish, three Gentile) become active in this exchange of greetings. Five of the six are also included in the greetings section of Philemon. Along with passing along the greetings of these associates, Paul adds notes of affirmation and appreciation.

Aristarchus heads the list of greeters. Aristarchus is a Macedonian, a native of Thessalonica, who shows up as a travel companion of Paul. He may have come into Christian faith in connection with Paul's ministry in Thessalonica (Acts 17:1-9). Aristarchus was in the thick of things with Paul at the time of the riot in Ephesus (Acts 19:29), was part of the delegation accompanying Paul to Jerusalem (Acts 20:4), and was with Paul en route from Caesarea to Rome (Acts 27:2). On the reasonable assumption that Colossians is written from Rome, it is probable that Aristarchus continues with Paul to and in Rome.

Paul calls him a *fellow prisoner,* a term used as "prisoner of war." The same designation is used of Andronicus and Junia (Rom. 16:7) and of Epaphras (Philem. 23). Paul at times refers to himself as a prisoner, but never with the Greek term employed here.

One may debate whether the term as used here means literal imprisonment or carries a metaphorical sense (implying "prisoner of Christ"). Paul's fondness for the military idiom (Rom. 7:23; 2 Cor. 2:14; 10:3-5; Eph. 6:11-17; 1 Tim. 1:18; 2 Tim. 2:3-4) argues for *fellow prisoner* being equivalent to "fellow Christian." (The NEB rendering is *Christ's captive like myself.*) However, since the expression *my fellow prisoner* does not here have any qualifier such as "of the

Lord" (cf. Eph. 3:1; 4:1; 2 Tim. 1:8; Philem. 1, 9), the literal meaning may be intended. Aristarchus may have shared Paul's captivity voluntarily for companionship and support (Ramsay, 1896: 316).

Mark, identified and credentialed as *the cousin of Barnabas*, is no doubt the same person appearing as John Mark in Acts. Apparently the church at Colossae is well acquainted with Barnabas. The source of the *instructions* is not at all clear. Paul may be adding his affirmation to a communication from someone else, such as Barnabas or Peter. There is no way to know if Mark ever made it to Colossae. However, there is a story behind the reminder of the previous instructions to *welcome him* if he comes to Colossae. (See below, in TBC.)

Jesus who is called Justus is mentioned next. All that is known about him is here in verse 11. Jesus was a common name among Jews until the second century, when it was dropped almost entirely from use by both Jews and Christians, presumably because of the association with Jesus, the Christ. It is the Greek form of the Hebrew/Aramaic name Joshua or Jeshua. His hellenized name, *Justus*, was also a favored one among proselytes and Jews who took a second name (Acts 1:23; 18:7; cf. 13:9, Saul/Paul). *Justus* means "the Just" or "the Righteous." Two others in the NT have this name, one of those proposed to replace Judas (Acts 1:23) and a man who opened his house to Paul at Corinth (Acts 18:7). Paul includes four comments about these three colleagues:

1. They are *of the circumcision*, a term generally (but not unanimously) accepted as meaning Jewish Christians. In several instances the term identifies the faction that was insisting that Gentile believers needed to be circumcised (Acts 10:45; 11:2; Gal. 2:12). In other instances the term is broader and refers to Jews who have become believers in Jesus as distinguished from Gentile believers. Since the issue of circumcising Gentiles does not arise in Colossians, the generic sense best fits the context.

2. These three are the *only* believers of Jewish background who stay by and work with Paul at this time. One senses a note of pathos in Paul's comment.

3. Paul calls them *co-workers for the kingdom of God*. *Co-workers* implies more than fellow believers. They do not distance themselves from Paul (a prisoner and generally unwelcome by the Jews, Acts 28:17-28), and they involve themselves in his work and mission. *The kingdom of God* usually has a future reference in Pauline usage, while the present aspect is termed "the kingdom of Christ." However, notable exceptions to that distinction (such as

Rom. 14:17 and 1 Cor. 4:20) open the way for the intended meaning here to be the kingdom in its present reality. Next to the person of Christ, the kingdom of God is the shaping reality for life and work.

4. Finally, these faithful colleagues become a *comfort* to Paul. The word for the drug paregoric is derived from the Greek word translated here as *comfort*. It is a medical term for a tonic. The meaning here is consolation or soothing action.

Epaphras is the first of three Gentile associates who add their greetings. As 1:7 infers, he has brought the gospel to the Lycus Valley. At the time of writing, he is with Paul (in Rome). Paul has four things to say about him:

1. The expression *who is one of you* is identical to what is said with respect to Onesimus (4:9).

2. The identification *servant* (or slave) *of Jesus Christ* is a strong statement. The slave imagery signifies the extent of commitment to the lordship of Jesus Christ. Paul uses the designation for himself (Rom. 1:1) and for himself and Timothy (Phil. 1:1; cf. James 1:1, 2 Pet. 1:1; Jude 1:1).

3. Epaphras *is always wrestling in his prayers* for the believers at Colossae. The wording requires a strong translation. Our word *agonize* comes from the Greek verb used here. Paul describes the intensity of his effort on their behalf with the same term in 1:29 and 2:1, translated there as *struggle*. A word from the same family describes the fervency of Jesus' prayer in Gethsemane (Luke 22:44). The word is associated with prayer also in Acts 12:5 and Romans 15:30.

The substance of earnest intercessory prayers by Epaphras coincides with Paul's goal (e.g., 1:9-11; 1:28—2:3). References to maturity, assurance, fullness, and God's will echo major emphases in the first part of the letter, and certainly allude to issues at Colossae—issues that greatly concern Epaphras as well as Paul. The parts of this purpose clause (4:12b) are likely related in this way:

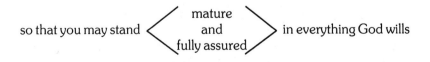

The potential of maturity echoes 1:28. *[Mature, p. 307.]* The compound word translated *fully assured* sometimes means "completed"

or "filled" (2 Tim. 4:5, 17) and sometimes "convinced" (Rom. 4:21; 14:5). Scholars are divided on the meaning here. Both nuances make sense, for Colossians stresses fullness in experience and firm conviction in contrast to inferior promises being offered. This reminder of the potential in Christ—completeness and full conviction in the whole will of God—emphasizes again the superiority of the gospel of Christ.

4. Paul adds a further tribute to Epaphras; he is a hard worker. More seems to be implied than that he works hard at prayer. We may assume that he has been the bearer of the gospel to Laodicea and Hierapolis as well as to Colossae (1:7). (See the Introduction on the proximity and relative location of the three cities of the Lycus Valley.)

Luke is with Paul, as he has been on and off earlier, according to the "we" sections of Acts (16:10-17; 20:5—21:18; 27:1—28:16). Here Paul calls him *the beloved physician*, which has led to the supposition that he is attending Paul as a personal physician. Luke is listed with fellow workers in Philemon 24, and as the sole companion of Paul in 2 Timothy 4:11. The fact that Luke is not included among those *of the circumcision* (4:11) is primary evidence that he is a Gentile. His native country is uncertain. Acts makes it seem probable that he is from Macedonia, even though a second-century prologue to Luke identifies him as from Antioch in Syria. A man named Lucius appears in Romans 16:21 as a relative of Paul, and a Lucius of Cyrene is listed in Acts 13:1, but it is unlikely that either of these is Luke.

The training of physicians in that day was closely supervised, with training centers at Tarsus, Athens, and Alexandria, though not much is known about the competencies of a first-century physician. His contribution as a colleague with Paul in the spread of the gospel goes far beyond his medical skills. He is best known as the author of Luke and Acts. It is fascinating for us to realize that the writers of both the Second and Third Gospels (and Acts) are together with Paul at the time when he is writing Colossians.

Demas is listed with only a name, no comment. In Philemon 24 he is part of those identified as fellow workers. Later Demas deserted Paul because he was "in love with this present world" (2 Tim 4:10).

It may be noted that Timothy is not among those sending greetings although he is included in the salutation (1:1).

Personal Greetings and Instructions 4:15-17

Paul makes a curious request. He asks the Colossian Christians to convey his greetings to the Laodicean Christians, but according to verse 16 the Laodicean church is also receiving a letter. A possible explanation is that Paul means for the ecumenical exchange to cultivate interchurch relationships. *Nympha and the church in her house* are singled out as recipients of Paul's greetings. Whether the name is feminine or masculine is determined largely by the pronoun modifying house. *[Text, p. 319.]* A church in someone's house was common in that era (Rom. 16:5; Philem. 2). *[House Churches, p. 297.]* Not until the middle of the third century did churches own property for assemblies. *Church* in these verses refers to a local assembly or congregation, in contrast to the universal meaning in 1:18, 24.

It is generally agreed that Nympha was at Laodicea. The wording of verse 15 (in Greek and in English versions) leaves open the possibility that there were two assemblies at Laodicea, one designated as *the brothers and sisters in Laodicea,* and the other *the church in her [Nympha's] house.* Thus there may well be several smaller house assemblies in the city that also meet as a whole, called in verse 16 *the church of the Laodiceans* (cf. Rom. 16:23, where Gaius hosts the whole church). The exact circumstances at Laodicea cannot be reconstructed from the available evidence.

Several baffling questions arise in verse 16 with reference to the exchange and reading of certain correspondence. What is *the letter from Laodicea?* Who wrote it? What happened to it? Why the directive to exchange and read the letters? Widely diverse opinions have been held through the centuries. (For a survey of the many ideas on this, see Lightfoot: 274-300.)

The phrase translated *from Laodicea* means the letter *that is at Laodicea* (Blass-Debrunner: sect. 437), not a letter from the Laodicean church. The repetition of *also* implies two letters of similar origin. Our best reconstruction is to see *the letter from Laodicea* as a letter from Paul to Laodicea that was also to be read at Colossae. Apparently Paul thinks the immediate conditions are such that there would be benefit in both letters being read in both settings.

The several references to reading indicate a practice of reading letters aloud before the assembly of Christians (see 1 Thess. 5:27 as an example of similar instructions). The same word was used for the reading of the OT in assemblies for worship.

The question of what happened to this Epistle to the Laodiceans has generated a lot of discussion. A Latin letter by that name has been judged to be a forgery fabricated toward the end of the fourth century. One view is that the letter to Philemon is the one referred to in Colossians. However, this view has Philemon living at Laodicea rather than at Colossae. This theory has not gained much support. Colossians 4:9 connects Onesimus with Colossae, and presumably that is also true of his master, Philemon. A more serious option identifies the letter with what we know as Ephesians, a letter now generally considered to have been intended for a circuit of churches in Asia Minor. Conceivably, the churches in the Lycus Valley could have been among the recipients of Ephesians. However, scholarly opinion places the writing of Ephesians after Colossians. *[Col. and Eph., p. 284.]* Reference to it in Colossians is therefore unlikely.

The conclusion of most commentators is that the letter in question has not survived. One guess about how it was lost is that it perished in the earthquake in the area in A.D. 60-61. In retrospect, the data indicate that three pieces of correspondence from Paul came into the Lycus Valley, one to the church at Colossae, one to the church at Laodicea, and the private letter to Philemon.

A special message is to be given to Archippus. We puzzle over why it is in indirect form rather than direct, with Paul addressing Archippus himself. One suggestion is that he lives at Laodicea rather than at Colossae. But Archippus is one of the persons included in the opening greeting in the letter to Philemon, along with Philemon, Apphia, and the church in Philemon's house. This scenario puts Archippus at Colossae. Perhaps Archippus needs words of encouragement from the whole congregation.

Archippus no doubt understands what Paul means by *the task that you have received in the Lord*, even though modern readers have no way of knowing the precise nature or content of the assignment. Here a specific *task* (lit., *ministry*, not as an office but a particular responsibility) has been received *in the Lord*. By adding *in the Lord*, Paul identifies the source and elevates the importance of the task. Perhaps Archippus is the successor to Epaphras as leader of the church at Colossae. (Another proposed reconstruction of the scene is explored in the comments on the letter to Philemon.)

Autographic Conclusion 4:18

Paul puts the final words in his own handwriting. The implication is that the letter up to this point has been dictated (cf. Rom. 16:22, where the secretary, an amanuensis, is named). Paul usually, perhaps always, concludes his letters in his own handwriting (as is explicitly evident also in 1 Cor. 16:21; Gal. 6:11; 2 Thess. 3:17; Philem. 19). Besides it being a personal style of the apostle, it also serves to make the letter genuine (cf. 2 Thess. 2:2, indicating forgeries).

The plea, *remember my chains*, is not a cry for pity, nor is it likely a reminder of his credentials of authority, for Paul has not made an issue of his authority even in the more confrontive sections of Colossians. It may be a request for prayer, although he does not make his imprisonment a subject for prayer in 4:3. Perhaps it is best to see in these words a reminder of the seriousness of life in Christ, thus encouraging depth of commitment and faithfulness on the part of the recipients. A plausible mental picture is that as Paul takes the pen to add his own greeting, the chains fastened to his wrist(s) are rattling.

The letter ends with a short, customary greeting. The final words are usually translated *Grace be with you,* supplying an implied verb *be* that makes the statement a benediction. The letter ends on this note of *grace. [Text, p. 319.]*

THE TEXT IN BIBLICAL CONTEXT
A Glimpse of Church Life

The final block of Colossians provides a verbal video clip of activity in and between first-century Christian congregations. Among the activities described and implied are these:

    corresponding (letters being written and delivered)
    traveling (messengers going great distances, if Paul is at Rome)
    gathering in assemblies
    reading letters before assemblies
    exchanging letters with another congregation
    oral reporting
    welcoming visitors
    praying/interceding
    supporting/encouraging
    expressing warm greetings

Greetings

Two-thirds of the NT letters include the terminology of "greet/greeting(s)"—all except Galatians, Ephesians, 1 Timothy, James, 2 Peter, 1 John, and Jude. Colossians has five occurrences. In the culture of the first century, people who met face to face greeted each other with an embrace, a kiss, or a handshake. Greetings were also expressed in other symbolic actions and in words.

In the Gospels we read of the rabbis enjoying public preferential greetings (e.g., Matt. 23:7). In his instructions to his disciples, Jesus attached considerable significance and power to greetings (Matt. 10:12-15; Luke 10:5-12). A greeting of peace could be conferred and withdrawn. Apostolic greetings are extended when arriving at and departing from a church (e.g., Acts 18:22; 21:6). NT letters normally begin and end with greetings. Paul apparently endorses a convention of the day. However, for him it becomes more than a customary formality. Greetings express affection. Paul adds a distinctive, personal touch with his handwritten greeting.

The exchange of greetings in the Pauline letters enhances a network of relationships between individuals and congregations. We may surmise that when a congregation hears a letter read asking that greetings be given to a named person, the greeting is acted out right then. One expression of mutual greeting among believers was "a holy kiss/kiss of love" (Rom. 16:16; 1 Cor. 16:20; 2 Cor. 13:12; 1 Thess. 5:26; 1 Pet. 5:14). Ecumenical greetings between congregations (as in Rom. 16:16 and Phil. 4:22) must surely have strengthened a bond of unity among the Christians scattered over the empire.

The John Mark Story

John (Mark) was with Paul and Barnabas on the first journey, to Cyprus and then on to the mainland in Pamphylia. John, as he is called in Acts, was along "to assist them" (Acts 13:5). Luke's choice of words indicates that John was an authority on the tradition about Jesus. (Luke uses the same term in Luke 1:2, translated as "servants of the word," along with eyewitnesses as sources of information about Jesus.) Peter likely trained John in the tradition about Jesus.

John left Paul and Barnabas and returned to Jerusalem. Why he decided not to continue with them "in the work" (Acts 15:38) is never explained. But reading between the lines, it seems probable that because of his close ties with the church at Jerusalem, he was not in agreement with Paul's acceptance of Gentiles without circumcision. After the Jerusalem conference (Acts 15), Paul refused to take John (Mark) along with him. Paul and Barnabas sharply disagreed about the matter, and as a result parted company. Barnabas does not appear again in the record until Paul mentioned him in 1 Corinthians 9:6, with no hint of the former rift. Mark does not appear again until mentioned in Colossians 4:10 and Philemon 24.

By piecing together the several brief references to John Mark, it seems likely that he had at least some acquaintance with Jesus. Mark's mother Mary owned a house where the early Christians gathered (Acts 12:12). That house may have been the location of the upper room where the believers gathered prior to Pentecost, and the guest room where Jesus met with the twelve for the Passover and Last Supper (Mark 14:13-15). Was Mark the man carrying a jar of water, and the one who escaped the soldiers, but without his clothes (Mark 14:51-52)? These are intriguing possibilities. If this is an accurate reconstruction, Mark, a resident of Jerusalem, could have had some contact with Jesus. (See Swartley, 1981:27-38, for a more extensive reconstruction of the John Mark story, and Appendix 1 of the same book for historical references to John Mark.)

Later Mark was valued by both Paul and Peter (2 Tim. 4:11; 1 Pet. 5:13). If, as seems plausible, Mark wrote the Second Gospel from Rome, he would have had access to both Paul and Peter. Colossians 4:10 has Mark among Paul's associates. Two reasons may have prompted Paul's affirmation of Mark. The practice of the early church to extend hospitality to traveling Christians was highly commendable, but also a source of problems. The Didache, an early second-century church manual on church life, gives explicit instructions for testing traveling teachers (11—13). Apparently there were charlatans who took undue advantage of Christian hospitality. Now Paul assures the Colossian church that Mark is okay. A second reason rests on the assumption that the church knows about the earlier dispute over Mark. Paul, therefore, makes sure that nothing out of the past will get in the way of Mark's acceptance.

The Person Paul Was

This final section adds a great deal to what Colossians says about Paul. The letter as a whole indicates what kind of person Paul was:

1. *A people person.* As in other correspondence, the names of colleagues and acquaintances were important to Paul. So was an exchange of news about personal circumstances. An aroma of personal caring permeates the letter.

2. *An appreciative person.* He had a warm way of identifying persons and he mentioned those who had been a comfort to him. This reveals a person who deeply appreciated the loyalty and kindness of those who stayed with him.

3. *An affirming person.* Many affirmations of character and con-

tribution surround the names of persons mentioned. What he said about Epaphras is a prime example.

4. *A team person.* Although Paul was more of a leader than a follower, he saw his ministry as shared with co-workers and fellow servants in the Lord. These verses indicate that he strongly supported his colleagues.

5. *A church person.* Far from being a free-lance preacher out there doing his own thing, Paul assumed church relationships as integral with the gospel. He worked at both intracongregational and intercongregational relationships.

6. *A spiritually concerned person.* What he affirmed in Epaphras was his own priority as well. His pastoral-care concern about maturity led to warning people, as well as building them up in the faith.

7. *A praying person.* The letter as a whole shows that Paul as well as Epaphras prayed earnestly for the Lycus Valley believers.

8. *A kingdom-oriented person.* When he lauded several associates who stayed with him as co-workers for the kingdom of God (4:11), he revealed his own orientation and priority.

9. *Christ's person.* This obvious characteristic colors all that Paul was and was doing.

A Servant (Slave) of Jesus Christ

This designation for Epaphras (4:12) carries meanings that may not be self-evident. A survey of usage helps to illuminate the concept. Paul uses the same identification for himself (Rom. 1:1; Gal. 1:10; Phil. 1:1). The term also occurs in James 1:1; 2 Peter 1:1; and Jude 1.

The Greek word for servant (slave), *doulos,* is the most common rendering in the LXX *[Septuagint, p. 316] of "servant" of God (Heb. ebed).* The exclusive nature of the relationship to God which the term conveys is borne out in Jesus' pointed words, "No one can serve two masters" (Matt. 6:24). Servant (slave) of God occurs rarely in the NT (Tit. 1:1 and James 1:1), but servant (slave) of Jesus Christ appears frequently, and in several forms.

The Greek term *doulos* is one of several related terms. *Diakonos* (translated servant, minister, deacon) emphasizes the servant function (Matt. 20:26; Col. 1:7, 23, 25). *Therapōn* (Heb. 3:5) denotes one who renders a particular service, often voluntarily. *Oiketēs* designates a household slave or domestic (Acts 10:7). *Hupēretēs* (lit., an under-rower) is used of one in a subordinate position (Mark 14:54). *Doulos* is the primary word for slave, with emphasis on the relationship between slave and master.

Two verb forms of this word family appear in the NT, *douleuō* (to be a slave, to perform the duties of a slave, e.g., Col. 3:24) and *douloō* (to enslave, to become enslaved, e.g., Rom. 6:18, 22). English versions often use "servant" for *doulos* unless the context clearly indicates human slavery. (NASB consistently uses "bondslave.") However, in passages such as Romans 6:16-23, the stronger term "slaves" is commonly used for relationships both to sin and to righteousness. Obedience determines enslavement (cf. John 8:34). The death and resurrection of Christ makes possible release from enslavement to sin, impurity, iniquity, passions, pleasures, and the elements of the universe—and freedom to come into a new obedience.

Jesus himself modeled the slave relationship. The confession found in Philippians 2:6-11 says he "emptied himself, taking the form of a slave." He also assumed the slave role when he washed his disciples' feet, an action which Jews hired Gentile servants to do. An extension of the paradigm "slaves of Jesus Christ" is the call to be slaves of one another in love (2 Cor. 4:5; Gal. 5:13).

"Welcome" in the NT Vocabulary

Paul reminded the church at Colossae to welcome Mark if he came there. The term *welcome* represents a specialized vocabulary in the NT having to do with receiving someone or something. The words are *lambanō* (plus two compound forms) and *dechomai* (plus six compound forms), widely distributed throughout the NT. (*Lambanō* usually conveys a broad meaning of receiving and taking. Our interest here is in usage that reflects a more intense meaning.) Some uses of these words have to do with hospitality, extending social amenities (e.g., Acts 17:7; 28:7). The early-church practice of hospitality for traveling Christians is reviewed more fully in comments on Philemon 22.

Several related uses throw light on Colossians 4:10 (and Philemon 17). (1) The words may refer to receiving Jesus himself, with varying degrees of seriousness and depth (e.g., Matt. 10:40; Luke 8:40; John 1:12; 5:43). (2) Two of the words frequently describe receptivity to the gospel message (e.g., Acts 2:41; 8:14; 11:1; 1 Thess. 1:6; James 1:21). (3) The words describe accepting persons with open arms, minds, and hearts—going beyond gracious hospitality. Illustrations of persons to be welcomed include bearers of the gospel message, persons given recommendation by known leaders, and fellow believers in general (Luke 10:8-10; Acts 15:4; Rom. 15:7;

16:2; Gal. 4:14; Phil. 2:29; 3 John 8, 10).

Welcoming is a serious matter. Believers were admonished not to welcome those whose teachings are false (2 John 10-11). Jesus made a connection between welcoming his commissioned disciples, welcoming himself, and welcoming God who sent him (Matt. 10:40; John 13:20). Thus Paul laid down his rule: "Welcome one another, therefore, just as Christ has welcomed you, for the glory of God" (Rom. 15:7). Therein is the measure and the motivation for Christian welcoming.

Grace as the Final Note

All thirteen of the letters attributed to Paul have a closing benediction that includes grace. Most of them have grace as the only ingredient, although several also include one or more of the following: peace, love, fellowship. Other general letters have a benediction that focuses on peace or none at all. Colossians 4:18 (along with 1 Tim. 6:21, and 2 Tim. 4:22) has the shortest form, and 2 Corinthians 13:13 has the longest.

The strong note of grace in the benediction is much more than the musical embellishment called a grace note. Without grace, God's grace in Jesus Christ, there is no gospel, no new life beyond limited self-reformation, no potential for genuine community and church, no forgiveness and reconciliation, no sure hope. As an element of the greetings in NT letters, grace is much more than a cliché or formality. Grace sounds the fundamental tone of the gospel chord.

THE TEXT IN THE LIFE OF THE CHURCH
Culturally Transferable Concepts of Church

A twentieth-century congregation in any part of the world, whether rural or urban, is a long way from the young first-century congregation in a city in the interior of Asia Minor to which Colossians was written. Since the circumstances then were so obviously different from those of most Christian churches today, what understandings of church arising out of 4:7-18 have modern value?

1. The church was viewed as people, not as an organizational structure or a developing institution. In an age when church structures are taken for granted, congregations and denominations need to hear the reminder from the early record that the church is people.

2. The church functioned as house fellowships. Both the family

nature and the relatively small size fostered a close-knit relationship among the members. Now, when church buildings are an option as they were not in the early centuries, more intimate clusters within the larger assembly can provide an essential experience of being the household of God.

3. Church leaders considered themselves servants, servants of the Lord and of the church. Certain persons were recognized as leaders, but without the trappings of office and hierarchy characteristic of the power structures of this world.

4. The kingdom of God gave shape and purpose to work in the church. Rather than being built around a human leader or a doctrinal distinctive, the early church found its identity and mission in being a local expression of the kingdom of God.

5. Interpersonal and intercongregational relationships provided mutual support and accountability. False notions of self-sufficiency and independence, as evidenced in individualism and congregationalism, keep persons and churches from the strengths and safeguards of a network of strong relationships, such as Paul fostered in the Lycus Valley.

6. Ongoing concerns for encouragement, maturity, assurance in God's will, and grace kept the church from complacency and stagnation.

7. The church moved forward in dependency on prayer. *[Church, p. 283].*

Working for the Kingdom of God

The designation *co-workers for the kingdom of God* (Col. 4:11) offers one focused way to express the goal of the efforts of Christians. Are we working first of all for the kingdom of God? This is a discriminating question that needs to be asked. Not all energy expenditures in the church seem to meet such a criterion. For the question to be useful, we need to have a clear understanding of what the Bible means by the kingdom of God. *[Kingdom Theology, p. 300.]*

Keeping a vision of the kingdom of God before the church will help to preclude several distortions and tangents. A certain amount of organizational structure seems inevitable and necessary, but church leaders need to avoid building empires of power. Programs are part of the church's life, but they dare not become the tail that wags the dog. Church buildings have become the way of life for churches in developed countries, but physical plants are not the kingdom of God.

Kingdom consciousness also provides several other values and safeguards. Working for the kingdom of God can keep the church from becoming provincial and sectarian. The concept includes the key foci of peoplehood and mission, inner group life and outward thrust into the world. Social as well as spiritual relationships are integral to the kingdom. We can evaluate both past performance and future projections in reference to kingdom values and goals. If we remember what we are working for in the church, that can go a long way in monitoring how church work is done, to ensure that the ways of working are consistent with kingdom objectives.

Interceding for Churches

The example of Epaphras (Col. 4:12) stands as a direct challenge for us to engage in intercessory prayer today. He prayed specifically and intently for a church. Releasing the power of God on behalf of churches through intercession is a spiritual activity too often reserved for times when all else has failed.

"History Belongs to the Intercessors"

Walter Wink asserts: "Intercession is spiritual defiance of what is, in the name of what God has promised. . . . In our intercessions we fix our wills on the divine possibility latent in the present moment, and then find ourselves caught up in the whirlwind of God's struggle to actualize it" (1992:298-304). Present circumstances will shape the content of intercession within the broader focus of prayer for God's reign coming and God's will being done on earth. The kingdom of God as a frame of reference serves to keep the human agenda aligned with the divine agenda.

In order to be a viable counterculture in the world, the church in its local expressions needs intercessors of the Epaphras kind who pray the future into being. Both the high calling of the church and the strangling grip of the powers [Powers, p. 308] require a network of faithful intercessors, not as a last resort but as a strategy of first priority.

Church Leaders Working Together

Church splits have generally occurred more because of clashes between leaders than because of substantive issues. Although the ver-

bal exchange may have focused on some aspect of doctrine or practice, the rift too often came as a result of key persons not being willing
to be reconciled with each other and work together.

The narrative that surrounds the final section of Colossians reveals leadership attitudes and actions that foster healthy relationships. Certainly there were problems. Paul's differences with John
Mark resulted in a parting of the ways with Barnabas as well. Colossians 4:10 indicates that reconciliation has taken place, the details of
which we do not know. Verse 11 seems to suggest a sense of disap-
pointment in some unnamed persons who either failed to identify
with Paul or left him. At least some of the hassles that often crop up in
interpersonal relationships among leaders are reflected in the story.

In Colossians the vignettes of various colleagues in ministry indicate no pecking order. Although Paul rather obviously was a key figure and expected his teaching and instructions to be respected, in
Colossians he did not flaunt his apostolic authority. In 1 and 2 Corinthians and Galatians, Paul did assert his authority from God to be
heard and to act. In those churches the integrity of the gospel hinged
on the integrity of apostleship. As noted in connection with Colossians 1:3-8, Paul demonstrated that he was a team person.

Competition, jealousy over turf and power, and empire building
are notably rare in what the records say about early church leaders.
The several instances of failure stand out in bold relief. Behind that,
we find a picture of leaders experiencing a healing of strained relationships and complementing each other in ministry in the kingdom
of God. The example of the early church is a rebuke of present-day
power struggles among leaders in the Christian church, and it is an
encouraging challenge for us to tap the redemptive potential in working together.

Synthesis: The Letter to the Colossians

Colossians touches on a wide range of topics. The breadth of interrelated themes becomes almost overwhelming for the reader and student of this letter. The subjects include Christian experience (conversion and growth), evangelism, nurture, church, leadership and ministry, baptism, suffering, the mind, prayer, ethics, interpersonal relations, marriage, parenting, kingdom, the powers, false religions and cults, hymnody, holiness, maturity, and many more. There are few issues faced by Christians-in-community in the world that are not touched on in Colossians.

Christology

Colossians discusses theology, but not in an academic way. In Colossians theology comes through as a way of understanding God's actions through Christ, with respect to the universe, the powers, the church, and individual Christians. Although it is all God's doing, the focus is on Jesus Christ. More than anything else, Colossians is about Christ. As the Christology of Colossians unfolds, with its far-reaching splendor, one can see why the panorama of topics comes into the discussion.

A notable feature of the Christology of Colossians is the vocabulary in which it is couched. Terms used include kingdom, redemption, forgiveness of sins, firstborn of all creation, all things (created, held together, to be reconciled), firstborn from the dead, preeminent, fullness, reconciler/making peace through the blood of his cross, fleshly body, afflictions for the sake of the church, church as his body, mystery of God, triumph over all powers and authorities, reality (contrasted with shadow), seated at the right hand of God, the Lord Christ, peace of Christ, word of Christ, name of the Lord Jesus, and more.

Conspicuously absent in the words and concepts of Colossians are a number of terms commonly used in talking about what God has done through Christ. For example, the vocabulary of Colossians does not include Savior/save/salvation, justification, righteousness, substitutionary atonement, law, satisfaction, foreknowledge, predestination, or new birth. Before quickly supplementing or forcing the vocabulary of Colossians into the thought forms and language of any particular theological tradition, we should listen carefully to the Christology of Colossians in its own terms.

The picture of Jesus Christ in Colossians is a composite of the overlays of several perspectives. Here is how we see Christ in Colossians:

1. *The preeminent Christ.* The Christ-hymn, 1:15-20, repeatedly affirms the priority and supremacy of Christ. Echoes are heard in 2:9-10, 17, and 3:1.

2. *The cosmic Christ.* Colossians breaks out of the confines of parochial human thought to reveal the one through whom and for whom all things were created, and who is before all things. This universe with whom Christ has to do includes the principalities and powers and the elements of the universe (1:13, 15-17; 2:15, 20). The work of Christ is greater than individual redemption and the creation of the new community, the church. It deals with estrangement and the power of sin in the cosmic arena. Victory encompasses all created reality.

3. *The redeeming Christ.* In addition to the specific affirmation in 1:14, a strong note of freedom can be heard in 2:13-23. Forgiveness and redemption come by way of the cross, Christ's death. The counterpart of deliverance from the realm of darkness is transference into the kingdom of Christ, into the new community of the redeemed.

4. *The triumphing Christ.* The key text is 2:15, which presents Christ as the one through whom God has exposed and disempowered the powers and accomplished a decisive victory over them through the cross.

5. *The reconciling Christ.* The reconciliation motif stands out in

1:20-22. Alongside the cosmic dimension of God's intent, the relational impact of Christ's death is also put in personal terms. Reconciliation is an implicit corollary of the mystery that brings Jews and Gentiles into the new creation.

6. *The revealing Christ*. Christ, as the image of God, reveals who God is (1:15). As the one in whom believers come to fullness, he reveals the human potential (2:9-10). The virtues to be put on (3:12-14) are the qualities found in Jesus.

7. *The nourishing Christ*. Growing, bearing fruit, and going on to stability and maturity—these all have their source in Christ. There is imagery of Christ as rootage and foundation, of believers being attached to Christ the head, and of the word of Christ dwelling in the community. All these affirm Christ as the source of life (2:6-7, 19; 3:3-4, 16).

8. *The adequate Christ*. The repeated appeal in 2:8-23 amounts to this: With all that is yours in Jesus Christ, why would you regress to inferior and worthless allurements? Contrasts between human philosophy or tradition and Christ, in whom the whole fullness of deity dwells; between shadow and substance; and between counterproductive do-it-yourself rules and the freeing Christ—these declare loudly the sufficiency of Christ.

Paul directed attention in Colossians to a holistic Christology. The affirmations about Christ and what Colossians says about the relevance of Christ for human experience lead to this conclusion. The significance of the wholeness of the Christology of Colossians can be seen by considering the gospel of Christ in five separate but interrelated sectors:

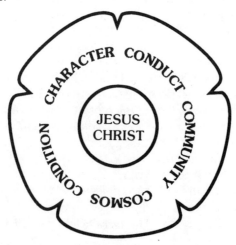

(1) *Condition* refers to what is commonly called status or standing with respect to God (1:14, 21-22; 2:13-14; 3:3). (2) *Character* refers to regeneration or inward transformation, expressed in Colossians as dying and rising spiritually and as change from the old self to the new self. (3) *Conduct* refers to behavior, the new walk. (4) *Community* has to do with the new collective reality which we call the body of Christ, the church, the family of God. (5) *Cosmos* identifies the relationship of Christ to "all things," the universe, the world (2:20).

The message of Colossians is that each sector is an integral and interrelated part of the whole. Christologies that fail to keep them all included and in balance, distort and misrepresent the gospel of Christ. When any one or a combination of several sectors predominate so as to depreciate or exclude any of the others, the gospel is in danger of becoming perverted. If one part of the gospel receives all the attention, even that part becomes deformed. The several parts are profoundly interrelated, and none are optional components of the gospel of Christ.

When we view the gospel as dealing almost entirely with a saved condition/status as a result of justification, we may conveniently distance or exclude the other elements from what is considered the basic work of Christ. The gospel message, then, becomes limited to release from guilt and assurance of heaven. Inner and outer change, the lordship of Christ, the demands of the gospel, and participation in the church of Christ come later, if at all. Consideration of Christ as the cosmic Christ is relegated to eschatology. Persons are told they are "saved" without being changed, discipled, or incorporated into the visible body of Christ. This "gospel" does not come from Colossians. Reconciliation is a key concept in the gospel according to Colossians.

When the gospel is viewed primarily as a matter of new birth or of a second blessing, experience becomes the central focus. Subjective experience becomes the evidence of God's work without adequate concern for the observable fruits of the new life and the new community of reconciliation. Questions about the nature and rightness of an individual's experience dominate the agenda, and theology is based on experience more than on biblical revelation and the discernment of a Spirit-led body. When emphasis on inner character dominates the scene, good intentions easily become a substitute for obedient living. The excitement of discovering deeper and previously untapped levels of spiritual experience should not be allowed to overshadow or displace the other equally significant aspects of the Christ-centered gospel.

When primary attention is narrowed to conduct, without due emphasis on the other facets of the whole gospel expounded in Colossians, people get the idea that being a Christian is a matter of adhering to a code of behavior. The crucial difference tends to be lost between discipleship as response to God's grace and conformity to the behavioral code as a means of being accepted by God (self-righteousness). Norms of conduct are all too easily set by tradition and the social mores of the particular group rather than having lifestyle and ethics shaped by Christology.

An emphasis on discipleship does not need to shift to legalism, but sometimes it has. C. S. Lewis (1960:175ff.) has effectively pointed out that "niceness" must not be separated from "newness" in an understanding of what it means to be a Christian. Concerns about Christian ethics are too often limited to private morality and private decisions about right and wrong. Issues of social ethics then receive little attention. Individualism interferes with the community of faith being the locus for moral discernment and support. These perceptions of morality and ethics do not reflect the teaching of Colossians or the NT as a whole.

When the community facet overshadows the other essential ingredients of the gospel, being a Christian may be perceived as basically a matter of church membership. The practice of baptizing babies rests on concern for the spiritual condition of babies and their belonging to the covenant community. But those who baptize infants fail adequately to consider the relation of personal belief to character and conduct. Reaction to this *corpus christianum* (state church) view has given rise to the term "born-again Christian," as if there could be any other kind. Christian community should provide support for living with inner direction. But, with an unbalanced emphasis on church, social pressure imposed by the group (outer control) becomes a substitute for inner control.

Primary focus on the cosmic Christ has the danger of making the gospel impersonal and distant from day-to-day human struggles. Most Christians need to be pushed out of their cozy, provincial cocoons and catch a vision of the Christ of the universe. But this exhilarating view of Christ does not readily translate into how one gets along with a spouse or equip one to reach out to a woman torn apart by postabortion guilt. The Christ who is triumphant over the powers and who is the agent of the reconciling of all things—this one is relevant to both personal and public life.

Deficiencies show up in one sector at one time and in another sector at another time. The balance between salvation and discipleship has tipped both ways. In late twentieth-century Western circles, individualism has become an obstacle to community in Christ. Unity, interdependence, and other related aspects of the gospel are ignored when individualism dominates the assumptions brought to the Bible and life.

Texts such as 1:15-20 and 2:9-10, 13-15 serve to correct narrow perceptions of the gospel that are all too common. The gospel that includes the cosmic Christ enables Christians to understand the unfriendly world and their own participation in Christ's mission in the world.

The whole ministry of Christ needs to shape the life and mission of the church. Colossians provides insights that will profoundly affect worship, prayer, life, and witness.

Pastoral Theology

A note of pastoral concern pervades Paul's letter to the Colossians. Through prayer, teaching, warning, and personal interest, the apostle gave practical substance to his pastoral theology. In Colossians we can observe what gave rise to Paul's concern for the Lycus Valley churches, the intensity of his concern, and the approach he took to assure spiritual health and progress.

Although the threatening influences in first-century Asia Minor are not identical with those experienced by Christians nineteen centuries later, the generic factors are remarkably similar. Based on what is known of the religious streams of the first century and from what may be deduced from Paul's critique in Colossians, a mixture of religious ideas posed a threat to the church. That brand of syncretism, the combining of various religious and philosophical ideas, seems to have borrowed from Greek philosophy, Eastern mystery religions, rabbinic Judaism, elements of Jewish thought modified by Greek influence (Hellenism), and local Phrygian expressions of religious paganism. [Religions, p. 313.]

A dangerous concoction of ideas seemed to offer a superior and more sophisticated view of life and the world to young, first-generation churches. The teachings were no doubt seductive and confusing because on the surface they were billed as an improved version of Christianity. According to Paul's analysis, Christology was the core issue. The added features actually devalued Christ in insidious and devious ways. Rather than being an improvement, the syncretic teachings led to a regression. The new religion was not only inferior; it resulted in a return to a deeper bondage to the powers.

Many contemporary fascinations are of a similar nature and attract people away from Christ: a variety of cults with their seductive perversions of the gospel of Christ, a lively interest in astrology and parapsychology, the mockery of satanism, wicca, witchcraft, and other dabblings into the supernatural, both ascetic and libertine values, the revival of human-centered mysticism drawing on Eastern religious practices, New Age influences, and neopaganism. Factors common to the first-century milieu include the mixture of religious streams, an aggressive appeal to those not thoroughly grounded in Christ, and an implicit if not explicit lowering of Christ. People may be confused by finding that in some of the current perversions of the gospel, not everything that is taught is totally wrong.

Paul's approach models a pastoral strategy for any age. First he makes a strong affirmation of spiritual health, a powerful reaffirmation of the excellence and adequacy of Christ, and a reminder of the seriousness with which he engaged in his ministry to the church. Next he brings several warnings and an exposé of the dangers involved. He strongly appeals to believers not to regress, and then he instructed and encouraged believers to keep on advancing in their individual and collective potential in Christ. Specifics about what to avoid—and why—seemed to be an important part of the antidote, but the bulk of Paul's response focused on positive teaching and encouragement. The wisdom of Paul's response commends itself as a pastoral strategy for helping Christians cope with today's confusing religious allurements. Paul's approach is helpful for equipping believers to recognize serious deficiencies in the gospel proclaimed by some avowed Christians and to spot the perversions of the gospel by various cults.

Mission

The agenda for those under the lordship of Christ goes beyond survival and includes mission. Although mission in the world is not given a specific mandate in Colossians, Paul assumes that participation in the spread and growth of the gospel movement is normal for those who have become believers-in-community. Enthusiasm for the gospel in a first-generation church needed only to be encouraged. Paul's testimony concerning the intensity with which he invested himself in his calling inspires involvement in the mission of Christ and the church.

Colossians offers a remedy for the lack of enthusiasm that characterizes the way the church often engages in its mission in the world. A dispassionate attitude about the relevance of the gospel of Jesus Christ results in a lethargy about mission. Paul reminded the church at Colossae of the uniqueness and superiority of Christ and the gospel. A fresh discovery and appreciation of the excellence of the gospel of the cosmic Christ, as portrayed in Colossians, stirs up mission fervor in any age.

Outline of Colossians

Philemon

A Letter of Love and Faith

Approaching Philemon

Philemon is the shortest of the letters carrying Paul's name, made up of 335 words in Greek. It is addressed to a *dear friend*, with no church responsibilities mentioned. Thus it is different from the pastoral epistles (1 and 2 Timothy and Titus), which are also written to individuals, but to recognized church leaders. Because Philemon is personal correspondence and Paul's shortest letter, it has been placed at the end of the Pauline letters in the NT canon. Third John is the only other NT letter to an individual that does not overtly deal with church matters. If a distinction can be made between letter and epistle, this is a letter. It is not entirely private, however. A church community is acknowledged both directly and indirectly. Although Paul does not specifically refer to himself as an apostle in this letter, a note of acknowledged apostolic authority comes through. However, Paul chooses not to exercise all the authority he knows he has.

All of the NT letters are more or less culturally and historically specific. A personal letter like Philemon is especially localized and dated. Since Philemon is in a class by itself in the Pauline collection, it is natural to wonder how it came to be included. We may reasonably suppose that Paul wrote other personal letters, but only Philemon has survived. One explanation comes by way of Ignatius, bishop of Antioch, in an epistle written in the second century to the churches of Asia Minor while he was on his way to Rome to be executed. There he identifies Onesimus as the bishop of Ephesus (*Ignatius to the*

Ephesians, 1:3). If this is the same Onesimus mentioned in Colossians and Philemon, Onesimus himself might be the link for getting the letter to Philemon into the collection of Paul's writings. Although Onesimus was a common name and Ignatius did not connect the Onesimus of Ephesus with the Onesimus of the NT, the possibility exists.

The Story Surrounding the Letter

We do well to recognize that a narrative underlies the letter to Philemon. However, not all the details of the story are given or are clear. Any reconstruction of the sequence of events referred to and implied in Philemon requires some interpretive decisions and imagination. According to the traditional understanding, Onesimus was a slave of Philemon who lived in Colossae. Philemon was known to Paul, likely having heard and responded to the gospel when Paul was in Ephesus. Onesimus ran away from Philemon's household, maybe stealing from his master when he left. He made his way to the big city, Rome. In some way he came in contact with Paul, who was in custody there. As a result Onesimus came to Christian faith and became a valuable help to Paul.

Paul wanted to have Onesimus continue as an associate with him in the service of the gospel, but he had neither a moral nor a legal right to retain him. So he sent him back home with this letter, requesting that Philemon receive him as a Christian brother, hinting that Onesimus be set free or returned to Rome to assist Paul, or both. The inclusion of the letter in the NT implies that the request was granted.

Several alternate versions of the story, with variations, are afloat. In the reconstruction proposed by Edgar J. Goodspeed and championed by John Knox (cf. also Lamar Cope), Onesimus was the slave of Archippus, rather than of Philemon. The letter was sent to Philemon as the overseer of the Lycus Valley churches. Colossians 4:17 is a key text in this view, mentioning a message for Archippus about completing the task he received in the Lord. This is taken as a direct reference to the request in the letter we know as Philemon, but there identified as *the letter from Laodicea* (Col. 4:16).

These interpreters do not agree on whether Archippus (and Onesimus) lived at Colossae or at Laodicea. The charge to be conveyed to Archippus (Col. 4:17) is seen by some to make more sense if he were not at Colossae. The reference to Onesimus as *one of you* (Col. 4:9) does not settle the matter of location if the Lycus Valley was considered to be one large community. Paul had the letter sent to Philemon and read to the church (implied from the church being included in the salutation, Philem. 2) to put additional pressure on Archippus. In this version of the story, Paul's goal was to have Onesimus come back to work with him after receiving his freedom.

Another attempt to fit the pieces together has been suggested by Sara Winter. Rather than Onesimus being a runaway slave, Winter proposes that he was a sent slave, sent to work with Paul. The letter was to the church, with Philemon as the church leader. The point of the communication was that Onesimus was no longer to be considered a slave in the Christian community. He was to be set free, and also to return to work with Paul.

Before making an assessment of the several versions of the story behind Philemon, we need to take into account all the relevant details of the text.

The Author of Philemon

Three times in the letter the author calls himself Paul (1, 9, 19). All of the evidence indicates that Philemon was included in the earliest collections of Paul's letters. It was part of the canon of Marcion (mid-second century) and of the listing in the Muratorian Canon (late second century). Only a few scholars have challenged its genuineness as a letter from the apostle Paul. About the only reason why its authenticity has been questioned at all is its obviously close connection with Colossians. If the content and style of Colossians is considered to require a date of writing later than Paul's time, then, it is argued, Philemon must also be later. However, the deductions can just as well support the argument that if Philemon is genuinely Pauline, then Colossians must also be by Paul.

The Affinity of Philemon and Colossians

The names common to these two pieces of correspondence attest to a common place and time of origin and a common community destination as well as common authorship. Nine persons are named in both: Paul, Timothy, Archippus, Onesimus, Epaphras, Mark, Aristarchus, Demas, and Luke. Although each letter mentions additional persons and the content of each is markedly different, Philemon and Colossians are uniquely linked together even though separated in the NT arrangement of Pauline writings.

Both letters were written while Paul was in custody. In both letters he refers to his *chains* (rendered *imprisonment* in Philem. 10). The where and when of that imprisonment are the same questions encountered with respect to Colossians (cf. "The Author and His Circumstances," pp. 24-26). Because of the relative proximity of Colossae and Ephesus (100 miles), an imprisonment at Ephesus is a possibility, one held by some highly respected scholars. However, Paul's first confinement at Rome runs into the least difficulties as the place and time for writing both Colossians and Philemon. An approximate date is A.D. 60.

Both letters speak to the slave-master relationship but in different ways. The household code in Colossians (3:22—4:1) and the personal appeal of the letter to Philemon complement each other.

Why Philemon Invites Our Attention

This brief letter does not deal with apostolic doctrine or with the challenges of church leading. Instead, it deals with Christian living in a particular social context. It addresses one social dimension of the new kingdom (Col. 1:13). A comment by Martin Luther reveals that reformer's appreciation for Philemon:

> This epistle gives us a masterful and tender illustration of Christian love. For here we see how St. Paul takes the part of poor Onesimus and, to the best of his ability, advocates his cause with his master. He acts exactly as if he were himself Onesimus, who had done wrong. Yet he does this not with force or compulsion, as lay within his rights; but he empties himself of his rights in order to compel Philemon also to waive his rights. (quoted by Lohse: 188)

Along with being an example of efforts to influence behavior, Philemon opens windows into the character of Paul. This brief letter greatly enhances our knowledge of the Christlike person Paul was.

The letter to Philemon addresses slavery on a personal level. In doing so it illumines how the early church came to process issues of the gospel and culture. From our distance we find ourselves wanting to ask why the apostle did not directly attack the institution of slavery. *[Slavery, p. 317.]* Philemon is an important part of what Paul did say about slavery, even though it does not answer all our questions about what he did not say.

A further significance of the Letter to Philemon is what it reveals about early church life. References to the house church and to experiences of koinonia are noteworthy. A related point of interest is the repeated reference to interpersonal spiritual refreshment. These and other matters addressed in the letter are topics for inquiry in a careful reading of Philemon. (See the Author's Preface and " A Letter Exalting Christ," pp. 15-27, for information about features of the commentary, the primary Bible version used, and the expository approach.)

Philemon 1-3

Salutation

PREVIEW

Paul's letter to Philemon is unique, but not because of the format of the salutation (or of the letter as a whole). It is written in the conventional pattern for letters of that time. (See comments on Col. 1:1-2.) However, within the formality of the introductory words, two details of content effectively establish the tone of the letter: (1) the way the author identifies himself, and (2) the way he addresses the recipients. Both what is said and what is not said become significant.

OUTLINE

Author, 1a

Recipients, 1b-2

Blessing, 3

EXPLANATORY NOTES

Author 1a

The self-descriptive phrase, *a prisoner of Christ Jesus*, is unique in the salutations of NT correspondence. Most times Paul labels himself an apostle. It is noteworthy that when he approaches Philemon as a peer, Paul does not call attention to his apostleship as a way of pulling rank. On the other hand, it is not in keeping with Paul's character to call attention to his imprisonment as a way to elicit pity.

Paul, it must be noted, considers himself a prisoner of *Christ Jesus*, not of Rome or of Caesar. This detail is Paul's way of saying that he is in custody because of his identity with Christ.

As in Colossians (and in 1 and 2 Thess., 2 Cor., and Phil.), Timothy is included in the salutation as an associate with Paul. The expression *I, Paul*, in the body of the letter (vv. 9, 19) shows that Timothy is not a coauthor. Since Acts 19:22 establishes that Timothy was with Paul in Ephesus, Timothy may be well-known by Philemon and others in the Lycus Valley. Although Paul often speaks of Timothy as "my son," here (and in 2 Cor. and Col.) he calls him *our brother*. *Brother* becomes a pivotal word in the letter (note vv. 7, 16, 20).

Recipients 1a-2

Paul lists three individuals and a house church in his salutation. Since he puts the names in grammatical parallel, it is not entirely clear who is to receive the letter. Further complicating the picture is the fact that in the phrase *to the church in your house*, *your* translates a singular pronoun. It is not clear, however, whether *your* refers to the person just named, Archippus, or to the person named first, Philemon.

The majority opinion is that Paul addresses the letter to Philemon. As noted above, Knox and others contend that Archippus is the primary addressee. Although Knox's view cannot be flatly rejected, the traditional understanding commends itself as the better choice. Bratcher and Nida offer this paraphrase to convey the likely intent: "To you, Philemon, our friend and fellow worker, and will you extend greetings to the church that meets in your house and to our sister Apphia and to our fellow soldier Archippus" (115).

From Paul's warm words we gather that *Philemon* is a valued friend and in some way a colleague in the work of the gospel. The ascription "beloved," here rendered as *dear friend*, occurs dozens of times in the NT. References to Philemon's love (vv. 5, 7) fill out a picture of a man and a community of love.

By calling Philemon a *co-worker*, Paul draws attention to their labors together in the kingdom of God. Since Philemon is not mentioned other than in this letter, the details of their joint efforts can only be surmised. Paul apparently never visited Colossae (Col. 2:1). His extended stay at Ephesus (Acts 19:1-20) is the most likely time for Paul to have become acquainted with Philemon. Not only does

Philemon come to Christian faith through Paul, he may also be engaging in an evangelizing ministry with Paul's encouragement and direction, even during Paul's time at Ephesus. In verses 7 and 20 Philemon is called *brother*.

Apphia is a name found frequently in Phrygian inscriptions. Paul calls her *our sister*. *Sister* refers to spiritual kinship; the designation is used also for Phoebe (Rom. 16:1). An intriguing conjecture is that Apphia is the wife of Philemon and that Archippus is their son. The order of the names here suggests the possibility, but it has no supportive evidence other than it has been a long-standing conjecture.

Archippus, mentioned here and in Colossians 4:17, receives the affirmation *fellow soldier*. In Philippians 2:25, the metaphor is also applied to Epaphroditus and there coupled with brother and co-worker. It connotes endurance and discipline in the spiritual warfare. Paul counts Archippus as a colleague in encountering the powers with the gospel (see on Col. 1:15-20 and 2:6-23, above).

Although the salutation includes *the church in your house*, it need not be deduced that the letter is to be read to the church. That kind of pressure would not be consistent with the tone of the letter. We assume that the church meets in the house of Philemon at Colossae, rather than in the house of Archippus (at either Laodicea or Colossae), as argued by several scholars. Since Philemon's house serves as a meeting place for a congregation, he is likely of above-average means. *[House Churches, p. 297.]* Including the church in the greeting serves to remind Philemon that he is part of a faith community and that his decisions are not purely private matters.

Blessing 3

The blessing is the same as in the salutations of Romans, 1 and 2 Corinthians, Galatians, Ephesians, Philippians, and 2 Thessalonians. The *you* is plural, which in this case means that it is extended to all mentioned above. Rather than the usual word of greeting in Greek culture (Acts 15:23; 23:26; James 1:1), Paul adopts a related word, *grace*, one full of Christian meaning. *Peace* represents the Greek word for the common Hebrew greeting shalom. The combination is richer than the words used independently. Grace is the ground of God's blessing; peace—with the meaning of restoration and wholeness—is the outcome. In these introductory blessings, the prayer is not for grace and peace to begin, but that the beneficiaries apprehend more fully what they are already experiencing.

Grace and peace do not come out of thin air. Almost always Paul specifies the source as *from God our Father* (1 Thess. being the only exception). When using only one address for God, Paul (and presumably the early church) says *our Father*. Jesus was the primary source of this Christian understanding and relationship (Matt. 6:9). (Cf. 1 Cor. 8:6 and Eph. 3:14 for elaborations on God as Father.) The additional words, *and the Lord Jesus Christ*, appear in all of the opening blessings except those in Colossians and 1 Thessalonians. The connecting word *and* is an affirmation of equality between God the Father and the Lord Jesus Christ. But rather than suggesting two deities, the additional words mean that the Lord Jesus Christ is the means of receiving grace and peace from God. Since "Lord" had many meanings in the Greek world (e.g., owner of slaves, the emperor, a respectful greeting equivalent to Sir), the full name/title leaves no question of identity.

THE TEXT IN BIBLICAL CONTEXT
Paul's Primary Self-Identifications

Paul does not always identify himself the same way at the beginning of his letters. Several times Paul calls himself "a servant (slave) of Christ Jesus" (Rom., Phil.) and "a servant (slave) of God" (Tit.). More often he introduces himself as "an apostle of Christ Jesus" (2 Cor., Eph., Col., 1 & 2 Tim.), "an apostle of Jesus Christ" (Tit.), "called to be an apostle" (Rom., 1 Cor.), or as "an apostle" (Gal.). Four times he specifies that his apostleship is "by the will of God."

At the beginning of his letter to Philemon, Paul identifies himself as *a prisoner of Christ Jesus*. The same designation, a prisoner of (for) Christ Jesus, or of (in) the Lord, also appears in several places other than in salutations (Eph. 3:1; 4:1; 2 Tim. 1:8). His use of a related term, translated imprisonment or chains (Phil. 1:7, 13-14, 17; Col. 4:18; 2 Tim. 2:9), helps to confirm the meaning. In all these instances, a physical confinement is undoubtedly meant, rather than a metaphorical bondage to the Lord. The expression "servant (slave) of Christ Jesus," however, is metaphorical.

Paul's choice of a primary self-identification seems to correspond with how he wants to be perceived by the readers. The three terms, *servant* (slave), *apostle*, and *prisoner*, have connotations appropriate to the various recipients of the letters. *Servant* (slave) is the most neutral of the terms, one that is equally applicable to all believers. *Apostle* calls attention to a right to be heard because of credentials from God. *Prisoner* brings into the picture the fact that faithfulness to the Lord and the gospel cost Paul his freedom.

The Church as Family

References in Philemon to brother (vv. 1, 7, 16, 20) and sister (2), to God as Father (3), and to a house church (2), are among many references and allusions in the NT to the church as a family or household. This seems to be the dominant figure (e.g., Mark 3:33-35; Luke 22:32; Rom. 8:15-17, 29; 1 Tim. 5:1-2; Heb. 2:11-18); it is used more extensively than body or building or any other analogies. The family imagery fits with Paul's comments on entrance by birth or adoption, and on relationships of nurture, sharing, and love.

Alongside the parallels between the family and the church, there are notable differences as well. Note some of the contrasts between factors composing the biological and spiritual families:

Biological Family	*Spiritual Family*
creation	redemption
involuntary	voluntary
flesh/blood	Spirit
ethnic	nonethnic
background/past	regeneration/change
genetic factors	becoming like Jesus

Jesus set a clear priority on the spiritual family over the biological family (Mark 3:32-35). In some respects the spiritual family is the model for the biological family rather than the other way around.

By reminding Philemon that he is part of a spiritual family, Paul brings to the forefront a whole range of values and resources relevant to the situation.

THE TEXT IN THE LIFE OF THE CHURCH
The Church as a Family System

Since 1970 a perspective on individual and family therapy, known as family systems theory, has gained credibility. One aspect of this perspective is relevant when considering how the letter to Philemon intersects with church life. The systems theory insists that individuals are so much a part of their family infrastructure that when one member of a family has a problem, it is in fact a problem involving the whole family.

Paul reminds Philemon that he is part of a church family system. That reminder, supported now by the insights of family systems, needs to be sounded in an age when individualism drowns out awareness and experience of the spiritual family.

Grace and Peace Experienced Corporately

Paul's form of initial blessing is true to the fundamental covenantal meaning of both grace and peace. In the LXX [*Septuagint, p. 316*] the Greek term for "grace" frequently renders a Hebrew term that "describes God's love and the steadfastness with which he keeps the covenant" (Barth: 74). Although grace includes forgiveness in individual experience, the primary connotation is the divine favor of God calling to himself a people. In the new covenant a major feature of the gospel of grace is the inclusion of Gentiles into God's people. OT usage leads to the conclusion that the Hebrew term *shalom* "is an emphatically social concept" (TDNT, 2:406). Thus both terms are directly associated with God's covenant and with the covenant people.

Modern Western understandings of grace and peace greatly limit the scope of both meaning and experience. With the mind-set of individualism, the blessing reads, May you each experience grace and peace. Paul means, May you together experience grace and peace. For Philemon and the church in his house, grace and peace entail doing away with a social barrier and accepting a slave as a brother. The church in every age needs this biblical understanding of grace and peace for members to accept each other and welcome new and different persons into covenant fellowship.

Philemon 4-7

Thanksgiving and Prayer for Philemon

PREVIEW

Before getting to the issue of the letter, Paul first writes some complimentary things about his friend, Philemon. Why does he take that approach? One suggestion is that it is the conventional way to write letters. It is good Hellenistic style to assure the addressee that the writer thinks of him faithfully and prays to the gods on his behalf. Paul seems to adopt and Christianize that cultural courtesy. It might be argued that this approach is "good psychology." The addressee will be able to handle the heavy agenda better if he is put into a good mood by first receiving praise. This tactic could be used in a wide range of strategies for warming up to a weighty request—all the way from genuine gentleness to manipulation.

A better way to explain why he begins with a paragraph of affirmation is that Paul is genuinely being Paul. He writes it because it is true, and because it is part of his Christian character to communicate encouragement and assurance. Most of the Pauline letters have a similar section following the salutation. However, it should not go unnoticed that at least seven key words in verses 4-7 recur in the core of the letter, verses 8-22.

OUTLINE

Thanksgiving to God, 4

Reasons for Thanksgiving, 5

Petition for Philemon, 6

Appreciation, 7

EXPLANATORY NOTES

Thanksgiving to God 4

What Paul has to say to Philemon, he first says to God. Speaking for himself (not including Timothy as in Col. 1:3), Paul says, *I always thank my God*. The expression *my God*, also in the thanksgivings in Romans 1:8 and Philippians 1:3, echoes the words of the Psalmist (e.g., 3:7; 5:2; 7:1, 3, 6; 13:3; 22:2; 25:2). It denotes intimacy, not exclusiveness.

The word translated *remember* can also have the meaning of "mention." The major translations are divided in their renderings here. The two meanings appear close together in Hebrews 11:15 and 22. If Paul is reporting his thinking out loud in prayer, the nuances blend together. Every time Philemon's name comes to Paul's mind and lips, he thanks God. Here and in verses 3-21, the pronoun *you* is singular, meaning Philemon and not including others mentioned in the salutation.

Reasons for Thanksgiving 5

Paul has not had any recent contact with Philemon, so his information about him is hearsay. From his sources, possibly Epaphras and Onesimus, Paul senses that Philemon has acquired a reputation of love and faith.

A literary device shows up in the Greek word order (lit., EDM):

. . .the love and faith which you have

toward the Lord Jesus and to all the saints

As indicated by the lines, the logical connection is between love and the saints, and between faith and the Lord Jesus (as in Col. 1:4 and Eph. 1:15). The meaning of the A B B¹ A¹ order is made clear in NRSV and NIV. This kind of literary structure is called *chiasmus* (cf. Col. 1:16). The chiastic order highlights the interior faith connection from which outgoing love flows.

Here Paul mentions *love* first, before *faith*, although he more often names faith first (Rom. 5:1-5; 1 Cor. 13:13; Gal. 5:5-6; Col. 1:4; 1 Thess. 1:3; 5:8). Love is an especially relevant virtue for the concern of this letter. Agape love implies action more than attitude. *Love for all the saints* connotes doing good for God's people without partiality. *[Holy, Saints. p. 296.]*

Hope is not included here with love and faith. *[Triad, p. 324.]* The focus of the letter to Philemon is on the present rather than the future. The current situation calls for faith that shows itself in love. Paul seeks to motivate Philemon to love Onesimus because of their common faith relationship with Jesus Christ.

Petition for Philemon   6

Commentators generally agree on the difficulty of verse 6: "This is notoriously the most obscure verse in this letter" (C. Moule, 1957:142). As we compare versions, we see a number of different ways this verse has been understood.

Several details deserve attention. Translators add the words *I pray* to identify what follows as the content of Paul's prayer for Philemon. The words *the koinonia of your faith* (EDM) convey the central concept on which Paul made his appeal (see TBC on "Koinonia"). This expression, found only here, can have several possible meanings: (1) the fellowship established with others by your faith, (2) your participation with others in the faith, (3) the sharing of your faith with others (NRSV, NIV), or (4) the generosity which springs from your faith. Dogmatic conclusions about the exact meaning are out of place. Although Philemon's anticipated generosity in receiving Onesimus may suggest meaning (4), the reason for receiving him is that he is a Christian brother, and that theme favors meaning (1). Viewed this way, *the koinonia of your faith* (EDM) is another way to express the sense of the chiasmus (v. 5).

The heart of the petition is that the fellowship of Philemon's faith *may become effective*. The word translated *effective* emphasizes activity and productivity (cf. Barclay, 1964:77-84). Papyri writings of that time use the word for a mill in working order and for land plowed and ready for producing a crop. (The same word is found in 1 Cor.

16:9 and Heb. 4:12.) The verb form in Galatians 5:6 expresses a related thought, "faith working through love."

The energy to be generated is to have a specific focus: knowledge. The strong word for knowledge found here encompasses both understanding and experience. *[Know, p. 304.]* (The same word occurs in Col. 1:9, 10; 2:2; and 3:10.) The focus is narrowed even more to knowledge of *everything good which is in us unto Christ* (lit., EDM). (For an alternate reading, see Essays *[Text, p. 321].*) *The good,* as used in the NT, refers both to what a believer receives (salvation), and to what is done for others. Both meanings fit the context here, but the modifying phrase *in us* (EDM) weights the meaning toward the good that God has given. The last phrase, *unto Christ* (EDM), may be no more than a stylistic variation of "in Christ" *[In Christ, p. 299],* although the preposition connotes direction and movement, as in leading to Christ or with Christ as the goal. Thus Lohse's translation: "all the good that is in us for the glory of Christ" (192).

Appreciation 7

This verse is not part of the prayer, but a further explanation of Paul's appreciation for Philemon. It serves as a bridge into his section of appeal, verses 8-22.

Paul says he has personally benefited from Philemon's love. This is the second reference to Philemon's love (cf. v. 4). The net result of Philemon's love is *much joy and encouragement* for Paul. Although the word translated *encouragement* can also mean request or admonition, here it has the sense of reassurance and inspiration. Older English versions render the word as comfort or consolation. In 2 Corinthians 7:4, 7, and 13, Paul also links joy and encouragement.

The last part of verse 7 implies that Paul experiences a vicarious benefit from Philemon's love. *Because the hearts of the saints have been refreshed through you, my brother* (Philemon), Paul is blessed. Paul cites no specific examples of love shown to himself or to *the saints.* Many versions appropriately have *hearts* for a term meaning viscera (*bowels,* KJV). It represents the whole person at the deepest level. *Being refreshed* or *being given rest,* recalls Jesus' words, "I will give you rest" (Matt. 11:28). Paul punctuates his affirmation for his friend with the warm words *my brother* (cf. v. 20).

THE TEXT IN BIBLICAL CONTEXT
Another Prayer Anticipating the Burden of the Letter

The letter to Philemon illustrates well one feature of the thanksgiving/prayer sections of the Pauline letters (cf. O'Brien, 1980). The introductory prayer anticipates what is called the "epistolary situation" of the main part of the letter. Note the key words in verses 4-7 that reappear in verses 8-20:

prayer(s)	4	22
love	5, 7	9, 16
koinonia/partner	6	17
good	6	14
hearts	7	12, 20
refresh(ed)	7	20
brother	7	20

Since the life situation of the recipient obviously shapes the content of Paul's prayers, these introductory thanksgiving/prayer sections are helpful in piecing together the story behind Paul's letters. They are especially useful when the situation is less than clear from the rest of the letter, as is the case with Colossians.

Koinonia in the NT

The most used Greek word in the NT for the various expressions of the common life of believers is *koinōnia*—now also an English loanword. It is translated as fellowship, sharing, community, participation, partnership, contribution, generosity, or communion. This noun is a form of the root adjective *koinos*, meaning common, shared, or public; in contrast to *idios*, which means private, individual, concerned only with oneself (the word from which *idiocy* is derived).

In secular Greek usage, *koinōnia* had several meanings: business partnership, marriage, and relationship with God. The NT speaks of koinonia with God, with Christ, and in (or of) the Spirit. The breadth and depth of meaning show what Christians have in common because they are Christians. The unique phrase *the koinonia of the faith* (EDM) in Philemon 6 establishes the link between being "called into the fellowship of his Son, Jesus Christ our Lord" (1 Cor. 1:9) and the "fellowship" to which the church was devoted following Pentecost (Acts 2:42). The inseparable relationship between the vertical and horizontal dimensions of koinonia is evident in 1 John 1:3, 6-7. Believers experience the resultant koinonia as a "fellowship of his

(Christ's) sufferings" (Phil. 3:10, EDM). Koinonia as community among believers is a creation of the Spirit, as evidenced in the post-Pentecost phenomena described in Acts 2:42-47.

Christian koinonia touches all levels of human existence and experience. "Sharing in the gospel" (Phil. 1:5) includes both experiencing the gospel and helping to spread the good news. Sharing to meet material needs is also called koinonia (Rom. 15:26; 2 Cor. 9:13).

Another form of the word is translated *partner*, as in Philemon 17. A close bond is implied. The verb form appears in Hebrews 2:14 in parallel with a synonym for *koinonia:* "Since, therefore, the children share flesh and blood, he (Jesus) himself likewise shared the same things."

Koinonia is akin to bonding. The intensity of the connection can be seen in the warnings about inappropriate fellowship. If a Christian participates in the sins of others (1 Tim. 5:22) and takes part in the shameful works of darkness (Eph. 5:11), that one becomes entangled in the guilt and judgment of those who do such things. The spiritual bond is strong between the Lord and believers, and between believers in the holy community. This bond is of such an exclusive character that Christians cannot have koinonia with unbelievers without compromising their true koinonia (2 Cor. 6:14-18). Koinonia (communion) at the Lord's table precludes idolatry and partaking of the table of demons (1 Cor. 10:16).

The koinonia of the faith is a pivotal factor for Philemon. It should be a basic ingredient in the lives of all who respond to the call to experience Christ and the church.

Refreshing the Hearts of the Saints

Paul's choice of words to commend Philemon for his help to others deserves a second look. The verb translated *refreshed* means to be at rest or to give refreshment to someone. Sometimes it has a literal application, meaning bodily rest or sleep (Matt. 26:45). When Jesus said, "I will give you rest" (Matt. 11:28), he used "rest" primarily as a metaphor for salvation. In Revelation 14:13 the word means eternal rest. In two passages Paul used the term in a sense parallel to Philemon 7 and 20. In 1 Corinthians 16:18, Paul said of three men, "They refreshed my spirit as well as yours." In 2 Corinthians 7:13, Paul rejoiced because of what the repentance of the church meant for Titus: "His mind has been set at rest by all of you." The meaning in Philemon, then, is not an emotional lift for the moment, but action that sets hearts and minds at ease.

The word translated *hearts* (v. 7) refers to the inward parts. It is not the usual word for "heart." The English word *viscera* reflects the meaning. In biblical usage the term often stands for the whole person, as does heart, mind, and spirit. The term is a synonym of "heart" in 2 Corinthians 6:11-12.

In NT usage the term often carries connotations of profound love expressed as mercy, compassion, and affection. Coupled with *compassion* (Col. 3:12) it denotes the virtue to be put on as heartfelt compassion. It is used in 1 John 3:17 in reference to shutting up the inner springs of compassion when faced with human need. The source of the heart's capacity to love is "the compassion of Christ Jesus" (Phil. 1:8). An association between refresh and heart (Philem. 7, 20) occurs also in 2 Corinthians 7:13-15.

These rich, multifaceted terms, used in combination, describe Philemon as a man who brings out the best in persons. He uses a gift for enabling persons to rise to increasingly higher levels of their potential in Christ. This commendable quality also shapes Paul's intent and approach in writing to Philemon.

THE TEXT IN THE LIFE OF THE CHURCH
Koinonia in the Church Today

Popular connotations of fellowship often fall far short of what the NT labels koinonia.

> Koinonia is more than meeting together from time to time; it is more than merely enjoying the presence of others; it is more than those feelings of well-being which warm our hearts when we greet our friends at church functions; it is more than common ethnic, cultural, linguistic, and historical ties (although these may well represent important psychological and sociological values); it is more than the organization of a congregation into a series of subgroups related to interest, age, and sex (such multiplication of activities can become a substitute for true koinonia). (Driver, 1976:29)

Koinonia is first of all an experience of commonality and community before it is something that people do. The reality of the bonding of human and divine in Christ, issues in genuine, tangible human relations that encompass the whole gamut of human existence. Believers are to experience the koinonia of faith in the worship assembly, and also in the social and economic aspects of life. The genius of true koinonia is in the intertwining of the spiritual and material in the sharing of life. It is not enough to confess a "spiritual" kinship with all Christians while failing to cross the social, racial, and economic fences of the prevailing culture in tangible and authentic ways.

Christian koinonia is too serious a matter to be trivialized and reduced into merely having a social good time. Koinonia will continue to be an essential element in church life and an attractive component of the gospel message for those outside of faith and thus outside of true koinonia.

Expressing Appreciation

Paul sets an example in his letters, and in Philemon in particular, that could change church life for the better. He freely shares his appreciation for his dear friend. He chooses not to say anything negative about Philemon. Paul is not blind to the faults of others. He becomes sharply critical at times, but he does not have a perennial need to cut other people down.

An urge to deflate others, to make sure they do not think too highly of themselves, is not learned from Paul. His security in Christ frees him from the destructive practice of discrediting others in order to feel superior to them.

Paul models a pattern for mutual support among Christians that is simple enough. It is a matter of telling God and each other about specific appreciations. Rather than complaining to God about what is wrong with a sister or brother, Paul's way is to thank God for what is right about that person. Expressions of appreciation must be sincere and truthful. Phony praise does not help. On the other hand, genuine appreciation lifts and strengthens both receiver and giver.

Philemon 8-22

Appeal on Behalf of Onesimus

PREVIEW
This main part of the letter opens a window to a view of Paul in action. Here he may be observed dealing with a delicate but profound matter. He has been criticized for being weak in his approach, yet he can rightly be called a truly Christian gentleman on the basis of these paragraphs to Philemon. Even more, this section demonstrates a style of exerting influence without coercing, of persuading without violating the personhood of the other individual. Here is a model for parents, church people, and leaders with vested interest in the outcome of others' decisions.

This section also raises intriguing questions about Paul's response to the institution of slavery. How does what he wrote to Philemon fit with other things he wrote about slaves and slavery? Why does he stop short of denouncing slavery in the name of the Lord?

OUTLINE
Basis of Appeal, 8-9

Subject of the Appeal, 10-14

Theological Comment, 15-16

Confident Appeal, 17-21

Hospitality Request, 22

EXPLANATORY NOTES
Basis of Appeal 8-9

The transition phrase, *for this reason*, refers to Philemon's love (vv. 4, 7) and builds on Paul's confidence in Philemon's character. Although asserting his freedom in Christ to *command* Philemon to do his Christian *duty*, Paul chooses to make an *appeal* to him *on the basis of love*. *Appeal* stands in sharp contrast to *command*. Paul does not go the route of issuing a directive as a ranking superior. *Love* is his key factor for direction and motivation. Whether Paul means their mutual love, the principle of Christian love, or Philemon's record of acting in love—this is not said or clearly implied. Paul trusts love to direct Philemon to do what he ought to do as a Christian, without spelling out what that should be.

Paul adds three "footnotes" in support of his love appeal. He uses his own name, *I, Paul*, as a reminder that it is not just anybody who is making the appeal, but a personal friend whose integrity stands with his name. He calls himself *an old man* or *elder*, perhaps suggesting that he deserves respect. The word Paul uses can also mean "ambassador," as it is usually rendered in Ephesians 6:20: "an ambassador in chains." Translators and scholars are divided on the meaning in Philemon. In spite of the close parallel with Ephesians 6:20, "ambassador" denotes an authority factor that Paul just said he would forego. A reminder of his age is consistent with his stated style of approach. Repeating the label *a prisoner of Christ Jesus* (cf. v. 1) serves to remind Philemon that Paul takes his faith commitment seriously, which is what he calls Philemon to do.

Subject of the Appeal 10-14

Paul went this far into the letter before mentioning *Onesimus*, the one who is the reason for the letter. According to inscriptions of that era, *Onesimus* is a name frequently given to slaves. The name is derived from a Greek word meaning useful or profitable. It is not clear whether this is the name Philemon gave him (as is usually assumed) or a new Christian name from Paul.

Several pieces of Paul's description of Onesimus may be noted:

1. He is now a Christian believer, having been "fathered" by a Paul in custody. The fact of Onesimus's conversion is clear. We can only guess how that came about and how Onesimus came in contact with Paul. Paul calls this Gentile slave *my child* (sometimes translated "son"), a warm expression Paul uses elsewhere within the imagery of spiritual parenthood (1 Cor. 4:17; 2 Tim. 1:2).

2. Onesimus is a changed person because of the gospel. Previously he was *useless* to Philemon, but had now become *useful* to both Philemon and Paul. The contrast between *then* and *now* is pronounced in Colossians (cf. 1:21-23). *[Before—After, p. 282.]* Although Phrygian slaves had a reputation for being good-for-nothing, the reference may be to something in particular that Onesimus did or did not do. A word play has been noted in Paul's choice of words. *[Grammar, p. 293.]*

3. Paul is *sending him . . . back* to Philemon. Paul has a right to provide refuge for a runaway slave for a time, but he is required to report the fact to the master. *[Slavery, p. 317.]* The word for *sending back* (v. 12) can also mean "refer" (e.g., Luke 23:7, 11; Acts 25:21). If that meaning is applied here, Paul is saying, "I am referring the case of Onesimus to you to decide his future." *[Text, p. 321.]*

4. Onesimus has become special to Paul. Sending him back is like giving up his *own heart*. This is the same term found in verses 7 and 20, a word that signifies the whole person. Paul says in effect, "Part of me goes with him."

5. Onesimus is useful in ministering the gospel (vv. 11, 13). Paul *wanted to keep him* in Rome. His help is especially needed, presumably because of Paul's confinement. The "slave" (*doulos*) could "minister" (*diakoneō*), *be of service . . . for the gospel*. He could even take Philemon's *place* in ministering.

6. Paul is determined to do nothing without Philemon's *consent* (v. 14). As a matter of principle, Paul chooses not to make the decision for Philemon, for to do so would make the *good deed* something *forced* rather than *voluntary*. *Your good deed* picks up the reference to *the good* in verse 6. In both instances it is left in general terms. Love will do its work, voluntarily.

Theological Comment 15-16

Before getting to the substance of his appeal, Paul adds yet another perspective, that of providence. Paul sees the potential of eternal gain coming out of temporary loss. Rather than saying specifically that Onesimus ran away, Paul states the case in what has been called "the divine passive": *he was separated from you*. Paul is not denying any wrong on the part of Onesimus but observing that human failures can be God's opportunities.

The words *have him back forever* do not address the possibility of release or of return to Paul. Instead, as verse 16 makes clear, the new element is that Onesimus is now *a beloved brother*, both Paul's and Philemon's. (Cf. other references to *brother* in the letter.) Becoming a brother does not automatically erase the slave-master relationship. Paul does not say "no longer a slave," but no longer *as* a slave. The slave is now *more than a slave*. Onesimus is dear to Paul, but the potential is *much more* for Philemon as their new relationship *in the Lord* transcends their relationship *in the flesh*.

Confident Appeal   17-21

Paul's appeal grows out of all he has said thus far. The grammar of *if you consider me your partner* (v. 17) shows that Paul assumes the statement to be true. *[Grammar, p. 293.] Partner* translates a word in the same family as *koinonia*. At this point in the letter, the expression *the koinonia of your faith* (v. 6, EDM) takes on practical significance. Paul refers not to a business association or a casual friendship, but to their commonality in the Lord. He goes beyond interceding on behalf of Onesimus and puts himself into the equation. Thus Paul reasons,

> You and I are brothers and partners in the Lord.
> Onesimus is now also our brother because he is in the Lord.
> Therefore, *welcome him as you would welcome me*, as a partner.

Paul backs his appeal with a sweeping promise. *If he has wronged you in any way, or owes you anything* (v. 18) assumes there was a problem. *[Grammar, p. 293.]* This comment is the strongest evidence, in the absence of a specific acknowledgment, that Onesimus has run away from his master and perhaps also stolen from him. Using a term from the business world, Paul says, *Charge that to my account*. At this place in the letter, Paul inserts a promissory note in his own handwriting.

Paul none too subtly reminds Philemon of his debt to Paul himself: *I say nothing about your owing me even your own self* (v. 19b). We may conclude from this comment that Paul has been an instrument in Philemon's conversion, either directly or indirectly.

The style changes with verse 20. It is less angular and more upbeat as Paul asks several favors for himself. The relationship between Paul and Philemon comes to the fore in verses 20-22. Onesimus is not mentioned again in the letter. Repeating the warm, intimate address, *brother*, Paul introduces his wish to *have this benefit from Philemon in the Lord. [Grammar, p. 293.]* Paul has commended Philemon earlier for refreshing the hearts of the saints (7). Here he says, in effect, "Do it again." *Refresh my heart in Christ.*

Except for the requested welcome in verse 17, Paul does not spell out what Philemon should do with respect to Onesimus. In verse 21 he expresses confidence that Philemon will *do even more* than Paul has indicated. This comment opens the door for Philemon to take the initiative to set his slave free and perhaps send him back to Paul. However, he leaves the particulars to Philemon's conscience. He does identify the decision as a matter of *obedience*, presumably obedience to Christ, since Paul has not given a command. In Paul's teaching (Rom. 1:5; 16:26), obedience is a faith issue, and that connection takes us back full circle to the references to faith in verses 5 and 6.

Hospitality Request 22

Paul has one more request. He assumes a welcome in Philemon's household and thus asks candidly, *Prepare a guest room for me.* A term generally meaning hospitality refers here to a place of lodging (cf. Acts 28:23). Hospitality shown to traveling Christians and to strangers was fostered in the early church. With the strong ties of friendship he has with Philemon, Paul can count on accommodations in Colossae.

Paul also assumes a readiness on the part of the church in Philemon's house to pray for his anticipated release. The pronoun *you* shifts to plural in verse 22. This change does not indicate that the letter is to be read to the congregation, but that with this tactful suggestion, Philemon would call the church to pray concerning Paul's coming. The anticipated visit has been interpreted as yet another pressure on Philemon to comply with Paul's wishes. Yet it is not consistent with the tone of the letter's appeal to think that Paul meant to say, Pray that I can come so I can check up on you. However, the prospect of Paul coming to Philemon's house could not but give added incentive to comply with the request.

The hoped-for visit to the Lycus Valley implies a hoped-for release from Roman custody. *Restored to you,* or *graciously given to you* (lit., EDM) means "the one who is 'given' escapes death or further imprisonment by being handed over to those who wish him freed" (Bauer: 876). The passive voice of the verb may well be another example of the divine passive (noted in v. 15), recognizing that release and safe travel are God's gracious gifts in response to the petitions of the church. Paul and Philemon have apparently met previously, perhaps in Ephesus. Although not personally known in the Lycus Valley (Col. 2:1), Paul wants to visit his friend Philemon and the church at Colossae. Before going to Rome, Paul looked forward to a trip to Spain (Rom. 15:22-24). In his letter to the church at Philippi, also written from prison, he expected to get to Macedonia. Whether any of these plans ever worked out is unknown.

THE TEXT IN BIBLICAL CONTEXT
Changed by the Gospel

The letter to Philemon illuminates several contrasting vignettes illustrating change effected by the gospel. On the one hand there is Saul of Tarsus, a good Pharisee, upright, and socially exclusive. Roman citizenship brings its special privileges, which he uses at times. Onesimus, on the other hand, is a Gentile, a slave with no rights, and he is in trouble. The gospel turns a useless runaway slave into a useful servant of the gospel. But for Paul to say of him, he is my child, a beloved brother, my own heart, one he wants with him—all this shows a dramatic change in Paul as well.

Nothing is reported about Philemon before he came to new life, but the qualities and actions for which Paul praises God, reflect how thoroughly Christ has changed him. Paul speaks of this Gentile, likely of some means, as a brother, co-worker, and partner. Paul expects the gospel to change Philemon even more as he works through accepting Onesimus as a brother.

Spiritual Parenthood

Paul employs the metaphors of having children and parenting (v. 10) to describe spiritual birth and growth in other NT instances as well. The analogy also conveys a parental mentoring relationship. In 1 Corinthians 4:15, Paul says, "In Christ Jesus I became your father through the gospel." Two verses later he speaks of Timothy as a "beloved and faithful child." (See also Phil. 2:22; 1 Tim. 1:2; and Titus 1:4.). Maternal imagery of parenting occurs in Paul's words to the churches of Galatia: "My little children, for whom I am again in the pain of childbirth until Christ is formed in you" (4:19).

Appeal Instead of Command

Paul tells Philemon that he deliberately chooses to appeal to him rather than to command specific action. On other occasions Paul gives instructions and orders with the authority of apostolic credentials. He lets Philemon know he has a right to demand dutiful response but prefers an appeal to love. Paul does not always approach people the same way.

The word translated *to command*, and the cognate noun, are strong ones, used when a superior gives authoritative orders (e.g., the commands of God, Jesus' orders to demons, and the commands of Herod and Ananias). Even apart from these specific words, Paul's tone is much more of command than appeal at times (notably in 1-2 Cor. and Gal.). The style of appeal and entreaty also shows up at many places in Pauline writings. The word Paul uses to identify his approach to Philemon, *parakaleō*, has a wide range of meanings: call, invite, exhort, encourage, comfort, and appeal. The meaning in verse 9 is deduced from the contrast with command. Although he opts not to enforce compliance, Paul's appeal always carries a lot of weight. Note the basis on which he made appeals on other occasions:

"on the basis of love" (Philem. 9)
"by the mercies of God" (Rom. 12:1)
"by our Lord Jesus Christ and by the love of the Spirit" (Rom. 15:30)
"by the name of our Lord Jesus Christ" (1 Cor. 1:10)
"by the meekness and gentleness of Christ" (2 Cor. 10:1)

Why did Paul sometimes use appeal and sometimes command? The difference seems to be determined by matters of trust, confidence, and maturity. When Paul saw a demonstrated ability to choose and do what is right, he refrained from making decisions for people and appealed to responsible behavior. Recipients of his letters had various degrees of maturity, and that obviously resulted in borderline cases requiring sensitivity to the Spirit. When the integrity of the gospel was threatened, Paul took a more aggressive stance.

Hospitality in the Early Church

Hospitality was a distinct part of the culture of the Near East in bibli-

cal times. Both pagans and Jews counted it a virtue to provide accommodations for traveling strangers. Christians adopted the practice and gave it theological significance as a Christian principle. Paul
had good reason to expect Philemon to open his home to him and to
do it gladly and well.

From the patriarchal period, Abraham and Lot are examples of
persons who treated strangers generously. Jesus both depended on
the hospitality of others and sent out his disciples with the expecta-
tion of finding it. For Christians, the practice had stronger motivation
than duty. Alongside the word *philadelphia* (love of the brother), they
also used *philoxenia* (love of the stranger). With this term, Romans
12:13 enjoins the practice of hospitality as a way to show genuine
love. Hebrews 13:2 encourages hospitality with a reference to the experience of Abraham. Believers are reminded in 1 Peter 4:9 to show
hospitality without complaining or, as Phillips puts it, to "be hospita-
ble to one another without secretly wishing you hadn't got to be!"

A generous attitude of hospitality among Christians facilitated the
spread of the gospel in the first century. Abraham J. Mahlerbe and
others (e.g., Del Birkey) note how hospitality and the house church
complemented each other in the early church. [*House Churches,
p. 297.*] While experiencing the benefits of hospitality for evangelism
and unity, the church did need to contend with abuses of the practice
(2 John 10-11; Didache 11-12).

Philemon and Paul's Other References to Slavery

In Philemon, Paul emphasizes the new spiritual relationship between
slave and master. Whether or not Onesimus is now a brother in Christ
is not left open for difference of opinion. However, Paul lets the decision about release up to Philemon, while indirectly nudging in that direction. How, it may be asked, does this stance harmonize with other
Pauline references to slavery?

No other passage speaks explicitly to the relationship of master
and slave after they are both converted to Christian faith. Christian
slaves and Christian masters are both instructed in the household
codes (Col. 3:22—4:1; Eph. 6:5-9) and in related texts (1 Tim. 6:1-2;
Tit. 2:9-10; 1 Pet. 2:18-21). It is not necessarily assumed in these
teachings that the counterparts are Christians. Colossians 3:11 (and
the nearly parallel text, Gal. 3:28) asserts that in Christ the social box-
es of slave and free no longer matter. These texts concur with the emphasis of Philemon. However, Paul does not ground his appeal on

the Stoic teaching about equality on the basis of all coming from the same seed and breathing the same air (O'Brien, 1982:297). For Paul, it is a matter of spiritual commonality in the new community because of being in Christ.

One other passage speaks of the possibility of a slave gaining freedom. While answering questions about marriage in 1 Corinthians 7, Paul recommends the principle of continuing in the station of life in which one is called to Christ (7:17). Then he applies that principle to the slave who becomes a believer (7:21). Opinions are sharply divided on whether Paul counsels slaves to take or not to take an opportunity for freedom (cf. versions and footnotes). Either way, freedom is not considered an automatic privilege when a slave becomes a Christian. Paul says, "For whoever was called in the Lord as a slave is a freed person belonging to the Lord, just as whoever was free when called is a slave of Christ" (7:22). That word resonates with the emphasis of Philemon.

There is a fundamental change in the relationship of master and slave when both know Christ. This overshadows the slavery factor but does not entitle the Christian slave to demand freedom. Paul does not champion the contention of the mystery religions [Religions, p. 313] that a slave who had been "initiated" was no longer a slave, but stood as a free person alongside his former master (Lohse: 203). Yet the "in Christ" relationship does inevitably and radically alter the master-slave relationship.

THE TEXT IN THE LIFE OF THE CHURCH
A Paradigm for Responsible Decision Making

Can Christians be taught in Christ's way and then trusted to do what is right? Paul's approach to Philemon offers a paradigm for influencing behavior in the church and in the home. It is a better way than (1) allowing persons to stumble through the issue alone, (2) taking over and deciding for them, or (3) appearing to leave responsibility with them while employing tactics of intimidation, coercion, and threat. Paul's way with Philemon involved three factors: (1) belief that faith in Christ will inform action, (2) use of encouragement and persuasion without violating the person's responsibility and integrity, and (3) appeal to the highest motivations.

Because of the influences of culture, tradition, and social pressure, a faith base is crucial for responsible decision-making by Christian individuals and by the church. Yet instruction in the right way does not assure compliance; humans are inclined to separate action from knowledge. Believers offer needed encouragement and persuasion to each other, but that can easily slip across the line into manipulation and coercion.

Leaders (and parents) are tempted to use their power to assure acceptable decisions and behaviors. It may be necessary for us to dictate and demand suitable responses for keeping children from harming themselves and others. The same procedures, however, rob adults of personal responsibility and an opportunity to mature. Adolescents need structure, guidance, and encouragement as well as freedom to make some mistakes. Not all who have come to faith in the church have moved through adolescence to maturity. Therefore, the paradigm of inspiring and encouraging persons to live out their growing faith convictions, with a focus on love, will be fruitful in church life and in parenting. Paul has modeled an excellent way of peer influence.

Motivations for Doing Right

Paul's appeal to Philemon brings to the fore the matter of motivations for behavior, especially for doing what is right. Churches that emphasize the call of Christ and of the gospel to right behaving as well as right believing cannot avoid consideration of the motivational buttons they choose to push. We can learn much from studying the motives that Paul did and did not utilize for compliance with the gospel's way.

Paul did not appeal to the Stoic virtues of clemency in forgiving runaway slaves (cf. Lohse: 196-197). He did not appeal to humanitarian ideals. He specifically refrained from making the issue a matter of duty. Although identifying the decision regarding Onesimus as a matter of faith obedience, Paul made no mention of the consequences of disobedience. He did not threaten his friend. Yet all these kinds of tactics have been used, sometimes exploited, in efforts to motivate people to take desired steps. Making deductions from Scripture's silence is always hazardous. In this letter it is clear that Paul consciously set aside heavy-handed pressure on Philemon.

Paul depended on two primary motivational factors, faith and love. Both accent voluntary response. Jesus did command love as an act of the will, but there is no such thing as compulsory love. For Philemon the appeal based on faith and love was backed up with several reminders that could help him say, "I want to do what is right."

These included the following: the good Philemon had been doing, respect for Paul's integrity, news of the newfound faith, usefulness of Onesimus, God's providence, and a solid partnership with Paul.

The nature of Paul's approach to Philemon serves as a reminder for us to appeal to the highest Christian motivations. This is a challenge to pastors, evangelists, teachers, and all who have reason to care about the right behavior of others. We need to take the risks Paul did in trusting God and the power of faith and love.

Why Did Paul Stop Short of Denouncing Slavery?

The Bible, including Paul's writings, has been used to defend the practice of slavery as well as to champion abolition. Indeed, the Scriptures seem to give mixed signals about slavery, on the one hand accepting the practice and on the other laying down principles incompatible with traffic in human lives. If Paul would have labeled slavery as sin, supposedly the church would have consistently opposed the practice through the centuries. So we ask, Why did Paul not denounce slavery?

The question assumes that Paul did not say or do enough because of either blindness or fear. But this assumption separates the gospel from the culture of the Roman world at that time [*Slavery, p. 317*] and fails to recognize how revolutionary his teaching was and is. Because Paul did not openly repudiate slavery does not warrant the conclusion that he approved of it. (See Swartley, 1983:31-64, for an analysis of the ways the Bible has been used both for and against slavery.) We note several attempts to explain why Paul and the early church did not attack the institution of slavery. One is that the possibility of a massive slave revolt was too big a risk. Another is that the slavery giant was too big for the infant church to confront. Presumably the same "reasons" explain why there is also no denunciation of imperial cruelty and injustice (yet see Rev. 17—18, especially 18:13).

Another explanation must be considered. The NT is directed to Christian believers rather than to the social order of the day. The relatively few and scattered Christians in the churches of NT times simply did not have a sense of responsibility for the social order. Rather than addressing and trying to solve the social issues of the day, Paul called on believers to practice the way of Christ in all aspects of life. The teachings addressed to slaves make it clear that it is possible to be a Christian and a slave. Similarly, the teachings to masters may be taken to infer that it is possible to be a Christian and own slaves. However, the teaching to masters has profound implications for the institution of slavery. As F. F. Bruce puts it, "What this letter [Philemon] does is to bring us into an atmosphere in which the institution [slavery] could only wilt and die" (1977:401). Mennonite writer Guy F. Hershberger highlights the relevance of Philemon for matters of social injustice:

> Certainly human slavery is incompatible with social justice, and yet Paul does not demand the abolition of slavery. Instead, he places the whole matter on a different basis by reminding both master and slave that they are brethren and that their relations, one with the other, must be on the basis of Christian love. Certainly, where this relationship actually exists, the institution of human slavery cannot continue; and it would seem that Paul's approach in this case is the Christian solution for every form of injustice. (217)

The radical message to masters and slaves did not sink deeply into the psyche of the Christian church until the nineteenth century. Yet Lightfoot said about the NT teachings, "A principle is boldly enunciated, which must in the end prove fatal to slavery" (325). The gospel did have some effect on slavery in the early centuries. Lightfoot documents that "one of the earliest forms which Christian benevolence took was the contribution of funds for the liberation of slaves" (326). He goes on to say:

> But even more important than overt acts like these was the moral and social importance with which the slave was now invested. Among the heroes and heroines of the Church were found not a few members of this class. When slave girls like Blandina in Gaul or Felicitas in Africa, having won for themselves the crown of martyrdom, were celebrated in the festivals of the Church with honour denied to the most powerful and noblest born of mankind, social prejudice had received a wound which could never be healed. (326-327)

Without speculating about Paul's intent and strategy, an emerging principle commands respect: if masters will treat slaves as Christian brothers, that will put the institution of slavery out of business. Similarly, if Christians would refuse to kill Christians in war, it would be a major step in shutting down war.

The gospel of Christ did intersect with the social disorder of the first century. Since the typical congregation included both slaves and slave owners as believers, the social implications of the gospel could not be ignored. Philemon and the rest of the NT had a relevant word for that era and continue to speak to the church today.

An Echo of the Theme

John S. Dwight (1813-1893) of Boston labored in the ministry six years before devoting himself to literary work. For many years he was editor of a journal of music. Several lines from his translation of a well-known Christmas carol, "O Holy Night," reflect what Paul wrote to Philemon about accepting Onesimus as his brother in Christ (from "Cantique de Noël," by Cappeau de Roquermaure):

> Truly He taught us to love one another;
>   His law is love and His gospel is peace;
> Chains shall He break, for the slave is our brother,
>   And in His name all oppression shall cease.

Philemon 23-25

Greetings and Benediction

PREVIEW

Compared with the other Pauline letters in the canon, Philemon is brief, but it includes the names of no less than ten persons besides Paul. Those sending greetings at the close of the letter comprise a list strikingly similar to what is found at the end of Colossians. As is his custom, Paul ends with a benediction.

OUTLINE

Greetings, 23-24

Benediction, 25

EXPLANATORY NOTES

Greetings 23-24

Certain persons with Paul are making use of the letter going to Philemon to include their own greetings to him. *You* in verse 23 is singular. *Epaphras,* a *fellow prisoner in Christ Jesus,* heads the list. Since those mentioned in verse 24 are called *fellow workers,* it is best to take *prisoner* in a literal sense. In Colossians, Aristarchus is called *fellow prisoner.* According to Colossians 1:7, Epaphras took the gospel to Colossae and likely to the other Lycus Valley cities.

The only comment made about *Mark, Aristarchus, Demas, and*

Luke is that they are *fellow workers* (as Paul called Philemon in verse 1). For further information about these associates of Paul, see this commentary on Colossians 4:7-18.

In Colossians, "Jesus who is called Justus" is included along with the five named in Philemon. Because of that unaccounted-for difference, it has been proposed that instead of reading *in Christ Jesus*, a comma would give the reading "in Christ, Jesus, Mark, Aristarchus, Demas, Luke," making the names the same as those in Colossians 4:10-14. This suggestion also requires a minor text change. *[Text, p. 321.]* Although the proposal is plausible and favored by several scholars, it has not been picked up by translators, even in marginal readings.

Benediction 25

The benediction embraces the congregation again, as did the blessing in verse 3. *Your* is plural. The wording is identical with that in Philippians 4:23, and the phrase *with your spirit* is also in Galatians 6:18. *Spirit* does not refer to an inner ethos of the church community or to one part of human beings as differentiated from body or mind. Here the term stands for the whole person. Thus, *with your spirit* is no different in meaning from the more common ending of Pauline benedictions, "with you" (TDNT, 6:435).

Grace, as noted in comments on the blessing in verse 3, is more than a word used in polite correspondence. *The grace of the Lord Jesus Christ* epitomizes the God-given linkage between God and his people. It is an appropriate last word in all circumstances. *[Text, p. 321.]*

THE TEXT IN BIBLICAL CONTEXT
Common Elements in Philemon and Colossians

We note several marked similarities in these two letters. Both name Timothy as being with Paul at the writing. Both are written out of circumstances of custody, expressed in similar terms. The persons extending greetings are almost identical. These factors are consonant with a common author, namely Paul. A common destination is also widely accepted, although a few scholars argue for Laodicea as the location of the recipient of the letter to Philemon.

We also observe several differences. Significant variations in vocabulary (e.g., in the thanksgiving and prayer sections) are to be expected because of different addressees and issues. In Colossians, slaves and masters are addressed (3:22—4:1) and Onesimus is mentioned (4:9), but Philemon is not. Yet we can naturally assume that Onesimus is with Paul when he writes Colossians with its directives to slaves and masters. We may also assume that the two pieces of correspondence were kept together even though separated in the NT arrangement of Pauline letters.

Synthesis: The Letter to Philemon

The Story Surrounding the Letter

Some parts of this human interest story become clearer with examination of the evidence, and some parts remain hazy. Here is a likely reconstruction of the circumstances and events.

Philemon was a man of above-average means living in Colossae in the Lycus Valley. He had become acquainted with Paul, probably during the apostle's stay in Ephesus. Philemon came to faith and new life in Christ through Paul's ministry of the gospel. Paul continued to value him as a friend and colleague in the gospel. Philemon made his house available for a local assembly of believers in Colossae. Apphia may have been his wife, and Archippus, who had been given responsibilities in the church, may have been their son. Paul looked forward to enjoying the hospitality of Philemon's household.

Onesimus had been a slave in this Colossian household, but he had not become a Christian. At some point he ran away and went to Rome, the capital of the empire. He may have stolen money and possessions from his master when he left, and he had definitely robbed him of time and service. Somehow, whether by Providence or personal initiative, the fugitive slave and the apostle Paul met in metropolitan Rome. The result was that Onesimus came to faith in Christ. He became especially close to Paul and a valuable asset to him in the ministry the apostle was able to carry on while in Roman custody.

The time had come for Onesimus to return to Philemon. We can readily understand the dynamics of the relationships. Paul found himself in the middle. He wrote this letter to accompany Onesimus, encouraging Philemon to accept the runaway slave as a Christian brother in faith and love. Onesimus probably did not travel alone, for he and Tychicus were to deliver the letter we know as Colossians and report orally to the congregation about Paul's well-being. Although Paul recognized the church community in the letter to Philemon, he did not intend that it be read to the congregation as a way to put that kind of pressure on his trusted friend. (This letter is not the one mentioned in Colossians as *from Laodicea*.)

We have only one side of the communication between Paul and Philemon. We may surmise, however, from its preservation and inclusion in the New Testament that Paul's appeal found a favorable response in Philemon.

The Value of the Letter

This brief piece of personal correspondence makes valuable contributions to the New Testament. Several observations on the significance of Philemon emerge from the study:

1. Philemon sheds light on the early Christian conscience regarding slavery. Although Paul's appeal did not condemn the institution of slavery and stopped just short of using the word "emancipation," it proclaims a reality of the gospel that transcends the social order.

2. Philemon complements and goes beyond the directives of the Domestic Codes (*Haustafeln*) and the admonition to slaves in 1 Corinthians 7. It does this by focusing on the inevitable mutual relationship between slave and master when both are in Christ.

3. Philemon profoundly attests to human dignity. It has been called the Magna Carta of Human Dignity. The base is in redemption, not merely humanitarian respect.

4. Philemon adds greatly to an understanding of the character of Paul. He reveals his sensitivity and tact as he takes an assertive but not an authoritarian role in a triangular situation.

5. Philemon stands as an instructive model of brotherly admonition. This model is not the only style of approach Paul takes, yet it commends itself as a fruitful way of persuading without violating the values of voluntary response. Paul appeals to motivations that come from an experience of Christ in Christian community.

6. Philemon attests to the power of the gospel to transform

messed-up lives and broken relationships. Christ takes people where they are and changes them and how they see each other. The intertwined lives of Onesimus, Paul, and Philemon are graphic examples of the faith and love that come through Christ.

7. Philemon shows the way the gospel works in the social, political, and economic world. It answers the charge that the gospel will not work in the "real world."

8. Philemon reminds us that the faith community and Christian friendships are integral parts of the resources of Christ for making responsible personal decisions. Mention of the church and individual persons is consistent with the point of the letter.

Outline of Philemon

Abbreviations

BAGD	See Bibliography under Bauer, Walter
Berkeley	*The Berkeley Version in Modern English*
Bruce	*The Letters of Paul, an Expanded Paraphrase*
CSEL	*Corpus scriptorum ecclesiasticorum latinorum*
DSB	The Daily Study Bible Series
EDM	Author's translations
GNB	*Good News Bible (Today's English Version)*
Goodspeed	*The New Testament, An American Translation*
IDB	See Bibliography under IDB
JB	*The Jerusalem Bible*
KJV	*King James Version of the Holy Bible*
lit.	Author's literal translation
LXX	The Septuagint, a Greek version of the Old Testament
ME	See Bibliography under ME
MT	Masoretic Text
NASB	*New American Standard Bible*
NEB	*The New English Bible*
NIV	*New International Version*
NRSV	*New Revised Standard Version*
NT	New Testament, in the Bible
OT	Old Testament, in the Bible
	Names of books of the Bible are abbreviated to the first letters, in a standard fashion.
Phillips	*The New Testament in Modern English*

RSV   *Revised Standard Version*
TBC   The Text in Biblical Context
TDNT   See Bibliography under TDNT
TLC   The Text in the Life of the Church
TR   Textus Receptus *[Text Variations, p. 319]*
UBS   See Bibliography under UBS

Other Ancient Sources

Apostolic Fathers
Barnabas   The Epistle of Barnabas
Clement   The First Epistle of Clement to the Corinthians
Didache   The Teaching of the Twelve Apostles
Ignatius   To the Ephesians
Ignatius   To Polycarp
Polycarp   The Epistle to the Philippians of Saint Polycarp

Aristotle   (The Greek philosopher)

Dead Sea Scrolls   (Qumran)
1QH   Thanksgiving Hymns

Josephus
Ant.   Antiquities of the Jews

Old Testament Apocrypha
Ecclus.   Ecclesiasticus, or Wisdom of Jesus Son of Sirach
2 Esdras   Ezra Apocalypse (4 Ezra)
1-2 Macc.   1-2 Maccabees
Wisd. of Sol. Wisdom of Solomon

Philo   (Philo Judaeus)

Pseudepigrapha
2 Baruch   (Syriac) Apocalypse of Baruch
Letter of Aristeas

Rabbinic Literature
Mishnah Aboth   The Sayings of the Fathers

Essays

OUTLINE

BEFORE—AFTER A then—now formula in the NT, primarily in the Pauline letters, calls attention to a sharp contrast between a pre-Christian past and the new situation in Christ. The Greek adverbs constituting the formula are *pote* or a few times *tote* (usually translated as "then" or "once"), and *nun* or the more intense form *nuni* (translated as "now").

Passages in which both members of the contrast formula are present (with the indicated change) include the following:

Rom. 6:20-22 (slaves of sin—> set free from sin)

282

11:30 (disobedient—> obtained mercy)
Gal. 1:23 (persecuting—> proclaiming the faith)
4:8-9 (did not know God—> know God)
Eph. 2:11-13 (far off—> near)
5:8 (darkness—> light)
Col. 1:21-22 (alienated—> reconciled)
3:5-10 (old nature—> new nature)
Philem. 11 (useless—> useful)
1 Pet. 2:10 (no people—> God's people)
(not received mercy—> received mercy)
Passages in which one member of the contrast formula and the concept
of the other is present include:
Rom. 7:1, 6 (the law is binding—> discharged from the law)
Eph. 2:1, 5 (dead—> made alive)
1 Pet. 2:25 (straying—> returned)
Passages in which the concept is found without the formulaic adverbs:
Rom. 5:10 (enemies—> reconciled)
1 Cor. 6:9-11 (numerous vices—> washed, sanctified, justified)
Many other passages fit the pattern "once you were, but now you are," in-
cluding Col. 1:12-13; 2:13; and 3:1-3. Most of the instances refer to a change
of status or condition, while several refer to change of behavior.

CHURCH IN COLOSSIANS Church is far more than an incidental theme
in Colossians. Besides the word *church*, a number of synonyms and figures of
church are scattered throughout the letter:
church (*ekklēsia*) 1:18, 24; 4:15, 16
saints (*hagioi*) 1:2, 4, 12, 26; 3:12 *[Holy, Saints, p. 296.]*
body (*sōma*) 1:18, 24; 2:19; 3:15
family/household (brothers and sisters) 1:1, 2; 3:16; 4:7, 9, 15
chosen ones (*eklektoi*) 3:12
beloved (*ēgapēmenoi*) 3:12
church in _____ house (4:15, cf. Philem. 2) *[House Churches, p. 297.]*
In some of these references, *church* refers to the church universal and in others to a local assembly or congregation. Although *church*, the term the early
church chose over *synagogue,* is the transformation of a Greek idea, the
word occurs frequently in the LXX with the thought of assemblage, and there
may well be an Aramaic equivalent in *keništa* (Marshall, 1973:359-364).
In 3:12 the terms *chosen ones* and *beloved* echo OT references to the
people of God. However, the designations "people of God" and "Israel of
God" do not occur in Colossians. The NT imagery of temple, bride of Christ,
flock, and field also do not appear. The terms and images for church in
Colossians reflect an understanding that the group is more than the sum of
the parts. For examples, the designations brother and sister require a family
entity, body is more than a collection of body parts, and saints are not produced in isolation. *[Holy, Saints, p. 296.]*
The concept of "corporate personality," with roots in the OT, lies behind
the body image of the church (although the word body is not explicitly used
in that sense in the OT). The Hebrews found individual identity in the corporate life of their family, tribe, and people—"the bundle of the living" (1 Sam.
25:29). Similarly, the individual believer finds identity in Christ by participating in the body of Christ.
The doctrine of church in Colossians accords with Paul's overall view of

the church. Although using an ordinary term for assembling in the first century (*ekklēsia*), Paul's model for community had more to offer by far than the contemporary competitors. For Paul, church meant people meeting for community life. The distinctive factors were "the character of the gatherings and the source of their dynamic" (Banks: 50).

COLOSSIANS AND EPHESIANS The kinship between these two letters is more pronounced than between any other Pauline writings. The similarities are evident in several ways. In vocabulary and phraseology, about one-third of the words in Colossians are found also in Ephesians and about one-fourth of the words in Ephesians are found in Colossians. The many parallels are about equally distributed throughout the letters, although the order is not entirely the same. The most extended verbal agreement is between Col. 4:2-4, 7-9; and Eph. 6:18-22. Word sequences of three to seven words add to the evidence for kinship (Col. 1:1-2||Eph. 1:1-2; Col. 1:14||Eph.1:7; Col. 1:25|| Eph. 3:2; Col. 1:26||Eph. 3:9; Col. 2:19||Eph. 4:16). Several expressions occur in both letters and are not found elsewhere in Paul: "making the most of the time" and "bear with one another."

These two letters are also similar in style. Laborious thought processes with complex sentences and common grammatical traits are peculiar to Colossians and Ephesians. The organization of the two follows the same broad outline. A predominately doctrinal section is followed by application, including the "put off/put on" motif and the *Haustafeln* (Domestic Codes).

Explanations offered for these similarities include dependence of one on the other (both ways), mutual dependence, and both drawing on common sources (cf. Reicke). The traditional view is that Paul is the author of both.

We note several important differences between Colossians and Ephesians. Some of the vocabulary seems to have differing nuances of meaning in the two letters. In Ephesians the now-revealed "mystery" is the inclusion of both Gentiles and Jews in the church. Colossians gives the term the same meaning (1:26-27), but also speaks of Christ himself as the "mystery" (2:2). In Ephesians, Christ's body, the church, is the "fullness" (1:22-23). In Colossians, the *fullness* of God is in the incarnate Christ (1:19; 2:9), with the added point that believers are filled in Christ (2:10). *[Fullness, p. 288.]* These and similar differences do not constitute sharply divergent uses of words. Instead, they are examples of an interplay of meanings. F. F. Bruce observes that in Col. 3:14, love is the bond of harmony; and in Eph. 4:3, unity of the Spirit is maintained in the bond of peace. Then he offers this perspective:

> This is the sort of thing which suggests that the relation between Colossians and Ephesians is not so much one of direct dependence by the latter on the former; it is rather the relation between two works which are the product of one mind around the same time. If Paul had the general idea of love and peace linked in his mind at this time with the idea of a unifying bond binding all the graces of Christian life together, that would sufficiently account for the similar, if divergent, modes of expression. (1957:282)

Several more differences should be noted. Ephesians refers to the Spirit eleven times, while Colossians mentions the Spirit only once. A plausible explanation for this scant reference to the Spirit in Colossians is that the climate in Colossae led Paul to use alternate ways to describe new life in Christ. Although the terms "Savior," "saved," and "salvation" all occur in Ephesians, none of them are in Colossians. For reasons unknown to us, Paul seems to have avoided certain terms when writing to the Lycus Valley believers.

Along with the notable similarities between these two letters, we see that each has its own character and emphasis. While both speak of Christ and the church, Colossians puts the spotlight on Christ, and Ephesians emphasizes the church. The letters complement each other. The evidence indicates that they were written by the same person. Thus the differentiating character of each one finds its best explanation in the respective purposes of each one and in the differing religious, social, and political climates into which they were sent.

The likelihood is that Paul wrote Ephesians shortly after Colossians. This is where Bruce comes out in his reconstruction of the story:

> It still appears most probable that Paul, having completed his letter to Colossae, allowed his thoughts to run on along the same line until he was gripped by the vision which finds expression in the companion letter, and began to dictate its contents in an exalted mood of inspired meditation, thanksgiving, and prayer. The resultant document was then sent as a letter to the Asian churches by the hand of the messengers who were entrusted with the Epistle to the Colossians. (1957:172)

ELEMENTS OF THE UNIVERSE   This term, occurring in Col. 2:8 and 20, causes problems for interpreters and translators because the word *stoicheia* (elements) has no precise definition in the NT. In the literature of the Greek world of the first century, the "elements" were commonly understood to be the basic four: earth, water, air, fire (with a fifth sometimes added: ether). Eduard Schweizer argues that this basic definition underlies NT usage, and that asceticism (Col. 2:21) and worship of angels (2:18) were attempts to break free from the power of the elements (1988:455-468). Colossians asserts that Christ is the superior power, and in him believers die to the elements of the world and rise again to seek the things above.

Walter Wink's research indicates that in first-century usage, *stoicheia* meant the most basic components of any entity or thing; the meaning must be determined by the context. We use the word elements in a similar way in speaking of chemical elements, of the Lord's Supper, and of wind and rain as elements of nature. Wink notes four different meanings in the seven NT occurrences (1984:77):
- The ABCs, the elementary or first principles of faith—Heb. 5:12; Gal. 4:9 (in part)
- The constituent elements of the physical universe—2 Pet. 3:10, 12
- The basic constituents of religious existence common to Jews and Gentiles alike (rituals, festivals, laws, beliefs)—Gal. 4:3, 9; Col. 2:20
- The first elements or founding principles of the physical universe—Col. 2:8

In this analysis the meaning of elements is different in Col. 2:20 from what it is in 2:8. Wink observes that early Christian theologians (after the NT) also defined the elements differently in different contexts (1984:164-165).

This term is related to but not identical with "powers" in the NT. *[Powers, p. 308.]* The elements of the world/universe are neither political personalities nor spirit beings. But they are real and powerful. One meaning of the term *archē* (translated *ruler* in 2:10) is first principle, and in that sense it is synonymous with element. The elements become idolatrous when people grant them an ultimacy they do not really have. As the shaping factor of physical, social, or religious existence, Christ is ultimate, not the elements of the universe. Wink comments on the modern choice of materialism in this way:

> Paul's prescience in Col. 2:8 is remarkable; he somehow understood something that our age, with all its feats of knowledge and technology, has been unable to grasp: that the fascination with first things—the elements of the universe—would inevitably lead to idolatry and to a subtle but insidious slavery to matter. The moment we declared these principles ultimate, we elevated them in value above ourselves. Having projected ultimacy onto matter, we could only bow before it. For whatever is ascribed ultimacy functions as a god, whether its devotees would describe it thus or not. And the preferential selection of matter as the ultimate reality of the universe, as its fundamental constituent and determining factor, meant that the entire spiritual dimension of reality was ruled illusory from the outset (1986:137).

ENDURANCE, PATIENCE Endurance (translated from *hupomonē*) and patience (from *makrothumia*) and their verbal counterparts occur numerous times in the NT (and less frequently in LXX). They occur together or in close proximity several times in addition to Col. 1:11 (e.g., 1 Cor. 13:4, 7; 2 Cor. 6:4, 6; 2 Tim. 3:10; and James 5:7, 8, 11).

Endurance, also sometimes translated as patience and as steadfastness, is the enablement that comes from God (Rom. 15:5) to accept and remain steadfast while experiencing difficulties and testings. Generally it has to do with accepting outward circumstances without wavering. Enduring is the opposite of complaining, grumbling, or becoming despondent. It is an outgrowth of faith and hope, rather than a matter of bravery or stoic acceptance.

Patience, sometimes translated as long-suffering, also has its source in God, the God who exercises divine restraint. It is a gift, listed as a fruit of the Spirit (Gal. 5:22), and goes deeper than rigorous self-restraint in outward response. In Col. 3:12 it is one of several "garments" to be put on by those who belong to Christ. Generally, patience is exercised toward people, rather than things or circumstances.

Endurance and patience, along with a related word, forbearance (*anochē*), have a distinctively Christian flavor. Except for the idea of perseverance in completing a job, Greek thought did not consider these attributes to be virtues. Christian faith enabled endurance of hardship and patient acceptance of persecution.

The early church found in the Christian grace of patience an alternative to warfare and other forms of violence. The Apostolic Fathers (leaders who followed the apostles) understood *makrothumia* (patience) and the Latin equivalent (*patientia*) to mean the endurance of injustice and persecution without doing violence to the evildoers. The meaning of the Latin term *patientia* is essentially what we refer to as nonviolence (cf. Hornus: 213-226; Driver, 1988:60-70). The source of this conviction was certainly not Greek or Roman society, but Jesus. Clement of Rome wrote near the end of the first century,

Let us, therefore, be humble-minded, brethren, putting aside all arrogance and conceit and foolishness and wrath, and let us do that which is written (for the Holy Spirit says, "Let not the wise man boast himself in his wisdom, nor the strong man in his strength, nor the rich man in his riches, but he that boasteth let him boast in the Lord, to seek him out and to do judgment and righteousness"), especially remembering the words of the Lord Jesus which he spoke when he was teaching gentleness and long-suffering (*makrothumia*). (1 Clement 13:1, tr. by Kirsopp Lake)

Writings by Tertullian (ca. A.D. 200; *Apologeticum [Apology]* and *De patientia [On Patience]*), Origen, Cyprian *(De bono patientiae [The Advantage of Patience])*, Lactantius, and many others extol the virtue of patience in the sense of nonviolent response to evil persons. Tertullian said that Christ unbelted every soldier. Augustine, who expounded the classic just-war theory (!), also left a memorable definition of a patient person as one who "prefers to endure evil so as not to commit it rather than to commit evil so as not to endure it" *(De patientia* 2, from Hornus: 220).

Endurance and patience are words people often forget about when all is going well for them in the world. However, the Bible is realistic about what Christians can expect to face, and it instructs us in the way to respond, following the teaching and example of Christ.

ETHICAL LISTS Paraenesis (from a Greek word meaning to advise or exhort) is the general term used for exhortations of an ethical or practical nature. Within this broad category, two types of ethical material found in the NT are relevant to studies in Colossians: (1) vice and virtue lists and (2) Domestic Codes *(Haustafeln)*. Several issues are common to both of them.

Much discussion has been focused on the source(s) for these NT ethical teachings. Teaching of a similar nature is common in the literature of Stoicism (Greek thinking) and Hellenistic Judaism (Jewish religion as affected by Greek culture). Some scholars have assumed that the early church needed to borrow an ethical framework or teaching from somewhere because of the delay in Jesus' return. Supposedly, the church was like a ship without a rudder and looked to Stoic, Iranian, or hellenized Jewish sources. The notion that the NT ethical lists represent a "Christianizing" of existing codes has been thoroughly challenged (by David Schroeder and others). The form is somewhat similar, but the content of the NT ethical teaching is significantly different.

For example, the cardinal vices and virtues of Stoicism are not in the NT lists. Conversely, humility and the fruit of the Spirit find no parallels elsewhere. Anyhow, asking what item was borrowed from where is shortsighted. NT ethical teachings come from a more immediate source: "The basic ethical conception of the NT codes—that without belonging to the world as such, one has responsibilities within the structures of society—takes us back to the teaching and example of Jesus himself" (Schroeder, 1976:547). After showing that the *Haustafeln* teachings are substantially and radically different from either Greek or Jewish sources, John H. Yoder offers this observation: "The only remaining source we very logically suspect is that somehow this tradition comes from Jesus" (1972:182).

Jesus did include a catalog of sins in his teaching: "For it is from within, from the human heart, that evil intentions come: fornication, theft, murder, adultery, avarice, wickedness, deceit, licentiousness, envy, slander, pride, folly" (Mark 7:21-22). This list is notably similar to other NT vice lists. Lane offers the comment: "It has frequently been held that the Marcan list reflects Hellenistic or Pauline influence, but there is no valid reason for holding that the list cannot go back to Jesus, at least in its essential form" (257).

Another part of the picture is the evidence of a genre of teaching in the NT that may well have become a traditional body of instructional material. Work done by Carrington, Selwyn, and others, demonstrates a recurrence of themes such as: put off/put on, be subject, watch and pray, and resist. These have striking parallels in the writings of Paul, James, and Peter. The evidence points to an oral tradition going back to Jesus that became more formalized as the church passed on the faith tradition to new believers.

But that raises another question. How shall we account for the differences in the several ethical lists, both in the put off/put on teachings and in the Domestic Codes? Part of the explanation may be that the formalizing of the tradition was still in process. But a more plausible explanation is in the dissimilar circumstances of the churches at different places. Things were not the same in Galatia as they were in Corinth or in the Lycus Valley. The apostolic instructions were undoubtedly shaped by the current needs of a given church. This does not mean that they do not have relevance for the church in every age. The genius of the NT ethical lists lies, not in discovering what is included or left out in any particular list, but in their christological base (see "Christological Ethics," pp. 159-161).

FULLNESS Plērōma is the Greek noun for fullness (also used as a transliteration), meaning "that which fills or completes," or "the resulting completeness." It occurs in the NT a number of times in a nontheological sense, e.g., in Mark 6:43 of the filled baskets of leftover fragments. In seven instances it has a distinct theological meaning:

John 1:16, "from his fullness we have all received"
Eph. 1:22-23, "the church, which is his body, the fullness of him who fills all in all"
Eph. 3:19, "so that you may be filled with all the fullness of God"
Eph. 4:13, "to the measure of the full stature [the stature of the fullness, EDM] of Christ"
Col. 1:19, *for in him all the fullness of God was pleased to dwell*
Col. 2:9, *for in him the whole fullness of deity dwells bodily*
Col. 2:10, *you have come to fullness in him*

In these texts, fullness applies to (a) God, (b) Christ, (c) believers who share in the fullness of Christ, and (d) the church. The texts from Colossians particularly stress (b) and (c), that all the fullness of God is in Christ, and believers experience fullness in him.

The roots of this theological sense of fullness are found in the OT. The word plērōma in the LXX usually has the meaning "everything in it" (e.g., Ps. 24:1; 50:12; 89:11; and 96:11). However, in related forms of "fill" and "fullness," the thought comes through that God fills the heaven and the earth (Ps. 72:19; Isa. 6:3; Jer. 23:24). While God's glory fills the earth or the temple and his presence and power are felt, biblical revelation is devoid of the notion of pantheism, that God is everything and everything is God.

As a word later used by Gnostics (particularly in Valentinianism), plērōma became a technical term with several shades of meaning. One concept had plērōma referring to the emanations that came from God.

[Gnosticism, p. 289.] Col. 1:19 and 2:9 stand in sharp contrast to the dualism that contends that God cannot be directly involved in the material world or human existence.

In Eph. 1:23, the church is called "the fullness of him who fills all in all," whereas in Col. 1:19 it is in Christ that "all the fullness of God was pleased to dwell." The difference is a matter of focus and emphasis, with the comment of Col. 2:10 providing the link, "and you have come to fullness in him." *[Col.& Eph., p. 284.]*

GNOSTICISM Gnosticism was an elaborate combination of numerous religions and philosophies that came into full bloom in the second century. However, many of its elements had pre-Christian roots. The term comes from the Greek word *gnōsis*, meaning knowledge. We cannot clearly know the extent to which Gnosticism was developed in Paul's time. Yet the seeds of this mixture of Greek philosophy, marginal Jewish speculation, and oriental mystery cults were growing as the early church spread out in the cities and provinces of the Roman Empire. Gnostic ideas can be seen in the troublesome teaching at Colossae.

While Gnosticism is a term used to describe various related schools of thought, several elements were characteristically present. Gnostics contended that special knowledge was disclosed to only a few. Their system of thought was basically dualistic, of the variety that sees the material (the body) as evil and the spiritual (spirit) as good. For some that idea led to asceticism; for others it led to license because they thought the body did not matter anyway. Any connection between God and humankind, from this dualistic point of view, would need to be through intermediaries (referred to as demiurges, aeons, or emanations). In each successively lower level of emanations, the divine element is weaker until contact with matter is conceivable. Such views affect the doctrine of creation and the doctrine of Christ, specifically incarnation. Gnostics spoke of a First Principle, of Plērōma (fullness), and of true Reality. Although not originating within Christianity, Gnosticism could and did incorporate some Christian ideas, with modification. Much of Christianity was in time affected by Gnostic influence and defined itself over against Gnostic teachings.

A mid-second-century work identified as The Gospel of Truth, part of the Nag Hammadi writings, is an example of "Christian" Gnosticism. Not a gospel in the sense of the four canonical gospels, it addresses the person and work of Christ from a Gnostic perspective. The basic human problem is viewed as ignorance rather than as alienation because of sin. The document illustrates the effect of Gnosticism on Christian thought, specifically in the contrast between Gnostic and NT Christologies (cf. IDB, 1976:923-926).

The Ophites represent one brand of Gnosticism that appears to have arisen in western Asia Minor. Scholars have pointed out three ingredients of Ophism: Judaism as it had evolved in Phrygia (with a reputation for speculation and syncretism), a veneration of snakes as a source of wisdom (popular in Asia Minor), and the mystery cult of the Great Mother (with Phrygian and Egyptian roots). (See Kroeger, 1986; 1992:153-170.)

One particular facet of the religious scene illustrates the relevance of Colossians for Christians in the pagan world. In Greek thought, hope focused on the human potential rather than on any deity. Hope at best was a human projection of the future. Stoicism had no interest in hope. Other religious streams, such as the Mystery Religions, gave primary attention to present ecstacies rather than to future expectations. Judaism, however, had a strong messianic/eschatological hope. Christianity gave life new meaning and power in that hope rests on what God has already done in Christ, breaking open the future and enabling life in the now-but-not-yet.

GRAMMAR NOTES
COLOSSIANS
1:3-8 In this long complex sentence, one main verb, *thank*, is followed by a series of clauses strung together in Greek with seven participles (*praying, having heard, being laid up, having come, bearing fruit, growing, having made known*), an adverb (*just as*, 3 times), and relative connectives (*that/which, who*) (EDM).
1:9-14 The structural flow of this block (shown on the left) is shaped by the syntax of these verses (right):

Structure		*Key Words of the Text (EDM)*	*Syntax*
Action	9	*we have not ceased praying/asking*	main verb (present tense)
Intent		*that you may be filled*	purpose clause
Result	10	*so that you may lead a life worthy and pleasing*	infinitive
Description		*bearing fruit . . .*	4 participles
		growing . . .	
	11	*being empowered . . .*	
	12	*giving thanks . . .*	
Reasons		*Father has enabled you . . .*	3 aorist verbs
(Father)	13	*he has rescued us . . .*	(past tense)
		and transferred us . . .	
Benefits	14	*redemption*	2 nouns
(Son)		*forgiveness of sins*	

1:20 The translation *having made peace* (NASB) accurately reflects the aorist (past tense) participle found here, pointing back to Jesus' death.
1:23 The expression introduced by *provided that* employs one of several ways the Greek language indicates conditions. This one assumes the condition is true. (See Eph. 3:2 and 4:21 for similar constructions.)
    Here is the sense of verse 23a, following the grammar in Greek: *Of course you must persist in the faith, having been given a solid foundation and firmly established, not being dissuaded from the hope of the gospel* (expanded, EDM). The main verb of the clause is *epimenō* (*persist*); followed by a perfect passive participle, *having been given a solid foundation;* an adjective, *firmly established;* and a present passive participle (with a negative), *not being dissuaded.* These explicit and implicit passives reveal that the capacity to persist is provided for the believer.
1:24 The double prefix and the present tense of *antanaplērō* (complete) denote a repeated supplemental contribution. The word occurs only here in the NT and is not used at all in the LXX (TDNT, 6:307).
1:28 The verb teach (*didaskō*) takes an accusative object, but *in all wisdom* is in the dative case. Therefore, wisdom is not so much what is being taught as descriptive of the manner of the warning and teaching (Bratcher and Nida: 42).
2:7 All three participles are in the passive mood, indicating God's action on

the believer. The first, *having been rooted*, is a perfect tense participle, imply-ing continuing effect of the action. *Being constructed* and *being made firm* are both present tense participles, implying that the action is still going on (EDM).

2:8 The imperative, (*You* [implied]) *see to it*, is plural. The object, *you*, is thus plural, implying group responsibility for each other, to guard against any being taken *captive*.

2:10 The perfect passive participle, literally, *having been filled*, draws atten-tion to divine action already accomplished, in which the believer stays filled (in potential, if not in actuality).

2:11 A parallel in the construction has a bearing on the meaning (EDM):
   by (en) the putting off of the body of flesh
   by (en) the circumcision of Christ
The parallel implies that both phrases speak of how spiritual circumcision is accomplished. G. Beasley-Murray states the idea: "The body of flesh was stripped off when Christ was circumcised" (1962:152). The reference is to Christ's death.

2:13-15 In each verse, a triad of three lines, the middle line has an active in-dicative verb, stating what God has done. The first and third of these indica-tives are aorist (past) tense; the second one is perfect tense (emphasizing the permanence of the removal). In each case the flanking lines have participles, with the first in the present tense (implying action coinciding with that of the main verb) and the other five in aorist tense (implying action prior to that of the main verb). The verb forms, then, along with the nouns and pronouns, clearly indicate the organization of thought.

The first participle in 2:15, *apekdusamenos*, is a middle form. If it is taken as a true middle, in a reflexive sense (as fits in 3:9), then the subject has changed from God to Christ, and we have a reference to Christ divesting himself of the powers. The emphasis is on Christ rejecting the powers and freeing himself from their control through his death. The church fathers and many commentators have followed this interpretation. The NEB follows this option, *On that cross he discarded the cosmic powers and authorities like a garment.*

If, however, it is a middle form with an active sense, then we have a refer-ence to God stripping the powers of their power. Several grammarians have shown that the Greek of the NT substitutes the middle voice for the active in certain verbs, this being one of them (e.g., Blass, Debrunner, para. 316). This view has God engaging in a frontal attack of the powers through the cross of Christ. (For a fuller discussion, see O'Brien, 1982:127.)

2:16 Negative prohibitions, in Greek, are expressed either by a present im-perative with *mē* (one of several negative words), meaning, "Stop doing what you are now doing"; or by an aorist subjunctive with *mē*, meaning, "Do not start. . . ." Since 2:16 has the present imperative, the implied meaning is, "Stop letting anyone do this to you," suggesting that it was already happen-ing. (See C. Moule, 1963:20-21, for a discussion of imperatives and prohibi-tions that comes out at a different place.)

2:18 Generally, a prohibition expressed with a present imperative (as here) prohibits continued action. (But see C. Moule, 1963:20-21.) NASB captures this point of grammar: *Let no one keep defrauding you.*

Four present participles follow the imperative, the main verb, in 2:18-19a. As in other instances, the organization of the sentence is implicit in the grammar of the text.

2:19 The phrase *from whom* has a masculine relative pronoun (in Greek) although it refers back to *the head*, which in Greek is a feminine noun. Normally they should agree in gender. However, the reference to Christ is so dominant that the rule of grammar is set aside in favor of clear meaning.

The participles, *being equipped* and *being joined together*, are both passives, indicating that these effects are what Christ supplies and not the result of purely human effort (EDM).

2:20 The middle-voice verb, *submit*, implies that the readers are in control and allowing the imposed regulations. The question means that they have a choice in the matter: *Why are you letting yourselves be regulated?* (EDM).

3:5 While the aorist tense might be expected to indicate point action rather than linear action, the rule is not absolute, particularly for imperatives (cf. C. Moule, 1963:20-21). The primary significance of the aorist here is the urgency of taking the action.

3:9 The widely accepted rule that a present imperative with *mē* implies, "Stop doing what you have been doing," presumably applies to the prohibition against lying. (But see C. Moule, 1963:20-21.)

3:9b-10a Scholars disagree on the issue of whether the aorist (past) participles in these verses are true participles, referring to what had taken place previously, or whether these are instances of an imperative meaning of participles, as is the case in some other NT texts, e.g., in Rom. 12:9-19. There participles, interspersed with imperatives, evidently have an imperatival sense. (David Daube has demonstrated a background of rabbinic usage for this phenomenon in "Participle and Imperative in 1 Peter," in Selwyn: 467-488.) Eph. 4:22-24, a passage similar to Col. 3:9-10, supports translating the participles as imperatives, although the passages are not grammatically parallel. Rom. 6:11 also confirms the understanding that counting oneself dead to sin and alive to God (or to use the language of Colossians, to put off the old self and put on the new self) is not a once-for-life action, but an ongoing process.

However, it is also true that Paul often refers in Colossians to the decisive life-changing event of being transferred into the new kingdom and transformed inwardly as a past experience (using aorist participles, 2:12; or aorist indicatives, 2:20; 3:1, 3). The fact that we have aorist participles in 3:9b-10a supports interpreting them as true participles, for when participles have an imperative meaning, they are predominately in the present tense. (Among scholars accepting these as true participles are Martin, 1978:106, and O'Brien, 1982:188-189; cf. TDNT, 6:644.) One might argue that both perspectives are true to Paul and the NT. The issue is the meaning here.

3:10, 12 The participle *have clothed yourself with* and the imperative *clothe yourselves with* are middle-voice forms of *enduō*. In Greek literature (secular, LXX, and Chrysostom) the middle voice of this verb "always means to surrender to the possession and control of, and to become the property of and to be dominated by" (Garber: 101). This meaning helps in understanding the admonition to "put on Christ." It also bears on being clothed with the new self (3:10) and on Christians clothing themselves with the qualities God gives (3:12-13).

3:13 *Bearing with* and *forgiving* (EDM) are both present middle participles. Some consider these to have the force of imperatives, similar to those in 3:9b-10a (above). However, here it makes good sense to take them as participles that further explain the meaning of the commands. The present tense indicates that an ongoing practice is intended. The construction of the (present subjunctive) conditional clause, *if anyone has a complaint*, implies that whenever the situation arises, this is how to respond.

3:16 All three are present active participles, identical in all ways, although *singing* (EDM) stands in a different word sequence. They should likely be seen as parallel to each other whether construed as true participles or as having the force of an imperative.

3:18 The use of the article, literally *the wives, the husbands,* etc., designates classes of persons, and the words of address imply, "You who are. . . ."

The present middle imperative carries the sense *be submitting yourselves to* (EDM).

4:2-6 The disciplined grammatical structure of these verses is much more apparent in Greek than in English translations. We have this sequence:

An imperative followed by two descriptive participles (2-3a).

Two purpose clauses, both using subjunctives and the same repeated infinitive (3b-4).

An imperative followed by a participle (5).

An implied imperative followed by a participle and two infinitives (6).

In addition, three of the four *en* phrases provide coherence.

4:3 NRSV and NIV translate the present participle, *praying,* as an imperative, *pray.* (See this essay on 3:9b-10a.) Understood as a participle, the word indicates a specific focus for the clear call to pray in verse 2.

4:6 There is no verb in this sentence in Greek. We can catch the intended meaning by supplying the imperative *let . . . be.*

PHILEMON

11 The name Onesimus means useful. Paul chose a synonym, with prefixes, to contrast *useless (achrēston)* and *useful* (euchrēston). There is a marked similarity between the sound of *chrēstos* and *christos* (Christ). This wordplay hints that Onesimus's conversion to Christ enabled him to live up to his name.

17 The construction of *ei* with the indicative connotes a condition assumed to be true.

18 The same grammatical construction as in verse 17.

20 The intensity of Paul's personal appeal can be seen in a literal translation: *Yes, brother, I from you may I have (let me have) benefit in [the] Lord* (EDM). An emphatic pronoun *I* is added when *I* is already implicit in the verb form, and *I* is set next to *from you.*

HEAD and BODY For understanding the meaning of head in relation to body, we need to keep in mind biblical usage of the term *head.* An outline of Hebrew OT, LXX, and NT usage follows:

Hebrew Old Testament. *Roš* (and related words of the stem) appears:

as a part of the body (Gen. 3:15)

as summit or top (Exod. 17:9; 2 Chron. 3:15; Ps. 118:22)

as a superlative, meaning best (Exod. 30:23)

as chief, elder of tribe (Exod. 6:14)

as first, firstfruits (Gen. 25:25; Lev. 2:12)

as beginning, the primary sense of the feminine form of the noun (Gen. 1:1; Prov. 1:7)

"Unquestionably the idea of authority or leadership often attaches to *roš*; but then a chieftain's authority in social relationships is largely dependent upon his 'seniority,' or 'priority,' in the order of being" (Bedale: 213).

Septuagint. The Hebrew word for head (*roš*) is sometimes translated into Greek as *kephalē* (head) and sometimes as *archē* (a word that can mean either ruler or beginning). The evidence suggests that the two Greek words were sometimes used interchangeably (e.g., Isa. 9:14-15, where both occur), although in classical Greek they have nothing in common. We may surmise that Paul was familiar with the meanings and associations of head in the OT (Hebrew and Greek). Of interest is the fact that these two words *kephalē* and *archē* both appear in Col. 1:18, translated as *head* and *beginning*, respectively.

In the OT, when head is used of chiefs or rulers, their subjects are not referred to as a body. God is spoken of as the head of Israel (2 Chron. 13:12), but the people of God are never called the body of God in any way parallel to the NT expression, body of Christ.

New Testament. *kephalē* occurs:
as a part of the body (Mark 6:24; 1 Cor. 12:21; Rev. 1:14)
as representative of the person (Acts 18:6; Rom. 12:20)
as descriptive of Christ (Col. 1:18; 2:10; 2:19; Eph.
    1:22; 4:15; 5:23)
as key position, "head of the corner" (Matt. 21:42; Acts
    4:11)
as descriptive of man/husband (1 Cor. 11:3-10; Eph. 5:23)

When head refers to Christ (as in all the occurrences in Colossians), several facets of meaning appear: superiority of Christ over all (Eph. 1:22; Col. 2:10), beginning (Col. 1:18), source of growth (Col.2:19), archetype (Eph. 4:15), and spiritual relationship (Eph. 5:22-33).

The Greek world conceived of head differently. Greek literature reveals an understanding of the universe as a big body. Zeus, or some other supreme god, was seen as the soul or head of the universe. Paul's use of the head-body figure did not follow the popular Greek notions of his time. Although Paul spoke of Christ as the head of all, he never used "the body of Christ" to refer to the universe, but rather to the church.

Biblical usage does not support the idea, deduced from modern understandings of physiology and neurology, that the head controls the body. The parallel Hebrew word in the OT (*roŝ*) means *primary* and *source* as well as *leader* and a *part* of the body.

Both Greek and Jewish popular understandings were that the heart, not the head, is the center of reason and will. The NT makes no direct or implied reference to the brain. Several NT passages use the head-body figure in ways that do not fit with the concept of brain control. In 1 Cor. 12:21 (in context), the head is one of several interdependent members of the body, with no suggestion of superiority or rule. In Col. 2:10 *head* carries with it the idea of "overlordship" as well as priority. But Col. 2:19 and Eph. 4:15-16, which picture the head as the cause and source of growth in the body, begin to make sense when the close connection between head (*kephalē*) and beginning/source (*archē*) is recognized. By allowing biblical usage to be a major factor in the meaning of Bible words, we can avoid reading into the texts meanings that have their origins in our culture and hence are foreign to the Bible milieu. In the Bible, *head* does not always have the same meaning. We must take care not to assign a meaning of superiority in all cases, because the word also frequently means source or a relationship of interdependence (cf. TDNT, 3:673-681).

HISTORY OF CHRISTOLOGY   Christology is the study of the person and work of Jesus Christ, including a disciplined articulation of an integrated understanding of the biblical data. Such efforts are valuable for communicating the faith and testing faithfulness in the contemporary world context.

The NT provides the primary data for Christology. Col. 1:15-20 and the several other similar passages arising out of the faith tradition are intentional statements of Christology, but none of these is fully comprehensive. Key elements of the data include the words of Jesus, the narrative records of his ministry, the names and titles for Jesus, the sermons and letters, and the analogies and figures used to communicate the effects of the work of Christ. In the postresurrection era, Christians began using the same language to speak of Jesus as they did to speak of God. The history of the affirmations about Jesus in the NT shows that "Christology formulations arose out of worship, and worship arose out of the Christians' experience of Jesus" (France: 34). It follows that "modern christological discussion, if it is to maintain its links with NT Christianity rather than set up a new discipline unrelated to historical Christian origins, must begin where Christology itself begins, in the worship of Jesus" (France: 36).

During the centuries following the apostolic era, the church found it helpful to develop careful formulation of christological understandings in response to distortions and denials of biblical doctrine. The person of Christ was the disputed issue. The NT affirms the paradox that Jesus Christ is both human and divine without trying to explain the paradox. Attempts at reasoned explanations often resulted in losing the paradox on one side or the other. Either Christ's divinity was overemphasized at the expense of his humanity, or his humanity was overemphasized at the expense of his divinity. For example, Docetism is the view that Christ only appeared to be human. Arianism is the view that Jesus was neither God nor human, but of an order in between. Modalism is the view that God, who is one, came in three different form/modes, Father, Son, Spirit. Adoptionism (as one example of subordinationism) is the view that Jesus became the Son of God at his baptism. Many other ideas about Christ were also afloat.

The intense debates and adopted formulations of Christology throughout the centuries brought into use an extrabiblical vocabulary. Some terms were borrowed from Greek thought, and some created for the occasion. Examples of borrowing: *essence, substance,* and *person.* Examples of minting new terms: *trinity, divinity, humanity,* and *preexistence.* We need to put biblical understandings into contemporary thought forms, but problems do arise.

Persons who influenced the thought and formulations that became standards of orthodoxy include Tertullian (ca. 160-220), Origen (185-254), Athanasius (293-373), the Cappadocian Fathers (late fourth century), and Augustine (354-430). Seven general church councils were held, with Christology a key issue: Nicea, 325; Constantinople, 381; Ephesus, 431; Chalcedon, 451; Constantinople, 553; Constantinople, 680; and Nicea, 787. Historic creeds include the Apostles' Creed, the Nicene Creed, the Athanasian Creed, and the Definition of Chalcedon.

These statements of dogma/doctrine primarily address issues about the person of Christ, although they also include the death, resurrection, and return of Christ. Even though they affirm the humanity of Christ, they do not mention his teachings and exemplary life or the present aspect of the kingdom of God. Because there is an integral connection between the doctrine of the church and the doctrine of Christ, it is important to note that the historic creeds (Nicene and Chalcedon) arose out of the state-church synthesis that came with Constantine. That context may have more to do with what they do not say than with what they do say about Christ.

Divergent views about the saving work of Christ came in later centuries. Western orthodox theology has generally followed the views of Anselm of Canterbury (11th century), characterized as the "satisfaction" theory of atonement. Peter Abelard (12th cent.) elaborated what is known as the "moral influence" theory. The "classical" view was prominent from the second through the seventh centuries and revived by Gustaf Aulén (20th cent.); it emphasizes Christ's victory over the powers.

Anabaptists of the sixteenth century were generally comfortable with historic orthodox understandings. Except for the unorthodox views of several leaders, they affirmed both the divinity and humanity of Christ and salvation through his death on the cross. However, they had a preference for using biblical language rather than creedal language. (See M. Miller: 147-150.) They stressed Christ's resurrection and the resurrected life of believers, the teachings and example of Jesus, and the church as the kingdom of Christ—biblical emphases they found lacking in both Roman Catholic and Protestant doctrine and practice.

Maintaining the paradox of Christ's full humanity and divinity, without compromising one or the other, has been a challenge in every age. The community confesses Jesus as Christ and as Lord and is concerned about discipleship; these both stem from biblical Christology. As is clearly evident in Colossians, Christology is a crucial factor for all Christian understanding and living. Although Christology is a central element of doctrine, not all Christians have the same Christology. "One might say, 'By their Christologies ye shall know them' " (Marshall, 1976:11).

HOLY, SAINTS The words *holy/holiness*, *sanctify/sanctification*, *dedicate/consecrate*, *holy ones/saints*, and various other translations of these words all have a common root. If we fail to recognize how this family of words is closely connected, we may stumble into sad distortions of meaning. This family of words is found in both Testaments, with the Greek *hagios* being the counterpart of the Hebrew *qadoš*, both translated as *holy*. (The several less-used synonyms will not be considered here.)

The primary Hebrew words in this family are the following:

qdš (root), primary meaning of separation from the common

qadaš (verb), consecrate, sanctify, prepare, dedicate, devote, make holy, be hallowed/sanctified

qadoš (adjective), holy, holy one, saint (plural is used of angels)

qodeš (noun), apartness, holiness, sacredness

miqdaš (noun), holy place, sanctuary, hallowed part

These words are applied to God, to individuals, to places and objects, and to the people of God. The prophet Hosea associates holiness with active love, rather than with wrath against sin. The moral sense of holiness is also present, as for example in the holiness code of Leviticus 19.

The primary Greek words in the family are the following:

hagiazō (verb), make holy, consecrate, set apart, sanctify, treat as holy, hallow, purify

hagios (adjective), holy, sacred, dedicated, consecrated

hagioi (plural substantive), holy ones, saints

hagion (neuter substantive), holy place

hagiasmos (noun, emphasizing process), consecration, sanctification
hagiotēs (noun, emphasizing attitude), holiness
hagiōsunē (noun, emphasizing resultant condition), holiness, sanctification
Of these words, Colossians has *holy* and *saints*, and Philemon has *saints*.
Several observations about this family of words are of note.

(1) Two related meanings make up the basic concept, somewhat like two sides of a door. On one side we have the meaning, set apart, and the various ways that is expressed. On the other side, we have the sense of moral purity. When God says, "Be holy, for I am holy," both meanings are involved, both for God and for those called. God sanctifies his people, setting them apart as belonging to him. His people sanctify God by setting him above all other gods. His people sanctify themselves, committing themselves exclusively to God. Appropriate moral behavior follows because they are set apart and committed to conform to the character and will of God.

(2) Ethical holiness is never a prerequisite to becoming God's people, nor is perfection an automatic result of God's consecrating action. Instead, the new status is to result in growth in holiness (Col. 3:12-14).

(3) Sanctity is not associated with asceticism or the denial of all pleasure.

(4) *Saints*, a frequent NT term, does not refer to an elite group within the church, but to the church or congregation as a whole. Paul's relief offering for "the saints in Jerusalem" was not for a morally superior part of the believers in Jerusalem. Paul could call the Corinthian believers "saints" and go on to point out their immaturity and faults. However, the term carries with it the upward call in Christ. (For a helpful discussion of the term *saints*, see *These Are My People*, by Harold S. Bender.)

HOUSE CHURCHES, HOUSEHOLDS Both Col. 4:15 and Philem. 2 speak of a church in someone's house. These are but two of many examples in the NT of a pattern of congregational grouping in the early church. The term *house* (*oikos*) carries several overlapping meanings. Sometimes it refers to a dwelling place, sometimes to a household or family, and sometimes to the church as a household (although including more than one family). The texts listed here include all three meanings, sometimes with a secondary meaning inferred:
   Mark 9:28; 10:10—house as a place for teaching disciples
   Acts 2:46; 5:42—houses as settings for life of the new community
   Acts 12:12—gathering in Mary's house for prayer
   Acts 16:14-15—household of Lydia baptized, house made available
   Acts 16:34—household of jailer (Philippi)
   Acts 18:7-8—house of Titius Justus, household of Crispus (Corinth)
   Acts 20:8-11—meeting in upper-floor room (Troas)
   Acts 20:20—proclaiming/teaching from house to house (Ephesus)
   Rom. 16:3-5—church in the house of Prisca and Aquila (Rome)
   Rom. 16:23—Gaius, host of the whole church
   1 Cor. 16:15—household of Stephanas
   1 Tim. 3:15—household of God
   Titus 1:11—leading astray whole households
In several texts the idea is present without the word *house/household:*
   Rom. 16:10-11—those of (the household of) Aristobulus, Narcissus
   Rom. 16:14-15—brothers and sisters, saints with named individuals
   1 Cor. 1:11—Chloe's people

This widespread phenomenon in the early church yields a number of valuable observations for understanding the early church:

1. The church adopted house churches even prior to the time when they needed a low profile because of persecution.
2. Both men and women are named with houses or households.
3. Not all believers were poor. Some were able to provide houses of adequate size for gatherings.
4. Large cities, such as Corinth and Rome, had more than one house church. This may account in part for the divisions at Corinth. Larger assemblies came together, made up of the smaller groups (Rom. 16:23).
5. The pattern facilitated the primary group nature of the church in its essence, providing for intimacy, accountability, worship, and fellowship.
6. The pattern allowed for the flexibility that mobility requires. It fitted well with the emphasis on hospitality.
7. The pattern assumed diversities of age and socioeconomic standing and turned them into opportunities.
8. The house-church phenomenon explains the spread of Christian faith and the vitality of churches in the early centuries.

Archaeological excavations of 1930-31 in what is now Syria uncovered a house church from the third century. This building at Dura-Europos shows evidence of being remodeled from a private dwelling into a place for also accommodating Christian church gatherings (cf. Birkey: 55-57). When churches began to erect their own edifices (from the fourth century on), house churches became obsolete, and the nature of the church changed.

Floyd V. Filson stimulated interest in the household concept of the church with a 1939 article, "The Significance of the Early House Churches." "It was the hospitality of these homes which made possible the Christian worship, common meals, and courage-sustaining fellowship of the group. The Christian movement really rooted in these homes" (109).

Renewal movements and a revival of the house-church concept have usually accompanied each other. A notable example from history is the Anabaptist movement of the sixteenth century. They met as house fellowships, not only because it was illegal and dangerous to meet publicly, but also because they recognized the values of this NT pattern. Small groups functioning as house churches were the strength of the Methodist movement. Today intentional face-to-face groups are emerging many places over the world as the most viable form of church.

(See also *Paul's Idea of Community: The Early House Churches in Their Historical Setting*, by Robert Banks; *Social Aspects of Early Christianity*, by Abraham B. Malherbe; and *Building the House Church*, by Lois Barrett.)

IMAGE OF GOD We need an awareness of the backdrop of biblical usage to give perspective to the several references to the image of God in Colossians. The concept emerges first in Gen. 1:27, where it says that humans are made in the image of God, and thus they have a distinct dignity separate from the animals. The original image is associated with humans being made male and female. The image of God is reflected in male and female together, and they share together in their God-given assignments to multiply and have dominion over the other creatures, plants, and trees (1:26-29; 2:15, 18). Murder is prohibited because humans are made in God's image (Gen. 9:6).

This image denotes the whole personal-physical being, with a capacity to commune with God. The image of God in humans was blurred by sin but not completely lost (Kraus, 1991:114; Roop: 321-323; TDNT, 2:391).

Although pagans commonly made images of deities, God prohibited that practice (Exod. 20:4; Lev. 26:1). God could be "seen" in what he did. The word *icon* is derived from the Greek word for image. Strictly speaking, an icon is a representation rather than an idol, but icons readily become objects of worship and thus idols. Idolatry is implied by the image of the beast in Rev. 13—16, 19—20.

In the NT, primary emphasis falls on Christ as the image of God rather than on the thought of humankind being in the image of God (echoed in 1 Cor. 11:7-12; James 3:9). Christ is the presence of God. In the person of Christ, the invisible God becomes visible (John 1:18). Jesus Christ, as the incarnate Son of God, reveals God's intentions for being made in the image of God. In 2 Cor. 4:4 and Heb. 1:3, we find statements parallel to Col. 1:15, regarding Christ as the image of God.

As the concluding link in the image connection, believers are being made into the image of Christ, who is the image of God. Rom. 8:29 calls us "to be conformed to the image of his Son," and in 2 Cor. 3:18 believers are "being transformed into the same image" (referring to the glory of the Lord). Texts such as Col. 3:10 and Eph. 4:24, on the new self being renewed according to the image of its creator (God), allow for the meaning that the creating (or re-creating) is in the pattern of Christ (cf. Col. 2:9-10; Eph. 4:13, 15). Christ is set forth as the prototype, the demonstration of God's intent. Salvation is more than a matter of restoring standing with God; it is a transformation in which God is at work *in* believers as well as *for* them.

The "image" analogy is that of children being like their parents (Gen. 5:3). That is, those remade in the image of God take on the identity and character of the family of God, with Jesus the firstborn of the family (Rom. 8:29). Col. 3:10-11 explicitly reminds us that the image is experienced in Christian community.

The verses mentioned thus far imply that being re-created into the image of Christ is present experience. Several texts indicate that the transformation is completed at the end, when Christ comes again (e.g., 1 Cor. 15:49 and 1 John 3:2).

"IN CHRIST" The expressions "in Christ" and the variations "in him/ whom" and "in the Lord" appear extensively in Paul's writings, some two hundred times. This wording is exclusively Pauline, although the concept is found elsewhere in the NT, notably in Jesus' words in John 15:4-10, "Abide in me." For Paul, this expression became a code phrase for the new life which God makes possible through Jesus Christ.

In Colossians, *in Christ* (and the variations) occurs nineteen times. In chapters 1—2 we find *in Christ,* and in 3—4 *in the Lord.* The meaning of the phrase is not the same in all cases. In about two-thirds of the occurrences, the words fit the Pauline pattern of using *in Christ* as a code phrase for the new life. A slightly different meaning comes with *in him* in 1:16-17, 19; and 2:9.

We need to bring several related phrases into the picture. The concept corresponding to *in Christ* is *Christ in you* (1:27), or as expressed in Jesus' words, "I in them" (John 15:4-7). *The peace of Christ . . . in your hearts* (3:15) and *the word of Christ . . . in you* (3:16) are similar expressions. The *in Christ* side of the experience is matched and balanced by the *Christ in you* side.

The other related phrase, also found in Colossians, is *with Christ.* Although it is not a code phrase to the extent that *in Christ* is, both phrases convey overlapping concepts. Note the implied contrast between being *in Christ* and *in the world* in 2:20, expressed in NASB: *If you have died with Christ . . . why, as if you were living in the world, do you . . . ?* In addition Paul used fourteen compound words beginning with *sun,* the preposition translated "with." Three of them are found in Colossians (EDM), *co-buried* (2:12), *co-raised* (2:12; 3:1), and *co-quickened* (2:13). The phrase *with Christ* conveys an intimate union, a personal identification with Christ.

The unfolding picture is this. By identifying with Christ in his death and being raised with him to newness of life, the believer comes into a relationship with Christ which Paul labeled as *in Christ.* The experience transcends the limitations of physical, spatial perceptions, especially when the matching experience of *Christ in you* is included. Although the experience has something of a mystical quality, several elements can be identified.

In Christ speaks of connectedness, of a vital union, best thought of in a dynamic rather than a static sense. Faith and obedience are as much a part of the experience as security. *In Christ* designates a sphere of identity. Through being in Christ the Person, humans experience the potential of personhood themselves. Paradoxically, a person *in Christ* is not absorbed into nonexistence, but enters into a realization of being in the image of God.

Not to be missed is the inseparableness of being *in Christ* and being in his body. Except when misread through the colored glasses of an assumed individualism, the NT texts explicitly and implicitly place the *in Christ* experience in a community setting. The corporate dimension should automatically come to mind when the code phrase *in Christ* is encountered.

Finally, being *in Christ* encompasses both present and future experience. *With Christ* is often used with a future reference, as in 3:4. Both expressions also serve to define and shape the believers' here-and-now life, with an unbroken continuity on into ultimate future blessing.

KINGDOM THEOLOGY   The reality of two kingdoms, the kingdom of Christ and the kingdom of this world, stands out in Col. 1:13. These kingdoms are as different as light and darkness. The fact of two kingdoms is generally recognized in Christian circles. Yet there is no uniform answer on how we should understand these two kingdoms and how participants in the kingdom of Christ should relate to the kingdom of this world. A theology of two kingdoms was a key element in the sixteenth-century believers church efforts to restore faithfulness to the NT. That perspective deserves serious attention as the church in each generation seeks to be intentional about the relation of the church to the culture of its world.

In the Anabaptist version of the doctrine of two kingdoms, "the kingdom of Christ was characterized by peace, forgiveness, nonviolence, and patience. The kingdom of the world, or Satan, was strife, vengeance, anger, and the sword which kills. Government belonged to this kingdom of the world" (Klaassen, 1981:244).

The believers church perspective on kingdom theology can perhaps be understood best by differentiating it from other views of kingdom relationships. Historically and currently, we can see the following alternate *kingdom theologies:*

1. In the state church that developed in the fourth century, the two kingdoms meld into one entity. In the *Constantinian synthesis,* as it is called, the

kingdom of this world adopted the church; thus a clear distinction of kingdoms was obliterated. The nature of the church changed as all citizens were included in the newly defined kingdom of Christ. This view of the church, commonly identified as *corpus christianum*, dominated the picture for more than a millennium, and it continued beyond the Reformation.

Nationalism, in which the church is given a favored place but regarded to be in the service of the state, is a modern example of the state attempting to swallow the church for political advantage. Rhetoric about separation of church and state does not change the priority of the state over the church.

2. As a reaction to worldliness in the church, some took a strategy of intentional withdrawal in the form of monasticism and asceticism. However, most considered that kind of separation from the world as the exception rather than the norm for all Christians; those who took that route were called saints.

3. Muhammad, six centuries after Christ, established himself and the Muslim movement with a kingdom view that can be called triumphalism. He rejected Christ's way of the cross, suffering, and redemptive love; accepted the offer of an army; and effectively used political and military power in a campaign of triumph according to his perception of the kingdom of God. The manner in which the kingdom is to be established is a crucial issue between Christians and Muslims.

The Crusades, carried out in response to Muslim conquests, revealed the same mentality. Church and state together engaged in the "Christian" cause of fighting for the faith and against the pagans.

4. One view recognizes the fact of two kingdoms, but sees them nearly on a par. In this view a Christian is equally a citizen of Christ's kingdom and a citizen of the nation-state. The result is a double standard of ethics. What one could not do as a private Christian (e.g., take human life), one is expected to do if so ordered by the state (e.g., kill as a soldier). In seeking to avoid the tension between the two kingdoms, the result is a somewhat schizophrenic Christian identity.

5. Another historic view of the kingdoms has the church using the power of the state to enforce the values and morality of the church in society as a whole. Methods of coercion, violence, and conquest, which characterize the kingdom of this world, have been not only condoned but utilized and blessed in the service of the church's cause. While enjoying the protection of the state, the church seeks to legislate and impose its values on the world's citizenry.

6. A common "solution" is the attempt by some to separate private and public existence. The individual in private life adheres to the rules of holy living that belong with the kingdom of Christ, but in public life the ways of "the real world" are accepted as normative. The idea of accountability in a discipling community is virtually foreign to this view of the two kingdoms.

7. A "chaplaincy" stance aptly describes what the church's relationship to society has often turned out to be. John H. Yoder explains the analogy:

> Whether in industry, in a university, in the military, or in the feudal prince's court from which the term is derived, the chaplain is called to bless the existing power structure. He is given this place by the authority in power; he is supported by that authority and in turn will put the stamp of divine approval upon what is being done there. His social posture is defined by this renouncing the liberty ultimately to challenge the selfish purposes of the

community which he serves and for which he prays at proper times. For him thus to stand in judgment upon this community would be first of all to condemn his own service to it, for his own ritual and moral support of that community's doing in the name of religion is itself the strongest claim the community makes to righteousness. (1971:119)

This chaplain role, which Yoder goes on to critique, grows out of a Constantinian understanding of the kingdoms.

8. A separatist attitude characterizes another category of kingdom theology. This designation is not to be identified with the separatist versus established-church dichotomy in sixteenth- and seventeenth-century England. Rather, it refers to a colony or isolationist concept. Those with this attitude are not anarchists, but choose to be nonparticipants in politics. Government is viewed as legitimate, but the church is not to be involved in such things. They say to the state, "We want to be left alone. We will not tell you how to govern. We choose not to vote, except maybe on wet-dry issues." This view assumes that God's standards are quite different for nations than they are for the church.

9. Some, with a popular and relatively modern view, see the kingdom of Christ as almost totally a future reality, and thus not of significant concern for Christian living in this dispensation. Such persons understand the church to be distinctly different from the kingdom. They consider the kingdom of this world to be real, dangerous, and under judgment, and they seek to escape from it in the rapture. Also, they tend to bypass the teachings and example of Jesus in the Gospels as not relevant for the church now.

10. Social activists are absorbed in making this world a better place; they represent a kingdom theology that assumes the kingdom of this world can be repaired. For them, social change takes priority over personal transformation. In reaction to that overoptimism, some have excluded all social concern from their agenda and concentrate on saving souls.

11. Many who accept the name Christian seem to be oblivious to the existence of two kingdoms, and they ignore or deny any fundamental tension between the kingdom of Christ and the kingdom of the world. This is especially true for those living comfortably. The result is a more or less unconscious accommodation to the values of the kingdom of this world. However, Christians living under oppression, deprivation, and misery can readily understand a two-kingdom theology. Many of them are finding the analysis of liberation theology and its hope attractive, even though some Christian liberationists may use violent methods for change.

A two-kingdom theology based on Christ and the NT resurfaced in the sixteenth century in the Anabaptist movement. It continues to provide a distinct alternative to the diverse kingdom understandings sketched above. Several pertinent features give shape to the believers church understanding of *the two kingdoms:*

1. There are two kingdoms. The distinction is in the acknowledged lordship of Christ. The confession "Jesus is Lord" is the watershed, and it is a political statement as much as it is a religious one.

2. God is sovereign. We live in a universe, not a "multiverse." The dualism of two kingdoms, with the accompanying tensions and clashes, is played out under the sovereignty of God. Even the kingdoms of this world serve the purposes of God (e.g., Jer. 25:8-14; Rom. 13:1-7).

3. The church of Christ is not identical with the kingdom of God/Christ,

but neither is it totally different. Although the kingdom of God/Christ is the bigger reality, the church is the primary locus of the reign of Christ.

4. The kingdom of Christ is present as well as future. Being transferred into the kingdom of God's Son (Col. 1:13) is a present experience, a partly realized eschatology which is a foretaste of more to come. A qualitative continuity between the present and future phases of the kingdom means that the love and peace that characterize the future kingdom are to be the ways of the present kingdom as well.

5. Participation in the kingdom of Christ profoundly affects the view of history, the value system, social ethics, and the view of nation-states (e.g., the kingdom of Christ is supranational in character). Members of this counter kingdom bear certain identifying marks. These are listed by Menno Simons: holy living, brotherly love, witness, and the cross/suffering (cf. J. Yoder, 1969:263-271).

6. Conformity to Christ necessitates a more-or-less radical nonconformity to the kingdom of this world and its ways. The believers church is convinced that the church is to be visible, that there is an identifiable and measurable boundary for the kingdom of Christ, and that the church is to be searching for tangible distinctives. Culturally dated external marks have often been adopted and later discarded. In spite of the limitations of historic attempts, faithful kingdom living seems to require a conscious nonconformity to the world while living out faith in a given culture. Until the truly radical nature of the kingdom of Christ is seen and accepted, the church too easily adopts an accommodationist attitude toward the world. For the church to be the church in the world, it will need to proactively structure life according to obedience to Christ as Lord. This means neither uncritically going with the world's flow nor automatically going an opposite direction, although it often turns out that the ways of Christ are an inversion of the ways of the world. (See *The Upside-Down Kingdom*, Donald B. Kraybill.)

7. Mission is an integral factor in kingdom living, more important than self-preservation. As John H. Yoder writes,

> The political novelty which God brings into the world is a community of those who serve instead of ruling, who suffer instead of inflicting suffering, whose fellowship crosses social lines instead of reinforcing them. This new Christian community in which the walls are broken down not by human idealism or democratic legalism but by the work of Christ is not only a vehicle of the gospel or fruit of the gospel, it is the good news. It is not merely the agent of mission or the constituency of a mission agency. This is the mission. (1969:274)

To what extent the church can or should be involved in matters of justice, be a prophetic voice to the political and economic systems of this world, and seek to influence change for the better—these are disputed issues. Since Christ is already head over all powers and authorities (Col. 2:10), his kingdom is not confined to the church. Hunger, misery, abuse, infanticide, and human bondage are contrary to Christ's heart and kingdom wherever they occur.

While some Christians limit their ministry in the world to responding to symptoms, others sense their mission to address systemic causes of human misery. William Wilberforce is one example of a believer working within the political system to bring an end to slavery in the British Empire. By carefully

critiquing both goals and methods, and by guarding against identifying causes and movements with the kingdom of God, some Christians maintain that
they can avoid going beyond the line of compromise and that they must be
involved. (E.g., *Completely Pro-Life* by Ron Sider advocates political influence.) The view of the cosmic Christ in Colossians challenges the position
that the church should concern itself only with spiritual matters. Reducing
suffering and helping people have a better life—this is only a part of what
Christ's peacemaking and reconciliation envision, but they are a part of the
agenda of Christ's kingdom. (Cf. P. Yoder, *Shalom*.)

In summary, for the church to apply NT kingdom theology to its life and
witness will mean coming to understand itself (1) as a distinct and viable alternative to the kingdom of this world, (2) as an example of the transforming
and reconciling power of Christ, and (3) as Christ's presence in the world to
announce his kingdom and denounce the powers of darkness.

KNOW, KNOWLEDGE   The Greek verb for *know* occurs at Col. 1:6; 4:8,
and the noun for *knowledge* at 1:9, 10; 2:2-3; 3:10. The compound forms,
epiginōskō and *epignōsis* could be expected to be stronger than the simple
forms *ginōskō* and *gnōsis*, but biblical usage shows little difference in meaning (TDNT, 1:689-719). They both appear in 2:2-3. A related verb, *to make
known*, occurs in 1:27; 4:7, 9.

Sometimes in the NT, knowledge has the ordinary meaning: information
(e.g., Col. 4:8). In most instances, however, knowledge has a theological
meaning that goes beyond factual data (cf. C. Moule, 1957:159-164).

The theological meaning of the words *know* and *knowledge* in the NT
builds on the difference between biblical Hebrew and classical Greek connotations of these words. To the typical Greek way of thinking, knowledge is intellectually acquired. From this perspective, the opposite of knowledge is ignorance. In the biblical view, knowledge includes observation and intellectual
grasp, but goes on to focus on experience, encounter, and engagement of the
will. Knowing God goes far beyond accepting the fact that God exists; it
means living in covenant obedience to God as revealed in Israel's experience. The opposite, from the biblical perspective, comes to a climax in disobedience and rebellion.

Christian usage of these terms builds on the OT concept, with several significant enhancements. Christ becomes the center of knowledge that is personal and relational. We come to know God in the person of Christ, who is
God's supreme action and self-revelation. Knowledge of God, of Christ, and
of the gospel includes intellectual awareness of God's actions in the Christ
event. The facts of the gospel are especially important to those who have not
heard of Christ before. But true Christian knowledge and truth cannot remain at the level of mental awareness and correct doctrinal statements. It
must engage the human will in response to the will of God. It must inform
obedient action.

Closely related words include understanding (*sunesis*), 1:9; 2:2; wisdom
(*sophia*), six times in Colossians; and truth (*alētheia*), 1:5-6. These also are
virtually equated with Christ.

In Gnostic views knowledge is seen as a special possession of the initiated
elite. Quite in contrast, in the Christian view all believers are to grow in the experiential knowledge of God in Christ. While some of the same vocabulary
appears in the writings of Paul (and other Christians) as in Gnostic writings, a
uniquely Christian perspective separates the meanings the words carry.

The biblical understanding of knowledge implicit in Colossians stands in contrast to several modern phenomena. The scientific worldview, which has until recently been largely unchallenged in Western culture, tends to define knowledge as observable facts (similar to the classic Greek view). Some try to stand against liberalism and humanism and yet also tend to adopt the tenets of reason, resulting in much emphasis on correct statements about God, the Bible, and faith, and in a more or less legalistic approach to private morality. The challenge before the church is to recognize that teaching and discipling must go beyond intellectual perception to engagement of the will in faith and in obedience to the person of Christ.

LITERARY STRUCTURE For a study of Colossians, it is especially valuable for us to pay close attention to the grammar and literary structure. If we want to understand the complex sentences and string-of-beads thought patterns of Paul's teaching, we need to observe the way words and phrases are arranged. Parts of speech, verb tenses, indicatives, imperatives, subjunctive moods, participles, person, number, gender, pronoun references, and other details of grammar are the basic elements. The organization of the material begins to become evident as we note what is dominant and what is supportive, the function of phrases and clauses (e.g., whether to give a directive, to describe, to explain, to amplify, to contrast, to warn, or to challenge), and the built-in connectives.

With a structural arrangement of the text of Col. 2:6-23, we can more readily see the relationship of the parts, parallels in syntax, and repeated and contrasting words. In the author's translation that follows, the positive lines are in italics and the negative lines in roman type:

(ADMONITION)
(6) *As therefore you received Christ Jesus the Lord,*
    so walk in him,
(7)   *having been rooted*
       and being built up in him
       and being established in the faith
         just as you were taught,
     overflowing with thanksgiving.
(WARNING 1)
(8) Beware lest anyone ensnare you
     through philosophy and empty deception
       according to human tradition,
       according to the elements of the world
       and not according to Christ;
(9) *because in him dwells all the fullness of the divine essence bodily,*
(10)   *and you have come to be filled in him*
   who is the head of all rule and authority.
(11)   *In whom also you were circumcised*
       with a circumcision not done by hand,
       by the putting off the body of flesh,
       by the circumcision of Christ,
(12)   *having been co-buried with him in baptism,*
   in whom also you were co-raised
     through faith in the activity of God
     the one raising him from the dead;

(13)   *and you being dead in your transgressions*
                and in the uncircumcision of your flesh,
        he co-quickened you with him,
                forgiving us all our transgressions.
(14)   *having canceled out the certificate of debt with its regulations*
                which was against us and hostile to us,
        he has taken it out of the way,
                having nailed it to the cross;
(15)   *having stripped the rulers and authorities,*
        he openly exposed them to ridicule,
                having displayed triumph over them in him.
(WARNING 2)
(16) Therefore, do not let anyone impose control over you
                in matters of eating and drinking,
                or in respect of a festival or a new moon or sabbaths;
(17)   which things are a shadow of the things that were to come;
                        but the reality belongs to Christ.
(WARNING 3)
(18) Let no one deprive you,
                being taken up with false humility
                        and worship of angels,
                venturing into visions he has seen,
                being inflated with empty conceit,
                        by his human way of thinking,
                and not holding on to the head,
(19)   *out of whom the whole body*
                        by its joints and tendons,
                        being equipped and joined together,
                grows according to the growth God supplies.
(APPEAL)
(20) *Since you died with Christ*
                out from under the elements of the world,
        why, as though participating in the world,
                are you subjecting yourself to its regulations?
(21)   Do not handle!
                            Do not taste!
                            Do not touch!
(22)   all referring to things destined to perish with use,
                    according to the ordinances and teachings of men,
                    regulations that lead—
(23)   though having a reputation of wisdom
                            in will worship,
                            in mock humility,
                            and in severe treatment of the body,
                            without any value whatsoever—
                    to indulgence of the flesh.

Structure and organization often provide keys to meaning. Structural analyses of several other sections of Colossians are included in this commentary. Such analysis is particularly fruitful in analyzing Col. 2:13-15. The structure and syntax of the Greek text reveal an organization that is not communicated in most translations.

MATURE IN CHRIST, PERFECT The goal of Christian experience identified in Col. 1:28 and 4:12 as *mature* or *perfect* has roots in the OT. Most of
the occurrences of the Greek word *teleios* in the LXX stand for two Hebrew
words, *šalem* and *tamim*, both of which mean whole, entire, complete, un-
blemished, blameless, upright. *Šalem* is based on the same root as the more
familiar word *shalom* (wholeness, peace). *Tamim* is used a few times in reference to God and his actions. A perfect sacrifice animal is one that is unblem-
ished (Exod. 12:5). When used of human character and conduct, the sense is
that of being upright, without being absolutely perfect (Gen. 6:9; 1 Kings
15:3). It also carries the sense of being completely loyal to God, serving with
a single heart (Deut. 18:13; 1 Kings 8:61; 1 Chron. 28:9).

Among Greek philosophers something is perfect when it "cannot be surpassed in its kind" (Aristotle). It was used of a musician or artisan who had
reached the apex of excellence. For Plato the perfect man was one who came
to that level through understanding and philosophical knowledge.

In the NT *teleios* occurs nineteen times. In a number of instances a contrasting condition is indicated:

Rom. 12:2, discerning God's perfect will or being molded by the world
1 Cor. 2:6 (cf. 3:1-3), spiritual or carnal, infants
1 Cor. 13:10, complete or partial
1 Cor. 14:20, adults or children
Eph. 4:13-14, mature or being tossed about, vulnerable to deceit
Heb. 5:12-14, ready for solid food or still infants needing milk

Absolute perfection describes God, but for humans the term seems to be
a relative one. In Christ the potential exists, but the realized perfection is less
than absolute. In Phil. 3:15 Paul calls himself mature/perfect while in the
context also acknowledging that he has not yet fully arrived. The ongoing debate regarding perfectionism hinges on different definitions of sin. Those
who teach sinless perfection define sin in terms of intention. Thus uninten-
tional failures do not negate perfection. Those who teach a need for continuing forgiveness and growth define sin in terms of the act, whether intentional
or not. The latter accuse the former of dishonesty and the former accuse the
latter of denying their potential.

Examples of two other forms of the word for mature/perfect give added
insights. The noun form appears in Col. 3:14, where the point is that maturity
or wholeness in the congregation is the result of the cohesive power of love.
The verb form in 1 John 2:5 and 4:12-18 also associates love and perfection,
as it does in Jesus' prayer for unity in God's love among believers (John
17:23).

In Colossians the concept of being perfect is closely related to fullness
(2:10), to the image into which believers are being made (3:10), and to knowing and doing God's will (4:12). The goals toward which Paul and Epaphras
strive stand as a reminder not to sell short the provision of the gospel of
Christ.

MIND *Mind* is the translation of a number of Hebrew and Greek words.
Members of one family of words appear four times in Colossians: 1:21
(*mind*), 1:28 (*warning*), 2:18 (*mind*), and 3:16 (*admonish*). Seven Greek
words make up the *noe-* family of concepts (cf. the English *noetic*), as shown
here with sample references:

noeō (basic verb)—understand, perceive mentally, consider, pay attention
    to (Mark 7:18; Eph. 3:4)

nous (simple noun)—mind, understanding, thought (Luke 24:45; Rom.
   12:2; 1 Cor. 14:14-19; Col. 2:18)
noēma—what is thought (2 Cor. 10:5; Phil. 4:7)
dianoia—understanding, mind, thought (Mark 12:30; Eph. 4:18; Col.
   1:21; 1 John 5:20)
ennoia—what takes place in the mind (Heb. 4:12; 1 Pet. 4:1)
metanoeō/metanoia—change of mind, repent/repentance, conversion
   (Mark 1:15; Acts 2:38; Rom. 2:4)
noutheteō/nouthesia—adjust the mind, correct, warn, admonish (Acts
   20:31; 1 Cor. 10:11; Col. 1:28; 3:16)
Another Greek word is translated mind in Col. 3:2, from another family
of words used extensively in Romans and Philippians (*phroneō/phronēma*).

POWERS References in Colossians to *thrones, dominions, rulers, powers,*
and *authorities* are part of a larger genre of terms in the NT that are commonly referred to as "principalities and powers" or simply "the powers."
These terms have been receiving more attention since 1962, when Hendrik
Berkhof's book, *Christ and the Powers*, first came out. Volumes by Walter
Wink provide the most thorough analysis of the subject to date: *Naming the
Powers* (1984), *Unmasking the Powers* (1986), and *Engaging the Powers*
(1992). Wink's research led him to affirm seven observations:
   1. "The language of power pervades the whole New Testament." Often
      the terms appear in pairs, or in longer series, such as in Rom. 8:38. A
      partial list includes: rulers, authorities, principalities, powers, domin-
      ions, world rulers, spirits of wickedness, and elements.
   2. "The language of power in the New Testament is imprecise, liquid, in-
      terchangeable, and unsystematic." The same word means different
      things, and the same thing is expressed with different words.
   3. "Despite all this imprecision and interchangeability, clear patterns of
      usage emerge."
   4. "Because these terms are to a degree interchangeable, one or a pair or
      a series can be made to represent them all."
   5. "These Powers are both heavenly and earthly, divine and human, spiri-
      tual and political, invisible and structural." Col. 1:16 is the clearest of
      examples.
   6. "The Powers are also both good and evil."
   7. "Unless the context further specifies, we are to take the terms for power
      in their most comprehensive sense." (Wink, 1984:7-12, 99-100)
   Wink's thesis, in his own words, is this:

I will argue that the "principalities and powers" are the inner and outer aspects of any given manifestation of power. As the inner aspect they are the
spirituality of institutions, the "within" of corporate structures and systems, the inner essence of outer organizations of power. As the outer aspect they are political systems, appointed officials, the "chair" of an organization, laws—in short all the tangible manifestations which power takes.
Every Power tends to have a visible pole, an outer form—be it a church, a
nation, or an economy—and an invisible pole, an inner spirit or driving
force that animates, legitimates, and regulates its physical manifestation in
the world. Neither pole is the cause of the other. Both come into existence
together and cease to exist together. When a particular Power becomes
idolatrous, placing itself above God's purposes for the good of the whole,
then that Power becomes demonic. (1984:5)

Defining the powers as "the structures of earthly existence" proves help-ful for understanding the meaning of the various terms. Five things can be said about these structures:

1. The powers/structures have been created in God's design for a useful purpose. The purpose may be stated as to regularize visible reality (J. Yoder, 1972:143).

2. The powers/structures share in a fallen world. They not only help to hold things together; they also separate and dominate, becoming masters in-stead of servants.

3. Even fallen, they are better than total chaos, and they continue to be under God's ultimate sovereignty.

4. The decisive victory over the powers/structures has been already ac-complished in the cross and resurrection, although they continue to act as if not defeated, when given opportunity.

5. The powers/structures face God's future, final action. They are pres-ent in the consummation.

Contemporary realities that fall in the category of these structures, called the "principalities and powers" in the NT, include the state, class, race, poli-tics, social struggle, public opinion, accepted morality, human tradition, na-tional interest, religious and ethical rules, the judicial system, ideas, ideolo-gies, movements, causes, corporations, institutions, bureaucracies, conglom-erates, methods, routines, and all idols (from lists by Berkhof and William Stringfellow).

These authors also call attention to the strategies and weapons of the powers: propaganda, terror, doublespeak, secrecy, surveillance, exaggera-tion, deception, division, demoralization, jargon, noise, and many more.

Expressed this way in the contemporary idiom, the powers are not to be dismissed as superstitions of an unenlightened past. "Far from being an indi-gestible burden to 'modern' man's credulity or faith, the references show that the immense problems facing modern man are still within the scope of the gospel" (Barth: 176).

Because the powers do bring some structure to human existence, "we cannot live without them." But because they also demand unconditional loy-alty and in fact enslave, "we cannot live with them" (J. Yoder, 1972:146). Therefore, the victory of Christ over the powers becomes a relevant and at-tractive part of the good news. Echoing through the NT is Christ's claim, "All authority in heaven and on earth has been given to me" (Matt. 28:18).

The existence of the church is itself evidence that the domination of the powers has been broken in the death and resurrection of Christ. "The church witness to the victory of Christ consists in creating new patterns of life free from the rule of the powers; acting to neutralize, relativize, demythologize, de-idolize, and debunk the powers; reducing their claims, scope, territory, au-thority, and power; taking them only as modest, limited, purely instrumental agents of service and submission to human life. Paul reminds us that we are at war with the powers, not in a state of peaceful coexistence, detente, or cease-fire. Christ has invaded their territory and domain, and we are his agents and representatives" (Wallis: 71). In what has been called the "chron-ological tension" of this present age, the tension between what is already now but not yet, the church both lives out the victory already won and waits in hope.

PROBLEMS AT COLOSSAE The tone of Col. 2:8-23 reveals the writer's concern about some sort of unhealthy influence on the Lycus Valley Christians. Discussions about the "Colossian heresy" have been going on for a long time without a consensus of opinion. One writer lists forty-four different ideas about the identity of the opponents at Colossae. Another writer, Morna D. Hooker, argues that there is no more evidence of false teaching at Colossae than at Rome or Philippi. She contends that the warnings apply to young believers dealing with the influences of pagan and Jewish neighbors, and give no sure clue that there were heretical teachers.

Much caution needs to be exercised when trying to reconstruct the situation at Colossae. All we have to go on is one side of a conversation. Nevertheless, warnings and other negative comments in the letter itself are the major features on which conjectures can be based, such as the following: the possibility of being deluded and deceived (2:4, 8); philosophy based on human tradition (2:8, 22); basing life on the elements of the universe (2:8, 20); deference to principalities and powers (2:15); dietary restrictions and special days (2:16); worship of or like angels, visions, and pride masked by false humility (2:18); and ascetic practices (2:21, 23).

We may deduce from the strong emphasis on Christ in Colossians that the false teaching in question lowered the position of Christ. Further, the teaching seems to have included something about Christ, however limited or distorted, rather than presenting itself as a non-Christian religion. It was thus similar to many contemporary Christianity-based cults that also claim to offer an improvement over biblical faith. Paul, in response, exposed the teaching as actually a regression from what is available in Christ.

Information about first-century streams of thought suggest several possible sources of the teaching that concerned Paul. *[Religions, p. 313.]* Although Gnosticism did not come into full swing until the second century, the ideas were forming before the Christian era. Notable Gnostic views that could be part of the problem at Colossae include claims to superior wisdom for a select few, speculations about creation and how the universe operates, and a concept of matter as evil (which resulted in both asceticism and indulgence of the flesh). *[Gnosticism, p. 289.]*

Elements of Judaism seem to be present in the troublesome teaching. Jews who had accepted influences of Greek culture (Hellenism) were living in what we call Asia Minor. Some features of the Essene sect of Judaism also parallel aspects of the views and practices addressed in Colossians. For example, Essenism is known to have included a stringent asceticism, a reverence for the sun, and a marked interest in angels.

The probability that Jewish mystical asceticism underlies the troublesome teaching at Colossae is supported by several citations from the Dead Sea Scrolls. Along with considerable interest in angels, the Qumran literature affirms fellowship with heaven without needing a mediator. This could account for Paul's insistence that Christ is exclusively the agent of creation and redemption (cf. Bandstra; Francis, 1975). Since the Essenes exhibit some of the key views later associated with Gnosticism, the Qumran community may be a more likely source of the error at Colossae than a budding Gnosticism. (See Lightfoot: 73-113, for an elaboration of Essene and Gnostic doctrines in the teaching affecting the Lycus Valley; also Nock.)

Using the available data, we cannot fully reconstruct exactly what concerned the apostle and where those ideas came from. However, there is broad agreement among scholars that the ideas that caught Paul's attention were syncretic, a mixture of several strands of thought. Specific ingredients and their relative strength continue to be points of difference (see O'Brien, 1982:xxx-xxxviii, for examples of major schools of thought). A combination of sources seems to fit the sketchy evidence. This includes Judaism (both Essene and Hellenistic varieties), pre-Gnosticism, Mystery Religions, perhaps local pagan cults, and some Christian overtones. *[Religions, p. 313.]*

An important value to be gained from Colossians is in seeing how the apostle responds to the threat—analyzing, exposing, warning, and challenging—all the while majoring in preventive maintenance. The centrality of Christ becomes the test for any system of thought.

RECONCILIATION Of the several metaphors for the work of Christ in the NT, *reconciliation* carries the major part of the freight in Colossians. The vocabulary of this letter does not include *ransom, justification, salvation,* or *propitiation. Redemption* appears in 1:14, with emphasis on the Lord of the new kingdom, in whom there is redemption and forgiveness of sins.

References to reconciliation are relatively infrequent in the NT compared with the theological significance of the concept. The verb form, *reconcile* (*katallassō*), occurs in Rom. 5:10 (twice); 1 Cor. 7:11; and 2 Cor. 5:18-20 (thrice). The noun form, *reconciliation* (*katallagē*), occurs in Rom. 5:11; 11:15; and 2 Cor. 5:18-19 (twice). A verb form (*apokatallassō*) with a prefix which likely adds intensity to the shorter noun, also means reconcile; it occurs in Eph. 2:16; Col. 1:20; and 1:22. (*Diallassomai*, with a different prefix coupled to the same base, is used in Matt. 5:24 in the sense of reconcile.)

These words do not occur in the Greek OT *[Septuagint, p. 316]*. The Hebrew OT has no equivalent for these Greek terms. They do appear in 2 Maccabees several times, revealing that Greek-speaking Judaism thought of God being reconciled under certain conditions: "May [God] hear your prayers and be reconciled with you" (1:5, JB); "If, to punish and discipline us, our living Lord vents his wrath upon us, he will yet be reconciled with his own servants" (7:33, JB). In that period Jewish piety understood that a return to grace required human initiative. Josephus and the rabbis of the time used these Greek terms to mean reconcile, placate, or appease. The gospel brings a different perspective.

In the NT such terms refer to restoring a disrupted or broken relationship, both between God and humans and between humans. To reconcile is to bring alienated parties into council again. By removing the barriers and enmity between parties, oneness is restored. The KJV translates the noun (*katallagē*) one time as atonement, in Rom. 5:11. In its primary sense of "at-one-ment," atonement is equivalent to reconciliation, but as theological terms, *atone* and *atonement* have taken on the connotation of making amends by paying a penalty, a concept not part of the biblical meaning of reconciliation.

Since reconciliation has to do with real relationships among people and primarily with God, the term is a literal reality as well as an image of a mystery beyond full human comprehension. "Colossians picks up this imagery of reconciliation as the foundation of the apostolic ministry. It presents the invitation to humanity to 'be reconciled' as extended to the entire cosmos" (Perkins: 82). Ralph P. Martin has also made a strong case that reconciliation is at the heart of Pauline theology (1981). Reconciliation is a relational concept rather than a legal one, such as justification. Although the term is not in the OT, the concept is at home in the covenant relationship of God and his people. If we put reconciliation near the top of the list of ways to describe what God has done in Christ, that is certainly in harmony with the overall tone of Colossians. (The conflict-victory-liberation motif is also prominent in Colossians, 1:13-14; 2:8-15, as well as in the NT as a whole.)

The meaning of reconciliation (as action and result) depends to a large extent on what the problem is perceived to be. Estrangement identifies the problem—but who is estranged from whom, and who needs to be reconciled with whom? Is the enmity that needs to be removed on God's side, the human side, or on both sides? The idea of an offended and angry deity who needs to be appeased is not part of the biblical revelation of God. Instead, human attitudes and actions of disobedience, rebellion, and hostility toward God cause the estrangement and stand in the way of restored relationships. In the biblical texts, God initiates the action and is said to do the reconciling: *you . . . he has now reconciled* (Col. 1:21-22); "in Christ God was reconciling the world to himself" (2 Cor. 5:19). However, we cannot conclude that humans are totally passive in the restoration, nor that nothing changes from God's side. God's wounded covenant love, expressed as wrath, prompts the self-giving love of Christ's death on behalf of sinners. (See "The Wrath of God," TBC for Col. 3:5-14, pp. 163-165.)

The most notable feature of reconciliation is that it includes being incorporated into a new community of peace. The invitation to accept reconciliation with God is at the same time an offer to participate in the new creation, the new order of human relationships. Reconciliation is personal but it is not limited to an individual relationship with God. Reconciled human relationships are an integral part of things being made as they should be in Christ.

Col. 1:20 says the goal of God's reconciling work through Christ is God's shalom for all of creation. What all this includes and how and when it is accomplished are big questions. Among the views held with respect to *all things* being reconciled are these (outlined by O'Brien, 1982:55-57):

1. Only humans and angels are in mind here since persons, not things, are reconciled.
2. Only humans are included.
3. Only the cosmic powers are included.
4. All that has been disturbed and disrupted is what is returned to order.
5. Of major concern is not who or what is reconciled, but who is the reconciler.
6. *All* is fully inclusive, although not necessarily that all persons will gladly accept Christ's lordship.

Some of these seem too limiting to be in accord with the context. On the other hand, if we accept an inclusive meaning, then the Pauline texts seem to be in tension with passages such as Matt. 12:31-32; Heb. 10:26-27; and Rev. 21:27; 22:14-15. Reasoned explanations of what God can or cannot do would seem to move beyond what humans can know. John Driver's words summarize what reconciliation means in the Bible:

Reconciliation refers to more than the mere removal of a person's guilt. As we have seen, it is called the making of peace (Eph. 2:14-17; Col. 1:20; cf. Rom. 5:1), a new creation (2 Cor. 5:17), and the creation of a new humanity (Eph. 2:10, 15). In reconciling humankind to himself, God has created a new order of human relationships. In Col. 1:20 reconciling and making peace are really parallel concepts. This offers us a valuable clue to understanding the biblical view of reconciliation. The goal of Christ's reconciling work is the establishment of God's *shalom* intentions for people. This peace leaves no part of our common life untouched by God's grace, and it will finally transcend the limitations of our historical existence in its ultimate fulfillment. (1986:186)

RELIGIONS AND PHILOSOPHIES OF THE FIRST CENTURY The early Christian movement did not spread out into a religious vacuum. The religious landscape of the first century included the competing religious loyalties encountered by Christianity and the ideas and philosophies that had the potential of modifying and perverting Christian faith. Four categories are noted here.

Judaism, in which Christianity had its roots, existed in several varieties alongside the emerging church. Palestinian Judaism shows up in the story of the gospels. Among the major parties were the Sadducees, who dominated the Sanhedrin, and the Pharisees, who were concerned about the details of the law. The Samaritans, also claiming to be descendants of the ancient Israelites, held only to the Pentateuch. The term *Hellenistic Judaism* identifies the Hebrew religious heritage influenced by Greek thought and culture. The Jews scattered throughout the Empire were supposedly more affected by Hellenism than the Palestinian Jews. However, Greek ideas seeped into most varieties of Judaism. Philo of Alexandria, Egypt, was a contemporary of Jesus and a prominent representative of Hellenistic Judaism. His writings show influences from Plato, the Stoics, and the Pythagoreans. The Qumran community, associated with the Dead Sea Scrolls, is an example of a relatively small separatist strain of Judaism, the Essenes, who lived near the Dead Sea and elsewhere. They practiced an austere community life with many restrictions and emphasized priestly rules, secrecy, ceremonial washings, and angels. (See Nock: ix-xvii.)

In the Graeco-Roman world many cities had their own gods and accompanying cultic practices. Of particular interest is the development of the state or imperial cult. Emperor worship, which accorded divinity to the ruler, clashed with the Christian confession, "Jesus is Lord." Paul spoke of the religious and political climate of the Roman world in 1 Cor. 8:5-6: "Indeed, even though there may be so-called gods in heaven or on earth—as in fact there are many gods and many lords—yet for us there is one God, the Father, from whom are all things and for whom we exist, and one Lord, Jesus Christ, through whom are all things and through whom we exist."

Mystery religions and cults were a prominent part of the religious scene of the first century. Their origins are largely Eastern, arising in Egypt, Asia Minor, Syria, and Persia. Common elements included secrets, initiations and other rites, and various ascetic practices. Most mystery religions held a dualistic view of the world and the Greek notion that the soul is imprisoned in an evil, material body. One such mystery cult was built around the Greek god Dionysus or Bacchus. Names associated with another mystery cult, spreading out from Alexandria, include Adonis, Osiris, Serapis, and Isis. The Oriental religion of the Great Mother (Cybele) was particularly strong in Asia Minor. The worship of Artemis in Ephesus was apparently closely related. Mithra, a Persian god, was the main figure of yet another mystery cult that spread through the Empire and was a serious rival of Christianity in early centuries.

Worship practices of Mithraism resemble the religious influences at Colossae which Paul critiqued. Mithraic sanctuaries were caves decorated to impress new members. The crypts had images and scenes on the walls and ceiling depicting the cosmic myth surrounding the Iranian god, probably lit dramatically during initiations (cf. Col. 2:18, *dwelling on visions*). Cultic practices promoted mystical religious experiences in which the worshiper could feel close to things divine (Willoughby: 154-155).

With respect to the attraction of mystery religions:

> The imperial age was a time when religion was turning inward and becoming emotional, while philosophy, converted to religion, was following the same trend. There was a cultivated antagonism between spirit and matter and the conscious endeavor to detach one from the other by means of ascetic practices. It was a period of world-weariness and other-worldliness. There was a demand for fresh emotional experience, and the culminating effort was to overleap the bounds of nature and to attain union with the divine in the occult region beyond. These were some of the currents that indicated the general direction of religious thought and feeling when the Christian era began.... (Willoughby: 269)
>
> The man of the early Empire felt that the ultimate control of his disordered universe was not at all in his own hands, but that it rested with supernatural powers on the outside. . . . Whether these powers were friendly or unfriendly or both or either according to circumstances, there was a great variety of opinion; but generally speaking there was no doubt of their power. . . . To such a fearing world as this, which stood in abject awe of supernatural powers, the mystery religions came with the message of salvation through union with the lord of the cult (Willoughby: 272-273).

As people moved over the trade routes, religions became mixed, syncretic. The Lycus Valley, situated on a major travel route, certainly had exposure to these cultic religions of the Empire.

A fourth category of potential influence was philosophy. In the tradition of Socrates, Plato, and Aristotle (in the fourth and fifth centuries before Christ), philosophy gave primary importance to intellect, reason, and wisdom. The various schools of philosophy, most of which predate Christianity, were not religions as such, although they had religious overtones. Most of them regarded matter as evil and the spirit or soul as good. Stoics were strong on ethics and asceticism. Epicureans aimed for mental happiness. Pythagoreans provided an interest in astral forces. Platonists (and later, Neoplatonists) championed mysticism as a way to curb the downward pull of material existence and exhibited a syncretic or eclectic character, incorporating borrowings from other philosophies.

Incipient Gnostic tendencies and ideas are also a religious philosophy that had an impact on the church of the first century. By the second century Gnostic myths are clearly documented. Gnosticism, a serious rival of Christian faith with influence extending into the present, is described in a separate essay. *[Gnosticism, p. 289.]*

We have incomplete information on the influence the contemporary religious streams had on the early church, and what threat they posed. Yet two important values come from our awareness of the religions and philosophies of the time. We are reassured by knowing that the gospel took root and the church grew in spite of the competition and opposition of imbedded cults and religions. God was in the Christian movement with power. Converts came out of varied religious backgrounds. Thus we can have confidence that the gospel centered in Jesus Christ is relevant to human needs and yearnings in any age.

SECRET The term *secret* (or *mystery* in many translations) occurs twenty times in Paul's letters, four are in Colossians, five in 1 Corinthians, and six in Ephesians. It appears once in each of the Synoptics (in parallel accounts) and four times in Revelation. The LXX uses the term nine times (all in Daniel). The word was prominent in Hellenistic (Greek) religions and in Judaism (Nock: 109-124). The "mysteries" were often associated with secret rites, not unlike practices of modern secret societies.

The several occurrences in the NT do not all have precisely the same meaning. To understand the meaning of the term in Colossians, it is important to see how it is used elsewhere. Jesus spoke of "the secrets of the kingdom" (Matt. 13:11; Mark 4:11; Luke 8:10). For the disciples the mystery was disclosed, and for unbelievers it remained concealed. A general category of meanings includes: things not openly made known, the yet-incomprehensible ways of God, and some unspecified matters (e.g., Rom. 11:25; 1 Cor. 4:1; 13:2; 14:2; 15:51; Eph. 5:32; Rev. 1:20).

Note the words used for the content of the mystery (EDM translations):
"mystery of the kingdom" (Matt. 13:11)
"mystery of God" (1 Cor. 2:1; Col. 2:2)
"mystery of the gospel" (Eph. 6:19)
"mystery of Christ" (Eph. 3:4; Col. 4:3)
"mystery of the faith" (1 Tim. 3:9)
"mystery of our religion" (1 Tim. 3:16)
Other associated concepts include knowledge, wisdom, and proclamation of Christ. "Jesus Christ is the essence and contents of the revealed secret" (Barth: 125).

Ephesians has the clearest uses of the major meaning of the term. "In former generations this mystery was not made known to humankind, as it has now been revealed to his holy apostles and prophets by the Spirit: that is, the Gentiles have become fellow heirs, members of the same body, and sharers in the promise in Christ Jesus through the gospel" (Eph. 3:5-6). Barth summarizes the contribution of Ephesians to an understanding of God's secret in these words:

This is the secret that is finally revealed to the saints: God loved them before the creation. He loves them despite their sins and death. He loves them notwithstanding the former division of Jews and Gentiles. He loves them with the intention that they praise his glory. Man did not know this love; the powers did not. But God did. It was God's secret because it was hidden in his heart, identified with his own being, his whole self. Now it has been laid bare. The whole, true God is no longer hidden and unknown. His very heart is opened. (127)

The action verbs associated with secret/mystery also help us to understand the concept: "made known," "revealed," "make everyone see." Obviously the secret is no longer a secret. There is nothing to suggest that it is to be guarded or kept hidden from unworthy people.

As a much-used word in Gnostic circles [*Gnosticism, p. 289*], secret/mystery had the sense of special insights for a select few, but not so in biblical usage. Although Paul used the word, there is no evidence that he borrowed his concept of secret/mystery from the mystery cults of the day. The word was translated into Latin as *sacramentum*, and an association of sacrament and mystery followed. But biblical usage does not have it associated with ceremony or ritual, as in the mystery cults.

The secret's most pervasive meaning (whether the secret of God, the secret of Christ, or the secret of the gospel) is God's unveiled plan in Christ to include both Jews and Gentiles into the church as a demonstration of his wisdom before the principalities and powers (Eph. 3:9-10). The new day was exciting news for some, and a threat to others. Proclaiming this good news was Paul's absorbing assignment.

In the old covenant God in love chose the Hebrews to be a blessing to all nations. Ps. 67 expresses the vision. God blesses his people. All the nations know his saving power. All the peoples praise him. But God's people lost this sense of mission to the nations. An exclusiveness developed that various prophets challenged (Isa. 42:10; 49:6; Jon. 4). The vision was not completely absent when Jesus came into the world. Simeon knew about it (Luke 2:29-32; cf. Matt. 23:15). Jesus' ministry included Gentiles (e.g., Matt. 4:23-25; 8:5-13; 15:21-28).

However, the early church did not come to accept Gentiles without a struggle (Acts 10-11). In the Jerusalem conference (Acts 15) James corrected the prevalent but faulty line of interpretation that supported Jewish exclusiveness and superiority when he acknowledged that indeed the OT anticipated the inclusion of Gentiles into God's people. Full acceptance of God's secret met with resistance until the destruction of Jerusalem in A.D. 70. Paul addressed the Jew-Gentile issue extensively in Galatians and Romans. Affirmations of the secret are found throughout the NT (e.g., Col. 3:10-11; 1 Pet. 2:9-10). Rev. 15:3-4 describes the end result of the miracle God is accomplishing, with praise given to the "King of the nations!"

SEPTUAGINT   The Greek version of the OT known as the Septuagint is an important link between the Testaments. This translation of the Hebrew canon (plus a number of other writings) into Greek was probably completed by the middle of the third century B.C. in Alexandria, Egypt. The name comes from the legendary story that seventy-two Jewish elders did the work in seventy days (Letter of Aristeas). The common abbreviation is LXX.

There are significant differences between the LXX and the dominant Hebrew text, the Masoretic Text (MT) which is the work of Jewish copyists in the Middle Ages. The LXX text is sometimes longer and sometimes shorter than a strict translation of the MT. Other times it is simply different. Proposed explanations for the variation between the MT and the LXX include (1) translation factors (free rendering of the text), (2) transmission factors (changes since it was translated), and (3) following a different Hebrew text. Option (3) is favored above (1) and (2) by many contemporary scholars. When the Jews were living in separated colonies in Babylon, Palestine, and Egypt, it is entirely possible that different families of their Scriptures were collected and preserved. No clear connection seems to exist between the LXX and the Qumran manuscripts (Dead Sea Scrolls). A number of times, modern versions of the OT follow the LXX rather than the MT; footnotes indicate this in the NRSV, NIV, and to a limited extent in NASB.

The LXX is valuable for NT studies. The NT quotations of the OT usually follow the LXX, even when it is different from the MT. This is one indication that the LXX was the chief OT text of the NT era. For that reason alone, we need to take the LXX seriously. The LXX also provides a bridge between the thought worlds of the two Testaments. Word studies are greatly enriched by noting how NT words were used in the LXX. In that way vocabulary and thought forms can be traced through cultural changes and adaptations.

SLAVERY Slavery has been a fact of life for much of human history. By definition, a slave is a person who is the property of another person. Slavery was a conspicuous feature of the world of the NT era. Estimates of the numbers of slaves and the percentage of slaves in the Roman Empire vary greatly because no comprehensive figures are available. Conservative estimates put the ratio at one slave for every three to five free persons. But evidence exists that in some areas the number of slaves far exceeded the free population. William Barclay's undocumented estimate is 60,000,000 slaves in the Roman Empire (1975b:270). The slaves of that era were predominately Caucasian. Sources of slaves included kidnapping, sale of slaves in border areas, indebtedness, self-sale, children of female slaves, and military captives. In peacetime, when military conquest and piracy supplied few slaves, a primary source was homebred slaves.

Slaves had almost no legal rights. Their lives were in the hands of their owners. They were not permitted legal marriage, although common-law arrangements were allowed. Slaves had no legal rights over the children born to them. They worked in labor gangs in mines and fields and served in all kinds of ways in households. Since much work was relegated to slaves, it came to be regarded as demeaning. Idleness and ease resulted in increased sensuality, and slaves were subjected to the worst passions of the masters and their families. Masters and mistresses had absolute power over their slaves, to order, sexually use, abuse, punish, and even kill them. How they fared depended on the kindness or callousness of their owners. Evidence of extreme cruelty to slaves is matched by evidence of movement toward improved treatment. Since they were considered nonpersons, merely chattel and tools, the gospel of Christ was unbelievably good news for them.

The Hebrews had practiced slavery for centuries with considerable humanizing restraints, compared with Greek and Roman rules. The laws of Moses governed slavery, not the least of which was the Jubilee provision of setting slaves free every seven years. The Israelites were reminded that they had once been slaves in Egypt and that Yahweh had set them free. (Representative texts include Exod. 21:1-11; Lev. 25:39-55; Jer. 34:8-22.)

Slaves were responding to the gospel and becoming part of the churches that sprang up across the empire. Percentages are impossible to determine. The presence of both slaves and masters in a congregation, irrespective of numbers, brought the church face to face with the dynamics of the slave system.

A runaway slave could expect to find temporary sanctuary in a household, at least in some parts of the empire. However, a fugitive was to be reported to the master. Harboring someone else's slave indefinitely was an offense against the owner, and the one harboring the slave could be held liable for the lost time (cf. Martin, 1978:144-147). The law also allowed for selling the slave and forwarding the money to the owner. Although severe punishment was the usual rule for returned runaways, Paul mentions nothing about punishment for Onesimus, and Philem. 15-21 implies that there will be none if Paul's appeal to Philemon is effective.

In general the NT assumes the practice of slavery. Certainly the teaching about equality in Christ addresses the relationship of slaves and master in the church. Slave trading is listed as an unholy and profane practice in 1 Tim. 1:9-11 (cf. Rev. 18:13). Following the NT era, church leaders insisted on humane treatment of slaves and encouraged Christians to free their slaves. The Essenes openly denounced slavery and refused to own slaves (Philo, *Every Good Man Is Free* 12.79; IDB, 1976:831, "Slavery in the NT"). An example of compromise with the social system in the fourth century is found in the *Apostolic Canons* (canon 82):

> We do not permit slaves to be ordained to the clergy without their masters' consent; for this would wrong those that owned them. For such a practice would occasion the subversion of families. But if at any time a servant appears worthy to be ordained to a high office, such as Onesimus appears to have been, and if his master allows it, and gives him his freedom, and dismisses him free from his house, let him be ordained. (Ayer: 388)

The practice of slavery persisted in spite of the NT and teachings that followed:

> Slavery was pervasive in ancient civilization. Early Christianity, by its teachings and actions, sought on balance to mitigate the abuses and inhumanity of the system, but it would be left mostly to later ages to realize fully the incompatibility of slavery with human rights and dignity and to seek its abolition. (McHugh: 855)

SOURCES OF COLOSSIANS 1:15-20 Several special features of this christological hymn point rather convincingly to it being a prior composition woven into Colossians. If so, where did it come from? Scholarly answers do not result in a consensus. Here is an abbreviated analysis of the evidence and arguments:

In addition to a discernible liturgical lilt in the lines that fits the composition for corporate oral confession, the style is markedly different from the context in other ways. These lines have third-person subjects, while what precedes has first person and what follows has second person. Yet this somewhat unique block meshes with its setting so well that the reader senses it is an integral part of the flow of thought.

On the assumption that an "original" form of the composition has been incorporated, likely with alterations, form critics have tried to reconstruct the original. Some of these scholars assume further that the original would have been fully symmetrical, and thus they have judged certain phrases to be the author's additions to a borrowed composition. Both assumptions, however, are questionable, and the several proposed reconstructions less than convincing. Kümmel comments,

> It certainly cannot be denied that 1:15-20 bears a hymnic character, but the numerous reconstructions of the hymn expanded by the author that have been undertaken since Lohmeyer's analysis have scarcely led to a really convincing result. Indeed, the assumption is not yet proved that *a hymn constructed according to a strict scheme* has been used and that accordingly every fragment of a sentence beyond the scheme must stem from the author of Col. What is far more likely is that the author of Col. himself [regarded by Kümmel as Paul] has formed the hymn, utilizing traditional material. (343)

Suggested sources of the original composition include (1) a pre-Christian Gnostic text—which does not account for either the OT overtones or the distinctively Christian elements of the original; (2) rabbinic Judaism—which draws attention to OT parallels (e.g., regarding Wisdom) but leaves some unanswered questions; and (3) Hellenistic Judaism—which also recognizes parallels in wisdom literature, but overlooks certain significant differences. (4) Another view is that Paul came to the insights of this hymn in his own faith pilgrimage, building on early-church beliefs and liturgy (Hunter, 1961:123-126).

Paul's background in rabbinic and Hellenistic Judaism most certainly acquainted him with Judaism's keen interest in the wisdom of God. Prov. 3:19 and 8:22-31 celebrate wisdom's part in creation. The extracanonical writings of Hellenistic Judaism also acknowledge the role of wisdom in creation (e.g., Wisd. of Sol. 9:9; Ecclus. 24:3-9). Col. 1:15-20 resonates with some of the contemporary views of wisdom but far surpasses Jewish horizons in its claims for Christ. No Jewish writer, for example, envisioned wisdom as the goal of all creation. Out of his encounter with the risen Christ on the road to Damascus, Paul may well have been the first to connect image of God, priority over creation, incarnation, and reconciliation with Jesus of Nazareth.

A comparison of Gen. 1:1; Prov. 8:22; and Col.1:15-20 reveals some striking affinities. The first word of Genesis, bere'šit, "in the beginning," is a combination of the preposition be, echoed in Col: 1:15-20 as in, through, and for, and the noun rešit, reflected in the words firstborn, before all things, head, and beginning. In the LXX archē stands for rešit in Gen. 1:1 (also in Prov. 8:22, about wisdom), and is a key word in Col. 1:15-20. Image appears in Gen. 1:26 (and in Wisd. of Sol. 7:26, about wisdom) and also begins the description of Christ in Col. 1:15. (See Wright, with an expansion of Burney's observations.)

Thus Paul ascribed to Jesus Christ supremacy and sufficiency in superlative terms. He did this either independently or in collaboration with the faith community. It is truly remarkable that such a view of Christ emerged within three decades of the cross and resurrection. Although not a comprehensive Christology, this hymn is impressive evidence of profound christological understandings in the early church.

TEXT VARIATIONS Differences in translations that affect the meaning may be the result of (1) interpretation of the text, or (2) translators following a different Greek text reading. There are now over 5,500 extant NT manuscripts, with many containing only fragments and others the whole of the NT. Of these, 50 manuscripts contain the entire NT, and none of them is the original autograph. Many variations are found in these manuscripts, most of which are of only minor significance.

Biblical scholars have developed ways of weighing the evidence and offering critical judgment as to what was most likely the original reading. Four families of manuscripts are commonly identified: (1) Alexandrian (including Vaticanus or B, and Sinaiticus or Aleph), given the most weight by most scholars, primarily because they are older and thus closer in time to the original writings; (2) Western (including Bezae or D, Old Latin, and quotations from ancient writers); (3) Eastern or Caesarean (including certain groups of manuscripts in lower case letters and important papyri); and (4) Byzantine (comprised of many later copies of manuscripts).

The first printed Greek text, hurriedly edited by Erasmus early in the sixteenth century, was based on a few late manuscripts from the Byzantine family. His fourth edition was used by other scholars and in time became known as the Textus Receptus (TR; Received Text), the more-or-less standard text for translations into English for the next three centuries. This is the text behind the KJV. Editions of the Greek NT today, such as those produced by the United Bible Societies, make use of a number of older pre-Byzantine manuscripts found in the nineteenth and twentieth centuries and witnessing to text traditions copied less often. (See David Ewert, *From Ancient Tablets to Modern Translations*; Frederic Kenyon, *Our Bible and the Ancient Manuscripts*; Bruce M. Metzger, *The Text of the New Testament*; J. C. Wenger, *God's Word Written*; and Paul M. Zehr, *Biblical Criticism in the Life of the Church*.)

Chapter and verse divisions and punctuation occasionally affect how the text is construed. Punctuation and separation of words were introduced into the Greek texts in the ninth century along with the change from capital letters called uncials, to cursive letters called minuscules (Beegle: 19). In the editions of the Greek text today, editors determine the punctuation. Chapter divisions are attributed to Stephen Langton in the thirteenth century (Kenyon: 190). Rabbi Nathan made verse divisions in the OT in 1448 (Kenyon: 226). The Stephanus Latin Bible of 1555 first divided paragraph units into the verses we know today in the whole Bible.

Although judgments need to be made between variations in text readings (the task of textual criticism), scholars have produced a good Greek text to study and translate. Most of the text variations for Colossians and Philemon are of little consequence for the meaning. Those that are more substantive do not affect major doctrinal issues. Additions to the text were apparently made by some copyists to clarify the meaning, to make it consistent with the context, or in some cases to make Colossians the same as the text of Ephesians. Here is a list of variations judged to be worthy of note:

COLOSSIANS
1:2 The addition on the end, *and the Lord Jesus Christ* (KJV), comes from TR, but is omitted in the UBS text and most translations today. Internal logic is that copyists would more probably have added it than omitted it.
1:7 Evidence is divided between *our* (RSV, NASB, NIV, GNB) and *you(r)* (KJV, NRSV). *Your* fits with the other pronouns in the context. *Our* conveys Paul's initiative in sending Epaphras to Colossae. This is the first of several first-person and second-person pronoun differences in the manuscripts of Colossians.
1:11 A difference in the location of punctuation, added by Greek text editors, accounts for a break after *patience* (NRSV, NIV, NASB, GNB) or after *with joy* (RSV, KJV). The verse division, which also was not part of the original text, carries little weight. Both options are grammatically possible and both make good Pauline sense. Patience, for Paul, was not a matter of grim, Stoic endurance. Recall Jesus' beatitude, "Blessed are you when people revile you and persecute you." On the other hand, giving thanks is not to be a solemn chore, but an exuberant overflow of God-given joy.
1:12 Some ancient manuscripts (mostly Western) have *called* rather than *enabled*. Who is enabled? Evidence is divided between *us* (KJV, RSV, NASB) and *you* (NRSV, NIV, GNB). Paul made a shift from *you* (plural) in 1:9-11 to an inclusive first person, *us*, in verse 13. The manuscripts do not all agree on which person Paul used in verse 12, and it makes little difference.
1:14 The words *through his blood* (KJV following TR) are not in the older sources, and they were likely transferred from Eph. 1:7.

Essays

321

1:20 Because of divided evidence, the words *through him* occur a second time in brackets in the UBS text. Inclusion of the phrase is reflected in KJV and NASB.

1:22 Textual evidence is divided between the active form of the verb, *he has reconciled you,* and the passive form, *you have been reconciled.*

1:28 The addition of *Jesus* (KJV) to *Christ* has only limited late manuscript support.

2:2 Of the eight different readings, the longest is represented by KJV, *of the mystery of God, and of the Father, and of Christ,* and the shortest by the JB, which contains no reference to Christ at all. Variations were likely introduced in an attempt to clarity the meaning. In the best-supported text (literally, EDM), *of the secret (mystery) of God, of Christ,* the three nouns (secret, God, Christ) are all in the genitive case, which leaves as a matter for interpretation whether Christ is equated with the secret or with God.

2:11 The TR reading accounts for the additional words in KJV, *the body of the sins of the flesh.* Omitting those words has strong textual support.

2:18 The Greek text behind KJV has a negative in the wording (*which he hath not seen*), apparently added to make one kind of sense out of the phrase. That reading has little support.

3:4 Manuscript evidence is divided between *your* and *our.* The UBS Greek text has *your,* which agrees with the *you* in the last part of verse 4. None of the verbs in verses 1-3 are first person. However, Paul did occasionally slip into first-person pronouns, as in 1:13, including himself (and all believers).

3:6 The inclusion of the phrase *on those who are disobedient* has sharply divided support. In the UBS text, it is in brackets. It may have been introduced into some manuscripts from Eph. 5:6, where the phrase has unquestionable support.

3:13 *Lord* has strong manuscript support and is found in most translations. Text variations include *Christ* (TR), *God,* and *God in Christ.* Different ideas about who forgives sins seem to be reflected, as well as interest in making the text agree with Eph. 4:32.

4:15 The ending of the accusative form of the name, *Numphan,* allows for either masculine or feminine gender. Therefore, the pronoun modifying *house* becomes the determinant. Textual evidence is divided between *her, their,* and *his,* in that descending order of weight. Most modern translations follow the UBS text, which has *her.*

4:18. The *Amen* and the note about the place of writing, found in KJV, are not part of the most strongly supported text here or at the end of Philemon.

PHILEMON

6 Both *we* (NRSV, NIV) and plural *you* (KJV, NASB) have strong textual support. A change by Paul to first person is more likely than a change to second-person plural when the surrounding occurrences of *you* are all singular.

12 Verse 12 suffered a lot of alterations by copyists. See KJV for a late version of the text.

23 Neither texts (with punctuation added editorially) nor translations (even in margins) have a comma between Christ and Jesus. For Jesus to stand as a separate name (starting the list of persons giving greetings), the Greek name would need an additional *s* at the end, a form without textual support.

25 Concerning the added *Amen* (KJV), see the comment on Col. 4:18.

THANKSGIVING Seven texts are scattered throughout the four chapters of Colossians, using the words *thank, giving thanks, thanksgiving, thankful,* and *gratitude.* These give Colossians an unmistakable aroma of thanksgiving, and each passage makes a distinct contribution to the total emphasis on thanksgiving. Each instance, and the composite even more so, models a pattern of thankfulness from which contemporary Christians may take lessons. The several texts and what they inspire are as follows:

Reference/Text	Explanations	Thanksgiving Today
1:3-6 *In our prayers for you we always thank God . . . for we have heard of your faith . . . and of the love that you have . . . because of the hope laid up for you in heaven.*	Regular thanks goes to God for others, specifically for evidence of fruits of the gospel in their experience as part of the progress of God's movement.	We are called to thank God for individual lives and for corporate life, for what the gospel is producing in them (quite apart from asking God to fix, change, or help them).
1:11-14 *Joyfully giving thanks to the Father, who has enabled you . . . . He has rescued us . . . and transferred us . . . redemption . . . forgiveness.*	Thanksgiving focuses on what God has done for us, giving attention to the fact of his powerful action as much as to the benefits.	Thanks can stem from reviewing God's actions in the style of Psalms that rehearse God's saving deeds, including specific instances up to the present.
2:6-7 *As you therefore have received Christ Jesus the Lord, continue to live your lives in him, rooted and built up in him and established in the faith, . . . abounding in thanksgiving.*	Personal experience of Christ as Lord, with focus on security and stability, results in an overflow of thanks.	Let thanksgiving arise out of a personal inventory of life in Christ, roots and growth, responding out of what has been experienced.
3:15 *And let the peace of Christ rule in your hearts, to which indeed you were called in the one body. And be thankful.*	Gratitude arises out of recognition that Christ, who is peace, enables peaceful relationships in the body. The community of faith is to let Christ do his peace	The church needs to acknowledge and celebrate that Christ is making community possible. Specific instances of Christ's "umpire" ministry are rea-

ministry and then give thanks for it.

sons for responses of thanks.

3:16 *Let the word of Christ dwell in you richly; teach and admonish one another in all wisdom; and with gratitude in your hearts sing psalms, hymns, and spiritual songs to God.*

The internalized word of Christ is to be experienced in corporate life and worship. The word of grace within is to issue in sound teaching and grateful singing.

With the word of Christ within, voice and heart, mind and spirit engage in a concert of praise and gratitude. Without that inner source, outward expressions lack integrity.

3:17 *And whatever you do, in word or deed, do everything in the name of the Lord Jesus, giving thanks to God the Father through him.*

"Doing" in his name is linked with thanksgiving. Having all of life sanctified in Christ is a privilege. To live all of life in the name/character of Christ is praise.

Thanksgiving is not to be separated from faithful living. In addition to individual praise-living, gathered worship is the counterpart of the scattered witness.

4:2-4 *Devote yourselves to prayer, keeping alert in it with thanksgiving. At the same time pray for us as well that God will open to us a door for the word, that we may declare the mystery of Christ, for which I am in prison, so that I may reveal it clearly, as I should.*

Thanksgiving is seen as an integral part of persistent, watchful prayer. Here thanksgiving is coupled with intercession, with focus on open doors and witness. A shared fellowship of the gospel is implied. (See also Philippians 1:5 and 4:6.)

Thanksgiving in the church is rightly coupled with recognition of privileges and opportunities, with acceptance of God's help, with acknowledgment of dependence, and with affirmation of those witnessing for Christ.

TITLES FOR CHRIST The several names and titles used for Christ in Colossians are primary evidence concerning the author's understanding of Christ. The designations in NRSV are consistent with the UBS Greek text. We find the following:

Christ, 25 times (alone and in combinations)

Lord, 13 times, plus the same word once translated as *Master*. (In several

instances the reference could be to Yahweh, but the same word is used
for both Yahweh and Jesus Christ in the N.T.)
Jesus, 6 times (never alone)
Son, 1 time

In combinations we find *Christ Jesus*, 3 times; *Lord Jesus*, 1 time; *Lord
Christ*, 1 time; *Lord Jesus Christ*, 1 time; and *Christ Jesus the Lord*,
1 time. Another essay discusses the expressions *in Christ, with Christ,*
and *in the Lord*—all three in Colossians. *[In Christ, p. 299.]*

A listing of these titles in Colossians yields several observations. *Christ*
predominates as the title in the first part of the letter, while *Lord* predominates in the latter part, particularly from 3:17 on. Along with that shift in usage, note that *in Christ* occurs only in Col. 1—2, and *in the Lord* only in Col.
3—4. *[In Christ, p. 299.]* "The believer is spoken of as being deeply rooted 'in
Christ,' but he is summoned to walk 'in the Lord' " (Schweizer, 1982:171).
    The several names and titles have important emphases of meaning. *Jesus*
is the human name given by special direction (Matt. 1:21; Luke 1:31). Jesus
was a common Jewish name, an equivalent to the Hebrew name Joshua or
Jehoshua, meaning Yahweh saves.
    Christ is the Greek equivalent to the Hebrew title Messiah, with a basic
meaning of Anointed. Christ is a messianic title, but in usage becomes also a
name. Jesus did not use the term concerning himself, preferring "Son of
Man." Peter's proclamation that God made Jesus both Lord and Christ (Acts
2:36) is highly significant.
    Lord is also a title that has become a name. In NT usage it has several
meanings. Sometimes it is no more than a polite form of address, like Sir.
Sometimes it means *Master,* as in Col. 4:1. In about two hundred occurrences in the NT, it designates Christ as Lord, with divine lordship implied.
The term has political overtones, for it puts Christ over against a Caesar who
calls himself lord. Saying "Jesus is Lord" is both a confession of faith, a commitment of obedience, and a declaration of allegiance in the midst of competing loyalties (1 Cor. 12:3).

TRIAD OF GRACES   The Christian triad, faith-love-hope (Col. 1:4-5), is a
combination that cannot be explained as mere coincidence. The eleven instances of the triad in the NT are as follows, with varied sequence of terms:

1 Thess. 1:3   your work of faith
                              and labor of love
                              and steadfastness of hope

1 Thess. 5:8   the breastplate of faith
                              and love,
                              and for a helmet the hope of salvation

Col. 1:4-5   your faith in Christ Jesus
                              and of the love that you have for all the saints,
                              because of the hope laid up for you

Eph. 4:2-5   bearing with one another in love . . .
                              one hope

	. . . one faith
Heb. 6:10-12	the love that you showed . . . full assurance of hope . . . through faith and patience inherit the promises
Heb. 10:22-24	full assurance of faith . . . the confession of our hope . . . to love and good deeds
Gal. 5:5-6	by faith, we eagerly wait . . . the hope of righteousness . . . through love
1 Cor. 13:13	faith, hope, and love abide
Rom. 5:1-5	justified by faith . . . boast in our hope . . . God's love has been poured into our hearts
1 Pet. 1:21-22	your faith and hope are set on God . . . genuine mutual love
1 Pet. 1:3-8	a living hope . . . protected . . . through faith . . . you love him

In addition to these occurrences in Paul, Peter, and Hebrews, the triad occurs also in the Apostolic Fathers (Barnabas, Polycarp). It does not occur in the Synoptics, Acts, or the writings of John. The combination is not always as compact as it is in 1 Cor. 13:13, but one cannot avoid the conclusion that these were three key words in the vocabulary of the early church. In several places, mention of one of the terms seems to have led to mention of the other two, even if not incorporated smoothly (e.g., 1 Thess. 5:8, which would most naturally read "the breastplate of faith and the helmet of salvation").

These three words (in several forms in the Greek text) occur in Colossians in the following places:

faith (noun) 1:4, 23; 2:5, 7, 12
faithful (adjective) 1:2, 7; 4:7, 9
love (noun) 1:4, 8, 13 (Greek: *the Son of his love*); 2:2; 3:14
love (verb) 3:19
beloved (participle) 3:12
beloved (adjective) 1:7; 4:7, 9, 14
hope (noun) 1:5, 23, 27

Palestine in New Testament Times

Abila · · Damascus
ABILENE

Sidon ·
Zarephath ·

Mt. Hermon ·

SYRIA

· Tyre
· Caesarea Philippi

PHOENICIA

GALILEE

Ptolemais ·
Chorazin
· Bethsaida
Capernaum ·
Mt. Carmel ·
Magadan · Sea of Galilee
Cana · Tiberias

Nazareth ·
· Gadara
Nain · Mt. Tabor

DECAPOLIS

· Caesarea

Salim ·
Aenon ·
Jordan River
Gerasa ·

Samaria
Mt. Ebal ·

SAMARIA · Sychar

PEREA

· Mt. Gerizim

· Joppa
+ Arimathea

Ephraim ·
Jericho ·
Emmaus
· + Bethany
· Azotus
Jerusalem ·
Qumran ·

JUDEA
Bethany ·
Bethlehem ·

Mediterranean Sea

Ascalon ·
Dead Sea
· Machaerus

· Gaza
· Hebron

IDUMEA

NABATEA

Map by Paula Johnson, Merrill R. Miller, and Jan Gleysteen

+ Means city has uncertain location

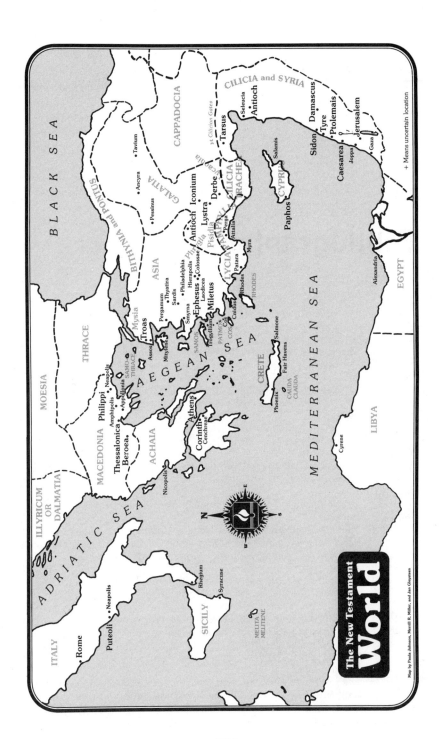

The New Testament World

Map by Paula Johnson, Merrill R. Miller, and Jan Gleysteen

BLACK SEA

CAPPADOCIA

CILICIA and SYRIA

BITHYNIA and PONTUS

Tavium

Ancyra

Pessinus

GALATIA

Seleucia
Antioch

Damascus
Tyre
Sidon
Ptolemais
Jerusalem
Gaza

St Cilician Gates
Tarsus

Iconium

CILICIA

Antioch
Pisidia
Lystra
Derbe
Perga
Attalia

Caesarea
Joppa

+ Means uncertain location

ASIA

Philadelphia
Hierapolis
Colossae
Laodicea

PAMPHYLIA

LYCIA

Salamis

CYPRUS

Patara
Myra

Paphos

Pergamum
Thyatira
Sardis

Smyrna

Ephesus
Miletus

Trogyllium

SAMOS
THRACE

PATMOS
COS

Caudos

RHODES

Rhodes

Cnidus

Salmone

Alexandria

Mysia
Troas

Assos

Mitylene

EGYPT

SAMOS

AEGEAN SEA

MEDITERRANEAN SEA

CRETE

Fair Havens

THRACE

MOESIA

Neapolis

Appolonia

Amphipolis

Philippi

MACEDONIA

Thessalonica

Beroea

ACHAIA

Athens

Corinth
Cenchrea

Nicopolis

Phoenix

CAUDA
CLAUDA

LIBYA

Cyrene

ILLYRICUM
OR
DALMATIA

ADRIATIC SEA

ITALY

Rome

Puteoli

Neapolis

Rhegium

Syracusae

SICILY

MELITA
MELITENE

N E S W

327

Bibliography

Allen, Roland
    1962   *Missionary Methods: St. Paul's or Ours?* Grand Rapids: Eerdmans.
Argall, Randall
    1987   "The Source of a Religious Error in Colossae." *Calvin Theological Journal* 22:6-20.
Augustine of Hippo
    1956   *De patientia* (On Patience). In *Nicene and Post-Nicene Fathers of the Christian Church*, 3:527-436. Grand Rapids: Eerdmans.
Ayer, Joseph Cullen, Jr.
    1949   *A Source Book for Ancient Church History.* New York: Charles Scribner's Sons.
Baggott, L. J.
    1961   *A New Approach to Colossians.* London: Mowbray.
Bandstra, Andrew J.
    1974   "Did the Colossian Errorists Need a Mediator?" In *New Dimensions in New Testament Study,* ed. by Richard N. Longenecker and Merrill C. Tenny, 329-343. Grand Rapids: Zondervan.
Banks, Robert
    1980   *Paul's Idea of Community: The Early House Churches and Their Historical Setting.* Grand Rapids: Eerdmans.
Barclay, William
    1963   *The All-Sufficient Christ.* Philadelphia: Westminster Press.
    1964   *New Testament Words.* London: SCM Press.
    1975a *The Letters to the Philippians, Colossians, and Thessalonians.* Rev. ed. DSB: The Daily Study Bible Series. Philadelphia: Westminster Press.
    1975b *The Letters to Timothy, Titus, and Philemon.* Rev. ed. DSB: The Daily Study Bible Series. Philadelphia: Westminster Press.
Barrett, Lois
    1986   *Building the House Church.* Scottdale, Pa.: Herald Press.

Barth, Markus
　　1974　*Ephesians.* Anchor Bible, 34-34A. Garden City, N.Y.: Doubleday
　　　　　and Company.
Bauer, Walter
　　1979　*A Greek-English Lexicon of the New Testament and Other Early
　　　　　Christian Literature.* Trans. and ed. by W. F. Arndt and F. W.
　　　　　Gingrich, rev. and augmented by Gingrich and F. W. Danker. Chi-
　　　　　cago: University Press.
Bauman, Clarence
　　1964　"The Theology of 'The Two Kingdoms.' A Comparison of Luther
　　　　　and the Anabaptists." *Mennonite Quarterly Review* 38:37-49,
　　　　　60.
Beasley-Murray, George R.
　　1962　*Baptism in the New Testament.* Grand Rapids: Eerdmans.
　　1973　"The Second Chapter of Colossians." *Review and Expositor*
　　　　　70:469-479.
Beasley-Murray, Paul
　　1980　"Colossians 1:15-20, An Early Christian Hymn Celebrating the
　　　　　Lordship of Christ." In *Pauline Studies,* ed. by D. A. Hagner and
　　　　　M. J. Harris, 169-183. Grand Rapids: Eerdmans.
Bedale, Stephen
　　1954　"The Meaning of *kephalē* in the Pauline Epistles." *Journal of
　　　　　Theological Studies* 5:211-215.
Beegle, Dewey M.
　　1960　*God's Word into English.* New York: Harper and Brothers.
Beker, J. Christiaan
　　1990　*The Triumph of God: The Essence of Paul's Thought.* Tr. by Lo-
　　　　　ren T. Stuckenbruck. Minneapolis: Augsburg Fortress.
Bender, Harold S.
　　1962　*These Are My People.* Scottdale, Pa.: Herald Press.
Berkhof, Hendrik
　　1977　*Christ and the Powers.* Tr. by John H. Yoder, 2d ed. Scottdale,
　　　　　Pa.: Herald Press.
Birkey, Del
　　1988　*The House Church.* Scottdale, Pa.: Herald Press.
Blass, F., and A. Debrunner
　　1961　*A Greek Grammar to the New Testament.* Tr. and ed. by R. W.
　　　　　Funk. Chicago: University Press.
Bosch, David J.
　　1983　"The Structure of Mission: An Exposition of Matthew 28:16-20."
　　　　　In *Exploring Church Growth,* ed. by Wilbert R. Shenk, 218-248.
　　　　　Grand Rapids: Eerdmans.
Bratcher, Robert G. and Nida, Eugene, A.
　　1977　*A Translator's Handbook on Paul's Letters to the Colossians and
　　　　　to Philemon.* Stuttgart: United Bible Societies.
Brown, Raymond E.
　　1968　*The Semitic Background of the Term 'Mystery' in the New Testa-
　　　　　ment.* Philadelphia: Fortress Press.
Bruce, F. F.
　　1957　*Commentary on the Epistle to the Colossians* (with *Commentary
　　　　　on Ephesians,* by E. K. Simpson). New International Commentary
　　　　　on the New Testament. Grand Rapids: Eerdmans.

1965   *The Letters of Paul: An Expanded Paraphrase.* Grand Rapids:
        Eerdmans.
1977   *Paul: Apostle of the Heart Set Free.* Grand Rapids: Eerdmans.
1984   "Jews and Christians in the Lycus Valley." *Bibliotheca Sacra*
        141:3-15.
1984   "The 'Christ Hymn' of Colossians 1:15-20." *Bibliotheca Sacra*
        141:99-111.
1984   "The Colossian Heresy." *Bibliotheca Sacra* 141:195-208.
1984   "Christ as Conqueror and Reconciler." *Bibliotheca Sacra*
        141:291-302.
Burney, C. F.
1926   "Christ as the *Archē* of Creation." *Journal of Theological Studies*
        27:160-177.
Caird, G. B.
1981   *Paul's Letters from Prison.* New Clarendon Bible. London: Ox-
        ford University Press.
Carrington, Philip
1940   *The Primitive Christian Catechism.* Cambridge: University Press.
Church, F. Forrester
1978   "Rhetorical Structure and Design in Philemon." *Harvard Theo-
        logical Review* 71:17-33.
Cope, Lamar
1985   "On Rethinking the Philemon-Colossians Connection." *Biblical
        Research* 33:45-50.
Cranfield, C. E. B.
1975   *The Epistle to the Romans.* International Critical Commentary.
        Edinburgh: T & T Clark.
Cullmann, Oscar
1959   *The Christology of the New Testament.* Philadelphia: Westmin-
        ster Press.
Driver, John
1976   *Community and Commitment.* Scottdale, Pa.: Herald Press.
1989   *Understanding the Atonement for the Mission of the Church.*
        Scottdale, Pa.: Herald Press.
1988   *How Christians Made Peace with War.* Peace and Justice Series.
        Scottdale, Pa.: Herald Press.
Dunn, James D. G.
1975   *Jesus and the Spirit.* Philadelphia: Westminster Press.
1980   *Christology in the Making: A New Testament Inquiry into the Or-
        igins of the Doctrine of the Incarnation.* Philadelphia: Westmin-
        ster Press.
Durnbaugh, Donald F.
1968   *The Believers' Church.* Scottdale, Pa.: Herald Press.
Eller, Vernard
1987   *Christian Anarchy: Jesus' Primacy Over the Powers.* Grand Rap-
        ids: Eerdmans.
Ewert, David
1983   *From Ancient Tablets to Modern Translations.* Grand Rapids:
        Zondervan.
Filson, Floyd V.
1939   "The Significance of the Early House Churches." *Journal of Bibli-
        cal Literature* 58:109-112.

Finger, Thomas N.
  1985-89 *Christian Theology: An Eschatological Approach.* 2 vols. Scott-
      dale, Pa.: Herald Press.
France, R. T.
  1982   "The Worship of Jesus: A Neglected Factor in Christological De-
      bate?" In *Christ the Lord,* ed. by Harold H. Rowdon, 17-36.
      Downers Grove, Ill.: InterVarsity Press.
Francis, Fred O., and Wayne A. Meeks
  1975   *Conflict at Colossae.* Society of Biblical Literature. Missoula,
      Montana: Scholar's Press.
  1977   "The Christological Argument of Colossians." In *God's Christ
      and His People,* ed. by Jacob Jervell and Wayne A. Meeks, 192-
      207. Oslo, Norway: Universitetsforlaget.
Friedmann, Robert
  1973   *The Theology of Anabaptism.* Scottdale, Pa.: Herald Press.
Gallardo, José
  1984   "Ethics and Mission." In *Anabaptism and Mission,* ed. by Wilbert
      R. Shenk, 137-157. Scottdale, Pa.: Herald Press.
Garber, S. David
  1974   "Symbolism of Heavenly Robes in the New Testament in Com-
      parison with Gnostic Thought." Ph.D. diss., Princeton Theological
      Seminary.
Getty, Mary Ann
  1987   "The Theology of Philemon." *Society of Biblical Literature Ab-
      stracts and Seminar Papers* 26:503-508.
Goodenough, E. R.
  1929   "Paul and Onesimus." *Harvard Theological Review* 22:181-183.
Goodspeed, Edgar J.
  1937   *An Introduction to the New Testament.* Chicago: University
      Press.
Grebel, Conrad
  1985   *The Sources of Swiss Anabaptism: The Grebel Letters and Relat-
      ed Documents.* Leland Harder, ed. Classics of the Radical
      Reformation, 4. Scottdale, Pa.: Herald Press.
Grimsrud, Ted
  1987   *Triumph of the Lamb.* Scottdale, Pa.: Herald Press.
Halteman, Jim
  1988   *Market Capitalism and Christianity.* Grand Rapids: Baker Book
      House.
Harms-Wiebe, Raymond Peter
  1987   "A Pauline Power Encounter Response to Umbanda." *Mission
      Focus* 15:6-10.
Harris, Murray J.
  1991   *Colossians and Philemon.* Exegetical Guide to the Greek New
      Testament. Grand Rapids: Eerdmans.
Harrison, P. N.
  1950   "Onesimus and Philemon." *Anglican Theological Review*
      32:268-294.
Hauerwas, Stanley, and William H. Willimon
  1989   *Resident Aliens.* Nashville: Abingdon Press.
Hendricks, W. L.
  1975   "All in All: Theological Themes in Colossians." *South Western
      Journal of Theology* 16:23-25.

Hershberger, Guy F.
  1946   *War, Peace, and Nonresistance.* Scottdale, Pa.: Herald Press.
Hiebert, Paul G.
  1992   "Spiritual Warfare: Biblical Perspectives." *Mission Focus* 20:41-46.
Hinson, E. Glenn
  1973   "The Christian Household in Colossians 3:18—4:1." *Review and Expositor* 70:495-506.
Hooker, Morna D.
  1973   "Were There False Teachers in Colossae?" In *Christ and Spirit in the New Testament,* ed. by B. Lindars and S. S. Smalley, 315-331. Cambridge: Cambridge University Press.
Hornus, Jean-Michel
  1980   *It is Not Lawful for Me to Fight.* Tr. by A. Kreider and O. Coburn. Scottdale, Pa.: Herald Press.
Horsch, John
  1950   *Mennonites in Europe.* Scottdale, Pa.: Mennonite Publishing House.
Hubmaier, Balthasar
  1989   "Eighteen Theses Concerning the Christian Life," 1524. In *Balthasar Hubmaier: Theologian of Anabaptism,* ed. by H. W. Pipkin and J. H. Yoder, 30-34. Scottdale, Pa.: Herald Press.
Hunter, Achibald M.
  1938   "Faith, Hope, Love: A Primitive Christian Triad." *Expository Times* 49:428-429.
  1959   *Galatians, Ephesians, Philippians, Colossians.* Layman's Bible Commentary, 22. Richmond, Va.: John Knox Press.
  1961   *Paul and His Predecessors.* Philadelphia: Westminster Press.
IDB
  1962   *The Interpreter's Dictionary of the Bible.* 4 vols. George A. Buttrick, ed. Nashville: Abingdon Press.
  1976   *The Interpreter's Dictionary of the Bible.* Supplementary vol. Keith Grim, ed. Nashville: Abingdon Press.
Jeschke, Marlin
  1983   *Believers Baptism for Children of the Church.* Scottdale, Pa., Herald Press.
Kenyon, Fredric
  1939   *Our Bible and the Ancient Manuscripts.* New York: Harper and Brothers.
Klaassen, Walter
  1973   *Anabaptism: Neither Catholic nor Protestant.* Waterloo, Ont.: Conrad Press.
  1981   *Anabaptism in Outline: Selected Primary Sources.* Scottdale, Pa.: Herald Press.
Knox, John
  1959   *Philemon Among the Letters of Paul.* New York: Abingdon Press.
Koch, Eldon W.
  1963   "A Cameo of Koinonia: The Letter to Philemon." *Interpretation* 17:183-187.
Kraus, C. Norman
  1974   *The Community of the Spirit.* Grand Rapids: Eerdmans.
  1987   *Jesus Christ Our Lord: Christology from a Disciple's Perspective.* Revised, 1990. Scottdale, Pa.: Herald Press.

1991   *God Our Savior: Theology in a Christological Mode.* Scottdale,
       Pa.: Herald Press.
Kraybill, Donald B.
1990   *The Upside-Down Kingdom.* Rev. ed. Scottdale, Pa.: Herald
       Press.
Kroeger, Catherine Clark
1986   "1 Timothy 2:12—A Classicist's View." In *Women, Authority,
       and the Bible,* ed. by Alvera Michelsen and James Hoover.
       Downers Grove, Ill.: InterVarsity Press.
Kroeger, Richard Clark, and Catherine Clark Kroeger
1992   *I Suffer Not a Woman: Rethinking 1 Timothy 2:11-15 in Light of
       Ancient Evidence.* Grand Rapids: Baker Book House.
Kümmel, Werner Georg
1973   *Introduction to the New Testament.* Rev. English ed. Nashville:
       Abingdon Press.
Ladd, George Eldon
1973   "Paul's Friends in Colossians 4:7-16." *Review and Expositor* 70
       507-514.
Lane, William L.
1974   *The Gospel According to Mark.* New International Commentary
       on the New Testament. Grand Rapids: Eerdmans.
Lederach, Paul M.
1980   *A Third Way.* Scottdale, Pa.: Herald Press.
Lewis, C. S.
1960   *Mere Christianity.* New York: Macmillan Publishing Company.
Lightfoot, J. B.
1875   *St. Paul's Epistles to the Colossians and Philemon.* Lynn, Mass.:
       Hendrickson.
Lohse, Eduard
1971   *Colossians and Philemon.* Hermeneia. Philadelphia: Fortress
       Press.
Longenecker, Richard N.
1970   *The Christology of Early Jewish Christianity.* Studies in Biblical
       Theology, 2d ser., 17. Naperville, Ill.: Alec R. Allenson.
Lucas, R. C.
1980   *Fullness and Freedom: The Message of Colossians and
       Philemon.* Downers Grove, Ill.: InterVarsity Press.
McDonald, H. Dermot
1980   *Commentary on Colossians and Philemon.* Waco, Tex.: Word
       Books.
McHugh, Michael P.
1990   "Slavery." In *Encyclopedia of Early Christianity,* ed. Everett Fer-
       guson, 854-855. New York: Garland Pub.
McKinnon, James
1987   *Music in Early Christian Literature.* Cambridge: University Press.
Mains, David
1989   *Thy Kingdom Come.* Grand Rapids: Zondervan.
Malherbe, Abraham J.
1983   *Social Aspects of Early Christianity.* 2d ed. Philadelphia, Fortress
       Press.
Marshall, I. Howard
1973   "New Wine in Old Wine Skins: V. The Biblical Use of the Word
       'Ekklēsia.' " *Expository Times* 84:359-364.

1976   *The Origins of New Testament Christology.* Downers Grove, Ill.: InterVarsity Press.
1982   "Incarnational Christology in the NT." In *Christ the Lord,* ed. by Harold H. Rowdon. Downers Grove, Ill.: InterVarsity Press.
Martin, Ralph P.
1964a   "An Early Christian Hymn (Col. 1:15-20)." *Evangelical Quarterly* 36:195-205.
1964b   *Worship in the Early Church.* Grand Rapids: Eerdmans.
1978   *Colossians and Philemon.* The New Century Bible Commentary. Grand Rapids: Eerdmans.
1981   *Reconciliation: A Study of Paul's Theology.* Richmond: John Knox Press.
Martyrs Mirror
1950   *The Bloody Theater or Martyrs Mirror of the Defenseless Christians.* Compiled by Thieleman J. van Braght, tr. by J. F. Sohm from the 1660 Dutch ed. Scottdale, Pa.: Mennonite Publishing House.
Mauser, Ulrich
1992   *The Gospel of Peace.* Louisville, Ky.: Westminster/John Knox Press.
ME
1955-59 *The Mennonite Encyclopedia.* Vols. 1-4. Scottdale, Pa.: Herald Press.
1990   *The Mennonite Encyclopedia.* Vol. 5. Scottdale, Pa.: Herald Press.
Meeks, Wayne A.
1983   *The First Urban Christians: The Social World of the Apostle Paul.* New Haven: Yale University Press.
Melick, Richard R., Jr.
1991   *Philippians, Colossians, Philemon.* The New American Commentary, 32. Nashville, Tenn.: Broadman Press.
Menno Simons
1956   *Complete Writing of Menno Simons.* J. C. Wenger, ed. Scottdale, Pa.: Herald Press.
Metzger, Bruce M.
1968   *The Text of the New Testament.* 2d ed. New York and Oxford: Oxford University Press. 3d ed., 1992.
Miller, John W.
1969   *The Christian Way.* Scottdale, Pa.: Herald Press.
Miller, Marlin E.
1990   "Christology." *The Mennonite Encyclopedia,* 5. Scottdale, Pa.: Herald Press.
Moule, C. F. D.
1957   *The Epistles to the Colossians and Philemon.* Cambridge Greek Testament. Cambridge: University Press.
1963   *An Idiom Book of New Testament Greek.* Cambridge: University Press.
1973   " 'The New Life' in Colossians 3:1-17." *Review and Expositor* 70:481-493.
Moule, H. C. G.
1902   *Colossians Studies.* London: Hodder and Stoughton.

Müller, Jac J.
  1955   *The Epistles of Paul to the Philippians and to Philemon.* New International Commentary on the New Testament. Grand Rapids: Eerdmans.
Mullins, Terrence Y.
  1985   "The Thanksgivings of Philemon and Colossians." *New Testament Studies* 30:288-293.
Nauck, Wolfgang
  1952   "Salt as a Metaphor in Instructions for Discipleship." *Studia Theologica* 6:165-178.
Nestle, E., and K. Aland
  1981   *Novum Testamentum Graece.* 26th edition. Stuttgart: Deutsche Bibelstiftung.
Newbigin, Lesslie
  1986   *Foolishness to the Greeks: The Gospel and Western Culture.* Grand Rapids: Eerdmans.
Nock, Arthur Darby
  1964   *Early Gentile Christianity and Its Hellenistic Background.* New York: Harper & Row.
O'Brien, Peter T.
  1974   "Colossians 1:20 and the Reconciliation of All Things." *Reformed Theological Review* 33:45-53.
  1977   *Introductory Thanksgivings in the Letters of Paul.* Novum Testamentum, Supp. 49. Leiden: E. J. Brill.
  1980   "Thanksgiving within the Structure of Pauline Theology." In *Pauline Studies,* ed. by D. A. Hagner and M. J. Harris, 50-66. Grand Rapids: Eerdmans.
  1982   *Colossians, Philemon.* Word Biblical Commentary, 44. Waco, Tex.: Word Books.
Ogilvie, Lloyd John
  1977   *Loved and Forgiven: Colossians.* Ventura, Calif.: Regal Books.
Ollenburger, Ben. C.
  1991   "Mennonite Theology: A Conversation Around the Creeds." *Mennonite Quarterly Review* 66:57-89.
O'Neill, J. C.
  1979   "The Source of the Christology in Colossians." *New Testament Studies* 26:87-100.
Osborne, Philip
  1989   *Parenting for the '90s.* Intercourse, Pa.: Good Books.
Patzia, Arthur G.
  1984   *Colossians, Philemon, Ephesians.* A Good News Commentary. New York: Harper & Row.
Petersen, Norman R.
  1985   *Rediscovering Paul: Philemon and the Sociology of Paul's Narrative World.* Philadelphia: Fortress Press.
Perkins, Pheme
  1982   *Ministering in the Pauline Churches.* Ramsey, N. J.: Paulist Press.
Pokorný, Petr
  1991   *Colossians: A Commentary.* Tr. by Siegfried S. Schatzmann. Peabody, Mass.: Hendrickson Publishers.
Polhill, John B.
  1973   "The Relationship Between Ephesians and Colossians." *Review and Expositor* 70:439-450.

Prieb, Wesley J.
    1986   "The Power of the Lamb." In *The Power of the Lamb*, ed. by John
           E. Toews and Gordon Nickel, 117-128. Hillsboro, Kan.: Kindred
           Press.
Ramsay, W. M.
    1890   *Historical Geography of Asia Minor*. London: J. Murray.
    1896   *St. Paul the Traveler and Roman Citizen*. New York: G. P. Put-
           nam's Sons.
Ramseyer, Robert L., ed.
    1979   *Mission and the Peace Witness*. Scottdale, Pa.: Herald Press.
    1984   "The Anabaptist Vision and Our World Mission." In *Anabaptism
           and Mission*, ed. by Wilbert R. Shenk, 178-187. Scottdale, Pa.:
           Herald Press.
Reicke, Bo
    1973   "The Historical Setting of Colossians." *Review and Expositor*
           70:429-438.
Richardson, William J.
    1968   "Principle and Context in the Ethics of the Epistle to Philemon."
           Interpretation 22:301-316.
Robertson, Archibald Thomas
    1931   *Word Pictures in the New Testament*, 4. Nashville: Broadman
           Press.
    1959   *Paul and the Intellectuals*. Rev., ed. by W. C. Strickland. Nashville:
           Broadman Press.
Rolston, Holmes
    1963   *Thessalonians, Timothy, Titus, Philemon*. The Layman's Bible
           Commentary, 23. Atlanta, Ga.: John Knox Press.
Roop, Eugene F.
    1987   *Genesis*. Believers Church Bible Commentary. Scottdale, Pa.:
           Herald Press.
Schäufele, Wolfgang
    1962   "The Missionary Vision and Activity of the Anabaptist Laity."
           Mennonite Quarterly Review 36:99-115.
Scherer, Paul
    1961   *Love Is a Spendthrift*. New York: Harper & Brothers.
Schroeder, David
    1970   "The Origin of the New Testament Ethical Codes." Paper, Cana-
           dian Mennonite Bible College, Winnipeg, Man.
    1976   "Lists, Ethical." *See* IDB, 1976:546-547.
Schweizer, Eduard
    1973   "Christ in the Letter to the Colossians." *Review and Expositor*
           70:451-467.
    1982   *The Letter to the Colossians*. Tr. by A. Chester. Minneapolis:
           Augsburg Publishing House.
    1988   "Slaves of the Elements and Worshipers of Angels: Gal. 4:3, 9
           and Col. 2:8, 18, 20." *Journal of Biblical Literature* 107:455-
           468.
Selwyn, Edward Gordon
    1952   *The First Epistle of St. Peter*. London: Macmillan & Company.
Shank, David A.
    1980   "Toward an Understanding of Christian Conversion." In *Mission
           Focus: Current Issues*, ed. by Wilbert R. Shenk, 137-157. Scott-
           dale, Pa.: Herald Press.

Sider, Ron
  1987   *Completely Pro-Life.* Downers Grove, Ill.: InterVarsity Press.
Smith, William S.
  1962   *Musical Aspects of the New Testament.* Amsterdam: Vrije
         Universtiet te Amsterdam.
Stringfellow, William
  1973   *An Ethic for Christians and Other Aliens in a Strange Land.*
         Waco, Tex.: Word Books.
Swartley, Willard M.
  1981   *Mark: The Way for All Nations.* Scottdale, Pa.: Herald Press.
  1983   *Slavery, Sabbath, War, and Women: Case Issues in Biblical Inter-*
         pretation. Scottdale, Pa.: Herald Press.
TDNT
  1964-76 *Theological Dictionary of the New Testament.* 10 vols. Ed. by
         Gerhard Kittel and Gerhard Friedrich; tr. and ed. by Goeffrey W.
         Bromiley. Grand Rapids: Eerdmans.
UBS
  1983   *Greek New Testament.* Stuttgart: United Bible Societies. Third
         corrected ed., with Greek text identical to that of the Nestle-Aland
         Novum Testamentum Graece, 26th ed., Stuttgart: GBS, 1981.
Wahlstrom, Eric H.
  1950   *The New Life in Christ.* Philadelphia: Muhlenberg Press.
Wallis, Jim
  1976   *Agenda for Biblical People.* New York: Harper & Row.
Waltner, Erland, ed.
  1990   *Jesus Christ and the Mission of the Church.* Newton, Kan.: Faith
         and Life Press.
Weaver, J. Denny
  1983   "A Believers' Church Christology." *Mennonite Quarterly Review*
         57:112-131.
Wenger, J. C.
  1966   *God's Word Written.* Scottdale, Pa.: Herald Press.
Westermann, Claus
  1978   *Blessing in the Bible and the Life of the Church.* Tr. by Keith
         Grim. Philadelphia: Fortress Press.
Westermann, W. L.
  1955   *The Slave System of Greek and Roman Antiquity.* Philadelphia:
         American Philosophical Society.
Williamson, Lamar, Jr.
  1968   "Led in Triumph: Paul's Use of *Thriambeuō.*" *Interpretation*
         22:317-332.
Willoughby, Harold R.
  1929   *Pagan Regeneration: A Study of Mystery Initiations in the*
         Graeco-Roman World. Chicago: University Press.
Wink, Walter
  1984   *Naming the Powers.* Vol. 1, *The Powers.* Philadelphia: Fortress
         Press.
  1986   *Unmasking the Powers.* Vol. 2, *The Powers.* Philadelphia: For-
         tress Press.
  1992   *Engaging the Powers.* Vol. 3, *The Powers.* Minneapolis: Augsburg
         Fortress.

Winter, Sara C.
 1987   "Paul's Letter to Philemon." *New Testament Studies* 33:1-15.
Wright, Nicholas T.
 1990   "Poetry and Theology in Colossians 1:15-20." *New Testament Studies* 36:444-468.
 1991   *Colossians and Philemon.* Tyndale New Testament Commentaries. Grand Rapids: Eerdmans.
Yamauchi, E. M.
 1964   "Sectarian Parallels: Qumran and Colossae." *Bibliotheca Sacra* 121:141-152.
Yoder, John H.
 1969   "A People in the World: Theological Interpretation." In *The Concept of the Believers' Church*, ed. by James Leo Garrett, Jr., 250-283. Scottdale, Pa.: Herald Press.
 1971   *The Original Revolution.* Scottdale, Pa.: Herald Press.
 1972   *The Politics of Jesus.* Grand Rapids: Eerdmans.
 1983   "The Social Shape of the Gospel." In *Exploring Church Growth*, ed. by Wilbert R. Shenk, 277-284. Grand Rapids: Eerdmans.
 1985   *He Came Preaching Peace.* Scottdale, Pa.: Herald Press.
Yoder, Marvin
 1984   *What We Believe About Children.* Mennonite Faith Series, 13. Scottdale, Pa.: Herald Press.
Yoder, Perry B.
 1987   *Shalom: The Bible's Word for Salvation, Justice, and Peace.* Newton, Kan.: Faith and Life Press.
Zehr, Paul M.
 1986   *Biblical Criticism in the Life of the Church.* Scottdale, Pa.: Herald Press.

Selected Resources

Barclay, William. *The All Sufficient Christ.* Philadelphia: Westminster Press, 1963. A good topical treatment of Colossians.

_____. *The Letters to the Philippians, Colossians and Thessalonians* and *The Letters to Timothy, Titus, and Philemon.* DSB: The Daily Study Bible Series. Philadelphia: Westminster Press, rev. ed. 1975. Helpful comments, especially on the world of the early church, although not all aspects of the text are treated.

Bratcher, Robert G., and Eugene A. Nida. *A Translator's Handbook on Paul's Letters to the Colossians and to Philemon.* Stuttgart: United Bible Societies, 1977. Insightful comments on the nuances of meaning in the words of the text.

Bruce, F. F. *The Epistle to the Ephesians and Colossians.* New International Commentary on the New Testament. Grand Rapids: Eerdmans, 1957. The section on Colossians is solid exegesis in concise style.

Lucas, R. C. *Fullness and Freedom: The Message of Colossians and Philemon.* The Bible Speaks Today Series. Downers Grove, Ill.: InterVarsity Press, 1980. This volume does well in bridging from the text to current life.

Martin, Ralph P. *Colossians and Philemon.* The New Century Bible Commentary. Grand Rapids: Eerdmans, 1978. A solid work on both letters and within the reach of students with little or no acquaintance with Greek.

Melick, Richard R., Jr. *Philippians, Colossians, Philemon*. The New American Commentary. Nashville: Broadman Press, 1991. One of the newer commentaries, from a Southern Baptist scholar.

O'Brien, Peter T. *Colossians, Philemon*. Word Biblical Commentary. Waco, Tex.: Word Books, 1982. The most thorough of contemporary works to date, but written for the trained scholar.

Review and Expositor 70 (1973). The whole issue is devoted to Colossians, with a number of excellent articles.

Schweizer, Eduard. *The Letter to the Colossians*. Tr. by A. Chester. Minneapolis: Augsburg Publishng House, 1982. This Swiss author offers a thorough study, with a helpful section on the relevance of Colossians. The scholarly references are kept to the footnotes.

Wright, Nicholas T. *Colossians and Philemon*. Tyndale New Testament Commentaries. Grand Rapids: Eerdmans, 1991. This commentary in the new Tyndale series focuses on the meaning of the text, with the general reader in mind.

The Author

Ernest D. Martin was born on a farm in eastern Ohio in 1924. Following studies at Goshen (Ind.) College and its Biblical Seminary (B.A., 1950; Th.B., 1951), he was called into ministry as associate pastor in his home congregation, Midway Mennonite Church, Columbiana, Ohio. In 1963 he became the lead pastor and continued in that capacity until retirement in 1989. A sabbatical in 1976-77 gave him opportunity for an additional year at Associated Mennonite Biblical Seminaries (Elkhart, Ind.), including a unit of clinical pastoral education.

Martin served as vice-president and president of the Ohio Conference of the Mennonite Church and on several conference commissions and committees. He continues as overseer of several churches and leads a pastor-peer group. Denominational assignments have included serving as a member of a reference group on membership instruction materials, the task group preparing the position statement *The Church and Biblical Interpretation*, and the Goshen College Board of Overseers. He has taught short-term courses and led seminars in various church settings and has participated in local and urban ecumenical groups.

Martin's publications include *Preparing for Church Membership: Leader's Guide, Experiencing Christ in the Church, Off to a Good Start,* and *Jeremiah: A Study Guide.* Over the past thirty years he has also written numerous Sunday school lessons for *Herald Adult Studies/Adult Bible Study Guide* and adult teacher sections for *Builder.*

Ernest and Rosetta (Blosser), his wife, continue to live at Columbiana, Ohio, and attend the Midway congregation. They are the parents of Timothy, Susan Beuscher, and Nathan. Ernest continues to be busy with family, several church assignments, volunteer work in several settings, and a variety of interests and hobbies.